CW00740660

ROUTES FOLLOWED BY THE 8TH BAT

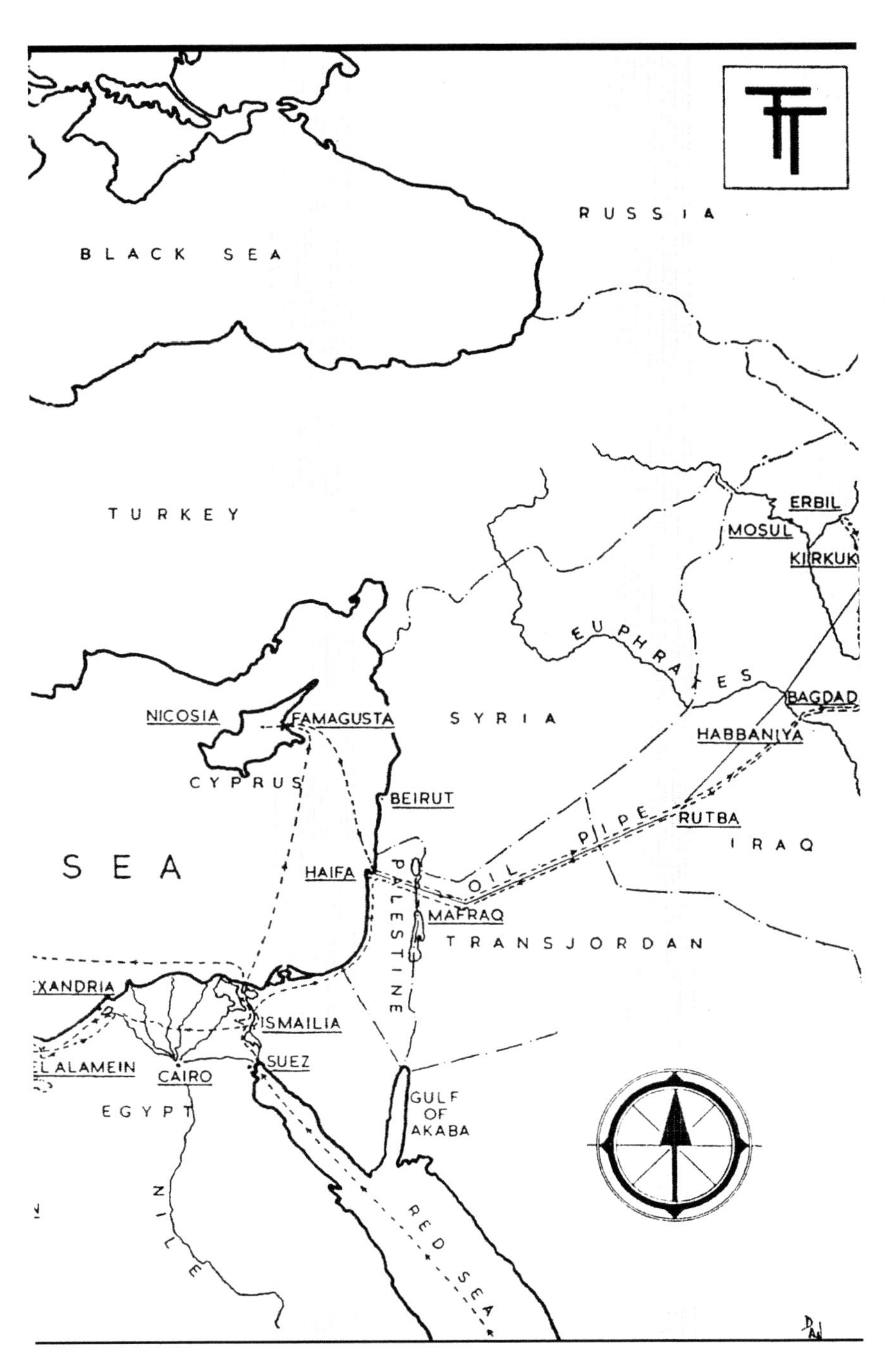

N IN THE MEDITERRANEAN THEATRE

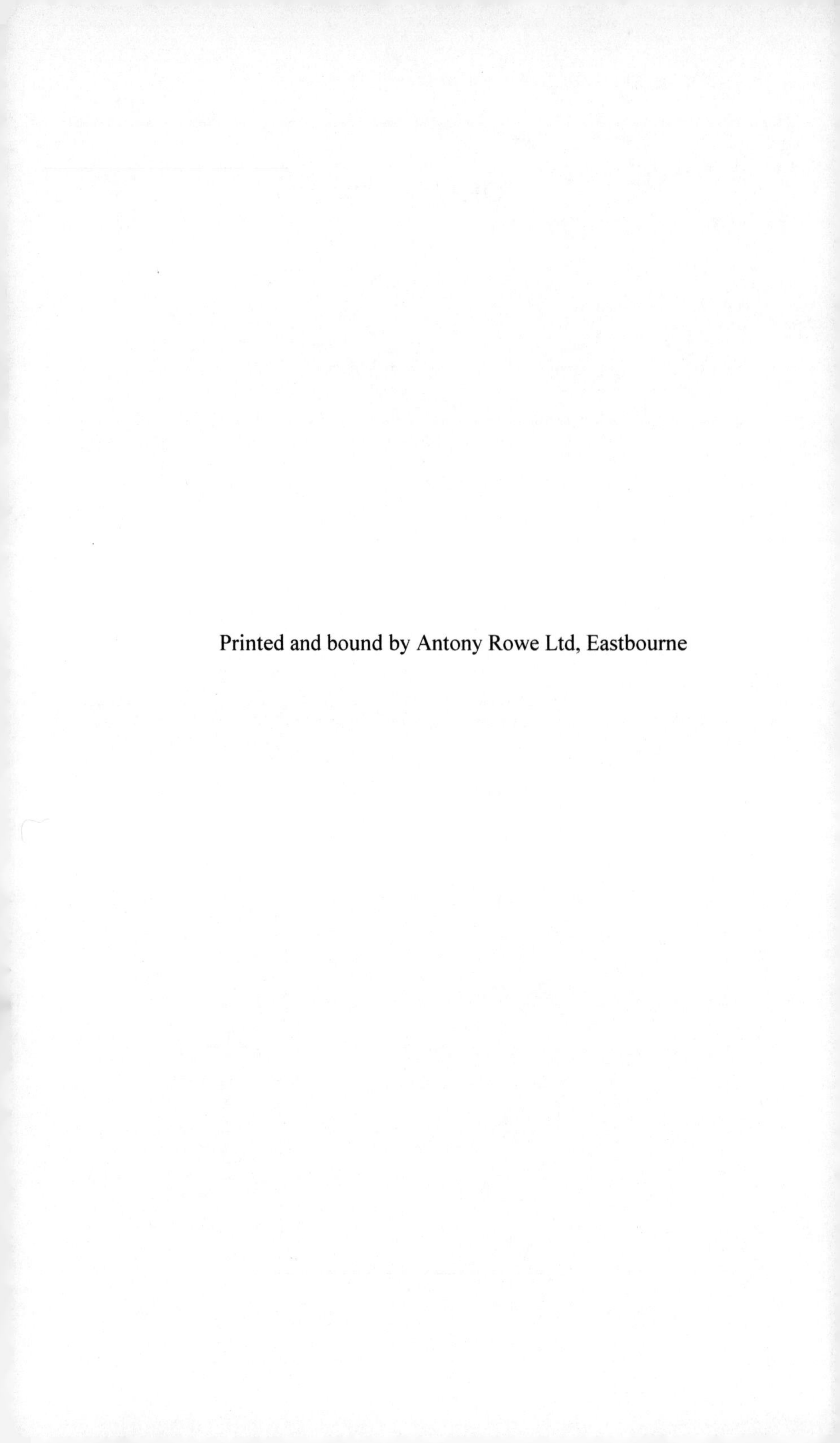
Printed and bound by Antony Rowe Ltd, Eastbourne

FOREWORD

BY

LIEUT.-GENERAL SIR BRIAN HORROCKS, K.B.E., C.B., D.S.O., M.C.

I regard it as a very great compliment to have been asked to write this Foreword to the History of the 8th Battalion the Durham Light Infantry, a worthy member of one of the most famous brigades in the British Army. This Durham Brigade of 50 Div. took part in more really hard fighting than did any other British brigade, and yet they were just as staunch when I last saw them on the " Island " north of Nijmegen in November, 1944 as they were in August, '42 when they first came under my command before Alamein, and when I first met them they were already veterans.

It is impossible in a short Foreword like this to mention all the battles in which the 8th D.L.I. took part, but three stand out in my memory.

Firstly Operation Supercharge, when the 151 Brigade our last infantry reserve carried out the final attack which broke the Germans at Alamein ; this was a vital attack which made history.

Then Mareth, a dour struggle which could only have been fought by experienced troops whose morale was high. Had it been possible to get the anti-tank guns over the Wadi Zigzaou nothing could have shifted 50 Div., of that I am certain.

Both the above were battles which received considerable publicity but little has been heard of the bitter fighting in which the Durhams took part at Gheel, yet this was a battle which had a decisive effect on the future course of the war.

I always had the greatest admiration for the 8th D.L.I. and the reason why they managed to maintain such a high standard over such a very long period is not far to seek. They always took a great pride in themselves and they were one of the happiest units that I have ever met.

This is a first-rate Battalion History and when you have read it you will agree with me that it must have been a fine thing to have served in this great Battalion, because every man that did so can now say to himself with pride, " I did more than my share to win the war."

B. G. Horrocks Lt Gen

30 Corps.

CONTENTS

APPENDICES

LIST OF ILLUSTRATIONS

LIST OF MAPS

Drawn by Major D. A. Neale, M.C.

ACKNOWLEDGMENTS

It has not been an easy task over the last three years to compile this History but it would have been infinitely more difficult without the valuable assistance which has been given to us by a number of people. We should like first of all to thank Colonel J. Turnbull, T.D., D.L., who has made it possible for this book to be produced and whose foresight and advice has helped us considerably on many occasions.

We are indebted to the following officers who have sent us their own accounts of various actions for inclusion in the book: Major R. S. McLaren, D.S.O., Major G. P. Chambers, Major J. A. Leybourne, M.C., Major H. S. Sell, M.C., Major R. I. Pitt, Captain W. G. Stray, M.B.E., Major D. A. Neale, M.C., Captain R. C. O'Conor, Captain P. G. Hampson, M.C., Captain J. G. Carruthers, D.C.M., Captain H. C. B. Catford (a veritable fountain-head of information), Captain W. S. Williamson, Captain W. H. W. Jalland and Lieut. A. W. Bark, M.M.

We are grateful to the War Office for the loan of the War Diary and official citations for gallantry; for the valuable assistance given in helping us to trace the names and addresses of past members of the Battalion and next of kin, so that we were able to circularise them about the History, and for the information from which the Roll of Honour was compiled. In this latter connection we must also thank Lieut.-Colonel W. H. Lowe, O.B.E., the Secretary of the Durham Light Infantry Association, for his great help and the trouble to which he went on our behalf.

Our thanks are also due to Lieut.-Colonel G. L. Wood, D.S.O., M.C., T.D., commanding the 8th Battalion the Durham L. I., for making all arrangements at Battalion H.Q. in Durham for the despatch of books and for allowing O.R.Q.M.S. W. H. Harper and Mr. R. Thornton leave to visit the Records Office at Exeter where they put in some very hard work on the compilation of the Roll of Honour and lists of names and addresses.

For the illustrations which appear in the book we have to thank the Imperial War Museum, the New York Times, Miss E. E. Turnbull, the officers whose portraits appear and Mrs. M. L. P. Jackson, and the officer commanding the Regimental H.Q. at Brancepeth and Major E. Brown, M.B.E. for loaning photographs taken by the late Captain J. N. Wheatley and subsequently presented to the Regimental Museum by his mother.

Last but by no means least we wish to thank our "back-room boys"—Mr. F. Rayner, Major R. I. Pitt and Major J. English—for the many long hours they have put in, checking the original manuscript and reading the final proofs, and also Mrs. Patricia Lewis, not only for her help with manuscripts and proofs, but for her unstinted co-operation in spite of her house being considerably disorganised for the sake of the History.

P. J. LEWIS.
I. R. ENGLISH.

J. Bacon Newcastle.

COLONEL J. TURNBULL, T.D., D.L.

INTRODUCTION

BY COLONEL J. TURNBULL, T.D., D.L.

Honorary Colonel of the 8th Battalion, The Durham Light Infantry.

The 8th Battalion, The Durham Light Infantry, having again acquitted itself so gloriously in another world war, it is fitting that its great deeds should be recorded. Many past and present officers and other ranks have readily co-operated in the production of this book, which I hope will be treasured not only by those who served with the Battalion, and their relatives, but by the many other close associates as well.

The achievements and trials of the Battalion, modestly recorded in this book, exemplify the splendid spirit of comradeship that existed amongst all ranks, and that dauntless determination to add lustre to the honour of the Regiment.

After heavy casualties, it was not always possible to have reinforcements of Durham men, but as officers and men of many honoured regiments joined the 8th Battalion they quickly sensed the friendly and family atmosphere and were proud to be adopted by, and to fight with, the " Durhams."

Having frequently met several of these officers and men from other regiments, I would like to thank them for honourable and gallant service which helped to further enhance the proud record of the Battalion.

On behalf of those who served in the Battalion, or who were associated with it, I thank the joint authors and all who have assisted in compiling this admirable and authentic record.

Having served in the 8th Battalion prior to the second world war and been associated with it for most of my life, I am proud to be allowed to write this introduction. I salute comrades alive and dead who have so worthily upheld the best traditions of our County Regiment.

The Battle Honours of the Battalion and the many awards gained by its members contribute with distinction to the record of noble services to our beloved Country at a time of its greatest need.

I commend with pride the following pages to all who are in any way concerned with the lives of these North-countrymen.

John Turnbull

THE MEMORIAL FUND

The publication of this book is in a large measure due to the generosity of the late Miss H. F. Turnbull who, in her life time, made substantial monetary gifts to the 8th and 11th Battalions of the Durham Light Infantry in memory of her brother, the late Colonel John Turnbull, C.M.G., V.D., D.L., who served in the 4th Volunteer Battalion the Durham Light Infantry, and later in the 8th Battalion the Durham Light Infantry from 1885 to 1912 and from 1914 to 1920, also was Honorary Colonel from 1929 until his death in 1937.

On the distribution of the estate of the late Miss H. F. Turnbull, the Old Comrades Association of the 8th Battalion also received liberal bequests in memory of Colonel Turnbull.

With the approval of the trustees these gifts to the two battalions and to the Old Comrades Association have to a considerable extent been used in defraying the cost of this History, and the authors and those associated with the publication gratefully acknowledge this financial assistance.

8th BATTALION
THE DURHAM LIGHT INFANTRY
1939-1945

CHAPTER ONE

EARLY DAYS IN ENGLAND

Mobilization—training in Oxfordshire—a new C.O.—a visit from H.M. the King—Embarkation for France.

THE 8th Battalion, the Durham L.I., commanded by Lieut.-Colonel E. A. Leybourne, T.D., was one of the many Territorial units to receive the order to mobilize during the afternoon of September 1st 1939. The message came through from Brigade H.Q. just before 3 o'clock and despatch riders were soon on their way from Battalion H.Q. in Gilesgate, Durham, to companies with the information. Little more than an hour later the code telegram ordering the embodiment of the Territorial Army was received at Gilesgate. By five o'clock the first members of the Battalion had reported to the company drill halls, and until nearly midnight the clerical staffs worked hard to absorb the men who were the peace-time backbone of what was destined to become a great fighting battalion.

For weeks, the possibility of Great Britain being involved in another European war had been the main topic of conversation whenever the men of the 8th had talked together—in the company canteens after a training lecture, on the rifle ranges, or on week-end schemes where, because of the appalling lack of equipment, coloured flags had been used to represent Bren guns and mortars. To the men of the 8th, the improvisation which was always so necessary within their own unit had made it quite clear that Great Britain's Territorial Army was not prepared for war. Those anxious weeks, with the storm clouds gathering rapidly over Europe, had been weeks of controversy and the men who jostled their way into the drill halls were glad that at last something definite was going to happen. Many of them were Durham miners ready to carry on the traditions of their fathers who had left the pits to fight in the 1914–18 war. Others were lorry drivers from several firms in Durham, many of whom were to make a name for themselves in the Carrier and M.T. Platoons, and there were clerks from office and factory desks, men from the Royal Ordnance factory at Birtley, and youngsters who only a few weeks before had been at school. All hurried home to bundle a few things together and report to their respective companies.

By the early evening of September 2nd the Adjutant was able to inform Brigade H.Q. that fifty-four officers and nearly eleven hundred men had reported for duty and much of the credit for the embodiment of the Battalion during these twenty-four hectic hours must surely go to the key parties which had been called up late in August. In spite of their many difficulties and blissfully ignorant of certain paragraphs in King's Regulations, the key parties had worked hard and earnestly to prepare for the embodiment of the Battalion and they carried out their job well.

With fifty-four officers and over a thousand men, it came as no surprise when Battalion Orders, issued during the evening of September 2nd, announced that the Battalion was to be divided into two units–the 8th and the 11th D.L.I. It was no easy task for Lieut.-Colonel Leybourne to detail some of his officers and men to form a nucleus of the new battalion, but he carried out this unpleasant task with characteristic fairness. Major J. Bramwell, T.D., was given command of the 11th D.L.I. The following day, at 11.15 a.m. on that memorable Sunday morning of September 3rd, all ranks at Durham listened to the broadcast from London of Mr. Neville Chamberlain. It was a silent audience which heard the Prime Minister announce quietly that a state of war existed between Great Britain and Germany, and that evening the various companies heard H.M. the King speak to his people throughout the British Empire. The challenge from Nazi Germany had been accepted.

As one of the three D.L.I. battalions of 151 Infantry Brigade of 50 Division, the 8th, like so many other Territorial units, had its teething troubles during those first hectic weeks after the declaration of war. To Captain A. B. S. Clarke the Adjutant and others on the administrative side must go much of the credit fo the smooth running of the unit. They brought order out of chaos during that critical period of the Battalion's history. September was indeed a month when there was so much to do and so little time in which to do it. Trenches were dug and sandbags filled as part of the air defence scheme, dozens of indents were sent in by the harassed Q.M. for the many and varied stores needed to bring the unit up to its War Establishment and the Medical Officer was busy all day inspecting, inoculating and vaccinating hundreds of tough-skinned miners.

The Brigade Commander, Brigadier J. A. Churchill, M.C., visited the Battalion and, after inspecting the men, he addressed the officers in the Mess at Durham. He spoke quickly and forcibly, stressing the importance of physical fitness and pointing out that the Territorial

Army was no longer a force of amateurs. The Brigadier's remarks about physical fitness were very soon driven home—the hard way. With all due respect to Field-Marshal Viscount Montgomery, there were several senior officers who had held extreme views about physical fitness long before the Field-Marshal had an opportunity to train his troops on these lines : one of them was Brigadier Churchill.

Whilst the companies carried out their training programmes, the C.O. and several of the senior officers attended a 50 Division exercise in Yorkshire where the Divisional Commander, Major-General G. le Q. Martel, D.S.O., M.C., expounded the role of the formation as a motorised striking force. Slowly but surely things were beginning to take shape and very soon the 8th was able to appreciate what was meant by direction from the top. With the Brigadier setting the pace, training schemes were originated by Brigade H.Q. which made some of the older hands wonder whether the Battalion would ever be able to make the grade for the British Expeditionary Force.

The administrative staff had the task of forming a National Defence Unit from the veterans of the 1914 war and also an A.T.S. company. The drill halls became hives of industry. As there was very little difference between the attestation papers of the men and women, there were some amusing errors, and on one occasion a veteran was issued with an A.T.S. skirt. The National Defence Unit was enlisted at Gilesgate and if few questions were asked by the recruiting staff about medical fitness and training, even fewer were answered by the veterans. " Why, man, here's me discharge papers," was the answer received by one young subaltern who tactlessly asked a veteran whether he could fire a rifle.

Throughout September the various teething troubles were disposed of until, towards the end of the month, the Battalion was beginning to function smoothly. A few days after a large church parade in Durham Cathedral, when the sermon was read by the Archdeacon, and twenty-eight days after the Prime Minister's speech, the Battalion received information that 50 Division was to be concentrated in Oxfordshire, with the D.L.I. Brigade billeted in the area of Charlbury, Chipping Norton and Shipston-on-Stour.

The move of the Battalion to Oxfordshire needed a lot of careful planning and inevitably, with the prospect of the early inclusion of the Division in the British Expeditionary Force, it became necessary to post veteran members of the 8th to Home Defence units. It was with regret that several of the best N.C.Os., including C.S.M. Rickaby of Gilesgate who had a record of long and distinguished service with the Battalion, were sent away. It was necessary to fill their places with newiy-promoted senior N.C.Os., a task which was not difficult because of the many excellent recruits who had joined the Battalion since the outbreak of war.

The last entry in the War Diary under the sub-heading ' Durham ' is a sad one for those members of the 8th who were with the Battalion during its pre-war Territorial days for it concerns the C.O. It was announced by Major J. G. Raine, M.C., who had been appointed

Second-in-Command during October, that Lieut.-Colonel Leybourne had decided to make way for a younger man. He had been a popular C.O. and Major Raine spoke of the long and sincere service he had given to the Battalion. He wished him every success in his new post of Quartering Officer, Northern Command, where Lieut-Colonel Leybourne remained until the conclusion of the war. The following letter was sent out to all companies and Major Raine took over command.

" On taking up another appointment I am compelled to-day to relinquish command of the Battalion with which I have been associated for twenty-five years.

" You will appreciate that this means a great wrench to me and I find it difficult to express my real feelings at this moment.

" I hope, however, that I may have some opportunity in the future of speaking to the Battalion when it is again concentrated.

" In the meantime, I wish you all good luck, in the confident knowledge that you will acquit yourselves well, and maintain the excellent traditions of the Battalion which I am so proud to have commanded."

Late in October 151 Brigade moved to Oxfordshire, the 8th by two trains to the Charlbury district where Battalion H.Q. and H.Q. Company were billeted in the pretty little village of Charlbury. The Carrier Platoon went to the White Hart, the Pioneer Platoon to the Bull Inn, the Buglers to the Victory Cinema, and the M.T. to Walcot Farm. Within a radius of ten miles of Charlbury the rest of the 8th was billeted in and around the villages of Enstone, Chadlington, Spelsbury and Dean. The inhabitants of these delightfully sleepy Oxfordshire villages, so different from the dusty and grimy Durham mining villages, gave a grand welcome to the northeners. The shops, village halls, and farmers' barns were taken over as billets and within two days the Battalion had settled down. Major R. S. McLaren, whose energy and enthusiasm had helped to keep the 8th going during the difficult Territorial days, returned from the Senior Officers' School at Sheerness to take over command of the Battalion.

Just before the move to Charlbury, it had been necessary to send some of the best N.C.Os. and men back to the Durham coal mines, where they were urgently needed. It meant that the 8th would be getting a replacement draft of militiamen and the Battalion waited with some misgivings. There is a terse entry in the War Diary for October 31st, " A draft of seventy-seven King's Own Scottish Border militiamen joined the Battalion . . . . a very smart lot of men." The Durham lads were favourably impressed, and in this particular case first impressions were right. Some of the Battalion's best N.C.Os. were produced from this Charlbury draft.

The last two months of 1939 in Oxfordshire will bring pleasant memories to the men of the 8th who were fortunate enough to be there. It was a period when all ranks really got to know each other and when that *esprit de corps*, which was so vitally necessary and quickly forthcoming in the difficult years that were to follow, first became apparent. Hard work there was and plenty of it but on the leisure side who will forget the achievements of Captain F. W. E. Goodenough's D Company at Dean, where a truly magnificent canteen, complete with bar, was built as a result of many foraging expeditions carried out by the company for wood and other materials ; the always successful Sergeants' Mess social evenings ; the generosity of Mr. Watney and many other locals who started friendships which were appreciated greatly at the time and are certainly not forgotten now. The other side of the picture was one of hard and exacting training, for General Martel had set a high standard of efficiency for the units in 50 Division. Most of the junior officers were sent away on tactical courses whilst, in the Battalion, courses were organised for the junior and senior N.C.Os. Major F. Taylor, the Q.M., was found to be unfit for service overseas and left the Battalion. His place was taken by R.Q.M.S. Marshall.

Further drafts of reinforcements arrived ; one from the 11th D.L.I. and a second draft from the K.O.S.B. Colonel J. Turnbull, T.D., D.L., the Honorary Colonel, visited the Battalion, as did many old friends and members of the Regiment. " There is no doubt that the old spirit is there," said Colonel Turnbull when he spoke to the men. " I am sure you will do as well as those that have gone before you." There were other distinguished visitors, including Sir Philip Chetwode, Mr. Anthony Eden, and Sir Ronald Tree. The standard of training improved greatly as each week brought the first wartime Christmas nearer and the changeover from individual training to battalion and company schemes was eagerly welcomed. The complex machinery of the unit, which had creaked rather uncertainly in the early days of the war, was beginning to run smoothly and there was an air of confidence about the 8th D.L.I.

One of the busiest members of the Battalion was the Medical Officer. With his hard worked staff he stood for hours on end, syringe in one hand and a piece of cotton wool in the other, as each company in turn was inoculated for tetanus. First H. Q. Company and then the rifle companies proceeded on seven days' leave ; A and B Companies were fortunate enough to get home for Christmas. Brand new carriers and trucks were parked at the White Hart and around Walcot Farm. New equipment was piled high in the Q.M. Stores ; Bren guns and mortars in their freshly painted green boxes, new boots, battledress, greatcoats, and all the miscellaneous equipment of an infantry battalion.

In the 8th it was by no means a typical English Christmas, as it certainly would have been if the Battalion had spent the holiday in those hospitable Oxfordshire villages. During December arrangements had been made for the whole Battalion to fire the Bren and Rifle Courses on the ranges at Castle Bromwich. It was hard luck, but it emphasised the desperate state of affairs in 1939 when speed was the essence of all training and not a day could be wasted. On Boxing Day Lieut.-Colonel C. W. Beart, M.C., already well known to some members of the Battalion, arrived from the 2nd D.L.I. in France to take over command. By the end of December, although there had been nothing official, the general feeling throughout the Battalion was that 50 Division would be leaving Oxfordshire before many more weeks had passed.

The first day of 1940 brought with it the message for which the Battalion had been waiting ; to prepare to move overseas at twenty-four hours notice any time after January 12th. It was a welcome New Year message. The last reinforcements of men arrived, the last parties were sent on embarkation leave and the Q.M. and Medical Officer redoubled their efforts to prepare the Battalion for the move to France. All the bulk baggage had to be marked with the unit serial number and distinguishing colour bands of red, green, red. Surplus stores had to be returned to Ordnance, and right up to the day before the move, the Q.M.'s three-tonner was the busiest vehicle in the Battalion. A new Medical Officer, Captain L. H. Wilkinson, R.A.M.C., who had joined the 8th early in the month, completed the last of the injections and, to the disappointment of some and the evident relief of others, he then carried out a final inspection and rejected seventy men as unfit for service overseas. It was hard luck on the majority, mostly elderly Territorials who had passed so many inspections only to be rejected at the last minute.

The impending move and the appalling weather in January made it impossible for any training during the month on a brigade level. Early in the month several officers and men had been sent on courses and there had been a Battalion M.T. scheme but, apart from these activities, the nerve centres were the Adjutant's office, the Q.M. stores and the M.T. and Carrier lines where the vehicles were being prepared for their journey.

The main event of the month was the inspection of the D.L.I. Brigade by H.M. the King in the main street of Chipping Norton on January 16th. On this particular morning it was bitterly cold and the companies marched to Chipping Norton without greatcoats, expecting to find that the Battalion transport had already arrived in the village with them. However, the trucks, which had frozen up during the night, were late and arrived only just in time to prevent His Majesty having to inspect a shivering Battalion ; the welcome greatcoats were put on just before the 8th marched into position. It is doubtful whether the King had ever inspected a healthier brigade of troops, for there was not a single man of the three D.L.I. battalions whose face had not been turned into the likeness of a rosy apple by the bitter cold. The King complimented the C.O. on the Battalion's turn out and steadiness in the ranks, and his praise was most welcome, for the 8th had improved beyond all recognition since those early days of the war. The dignity of the proceedings was somewhat marred by the band instruments freezing up as the Battalion was about to leave Chipping Norton and there was a pathetic series of the most extraordinary noises. Cpl. Fletcher and his bandsmen made a valiant but unsuccessful attempt to play "Blaydon Races" as the 8th swung out of Chipping Norton, and the Battalion left the village to surely the most ghastly wails which have ever been made by the instruments of a Regimental Band of the Durham Light Infantry.

After the King's inspection it was time for the Battalion to say goodbye—*au revoir* in many cases—to those many good folk who had made the stay of the 8th in the Cotswolds so memorable. Lieut.-Colonel Beart thanked the people of Charlbury for their many kindnesses to the northerners who had enjoyed their hospitality, and the villagers were pleased to return the C.O.'s thanks, for the 8th had been very popular. On the other side of the English Channel two officers from the Battalion–Captain J. H. Dixon and Lieut. R. I. Pitt–were busy requisitioning accommodation in the dirty little French village of St. Remy du Plain, twenty miles north of Le Mans.

On January 22nd, the transport and carriers, under the command of Captain J. W. Walton, left for Southampton. The night before had been a nightmare for the M.T. and carrier personnel ; the cold was so intense that every half hour it had been necessary to start up and run the engines for a few minutes to prevent a complete freeze up. It was a weary M.T. Platoon and Carrier Platoon which set out just after 6.30 a.m. on the eighty mile journey to Southampton, with 2/Lieut. I. R. English as pace-setter in the leading carrier and 2/Lieut. G. Blagdon bringing up the rear of the column with a large red flag on his vehicle. The convoy of sixty-three carriers and trucks and fourteen motor-cycles rumbled through the sleeping village of Witney, on through Abingdon, Newbury, Andover and Romsey to Southampton. They arrived at the docks just six hours after leaving Charlbury, having had no breakdowns *en route*. Three days were spent at Southampton whilst the ships were being loaded, and by January 26th the Carriers and M.T. were on their way to France.

The day that the road party arrived in St. Remy du Plain—on January 28th—the rest of the Battalion left Charlbury. It was one of the coldest days Oxfordshire had ever known, just the sort of day one would expect to leave England. The night before, A Company had marched in from Enstone and early on the Sunday morning they entrained at Charlbury Station with H. Q. Company. They travelled in luxury compared with what was in store for them ; in those days it was still eight men to a compartment and only six for a corridor train. It was a fearful day, remembered everywhere because of the wide-spread storms which so disrupted traffic throughout the country. D Company marching from Dean, and B Company from Chadlington had to plough their way through deep snow in the teeth of a blizzard and arrived at Charlbury Station almost exhausted. There were the usual last minute administrative queries about billets, latrines, keys and frozen pipes and then it was " good-bye to Charlbury."

No families or visitors were allowed at the railway station or the port of embarkation, and the Battalion was forbidden to use that last link with home, the telephone, when it detrained at Southampton. By early afternoon the 8th had embarked ; the trooper pulled out and anchored off the bar in the Solent until darkness blotted out the English coastline, then her engines throbbed as she got under way and moved out into the Channel. Next morning, after a somewhat stormy passage, dawn brought the coast of France and the port of Cherbourg into view.

CHAPTER TWO

WITH THE BRITISH EXPEDITIONARY FORCE

Hard training at Oissy—digging defences at Gondecourt—Germany attacks—the move into Belgium—the Battle of Warlus—a skirmish in Carvin—the rearguard action on the Ringsloot Canal—on the beaches at Dunkirk.

THE trooper nosed her way slowly into the quayside and down went the gangways. It was pouring with rain and the French skies were dark as the long lines of khaki-clad men filed off the ship. For the rest of the day the troops spent their time wandering around the town in the drenching rain, and they were not very impressed with their first sight of "La Belle France." An hour before midnight the 8th left Cherbourg railway station and the train crawled through the night as only French trains can do, puffing noisily into Carentan and beyond to Bayeux and Caen. There were several members of the Battalion destined to travel the same route in much less peaceful circumstances four and a half years later.

After detraining at La Hutte the Battalion travelled east about six miles to St. Remy du Plain. The French billets were poor compared to the billets in Oxfordshire, the weather was atrocious and it was far from easy to keep warm and dry. There was an extraordinary atmosphere in the France of early 1940 and many of the French people made only a half-hearted attempt to justify their country's declaration of war. If the British Expeditionary Force had experienced long months of inactivity there is no doubt that the morale of the troops would have been adversely affected. As it was, they were merely puzzled by the *laissez faire* attitude of their allies.

The German Fifth Column was already operating and there were frequent spy scares which, however, never came to anything. Another feature of the early days in St. Remy was the fantastic claims made by the locals for any loss or misfortune which could be blamed on the British troops. The buxom Frenchwoman who ran the village estaminet was disgusted with the behaviour of the Battalion, for nothing she could do or say would persuade the troops to raid her wine cellar. The previous battalion billeted in St. Remy—a hard-drinking Scottish unit—carried out a lightning raid one night and lifted some hundreds of bottles which the Messing Officer paid for at retail prices. Madame quickly stocked her wine cellars again when the arrival of Captain Dixon and Lieut. Pitt made it evident that another battalion was going to be billeted in St. Remy but the opportunity of selling her stock wholesale at retail prices did not occur again, in spite of her frantic unofficial appeals to the troops to help themselves. The stay of the 8th in this inhospitable French village was prolonged due to the bad weather which held up all road movement, and orders were not received for the move forward to the north-east until well into February.

The first stop was Longny, a charming little French village which was delightfully refreshing after the drabness of St. Remy. The villagers could not have been more hospitable and everyone was delighted when another break in the weather held up road movement and lengthened the stay in the excellent billets of Longny for a further week. Meanwhile the Carrier Platoon had gone by rail from St. Remy du Plain to the Amiens area where they were attached to the 4th Green Howards of 150 Brigade.

From Longny the Battalion moved by road to the G.H.Q. Training Area which was about fifteen miles west of Amiens. H.Q. Company and A Company were billeted in a dilapidated old chateau at Oissy, unoccupied since the days of the 1914–18 war. Dust lay thick on the furniture which stood exactly as the last occupants had left it and cobwebs were everywhere; the chairs and tables almost fell to pieces at a touch. The dusty furniture was bundled outside, the cobwebs removed and the chateau given a spring clean. Newspapers dating from the 1914–18 war were found, and two rusty old service rifles showed that British troops had been billeted there before. Poverty had indeed stricken the dilapidated village of Oissy or perhaps it had never recovered from the effects of the last war; the streets were ankle deep in mud, the houses lath and plaster sided. The walls were so thin that on one occasion a Battalion bicycle was leant against the wall of a house and fell through, much to the amazement of its owner.

It was a strenuous month at Oissy, a month of hard, exacting training when Battalion, Brigade and Divisional exercises followed one another in quick succession. Brigadier Churchill drove the Battalion to the limit and himself displayed tireless energy and enthusiasm. The 8th, training hard for its role of an infantry battalion in a motorised division, practised long approach marches in transport to a debussing point, followed by a quick attack and consolidation. Troop-carrying transport was provided by a R.A.S.C. company with three-ton lorries. At Oissy the art of embussing and debussing, a somewhat complicated drill which had been devised by General Martel, was finally mastered until the Battalion could carry out the drill so mechanically that it pleased the Divisional Commander. No one was sorry when news of another move forward came through, this time to Gondecourt, eight miles west of Lille. The Battalion went by train early in April; for the first time but certainly not the last, the troops piled into cattle trucks, a method of transport which had been such a feature of the 1914–18 war. These high wagons with their large iron wheels have one thing in common—they all carry a notice which informs the curious that they are capable of carrying forty men or eight horses. No one will ever know, but the general opinion is that the horses probably have a more comfortable journey than the men.

In April 1940, the B.E.F. consisted of three corps of about nine infantry divisions with ancillary troops. 1 and 2 Corps were holding a sector of the frontier east of Lille and were busy on the construction of field defences, pill-boxes and anti-tank ditches. 3 Corps included 50 Division and was made up of Territorial units, not all of which had arrived in France.

Since the previous November a sector of the Saar front had been allotted to the B.E.F. and several brigades had spent periods in the line, where vigorous patrolling and daily brushes with the enemy had given the British troops valuable battle experience. At the end of April Lord Gort assumed responsibility for a divisional sector of the Saar front and moved up 51 Division to relieve a French division. Whilst this blooding of some of the British regular battalions was being carried out in the Saar the 8th, together with other units of 50 Division, was given the task of constructing defences on the 2 Corps reserve line, a few miles east of Gondecourt.

The Battalion spent most of the time in denims and gum boots on the construction of anti-tank ditches, which had been left unfinished by other units, and the 8th had the task of turning chaos into order. It was just the sort of job for a battalion of Durham miners to tackle and as a result of their determined efforts a sorry-looking ditch, unrevetted and collapsing like a child's canal dug in soft sand at the seaside, became a trim, shapely, well-revetted anti-tank ditch of text book specification. There was an amusing mass wager between the commanders of B and D Companies, each betting three pints of beer per man that his company would beat the rival one in completing its section of the ditch. B Company, with a fairly dry section, was the favourite whereas the D Company section was a morass of wet, slimy mud. Much to the annoyance of the Brigade Commander, D Company only turned out on fine days, but in spite of this they won the bet comfortably. When they did work in the ditch, they did so like men possessed. The debt was honourably but rather noisily paid off one night in the village of Herrin, not far from Gondecourt, at a joint smoking concert sponsored by the rival company commanders. In fairness to B Company it should be put on record that, although D Company won the bet, the B Company section was a more professional job.

Those early days in France were probably the happiest of the war. There was a very good spirit in the unit which made it the military equivalent of a happy ship. Lieut.-Colonel C. W. Beart still commanded, with Major R. S. McLaren as his Second-in-Command. H.Q. Company was commanded by Major J. G. Raine, A Company by Captain J. H. Dixon, B Company by Captain F. B. Kirkup, C Company by Captain J. W. Walton, and D Company by Captain F. W. Goodenough. Lieut. G. Ferguson acted as Adjutant whilst Captain A. B. S. Clarke was on leave.

The Territorials in the Battalion had all volunteered to serve with the 8th ; during the months of leisure and training since the outbreak of war they had got to know each other really well and the men of the

Charlbury draft were settling down quickly in this battalion from County Durham. The war—although described as "phoney" in some quarters—was still an exciting business and there was a novelty about living in this strange country which was only just recovering from the devastation of the 1914–18 conflict. The town of Lille was only fifteen miles away with theatres, cinemas and those typically French bars where a pianist sits at a dilapidated old piano with a cigarette dangling from his lips and conjures "Avalon" from the keys.

On May 10th the "phoney" war came to an abrupt end and so did the Battalion excursions to the fleshpots of Lille. Hitler's Luftwaffe and armoured divisions crossed the frontiers of Holland, Belgium and Luxembourg. General Georges, the Allied Commander-in-Chief, immediately gave orders for the French and British forces to move forward into Belgium according to plans which had previously been worked out in detail. The long columns of guns, tanks and troops were soon on the move and crossed the Belgium frontier to race for positions on the line of the River Dyle, sixty miles inside Belgium. The Allied line on the river stretched from Namur in the south, through Wavre and Louvain and then north to the port of Antwerp. The sector allotted to the B.E.F. extended from Wavre to Louvain with the French First Army on the right of the British force, and on the left the French Seventh Army commanded by General Giraud.

A few days prior to the move 50 Division had lost its R.A.S.C. troop-carrying lorries and was no longer motorised. The Division was now part of G.H.Q. Reserve with an immediate task of providing local defence for the area south-west of Lille. The first few days were peaceful enough for the Battalion and the only warlike incident occurred when a German bomber was shot down near Gondecourt, bullets from the victorious R.A.F. fighter drilling a neat pattern of holes in the door of B Company's dining hall. There were, however, daily spy scares and false alarms about parachutists. It was all part of the German Fifth Column Plan which betrayed France from within her own frontiers with such tragic consequences.

By the night of May 15th, the timetable of the B.E.F. which had moved so swiftly and efficiently into Belgium, was running ahead of schedule and, two days earlier than had been expected, General Martel received orders to move his Division–as G.H.Q. Reserve–to the line of the River Dendre, west of Brussels. At the same time serious news came from the Ardennes where German armoured and motorised divisions had crossed the River Meuse between Sedan and Mézières with unexpected ease to attack the weak French Ninth Army with great force. This thrust had succeeded in effecting a break-through and by May 15th the enemy had also penetrated the front of the French First Army on the right of the B.E.F., thus threatening the flank of the British 2 Division.

On May 16th, the men of 50 Division moved forward into Belgium. The long column of troop-carrying lorries which had been allotted to the 8th rumbled through Roubaix and Tournai to Grammont, a town on the River Dendre where Major McLaren was waiting with the advance party. This party had left twenty-four hours before the Battalion and had first of all made arrangements for billets in Brussels, then in a village about ten miles south of Grammont, and finally in frantic haste and at only one hour's notice in Grammont itself. The Battalion arrived at 4 p.m. and when the drivers of the troop-carriers switched off their motors the buzz of countless aero engines could be heard above the low clouds which blanketed the town. The debussing drill did not work out in practice as well as it had done on exercises, and it was well that Grammont was hidden from the Luftwaffe. Fortunately no German airmen ventured below the clouds where a solitary Lysander acted as air cover, otherwise the target presented by the congested troop-carriers at the debussing point would certainly have resulted in the Battalion being subjected to its first air attack.

Meanwhile, owing to the deteriorating position in the south it had become clear that a prolonged defence of the River Dyle position was impracticable. Accordingly, orders were issued for the Allied forces to be withdrawn, part of the B.E.F. falling back through Grammont. The troop-carrying vehicles had hardly left the Battalion area before the rifle companies were hurried forward to the line of the river where they took up defensive positions to cover the withdrawal of units of the B.E.F. across the River Dendre at Grammont Bridge. Next morning it became obvious to the Battalion that things were in a bad way. At about 9 a.m. Captain Burdon-Taylor, who had been posted from the 8th to the 2nd D.L.I. the previous November, passed through the village. He had been wounded and gave a graphic account of the 2nd Battalion's battle on the River Dyle and the disastrous collapse of the French on the right flank of the British 2 Division; battle-tired and weary, the men of the 2nd D.L.I. moved back through Grammont. Before nightfall the 8th had received orders to prepare to move early next morning. The situation in front was very vague and just before midnight on May 17th, when the C.O. was at Brigade H.Q. receiving orders for the move, a motor-cyclist roared through Grammont, slowing down his bicycle sufficiently to shout that the Germans were only four miles away. Lieut. R. I. Pitt and 2/Lieut. P. Lucas on motor-cycles and a Carrier patrol under 2/Lieut. I. R. English were immediately sent out to verify this startling news, but the information proved to be entirely false and the most likely explanation is that the motor-cyclist was a German agent.

At 8 a.m. the Battalion moved by march route to Helchin near Courtrai, about twenty-seven miles to the rear. After marching for about two hours, the Tournai-Brussels road was reached. It was jammed with masses of refugees and Belgian soldiers on bicycles, all moving frantically westwards. The orderly move of the refugees which had been evident on the move up to the Dendre had become a chaotic, panic-stricken flight, completely out of control. It was a tragic sight to see these unfortunate people streaming back along the cobbled roads; the farm carts and lorries piled high with furniture, mothers carrying their babies, the faces of the old women who had seen the destruction of their country by the Germans in the 1914 war—puzzled, a little frightened, but still determined. Here and there a car, abandoned for lack of petrol, had been pushed off the road or a party of refugees lay stretched out on the grass verge, utterly exhausted and quite oblivious of the rumbling carts and lorries and the marching feet. The Battalion arrived in Helchin about 8 p.m. very weary and footsore, and was disposed in tactical positions along the canal bank. Working at Gondecourt in gumboots on the anti-tank ditch had softened the men's feet and the twenty-seven mile march along the cobbled roads had been very painful. Late that night Major Raine rejoined the Battalion, having blown the bridge at Grammont at 5 p.m. after the last units of the B.E.F. had crossed.

Next morning the Battalion continued the march back. After another day on the refugee-congested roads the 8th arrived at Toufflers near Roubaix and had just settled down in billets when troop-carrying lorries arrived and the Battalion was on the move again. Shortly after midnight the troops debussed in Provin, not far from Gondecourt, and went thankfully into billets for the night. It was here that Captain Clarke and a leave party rejoined the Battalion.

Meanwhile, the enemy breakthrough at Sedan by a force including five armoured divisions had been completely successful and the German thrust had now reached Amiens and the line of the River Somme. Rail communications had been severed at Amiens and there was a danger that the rest of the lines of communication would soon be cut. The troops of the B.E.F. who had been withdrawn from the River Dyle were now holding positions on the River Escaut, only a few miles east of the Franco-Belgian frontier, and a defensive flank facing south had been formed along La Bassée Canal and the Canal du Nord. By May 21st the German breach had widened and now extended from Amiens north-east to Arras, a distance of nearly forty miles. The German armour appeared to be directed on two main objectives : the town of Abbeville on the River Somme, and then up the coast to the Channel ports with a view to encircling the Allied armies in northern France and Belgium. In order to close this gap it was decided to attack with the British 5 and 50 Divisions and the British 1 Army Tank Brigade ; this force was to be known as Frankforce. It was agreed that French divisions would co-operate by attacking on either side of Frankforce, and that other French formations would attack southwards in an attempt to link up with their forces on the Somme. In fact, very little French support was forthcoming and eventually the effort to close the gap was made entirely by a brigade of 5 Division and 151 Brigade of 50 Division with some elements of 1 French Light Mechanised Division co-operating on the right of the D.L.I. Brigade.

Very little information was available concerning the disposition of the German forces. From the time of the initial attack against Belgium and Holland until the evacuation from Dunkirk the scarcity of reliable information about the enemy movements was one of the main features of the campaign. As far as our own troops were concerned, the town of Arras was held by 150 Brigade of 50 Division and a battalion of Welsh Guards. Brigadier Churchill's plan for 151 Brigade was for the 8th D.L.I. on the right and the 6th D.L.I. on the left, using Arras as a pivot, to advance and make good the line of the Arras-Doullens road, which was then to be used as a start line for further attacks south and south-east of Arras. The 9th D.L.I. was to remain in reserve to protect the right flank of the 8th Battalion.

The 8th was ordered to move to Vimy Ridge and the troops marched towards the village of Annay where troop-carriers waited for them. Annay had been heavily bombed and it was decided to lay up until nightfall before moving on to Vimy. In the early hours of the following morning—May 21st—the 8th left the village in troop carriers. Dawn had hardly broken before the arrival of the Battalion on Vimy Ridge where tactical positions facing south-west were taken up in the woods along the crest of the famous ridge. D Company manned trenches held by the Canadians in 1916 when Vimy Ridge had been the scene of such hard and bitter fighting. At 10 a.m. Lieut.-Colonel Beart issued his orders for the advance to the Arras-Doullens road. The Battalion had in support fifteen tanks of the 7th R.T.R., a battery of the 92nd Field Regiment, a battery of the Norfolk Yeomanry Anti-Tank Regiment and a scout car troop of the Royal Northumberland Fusiliers. The Battalion axis of advance was from Vimy to St. Waast, and then on to an assembly area at Maroeuil, where the supporting arms were to join up with the Battalion. The column, with the tanks leading and D Company as the advance guard company, was then to push on through Duisans and Warlus to the Arras-Doullens road.

Speed was vital; there was no time to prepare a quick meal or to issue haversack rations and within an hour of the C.O. issuing his orders the Battalion was on the move. The squadrons of German aircraft overhead fortunately did not pay any attention to the advancing infantry and the 8th first came under fire near Maroeuil. German gunners were ranged on the village and an odd shell came whining over. Maroeuil was also under small arms fire which delayed the assembly of the column and the tanks, moving off too soon, disappeared in the distance. That was the last the rest of the column saw of them. Contact was lost with the officer commanding the tanks and his liaison officer with the Battalion was unable to get in touch with him at any period during the battle.

When the column moved on and the leading troops reached the Arras-St. Pol road they found ample evidence that the British tanks had passed that way. German vehicles, burnt out and damaged—some of them with their drivers dead at the wheel—were strewn about the road. Enemy infantry in their field grey uniforms lay where they had fallen to the Vickers guns of the tanks. There were also a few dozen German prisoners in the hands of the crews of French tanks which had worked up to the road on the right flank of the Battalion. Some of the Germans from the burnt out and damaged vehicles had taken refuge in the woods around the village of Duisans; B. Company soon routed them out and took their first prisoners.

A and D Companies, the Carrier Platoon and parts of H.Q. Company and Battalion H.Q. now went forward towards the village of Warlus whilst B and C Companies, under command of Major McLaren, took up defensive positions around Duisans. The Battalion remained split up in this way and fought as two separate units for the rest of the battle. C Company was soon in action. Supported by a few French tanks they attacked a cemetery about half-a-mile to the west of Duisans where over a hundred Germans had taken refuge when the British armour had passed through the village. The French tanks raked the cemetery area with machine-gun fire and when the infantry advanced they found only eighteen Germans alive. The remainder had been mown down by the French gunners. The survivors were handed over to the French who stripped them to the skin and forced them to lie face downwards in the road until it was time to take them away.

It should here be mentioned that, having joined battle with the enemy three thousand yards short of the proposed start line on the Arras-Doullens road, the Battalion was completely without reliable information about German movements or locations. At about 5.30 p.m., just after passing through Warlus, A Company ran into heavy small arms and mortar fire from enemy holding positions on the Arras-Doullens road and was forced to take cover. At the same time German dive-bombers attacked the Battalion ; the sky seemed to be full of aircraft. Advanced Battalion H.Q., D Company H.Q., a reserve platoon and three French tanks were halted on the southern outskirts of Warlus and heavily dive-bombed and machine-gunned. For twenty minutes there was the high-pitched whine of the Stukas, the whistle of falling bombs and the clatter of machine-guns as the planes came down low to strafe. This first air action against the Battalion coincided with an attack by German tanks coming from the front and right flank. The French tank crews were taking cover under their tanks from the low-flying planes and knew nothing about the German threat until Major Raine dragged one of the gunners out feet first and indicated the danger in no uncertain manner. The Frenchman brought his gun into action quickly enough to stop the frontal attack whilst on the right flank the German armour was kept at a distance by the accurate fire of guns from a troop of the Brigade Anti-Tank Company.

Just before evening, A and D Companies, the Carrier Platoon and part of the Mortar Platoon were in defensive positions in and around Warlus. Whilst the troops dug in, the men who had been wounded during the air attack—the Battalion's first casualties since landing in France—started their journey back to England. This was the first time the 8th had been subjected to direct and heavy dive-bombing and machine-gunning. It was remarkable that in spite of the attack lasting twenty minutes and being virtually unopposed from the air or ground, only about ten men had been wounded and two vehicles destroyed. However, the effect on morale had been considerable. Many of the troops were in a dazed condition and it was only with the very greatest difficulty that they were persuaded to get to their feet and to move on again. The Battalion was soon to become used to this form of attack and to realise that the effect of the Junkers 87 dive-bomber is all bark and very little bite.

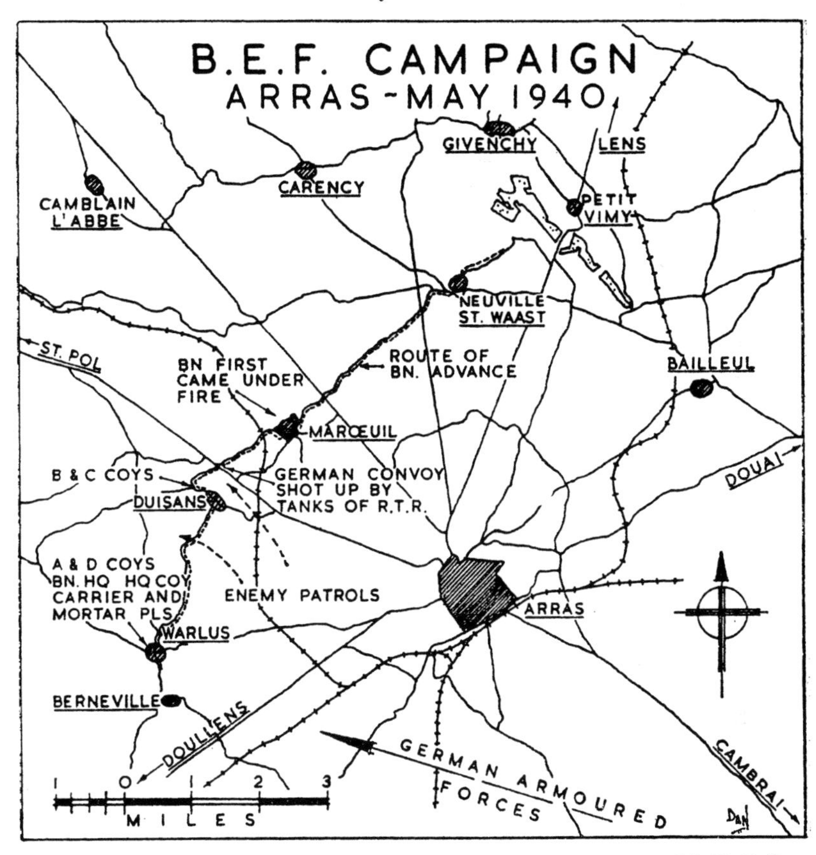

THE B.E.F. CAMPAIGN. The battle in the Arras area when the 8th Battalion, in an attempt to reach the Arras-Doullens road, became engaged in fierce fighting for the village of Warlus, west of Arras.

The rear half of the Battalion also came in for some attention from the Luftwaffe but the main excitement was caused by some French tanks which had taken a long cast round the right flank. They came out of a wood and machine-gunned B Company on the outskirts of Duisans. Tank recognition in the B.E.F. was not good in those days and within a few minutes four out of the five French tanks had been put out of action by the anti-tank gunners on B Company's front. Things had by this time reached such a state of confusion that the gunners might well have fired on the tanks under the impression that Germans manned them. This unfortunate incident drew some bursts of enemy machine-gun fire which drove the anti-tank gunners away from one of their guns, standing in a very exposed position. A British tank, passing through Duisans at the time, obligingly went forward accompanied by the gun crew and towed the gun back to cover.

When darkness came the advanced half of the Battalion in and around Warlus was attacked by a strong force of German tanks and infantry, and Lieut.-Colonel Beart withdrew all his troops into the village where they formed a close, all round defensive position. The German mortar fire was particularly accurate, several houses being set on fire by incendiary mortar bombs ; the blazing buildings lit up the village and the crash of bursting grenades and mortar bombs, mingling with the rattle of the Bren guns and German automatic weapons filled Warlus with noise. It was during this confused and bitter fighting that Sgt. A. Skorochod, the French interpreter attached to the Battalion from the French Military Mission, won the Distinguished Conduct Medal. A German tank advanced towards some 8th Battalion men and without hesitation Skorochod seized a Bren gun, threw himself down in the road and fired several magazines at the tank's armour plating from almost point-blank range. The tank withdrew under this hail of fire and a very serious situation was averted.

Whilst the battle raged in Warlus German armoured patrols struck round the flank of the village to reach the Warlus-Duisans road and sever communications with the rear half of the Battalion in Duisans ; other enemy patrols reached the Duisans-Maroeuil road and cut communications between Duisans and Brigadier Churchill's H.Q. in Maroeuil. The position in Warlus, where Lieut.-Colonel Beart and his men were now completely surrounded, seemed hopeless. Several attempts to communicate with the rear failed until 2/Lieut. R. Potts, the Mortar Officer, rode his motor-cycle flat out through the German cordon and reached Brigade H.Q. in Maroeuil at 2.30 a.m. on May 22nd. He received orders for the 8th to withdraw and once again broke through the German patrols to reach Major McLaren and B and C Companies in Duisans. However, by this time it was absolutely impossible to get through to Warlus and 2/Lieut. Potts stayed with these two companies until they withdrew from Duisans.

In Warlus the battle was moving swiftly to a climax. Heavy casualties had been inflicted on Lieut.-Colonel Beart's force, ammunition was running low and German reinforcements had been rushed up to deal with this intrepid body of men who had delayed the advance so long. Soon after midnight something happened which must have seemed like a miracle to the tired men in Warlus. Six French tanks with two armoured troop-carriers smashed their way through the German cordon and rumbled in to the village. The tanks had arrived just in time and a plan was quickly drawn up for a break-out. At 3.30 a.m. every Bren carrier and truck which had not been hit during the battle was used to evacuate the survivors of the small force which had held Warlus so gallantly. With the French tanks covering them the vehicles ran the gauntlet of German fire and raced out of the burning village. This unexpected and daring move took the enemy by surprise and, although some of the trucks and carriers were hit, the sortie was successful and the overloaded vehicles rejoined the rest of the 8th D.L.I. at Petit Vimy.

The Battalion had paid a heavy price in dead and wounded for its first action. A and D Companies between them had lost over a hundred men. The company commanders, Captain Dixon—who had been wounded—and Captain Goodenough were prisoners; Lieut. Rodger and C.S.M. Tellis were wounded and taken prisoner, and Lieut. Dees of D Company was also missing. In fact, Dees was not captured by the Germans in Warlus but escaped from the village only to be taken prisoner some days later whilst fighting with a mixed force at G.H.Q., Hazebrouck. B and C Companies, which had been in Duisans, were almost intact although C.S.M. Curry of C Company was missing and was later reported as a prisoner of war. Lieut.-Colonel Beart had been wounded in Warlus early in the action but had continued to direct operations with such calmness that he might have been on a training scheme. It was a great inspiration to see him, in spite of his wounds, moving about where the fire was heaviest. Most reluctantly he allowed himself to be evacuated and Major McLaren took over command of the Battalion.

During the afternoon of May 22nd the Battalion moved north along Vimy Ridge to Givenchy where Battalion H.Q. was set up near the village school; B Company was posted to defend the northern outskirts of the village with C Company covering the south-western approaches. The right flank of the Battalion was open but French tanks were known to be operating there, although contact could not be established with their H.Q. The Carrier Platoon sent out constant patrols to the south where the British 5th Division was holding the front a few miles away.

Next day Givenchy was a target for the German bombers. Casualties were caused to civilians as well as to troops and several carts loaded with refugees received direct hits as they passed through the village. When the smoke and dust had cleared away the long column of refugees moved on again, beyond the bomb craters and wreckage, out into the country. It was part of the German plan to break the French morale—this bombing of civilians along the roads and in the villages. These unfortunate people were by this time in a sorry plight; they had started the long trek back when the Germans invaded Belgium only to find their way to the south-west and safety blocked by the German break-through to the Somme. All day the refugees passed through the village, hoping to find a quiet spot in a world gone mad.

In the early afternoon there was a very heavy bombing raid just as a column of ammunition trucks from 5 Division were withdrawing through Givenchy. Several of the trucks were set on fire and whilst the troops fought the flames a direct hit set the village school blazing and some sheds nearby where the Battalion cooks' trucks had been hidden. C.Q.M.S. Marsden of B Company, with a complete disregard for his own safety, went into the blazing sheds several times to drive the trucks out through the flames. Several large bombs fell in the courtyard of the village church, killing some of the Battalion signallers and wounding Major Raine and also Major Forrester of the Norfolk Yeomanry. One of the signallers killed in this raid was Pte. Pratt, the Padre's right hand man in the reading rooms which had been established under more peaceful conditions in the various billeting areas. By his courage and buoyant spirits within a frail body Pratt had shown everyone a magnificent example during those hectic days since the Battalion had first come under fire near Maroeuil.

By 5 p.m., after units of 5 Division had been passing through Givenchy all the afternoon, news came from Brigade H.Q. that this Division had been withdrawn and was no longer holding positions to the south of 50 Division. On receipt of this information Major McLaren quite rightly supposed that the Germans would very soon mount an attack against 151 Brigade, but although the bombing continued until dark the enemy did not approach the main defensive positions. It may well be that a most aggressive patrol by Sgt. Carruthers and a section of carriers accounted for this German reluctance to launch an attack before dark. The carriers were on standing patrol just below the crest of Vimy Ridge near Carency when Sgt. Carruthers spotted German infantry and anti-tank guns moving in to position west of the ridge. The enemy artillery fire was very heavy at the time and he showed great courage and coolness in dealing with this new threat. The Bren guns were already out of the carriers, mounted for ground action, and when the gunners opened fire under the direction of Carruthers their accurate and steady shooting threw the German troops into complete confusion. When the last magazine had been fired none of the German anti-tank guns were in position and the enemy had suffered heavy casualties. The carrier section rejoined the Battalion in high spirits, having come through unscathed. For his part in this action Sgt. Carruthers was awarded the Distinguished Conduct Medal.

Back in Givenchy the bombing continued until darkness cloaked the village. The sky swarmed with German planes but not a single British machine was seen overhead. The reason is well known today but at that time the lack of British air support caused some bitter comment about the R.A.F. Some of the enemy planes which dive-bombed the Battalion were biplanes and were certainly not German Air Force machines. Several years later it was disclosed that they had been Dutch planes, seized by the Germans during the advance into Holland.

In the evening the 4th Battalion Royal Northumberland Fusiliers moved up on the right of the Battalion and took up defensive positions in the Bois de Givenchy. All night the crackle of rifle fire and the clatter of automatic weapons could be heard from the direction of the wood but the Battalion was not involved. About 2.30 a.m. orders were received for another withdrawal as Frankforce had become dangerously hemmed in by German penetration round the right flank.

It was a disappointment, as the 8th had hoped to fight it out on Vimy Ridge. At dawn, the Battalion left the bomb-scarred village of Givenchy in troop-carriers and, covered by the Carrier Platoon, retired through Petit Vimy, Rouvray and Henin-Leithard to Carvin. As the lorries left Givenchy the war memorial on the famous ridge where the Canadians in the 1914–18 war had fought for many months stood silhouetted against the sky.

The journey along the congested roads through Henin-Leithard and over the only bridge left intact across La Bassée Canal was a miracle of deliverance. Long before the Battalion reached the bridge the troop carriers were forced to proceed at less than walking pace. In broad daylight and under the watchful eye of a German Feisler Storch reconnaissance aircraft, known by now to all the B.E.F. as " Charlie," the vehicles crawled along three deep and nose to tail. Why the Battalion was not bombed has been the subject of much discussion since. Theories advanced vary from the Luftwaffe having run out of petrol and bombs to an alleged belief that the Germans wanted to see the Brigade across the canal rather than block the escape route and force a battle on the southern side.

In Carvin the 8th was ordered to hide up in a factory but after a meal the Battalion was sent to rest in the Bois d'Epinoy, on the left of the road from Carvin to Libercourt. Just after moving into this wood, a French Moroccan Division marched into the Bois d'Epinoy on the opposite side of the road under full view of German aircraft. Now the Luftwaffe was bombing again and the French received a thorough strafing for their carelessness, a few of the " overs " falling in the Battalion area. After digging slit trenches the troops settled down thankfully to their first long sleep for days. The following day was spent, between air raids, in washing, sleeping and eating. Apart from 2/Lieut. R. Worthington, who was wounded, the Battalion suffered no casualties, although some of the vehicles were damaged.

The C.O. now attended a conference at Brigade H.Q. where he learnt that another attack with two British formations—one of them 50 Division—the French Cavalry Corps and one division had been planned to take place on May 26th in conjunction with a large French force attacking from the south ; this was the famous Weygand plan. Meanwhile, however, the position on the left of the B.E.F. had deteriorated. The Belgians had been forced back causing a gap to appear between them and the British left flank on the Escaut. At the same time the Germans were delivering strong attacks from the direction of the Somme north-eastwards towards St. Omer, twenty-five miles from Boulogne. Communications with Dunkirk were endangered, Boulogne had fallen and Calais was invested. In view of the threat to the B.E.F., Lord Gort had no alternative but to order the only divisions he had in reserve—5 and 50—northwards to the Ypres area to fill the gap caused by the Belgian withdrawal, and so the attack southwards was finally abandoned.

Dawn broke on May 26th after a night of shelling. The German gunfire increased in intensity as the daylight hours approached and when it was light enough to take stock of the position it seemed that the 8th was in the midst of some sort of battle although the Battalion was not actually engaged. However, when Major McLaren and some observers climbed a nearby pit heap which provided excellent observation over the flat, wooded country they could see nothing except the smoke from shells, bursting in the rear of the Battalion. About 7 a.m., 2/Lieut. G. P. Chambers—the Signal Officer—who had been sent to Carvin to find out the situation returned with news of a French Algerian division. The French troops, hard pressed by the Germans who had crossed La Bassée Canal, had implored the British officer to send help, particularly in the way of light automatic weapons. Major McLaren had a difficult decision to make. He reasoned that the Battalion might be ordered to move elsewhere and did not want to go with an incomplete unit. However, he agreed to send the Carrier Platoon to Carvin, subject to recall if necessary, and 2/Lieut. English, Sgt. Skorochod and the Carrier Platoon, now reduced to only six carriers, were soon on their way to the H.Q. of the Algerian division in the northern outskirts of the town.

The carriers had been gone just over an hour when the Battalion was ordered to move to the Ypres area and the troop-carrying company was sent on a short distance to an embussing point in the village of Camphin. As the marching troops moved out of the wood they had their first experience of saturation bombing ; it was a particularly heavy raid and there were several casualties. The Battalion had always been dive-bombed on previous occasions and the troops liked this new German technique no better. The enemy planes flew fairly high, and keeping in close formation released all their bombs at the same time, most effectively covering the Battalion area. Once clear of the wood, the companies spread out in extended order ; it was a wise move, although it did not prevent the troops being bombed again several times as they crossed the open fields. They arrived in Camphin to find that the troop-carriers had not turned up and, whilst the companies settled down in the orchards around the village to wait for the transport, Major McLaren was greeted by a staff officer of 46 British Division who took him off to see General Curtis, the Divisional Commander.

General Curtis told Major McLaren that Carvin had been overrun by the enemy and that the 8th must counter-attack and recapture the town. If this information was correct, the Carrier Platoon had also been overrun. Efforts had been made to contact 2/Lieut. English after orders had been received for the move to Ypres, but all the despatch riders who tried to get through to Carvin had failed. German artillery was ranged on the approach road which was also frequently bombed from the air. Some of the motor-cyclists were blown off their machines by blast from the bursting bombs or shells whilst others were sent careering wildly off the road, with broken telegraph lines entangled in the wheels of their machines.

When the Brigade Major of 151 Brigade, Major A. Clive, arrived in Camphin and stated that the Battalion's presence in Ypres was not

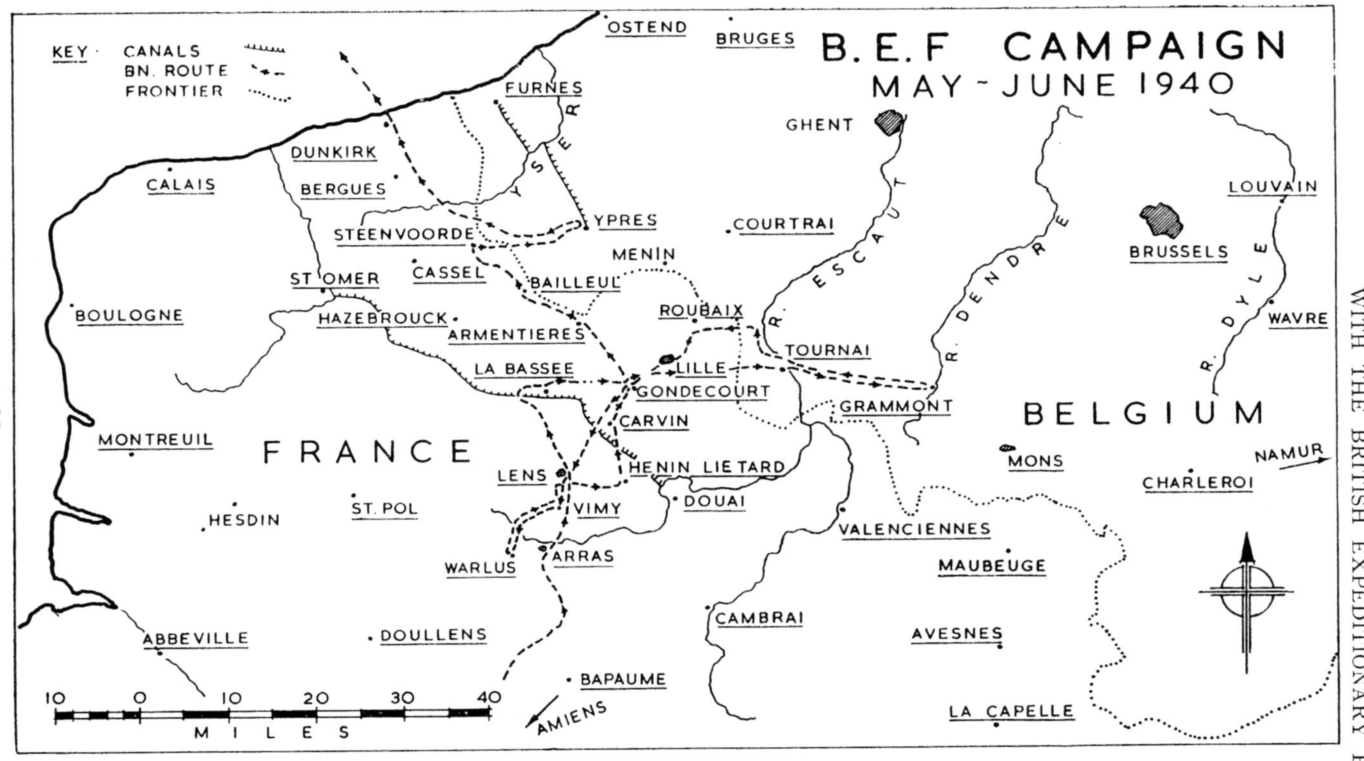

THE B.E.F. CAMPAIGN. The routes taken by the 8th Battalion during the fighting which took place in northern France between the time of the initial German attack and the evacuation from the beaches of Dunkirk.

immediately essential, it was decided to put in an immediate counter-attack against Carvin. Speed was essential to restore the situation which was on the point of breaking down. Major McLaren collected the Battalion and moved forward in close co-operation with Allied tanks only forty minutes after receipt of orders. The advance, made difficult by the constant shelling and frequent bombing, was carried out under his personal leadership with great elan and was entirely successful in restoring the situation. The speedy and successful attack of the Battalion had a marked effect on all Allied troops in the area. For his outstanding part in this action and his brilliant leadership during the remainder of the B.E.F. campaign, Major McLaren was awarded the Distinguished Service Order.

It is now necessary to leave the Battalion for a while in order to follow the fortunes of the Carrier Platoon which, after an uneventful journey, arrived in Carvin where 2/Lieut. English and Sgt. Skorochod reported to the French commander at his H.Q. He was in one room with eight or nine of his staff officers, all of them shouting at each other and gesticulating excitedly as they argued over the maps spread out on the table. Everyone was talking at once and it was only the badges of rank which defined the French commander. When the British officer and his interpreter walked into the room, the French stopped talking for a moment and then wildly acclaimed the two men in khaki battledress. When the chorus of " Bravo les Anglais " had died down the situation was explained. The Germans had crossed the canal near the Carvin-Lens road, but had not advanced very far. The Algerian troops, who had been in the line for some days, were tired and English was asked to report to a French colonel who would dispose the British troops in positions covering the southern exits of the town astride the Carvin-Lens road.

The streets were deserted as the carriers clattered through Carvin and although the colonel could not be found, a French major directed the platoon to its positions. Very soon they were digging in without enemy interference. News came through at about 11 a.m. that the French were going to counter-attack towards the canal. Shortly afterwards French gunners shelled the German positions, and infantry and tanks moved forward. Very little progress was made in this attack, which did not include the Carrier Platoon, and the situation was most confusing.

During the morning Sgt. Carruthers noticed a British vehicle out in front and two khaki-clad figures walking away from it. The men turned out to be the Padre of the 8th, Father Duggan and his batman, Pte. Deveney. They were obliged to abandon the Padre's car when it ran in to a ditch and were not at all impressed when informed that they had been out in No Man's Land, nearer to the German positions than to our own. The Padre's infectious humour soon cheered everybody. His explanation to a French major in rudimentary French, spoken in best Irish manner, about the British officer and the function of the vehicles under his command was most amusing to everyone but the major, who thought the English soldiers were quite mad. Padre

Duggan then established an unofficial Regimental Aid Post in a house in the main street where he worked untiringly all day, tending the wounded and showing a complete disregard for the German shelling, which was most accurate and caused a lot of damage to the town.

During the afternoon some Algerians took up positions near the Carrier Platoon. Their arrival was most welcome as the three sections of British troops had been isolated all day and had not seen any other Allied forces. The Algerian company was commanded by a French lieutenant who boasted that they meant to hold their positions " no matter what the Sal Bosche did." Then it began to rain in torrents, which damped the spirits of everyone and especially those of the North African troops. There followed some heavy and accurate shelling and, after a few minutes of this, the French lieutenant shouted " Allez, toute suite " and led the undignified withdrawal of his troops who hastened back to Carvin at the double. The Carrier Platoon was once more left on its own to defend the southern entry into the town. Soon afterwards enemy shelling grew heavier and German infantry appeared on the right only to withdraw when accurate Bren gun fire was opened at them.

It was now about 5 o'clock in the afternoon and the Battalion had just started to counter-attack Carvin, supposedly held by the Germans. C Company, under Captain Walton, was right forward ; D Company, commanded by 2/Lieut. Potts, was in the centre ; A Company, commanded by Lieut. Clark was left forward company, and B Company, under Lieut. Kirkup, was in reserve. The advancing troops were shelled as they approached the town and Lieut. Clark was wounded ; there was also some sniping from the direction of Carvin, probably the work of fifth columnists, the town being still held by the French. The Battalion arrived to find that no Germans had ever been in Carvin and it was the men of A Company who first found the Carrier Platoon on the southern outskirts, in action against German troops who had crossed the canal near the broken bridge on the Carvin-Lens road but had made no effort to advance. By this time the whole Battalion was occupying positions in the town and the Carrier Platoon reverted to command of the 8th, continuing to hold their positions on the southern outksirts. Intermittent but accurate shelling continued until dark and D Company had about twenty casualties from the German gunfire. At 11 p.m., Major McLaren called for a volunteer to locate the position of the leading German troops on the Carvin-Lens road. L/Cpl. McTiernan of the Carrier Platoon volunteered and was told to " go on down the road in your carrier until you're fired on." McTiernan did precisely this, his noisy vehicle drawing the fire of a German anti-tank gun about three-quarters of a mile north-east of the broken bridge on the Carvins-Lens road. The carrier returned safely with this valuable information.

The earlier orders for 50 Division to move to Ypres now came into force and at 2.30 a.m. on May 27th the Battalion withdrew from Carvin, embussing in the northern outskirts of the town. The troop carriers rumbled through the night, without lights, beyond familiar

Gondecourt to Armentières, Baileul and a place called Steenvoorde, where the Battalion arrived just after eight o'clock in the morning. Captain Clarke had gone ahead the day before to find billets in Steenvoorde but could not be traced anywhere, and no one else had the slightest idea where the Battalion was to be billeted. By this time the German fighter and bomber squadrons had made their appearance; Steenvoorde was no place for the 8th. The Battalion moved out on the road to Cassel to await further orders. The companies had only just settled down when a small German tank force put in a lightning attack from the west. This German attack was not pressed home and the tanks were obviously part of the left arm of the enemy pincer movement which was reaching out towards the coast; the commander probably did not want to get involved in a battle with a strong British force and sheered off when the Battalion showed some fight.

About 4.30 p.m. Brigadier Churchill arrived and ordered the Battalion forward to the Ypres Canal area. The D.L.I. Brigade had been given the task of holding positions north of Ypres along the canal facing east, with the 9th D.L.I. on the right and the 6th D.L.I. on the left. The 8th was in reserve for the first time and the Battalion had settled in by 10.30 p.m.

Orders were received at ten o'clock next morning for the 8th to move to come under command of Brigadier Haydon's 150 Brigade. The Brigadier had put in an urgent request for the Battalion to stop a reported German infiltration through a gap to the south of Ypres, between his brigade and the formation on the right. The Carrier Platoon went ahead to occupy the Dickebusche crest, scene of much bitter fighting in the 1914–18 war, and the rest of the Battalion followed on foot. The infantry companies took over from the Carriers and quickly settled down in the new positions. There was considerable shelling but no German attack was launched. The 4th Battalion Royal Northumberland Fusiliers moved up on the right flank and the 8th remained in position all that day, until relieved by a battalion of the Bedfordshire and Hertfordshire Regiment, and a battalion of the Manchester Regiment. To the surprise of the troops in the so-called front line, the battalion of Manchesters marched in from the front in excellent order to take over.

After this uneventful day, the 8th rejoined 151 Brigade as darkness fell and, at 2-30 a.m. next morning, the D.L.I. battalions withdrew several miles to the village of Woeston, where the 8th took up positions as left forward battalion of the Brigade and flanking unit of the Division with the Royal Ulster Rifles of 3 British Division on the left. By ten o'clock in the morning of May 29th the Battalion had dug in with D Company on the right, B Company in the centre, C Company on the left and A Company in reserve. The Carriers, under 2/Lieut. English, patrolled out in front and withdrew through the Battalion forward positions at midday, having watched the Germans launch a formal attack across the Ypres Canal against positions which the Brigade had evacuated six hours previously. On the way back the

Carriers had a skirmish with German troops in the village of Elverdinghe, only a mile from the Battalion forward positions. By early afternoon the Germans had closed the gap ; shortly after 6 p.m. enemy gunners registered the company areas.

At about this time news came through that the Belgians had asked for an armistice. The men of 50 Division and the rest of the troops in the B.E.F., tired to the point of exhaustion, were not particularly interested in the long term results of King Leopold's decision but it meant the collapse of the left flank of the Allied line and the probable encirclement and destruction of the B.E.F. Grimly and defiantly Lord Gort's sadly depleted army turned to meet the new German threat.

Just before 8 o'clock the Battalion received orders to withdraw once again, an hour later at 9 p.m. in broad daylight and under close enemy observation. Half-an-hour before the companies were scheduled to pull out of their positions German artillery and mortar fire increased and a heavy attack was launched against C Company. With characteristic thoroughness the Germans chose a weak point in the line, the junction between C Company and the Royal Ulster Rifles of 3 Division. Within a short time the momentum of the German attack had surrounded C Company and cut the withdrawal route. For the rest of that night the three platoons of C Company fought a losing battle against the superior German forces. Outnumbered, outgunned and isolated from the rest of the Battalion, the company was finally overrun. Only two men escaped to tell the story of the battle ; of the remainder, those who had not been killed or wounded were taken prisoner. Meanwhile the rest of the Battalion had withdrawn as planned. The heavy and accurate German shelling had kept the troop carriers out of the village and the troops embussed north of Woeston. The German follow-up was swift. As the last Battalion vehicle—a carrier—clattered out of the village, the leading German troops moved in.

By the night of May 29th/30th what remained of the B.E.F. had withdrawn to the Dunkirk perimeter. In view of the collapse of the Belgian Army and the precarious position of the French and British Armies, it had been reluctantly decided to evacuate the B.E.F. and as much of the French First and Seventh Armies as possible from Dunkirk. The British sector of the perimeter was about two miles from the town, based along the canals from Bergues to Furnes and Nieuport. There was a quick redistribution of the remaining British formations and 50 Division was transferred to 1 British Corps. General Martel was ordered to move his brigades into position to hold a sector of the perimeter near the Franco-Belgian frontier.

After leaving Woeston the Battalion withdrew across the Bergues-Furnes Canal at Houthe and came into Brigade Reserve in the area of the chateau at Moeres. Here, orders were received to destroy most of the vehicles including the carriers. This caused amazement and consternation but there is no doubt that it was a wise order, for by this time there was an uncontrollable concentration of vehicles in the

Dunkirk perimeter. To have allowed these vehicles to remain mobile would have invited chaos on the roads which had to be kept clear until the last. Most of the Battalion trucks were destroyed or damaged by the redoubtable Sgt. Glendenning of the M.T. Platoon, who did not confine his activities wholly to the Battalion transport and must have put hundreds of vehicles out of action during those last few days in the perimeter. He had several methods. One was to leave the engine running hard and then put a few rifle shots into the sump so that the oil drained out ; another was to mix handfuls of sand with the oil in the sump, then race the engine. A third method was to set a seven-second fuse on a hand grenade and place the bomb on the engine near the carburettor. Unfortunately the explosion set the engine on fire and resulted in the vehicle bursting into flames, which was forbidden for reasons of morale. The four remaining carriers escaped this drastic treatment until they were taken to the rear and destroyed on the beaches when the Battalion withdrew from the perimeter.

In the Brigade reserve position, the Battalion defended a wide ditch known as the Ringsloot Canal to the south-east of Moeres. May 30th was a fairly quiet day for the 8th but the 9th D.L.I., as left forward battalion of the Brigade, was under continual fire. During the day the Germans dropped leaflets showing a map of the B.E.F. dispositions. According to the enemy, the British Army occupied a very small area around Dunkirk and was almost completely surrounded by the Germans. In bold type, the leaflets had a message in English " The game is up, the innings is over ! There is no alternative but to surrender." The hard-pressed troops of the B.E.F. laughed at this German propaganda and did not believe a word of it. Later on, of course, they learnt that this particular piece of propaganda was one of the few occasions during the war when the Germans told the truth.

On May 31st a most welcome batch of reinforcements arrived from 70 Brigade, a formation which included the Battalion's second line unit, the 11th D.L.I. Commanded by Captain Shipley the reinforcements, one hundred strong and all volunteers, were organised into platoons to strengthen A and D Companies. The troops arrived at a time when German pressure against the Brigade front was increasing. During the afternoon the 6th and 9th Battalions were driven back by the ferocity of the German attack on to the 8th D.L.I. positions, where they dug in and thickened the defences.

The shelling in the area of the chateau, where 8th Battalion H.Q. had been established, was intense ; casualties came in fast and the familiar cry of " stretcher bearers " became more frequent. Lieut. Wilkinson, the Battalion Medical Officer, with Captain Rutherford the Medical Officer of the 9th D.L.I. established a joint Regimental Aid Post in the cellars of the chateau which was soon blazing above their heads. Assisted by the redoubtable Padre Duggan they did some excellent work. Throughout the afternoon the figures of the Padre and Cpl. Fletcher, the Stretcher Bearer Sergeant, could be seen wherever the shelling and casualties were heaviest. Journey after journey was made by the two men to carry in the wounded to the cellars of the chateau, where the Padre's cheerful humour was like a tonic to the long lines of men who lay on the floor waiting to be evacuated. He seemed quite oblivious to the heavy shelling, and his coolness, energy and courage undoubtedly calmed as well as kept up the morale of the wounded men in his care. Padre Duggan was awarded the Military Cross.

Just before dusk two machine-gun battalions, the 4th Gordons and the 1st Royal Northumberland Fusiliers, moved up and gave a magnificent performance of defensive fire across the Battalion front until the Vickers guns ran short of ammunition. Darkness brought a welcome easing of the German pressure. Brigadier Churchill quickly seized this opportunity to reorganise his command. He put the right of the Brigade front, by now a jumble of several units of the Brigade, under command of Lieut.-Colonel Percy of the 9th D.L.I.; the left sector under command of Major McLaren. The night passed fairly quietly for the British troops but not so quietly for the Germans on the Brigade front, who were bombarded by the guns of H.M.S. *Nelson*, steaming off the French coast. The huge shells went over like express trains to explode with a deafening roar in the German lines.

At 2-30 a.m. on June 1st the Battalion was ordered to break contact with the Germans on the Ringsloot Canal and, covered by the Carrier Platoon, withdrew in good order to the sand dunes some six miles to the east of Dunkirk. It is interesting to note that the withdrawal of the Battalion on foot and in two columns was not interfered with by the German forces who had been trying so persistently to break the Brigade's hold on the canal line.

Back in the sand dunes the battle-weary troops of 151 Brigade gratefully settled down to rest. By this time there was not a single man in the Brigade who was not tired to the point of exhaustion. The last fourteen days had been a nightmare, and the uncertainty and lack of news about the battle as a whole was not good for the morale of troops who had been continually withdrawing. The fighting had been heavy, and during the periods when the Battalion was not in action the troops had been continually on the alert. No one had ever been able to look forward to a complete night's sleep, for there was every chance that before the night was out the Battalion would be on the move again and only odd moments of sleep were snatched at infrequent intervals. The ceaseless bombing from the air and the continual German shelling had shattered the nerves of some of the troops and the strain was beginning to tell on everyone. Those men who sat down for a few moments rest were almost invariably over-powered by an irresistible urge to sleep. The voices of people talking seemed far away as though the listener was going under an anaesthetic, and the strain of fatigue and the lack of sleep will be remembered by those who took part in the campaign long after the fighting and dive-bombing has been forgotten.

The Battalion was shelled a little in its position in the sand dunes but the full force of the German attack was directed against the troops who were being evacuated, and all morning the Luftwaffe squadrons bombed the beaches and waiting transports. Those men of the Battalion who were not too tired to watch saw the epic of the little ships at Dunkirk. They watched this odd assortment of craft with their intrepid skippers dart in close to the beaches, pick up the troops and set course for England, their gunwales awash in many cases. They saw several British destroyers sunk, their guns firing to the last, and at midday they cheered wildly when R.A.F. fighters appeared over the beaches to send several of the German bombers spiralling down in flames. To see the R.A.F. roundels again after fourteen days of the Luftwaffe and not a single British plane was a great tonic. During the afternoon the German Air Force made only one or two appearances and the men of the B.E.F. took back the bitter words they had spoken about the R.A.F. earlier in the campaign ; the British fighters were obviously doing great work elsewhere.

Meanwhile, the dunes had come under long range German machine-gun fire and at noon Brigadier Churchill called a conference at Brigade H.Q. The Brigadier looked absolutely worn out as he quietly explained that it was most unlikely that the Brigade would be evacuated from Dunkirk. The infantry battalions and the assortment of attached troops were to be organised into two columns. One column, commanded by Lieut.-Colonel Percy, was to be a marching column whilst the other, commanded by Major McLaren and made up of the 8th D.L.I. and a hundred Grenadier guardsmen, was to be mobile. The columns had been given the task of smashing a way out of the Dunkirk defended area and attacking the German forces, causing as much damage as possible, so as to create a diversion whilst the remainder of the B.E.F. was embarked. The survivors were then to fight their way back to the beaches at Dunkirk, with the bare possibility that they would be evacuated if it was not too late. The Battalion was quickly organised for this new role. There were only a few Bren guns available but a visit to the beaches by some of the troops soon provided all the guns and ammunition required for the operation. The beaches were littered with every sort of weapon, abandoned by men who had swum out to the ships lying just offshore.

This suicidal operation was never carried out, for by 2.30 p.m. the untiring efforts of the R.A.F. had eased the situation at Dunkirk considerably and the foray of the two columns was cancelled. Instead, the Battalion received an amended order to move down to the beaches for embarkation. The remaining Battalion vehicles were destroyed and the troops set off on foot along the beaches towards Dunkirk, carrying all their weapons. Sgt. Malone of A Company shouldered a Lewis gun which he had found during the early stages of the battle and carried for ten days. Although a very heavy weapon when compared with the Bren he much preferred " something solid rather than them new-fangled Brens." L/Cpl. Wilson, the P.R.I.[1] canteen steward, trudged along with an alarm clock slung round his neck, and carrying a sandbag full of small change in French currency

[1]President of Regimental Institute ; administrator of a fund for the benefit of Other Ranks of the Battalion.

which had been in the till " when the balloon went up." The contents of the sandbag were eventually exchanged in England for forty good English pounds.

The march along the beaches was not without incident. Twice, German planes swooped down low over the Battalion to strafe the troops but fortunately they caused no casualties. By 6 p.m. the Battalion was dispersed on the beach at Dunkirk near the end of the famous mole and once more the troops dug themselves in. The situation was very vague. No one could be found who knew anything about embarkation orders for the 8th D.L.I. and Major McLaren went into the town to get some information. After wandering around Dunkirk for some time he found Divisional H.Q. but still could not get any definite news about the future movement of the 8th. He returned to the Battalion at about 9 p.m. to find a long column of men in threes, both British and French, forming up in broad daylight at the approaches to the mole ; an atmosphere of " first come, first served " was rapidly developing. Infantry, gunners, engineers, tank crews, R.A.S.C. personnel—men from every arm of the service were forming up although there was no ship in sight. It made a wonderful target for the German Air Force which fortunately did not put in an appearance. Then Brigadier Churchill arrived and in his own inimitable way soon arranged things differently. He produced a priority list on the spot which inevitably did not satisfy the many British and French troops involved, but the priority was enforced and what might have been an unpleasant situation averted.

The Battalion remained in slit trenches until ordered forward to take its place in the queue. There had been doubts as to whether the 8th would embark that night and it was with a feeling of relief that the anxious men climbed out of their slit trenches. The long line of troops moved slowly along the mole with British on one side of the causeway and French on the other. The beaches and harbour were under light shellfire and in the town of Dunkirk many large fires were burning. The mole itself and the ships alongside, mostly minesweepers were not under fire and a group of British and French soldiers had been stationed just short of the ships to regulate the flow of men to ensure that the Allied troops were embarked in equal numbers. The few French soldiers who still carried rifles had fixed bayonets and impaled loaves of bread on the steel ; most of them were Moroccans who laughing and shouting excitedly behaved like small children. It did not make the task of the regulating party any easier and they deserve a complimentary mention here for the tactful way in which they dealt with the odd assortment of Allied troops.

After passing the regulating party, the men of the 8th Battalion scrambled thankfully over the low rails of a destroyer and were at sea within a few minutes. The embarkation was a complete anti-climax. Early that afternoon the men of the 8th had expected to die fighting in a desperate break-out from the Dunkirk perimeter, and now, less than twelve hours later, they were in a British ship on the way to England. Many battalion histories will tell a different story about Dunkirk but for the 8th D.L.I. there were none of these epics of supreme gallantry which were later pictured in the pages of the *Illustrated London News*. There was no swimming out to small boats, no murderous bombing and shelling of the beaches. In the quiet times of peace many a week-end tripper to France had a more exciting leave-taking.

The flames in Dunkirk reached up to the night skies and the dull boom of gunfire came from somewhere inland. The ship set course for Dover and suddenly everything seemed quiet and peaceful. It was, after all, the English Channel and to the tired troops on board the destroyer it was a bit of old England.

The officers of the 8th D.L.I. at Charlbury, Oxfordshire in December 1939.

Back row. 2/Lieut. T. Coates, 2/Lieut. C. L. Beattie, 2/Lieut. G. Blagdon, 2/Lieut. R. Potts, 2/Lieut. T. Preacher, Lieut. G. Clark.

Middle row. 2/Lieut. I. R. English, 2/Lieut. E. L. Dees, 2/Lieut. J. A. Leybourne, 2/Lieut. J. A. Robinson, Lieut. (Q.M.) T. Marshall, Lieut. G. T. Ferguson, 2/Lieut. G. R. Rodger, 2/Lieut. G. P. Chambers, 2/Lieut. J. F. Gedge.

Front row. Captain L. H. Wilkinson, R.A.M.C., Captain G. F. Cook, Captain F. W. E. Goodenough, Captain J. W. Walton, Major R. S. McLaren, Lieut.-Colonel C. W. Beart, M.C., Captain A. B. S. Clarke, (Adjutant), Major J. G. Raine, M.C., Captain A. M. K. Martin, Captain A. Gordon, (not of the 8th D.L.I.). Lieut. F. B. Kirkup

New York Times.

A French soldier watches British troops marching through Dunkirk on their way to the beaches where an odd assortment of craft waited to take them to England—and safety. A burning searchlight lorry is in the foreground.

CHAPTER THREE

WAITING FOR THE INVASION

Home again—coastal defence—invasion is imminent—training at Yeovil and Honiton—mobilization for service overseas.

FOUR o'clock in the morning—the time of the Battalion's arrival at Dover just as light was breaking on June 2nd—is an unearthly hour to arrive anywhere but on this particular occasion there were no grouses. It was wonderful to be back in England again. There had been several alarms during the journey from Dunkirk but no attacks, and a cheerful though weary body of men formed up on the quayside. A disappointment was, however, in store for them ; the Battalion was ordered to hand in all rifles and Bren guns. There were some who were only too pleased to get rid of their burden but the majority of the troops felt that it was most unfair to be deprived of rifles and Brens which had been carried from Belgium to Dunkirk, and then across the Channel. Twice during the previous day at Dunkirk orders to destroy all weapons had been ignored, as it was thought that the instructions had been given to prevent them falling into the hands of the Germans. Actually the Navy had asked for the weapons to be left behind as they did not want the extra weight on their already overloaded ships. Many times during the summer months that were to follow when the Battalion had only a few automatic weapons, and those of strange makes, the companies could have made good use of the Brens they left lined up on the quayside at Dover.

From Dover the 8th was sent to reception camps in the Aldershot area. The troops climbed thankfully into English railway carriages, and those who could not find a seat lay stretched out in the corridors or on the floor of a carriage between the seats, dead to the world. History will never record that the men of the B.E.F. were shunned as a defeated army. Far from it—they were given a tremendous welcome by the people of the southern counties and the way in which they treated the 8th was typical. At every stop, and there were many of them between Dover and Aldershot, hastily organised parties of the fair sex distributed gifts of cigarettes, chocolate, food and good English cups of tea. Most important of all, these people who had heard with dismay of the defeat of their army in France, spoke words of encouragement. The B.E.F. was out of the ring but England stood steady. It was grand to listen to them and to know that there was going to be no collapse like that of France. These heartening thoughts were, however, sobered by the prospect of how the delightful peace and quiet of the Kentish countryside, through which the train had passed, would inevitably be shattered by the bombs and machine guns of the Luftwaffe.

In Aldershot an enthusiastic welcome awaited the Battalion from the men of various units, some of them Canadian, who had not been to France. After a few days of warm hospitality, the troops of 50 Division were taken in special trains to Knutsford Park, Cheshire, where the various units—which had become hopelessly mixed up during the last days in France—were able to sort themselves out. A few days after arriving at Knutsford, ten days leave was granted, and altered at the last moment to forty-eight hours because of the danger of invasion. It was, as everyone now knows, a very real danger and the situation was critical. Although upwards of 230,000 men of the B.E.F. had been brought back from Dunkirk, very nearly all the stores, equipment and vehicles of the force had been lost. No stores were immediately available to re-equip the B.E.F. and the defence of the country was in the hands of the few divisions which had not been to France.

When the men of the 8th returned from their short leave they were sent on to Rugeley in Staffordshire, where the three D.L.I. battalions went under canvas in a camp just outside the town. The Brigade continued the task of re-forming and drafts were sent to bring the battalions up to strength. The 9th Battalion was re-inforced by men from the King's Shropshire Light Infantry and the 6th Battalion had a draft from the Argyll and Sutherland Highlanders. The 8th was pleased to welcome three hundred and fifty D.L.I. from the Regimental Depot.

Lieut.-Colonel C. W. Beart, returned from hospital and took over command again from Lieut.-Colonel R. S. McLaren, and ten officer reinforcements arrived, the majority of whom were from the Royal Ulster Rifles and included 2/Lieuts. R. H. R. Robinson, D. A. Neale, and J. N. Wheatley. Major P.C. Parker, M.C., and 2/Lieut. P. H. Bower came from the West Yorkshire Regiment Infantry Training Centre and 2/Lieut. I. S. Turnbull, who had broken his arm on an exercise at Charlbury before the Battalion left for France, rejoined the unit. R.S.M. W. G. Stray received a well-deserved commission as Quartermaster, and with R.Q.M.S. Lightfoot was to look after the Q side of the Battalion admirably and without a break until the 8th went into suspended animation in 1945. Major D. A. Gray returned from Divisional H.Q. to take over H.Q. Company from 2/Lieut. R. Potts who had commanded the company during the closing stages in France, and who took over the Mortar Platoon again. Lieut. G. T. Ferguson became Adjutant, and Lieut. R. I. Pitt remained as Intelligence Officer. The company commanders and company sergeant majors were: A Company—Captain B. Holroyde (from the 6th Battalion) and C.S.M. Cockburn; B Company—Captain F. B. Kirkup and C.S.M. Wood; C Company—Lieut. C. Burdon-Taylor and C.S.M. Craggs; and D Company—Captain A. B. S. Clarke and C.S.M. McQuaid.

On June 22nd the Battalion received orders to move to the south coast near Weymouth to take over duties of coastal defence. After staging at Cattistock in Dorset the 8th, with the 72nd Field Regiment and 151 Brigade Anti-Tank Company under command, took up positions east and west of Weymouth from Osmington Mills to Abbotsbury. The field regiment had not a single gun of any sort and was organised as four rifle companies and the anti-tank company, without any anti-tank guns, was made up as one rifle company. Battalion H.Q. was at Upwey, a few miles north of Weymouth, where D Company, the Carrier Platoon without carriers, and the Mortar Platoon without mortars became Battalion Reserve.

The fourteen-mile long front was divided into two halves for tactical reasons. Lieut.-Colonel Mould Graham of the 72nd Field Regiment, with his headquarters, commanded the left sector known as Lodforce and Major Parker the right sector, christened Fleetforce. Both sectors were the responsibility of the C.O. of the 8th. Fourteen miles of vital coast defended only by riflemen ! It was only one stage removed from bows and arrows and there is no doubt that only the Channel and courage of the British people stood between England and Nazi Germany.

Shortly after the Battalion arrived in the coastal sector Lieut.-Colonel Beart left to command Weyforce, the defences of Weymouth, and Lieut.-Colonel McLaren took over command once more. The Battalion settled down in the coast defences. It meant much hard work ; weapon pits and command posts had to be constructed along the whole front and barbed wire erected. In that memorable mid-summer of 1940, with the ever-present danger of invasion, the forward companies " stood-to" at 10.30 p.m. and again at 4 a.m., just before dawn. There was little time for sleep between the "stand-to" periods, for almost every night brought a scare of some sort such as flashing lights or the sound of gunfire somewhere out there in the darkness over the Channel. Whether the scare was false or not it meant that the Battalion had to "stand-to" until dawn showed that all was well. Then a hurried breakfast was followed by another hard day's work on the beach defences.

The routine in the 8th during the month of July was typical of what was happening to the infantry battalions stationed along the threatened coastline of southern England. Night and day there were air raid alarms as the Luftwaffe made for Portland and on one occasion two bombs fell near E Company H.Q. at New Barn Farm. There were fifth column scares and reports of lights being flashed to German aircraft to guide them in over their targets. The reserve company usually had to turn out to investigate these mysterious flashing lights, and although they never found any fifth columnists there is no doubt that some elusive person did signal to German planes from the hills near Dorchester.

At 4 a.m. on July 11th a message was received that enemy surface craft were approaching Portsmouth and the Battalion " stood-to." Was this the long-expected invasion ? The Intelligence Officer went on a reconnaissance along the coast but could find nothing suspicious happening out at sea, and at 6.30 a.m. a message was received from Brigade H.Q. that it had been a false alarm. Thankfully the Battalion "stood-down," but a busy day was ahead. Just after midday fifteen bombers with a fighter escort dive-bombed Portland. Five enemy planes were brought down and A Company was sent to pick up an airman who had been seen to bale out of one of the crashing planes. It was another false alarm. Two days afterwards the Luftwaffe raided Portland again. Fifteen enemy planes came over and three were shot down for the loss of two of our own.

There are certain milestones in the history of the Battalion and one of them must certainly be linked with the month of July. A tall, very smart C.S.M. reported to the Adjutant one day from the Infantry Training Centre. There was nothing unusual about his name—just plain Jennings—and he had been posted to the Battalion as the new R.S.M. But to put it mildly, he was a very unusual man, and it would not be unkind to the many other excellent R.S.Ms. of the 8th Battalion to say that "Spike" Jennings, as he was very soon christened by the troops, was the best R.S.M. the Battalion has ever had. At about the same time, two new officers—2/Lieuts. B. Lindsay and D. T. M. Hopcroft—joined the Battalion with a draft of fifty other ranks from the D.L.I. Infantry Training Centre.

During the month of July the defences were inspected by the Corps Commander. His name in those days did not mean much to the Battalion but before the end of the war the 8th was destined to fight many a hard battle under the brilliant leadership of the alert little man, who missed not a single detail when he visited the forward companies on that afternoon in July 1940. His name was Montgomery.

The end of July brought with it a most amusing incident at the expense of Lieut. R. I. Pitt, the Intelligence Officer. One night the ever vigilant Home Guard sent a message that they had found signal flags on Friar Waddon hill, and shortly afterwards they reported that an enemy plane had flown low over Friar Waddon to drop red and yellow flares. The following morning the Intelligence Officer saw three red and yellow flags on a tripod at Friar Waddon. Obviously this was the work of fifth columnists and Lieut. Pitt went immediately to report the information to his opposite number at the R.A.F. Station, Warmwell. As the two officers were discussing ways and means of setting a trap, a party of Royal Engineers arrived at Friar Waddon to take away the flags which had been left there the previous day for surveying purposes. It was some time before Pitt was allowed to forget this episode.

At the beginning of August the Battalion was relieved on the beaches by the 4th East Yorks and withdrawn to Maiden Newton and Cattistock to become Brigade Mobile Reserve. Twenty antiquated and by no means always mobile civilian motor buses of the 25th Motor Coach Company came under command, as well as a number of cars and motor-cycles. The latter were formed into a Motor-Cycle Platoon under command of Lieut. I. S. Turnbull. August was a happy and busy month. There were strenuous platoon, company and battalion exercises and the 8th was able to operate once more as a compact unit after its wide dispersal on the beaches. During August the Battle of Britain was at its height and there were many aerial combats overhead. On several occasions enemy planes were shot down in the Battalion area.

The reserve role came to an end on September 1st, when the Battalion moved back to the beaches and took over from the 9th D.L.I. that delightful stretch of coast from Burton Bradstock to Lyme Regis. Battalion H.Q. was at Morecambe Lake and in the most glorious weather the companies settled down to improve defences, lay mines and erect wire. Lieut.-Colonel Beart returned from Weyforce to assume command once more, and that same night code word " Cromwell " was received from Brigade H.Q. ; this meant "stand-to in battle positions."

Invasion was imminent and British troops along the whole length of the south and east coasts moved to their action stations. For eleven days the Battalion "stood-to" ; it was a nerve-racking period, and the news on September 15th that the weather was becoming unsuitable for enemy landings was welcomed by those who knew and understood the weakness of the British defences. Hitler had missed his chance. The following day the weather broke and the high seas pounded and damaged the anti-tank blocks, put the telephone lines out of action, and filled many of the pillboxes in forward positions with water so that they were untenable. On September 18th "Cromwell" was cancelled and the Battalion "stood-down".

Whilst the code word was in operation a reinforcement company had been formed under command of Lieut. R. I. Pitt, and 2/Lieut. D. A. Neale became Intelligence Officer. Sgt. J. Carruthers having now been granted a well-deserved emergency commission, took over the Carrier Platoon from 2/Lieut. I. R. English, who went to Brigade as Transport Officer. Early in October the newly formed reinforcement company occupied the beach defences whilst the rest of the Battalion carried out a Divisional Exercise in the Dorchester area. The weather was bad and it poured with rain for the duration of the scheme, which was also marred by a most unfortunate incident. Just after dark a marauding German plane spotted the lights of some of the battalion vehicles and dropped a stick of bombs. Pte. Splevins, the C.O.'s driver, was killed and Major A. B. S. Clarke wounded. Shortly after this, another enemy plane came down low to strafe Battalion H.Q. but there were no further casualties.

Not long after the Divisional Exercise the Battalion was warned for foreign service and moved to Yeovil in Somerset whilst the beach defences were taken over by a battalion of the Essex Regiment. At Yeovil H.R.H. the Duke of Gloucester visited the D.L.I. Brigade and saw the Battalion training and after a month of intensive preparation, 50 Division became part of G.H.Q. Reserve. This entailed a move to Honiton in east Devon.

The training programme which had been started at Yeovil continued and there were numerous exercises and schemes. Some of these lasted several days, and took place in bitter weather on the heights of Exmoor. Snowstorms and blizzards meant that the exercises were carried out under the most miserable conditions. It was a hard testing ground but it certainly toughened up the 8th D.L.I. However, it was not all work and no play, for there were Battalion dances—all of them successful and most of them hilarious—E.N.S.A. concerts in the N.A.A.F.I., rugger games against Honiton Town and soccer fixtures.

About the middle of December the 8th received orders to mobilize for service overseas, with a probable date of embarkation in January. Most of the Battalion had been on leave by the turn of the year, but the date of departure was postponed and news received that 50 Division would not be sailing for some time. The winter months turned to spring and the 8th had become a well-trained and equipped battalion. Early in the year a lantern lecture, "The Wonders of Egypt," gave a good indication of the probable destination of the Division and when khaki drill and topees were issued the odds throughout the Battalion were on Egypt. There was a further spell of leave and the men knew embarkation would not long be delayed when the M.T. and Carrier Platoons left for a secret destination. H.M. the King visited the Battalion with General Alexander, who was G.O.C. in C. Southern Command, and saw a demonstration by two platoons of A Company and one of C Company near Wells in Somerset. Colonel J. Turnbull, T.D., D.L., always a welcome visitor, was with the Battalion for Guest Night.

Honiton saw many changes, but it was one affecting the whole Brigade which meant so much to the men of the 8th ; Brigadier Churchill relinquished command of the three D.L.I. battalions which he had led in France. His magnificent leadership during those critical days had endeared him to the troops. Another grievous loss was Padre Duggan ; his gallantry and continual cheerfulness during the hopeless situations which were all too characteristic of the French campaign had earned the respect of every member of the Battalion. Padre Nesbitt succeeded him. One of the old Territorial officers, Major D. A. Gray, left owing to ill health and his place was taken by Major P. Greenwell of the Regiment. Captain Wilkinson, the Medical Officer, was replaced by Lieut. Fish of the R.A.M.C. and Captain I. R. English returned from Brigade H. Q. to take over the Carriers once more. Captain G. P. Chambers became Adjutant, and Lieut. J. Kailofer, who had joined the Battalion at Honiton, became Signal Officer. Officer reinforcements came from various sources, including Lieut. C. L. Beattie from the Brigade Anti-Tank Company, and 2/Lieuts. D. C. Petrocochino, P. G. Hampson, E. N. Strickland, C. J. Woods and E. W. Venn.

There were also many changes amongst the Warrant Officers, N.C.Os. and men but most of the old hands, in spite of the efforts of the new Medical Officer to downgrade them as unfit or too old for service overseas, stayed with the 8th. Since the outbreak of war they had become well versed in the art of hoodwinking medical officers ; they were proud to belong to the 8th and the Battalion was proud to have them. To mention just a few of these real old soldiers : there was P.S.M. Bond—the Pioneer Sergeant, C.S.M. Craggs, Sgt.

Harrison—the Sergeant Cook, Bugle-Major Carr, Sgt. Boyle of the M.T. and Sgt. Fletcher of the Stretcher Bearers.

On May 21st 1941 the Battalion entrained for an unknown port of embarkation. They had been happy days in Honiton and the 8th did not quickly forget the kindness and hospitality which had been shown during the stay there. It was a long train journey which came to an end next day on the quayside at Gourock, where H.M.T. The *Duchess of Richmond* waited to take the troops aboard. The Battalion filed up the gangways to join Brigade H.Q., the 6th D.L.I., some small technical units, and about eight hundred R.A.F. officers and men who had already embarked. Very soon the *Duchess of Richmond* was packed to capacity and the troopship was nosed out into midstream by the fussy little Gourock tugs. Her sides were lined with khaki-clad figures ; some of them were leaving England for the first time but most of the members of the 8th had served in the B.E.F. campaign. Very few of them could have thought that it would be three years before they saw their homes again.

CHAPTER FOUR

THE VOYAGE TO THE MIDDLE EAST

Dodging the Bismarck—Freetown—South African hospitality in Durban—a tragic accident—through the Red Sea to Suez.

For two days the *Duchess of Richmond* lay in the Clyde and then on the evening of May 23rd her engines quickened their rhythm and the crowded trooper got under way. It was a depressing farewell to the old country ; fine drizzle and rain blotted out a last view of the shore and very soon most of the troops who lined the rails sought the warmth and shelter below decks.

Next morning the trooper was well clear of the Clyde and cutting through a choppy sea. The watchers on deck passed their time identifying the other ships in the convoy ; some were troopships and others were fast cargo vessels whilst the Commodore's flag was flown on the *Georgic*. There was also a most impressive escort consisting of H.M.S. *Exeter*, an anti-aircraft cruiser, an aircraft carrier and nine destroyers. It was reassuring to see the efficient way in which the sleek, grey destroyers shepherded the convoy, their Aldis lights winking at intervals to the *Exeter* ; but it was disturbing to realise that there were more escort ships than troopers and cargo vessels.

The convoy had only been at sea a few days when bulletins were posted on the notice board with the almost unbelievable information that H.M.S. *Hood* had been sunk off Greenland by the German battleship, *Bismarck*. To the people at home, the sinking of the *Hood* with such a heavy loss of life was one of the great tragedies of the war, and it was equally shocking to the men on board the *Duchess of Richmond*. They had lined the rails of the trooper to admire the warlike lines and massive superstructure of the great battle cruiser when she sailed majestically down the Clyde only a few days before the convoy left. Coinciding with this news about the *Hood* the convoy suddenly retraced its steps to the east and on one occasion all the escort ships, with the exception of H.M.S. *Exeter*, deserted the troopers and cargo ships and raced full speed for the skyline. It was fascinating to watch the destroyers cutting through the choppy sea at speed, their sharp bows throwing up great clouds of spray. Later it became known that the convoy had been very close to the track of the *Bismarck* as the German battleship raced for the shelter of Brest, with the avenging *Prince of Wales* and other British warships hard on her heels. It was indeed fortunate that the *Bismarck* was otherwise occupied for, had her commander been able to attack the British convoy, a history of the 8th Battalion would probably never have been written.

However, the danger passed and life on board the *Duchess of Richmond* settled down to the normal peace-time routine for troopships with the addition of training. The fact that the 8th was on board ship did not mean any slackening in the toughening process ; there was P.T. on the promenade decks and on the fore and aft cargo hatches each day and some of those mornings, as the ship ploughed her way through the North Atlantic, were bitterly cold. During the daylight hours the Officers' and Sergeants' Messes and every available square yard of deck space was utilised for training purposes. Small groups of officers, N.C.Os. and men brushed up their knowledge of tactics and weapon training and the Battalion was lectured on security, censorship and behaviour in foreign countries.

By night, with every porthole battened down as part of the strict black-out measures, the atmosphere below decks was stifling. For those who were fortunate enough to be on deck it was just possible, by peering into the darkness, to pick out the dark bulk of ships fore and aft. The way the convoy kept position and changed course during those pitch black nights without mishap was almost uncanny. It was impossible not to admire the casual efficiency of the Royal and Merchant Navy crews.

One week passed and the days had become monotonous with the regular routine and the perpetual expanse of ocean. If there had been a theme song on board the *Duchess of Richmond* it would have included Fred Astaire's famous lines "And what did we see ? We saw the sea." At the end of the second week, by which time the convoy was out of dangerous waters and most of the escort vessels had left to take up another assignment, the troops heard the welcome news that the ships were due to call at Freetown on the West African coast. Soon after this and with H.M.S. *Exeter* still in attendance the troopships and cargo vessels dropped anchor within sight of swaying palms and native mud huts on shore. To those who had not been out of England before it looked from afar like a tropical paradise, and for two days there was something else to gaze at apart from a wide expanse of ocean. But no one was allowed ashore at this fever-ridden port of call which, although it looked most desirable from the decks of the *Duchess of Richmond*, was in fact a miserable station for the handful of British army and navy personnel who had the ill fortune to be posted there.

The convoy lay off Freetown for two days and on several occasions French Air Force machines from Dakar flew high above the ships on photographic reconnaissance, whilst every gun in the convoy opened fire without scoring a hit. Freetown will best be remembered by the 8th and by the thousands of troops who lay off the town in convoys during the early years of the war, because it was here that the British Tommy first met and had dealings with the species "wog." These dark-skinned gentlemen in their frail-looking canoes, most of which bore painted texts from the Bible, circled slowly round the anchored ships offering for sale such goods as monkeys, bananas and pineapples at prices which would shame a modern black-marketeer. These travelling salesmen from Freetown had a masterly knowledge of certain words in the English language which do not appear in our dictionaries but play a prominent part in the military vocabulary. To the delight of the troops who lined the sides of the *Duchess of Richmond* the natives kept up a non-stop patter of obscene language as a part of their sales talk. This was a practice which caused a great deal of embarrassment later in the war when the troopships which called at Freetown carried a number of W.A.A.F., W.R.E.N. and A.T.S. personnel. The natural curiosity of these ladies was invariably rewarded by phrases shouted from the canoes which sent them post haste and red-faced to the shelter of their cabins. A fair trade was carried on with the "wogs" from the decks of the *Duchess of Richmond* by means of baskets on pieces of string, hauled up from the canoes by the troops on deck. This bartering came to an abrupt stop when a senior officer spotted a gas cape being exchanged for a pineapple, and from then on the natives were kept at bay by the ship's fire hydrants.

The convoy slipped away from Freetown as quietly as it had arrived and headed for the Cape of Good Hope. As the troopships sailed south-east into the tropics, conditions below decks on the *Duchess of Richmond* became almost unbearable. The ship had originally been built for the North Atlantic run and her ventilation system was entirely unsuited to a tropical climate. A few of the old soldiers who had realised what it was going to be like were the first to apply for permission to sleep on deck, but the accommodation beneath the stars was limited and the majority of the troops tossed and turned in their hammocks each night as the trooper made for Durban at a steady fourteen knots.

Shortly after leaving Freetown the convoy crossed the line and there was the usual boisterous ritual. It was a wonderful opportunity for the Battalion to have some fun at the expense of R.S.M. Jennings, who was to be a star turn at the " crossing the line " ceremony. The R.S.M. had other ideas, and indignantly maintained that he had already crossed the line as a member of the 1st Battalion when voyaging from China to Singapore. There were no ex-members of the 1st Battalion who could confirm or disprove this statement, but there were many members of the 8th Battalion who were quite certain that troopers on the China to Singapore run did not sail far enough south to cross the line. "That's my story and I'm sticking to it" said "Spike" Jennings, when challenged on this point, and he managed to get through the day unmolested.

The convoy docked at Durban on the morning of Friday June 20th. It was almost four weeks since the passengers on the transports had set foot on dry land, and they all looked forward eagerly to enjoying the hospitality of the South Africans, of which they had heard so much. After lunch on board ship the troops went ashore to experience the astonishing kindness of the people of Durban, whose sons and husbands were fighting with the Desert Army. There was scarcely a man in the huge convoy who was not whisked off by one of the dozens of cars parked outside the dock gates or which cruised through Durban looking for unescorted "Tommies." In most cases they were taken for a run round the city and hinterland and then entertained to a sumptuous tea. None of these Durban families had known anything about the arrival of the British convoy until the ships were sighted out at sea that morning, and the fact that their welcome was spontaneous and unorganised made it all the more acceptable.

There were well-stocked shops to explore and dances quickly organised in honour of the men from the convoy, rides in rickshaws pulled by South African natives in their colourful headress, who padded silently through the streets. But, like all good things, Friday June 20th came to an end and the troops returned to their hammocks on board ship to sleep it off. The following day, the 8th went for company route marches and it was a perfect example of the morning after the night before. Nevertheless the majority of those who vowed "never again" as they marched miserably in the sunshine were first out of the dock gates for another afternoon and evening in Durban.

On Sunday morning the Battalion attended a convoy church parade on a Durban cricket ground. It was an impressive ceremony under the hot South African sun and thousands of men stood bareheaded on the green-sward. On the way back to the docks newsboys held up specially printed bills with the incredible news that Germany had marched against Russia, and on board the *Duchess of Richmond* the men of the 8th crowded round the loudspeakers to hear the good news confirmed by a B.B.C. announcer.

Sunday afternoon was spent in Durban but there was no shore leave on Monday, as the convoy sailed in the afternoon. A Durban pleasure steamer, her rails lined by the youth and beauty of the town, escorted the troopships out to sea, and then with a last reassuring hoot from her siren she turned back. The people of Durban will always be remembered with gratitude and affection by the thousands of British and Dominion troops who were fortunate enough to spend a few days there on their way to the Middle East.

The next stop was Aden at the mouth of the Red Sea, and as the *Duchess of Richmond* headed north through the Indian Ocean the troops talked less about Durban and more about the probable destination of the Battalion. The R.A.F. contingent had disembarked at Durban *en route* for the Far East and their place had been taken by New Zealand and Indian troops, returning to the Middle East after escorting Italian prisoners of war. There was little doubt that the trooper was headed for Suez and those members of the Battalion who were quite certain that the 8th would be sent straight into the Western Desert watched the daily news bulletins from the Desert Army with a morbid kind of interest.

The voyage to Aden would have been as uneventful as the voyage from Freetown to Durban if it had not been for a most unfortunate accident. H.M.S. *Exeter*, the sole escort ship since leaving Durban, carried a Walrus aircraft which was launched by catapult in fine weather, to give the convoy anti-aircraft gunners some practice shooting. The sturdy looking old biplane would fly over the ships towing a target and carrying out feint dive-bombing attacks. One day the Walrus went in to one of her bombing runs but, as the pilot pulled out of the dive, the watchers on board the troopships were horrified to see the wings bend slowly back and break away from the fuselage, which plumetted straight into the sea like a stone. Both the pilot and observer were killed. It was all over in a few seconds and the fact that it happened in glorious weather as the convoy sailed through an azure sea made it all the more tragic. It was no setting for sudden death.

The convoy split up at Aden and the *Exeter* set off for the Far East. From then on the *Duchess of Richmond* was unescorted and after replenishing with oil she made for Suez through the sweltering heat of the Red Sea. The heat at night below decks was worse than at any other time during the voyage, and the only consolation was that the trooper had speeded up considerably since leaving Aden and was now doing a steady eighteen knots. She was at least getting somewhere quickly. There was a following wind which gave no respite from the heat and it was indeed a relief when the mountains of Sinai were sighted early on July 8th. That afternoon the trooper dropped anchor off Suez and as she came to a standstill the breeze was felt at last ; a mile or so away across the water was Egypt, land of the Pharaohs and vital key to the whole of the Middle East.

CHAPTER FIVE

FIRST MONTHS IN THE MIDDLE EAST

Qassasin Camp—the move to Cyprus—hard work on the Island defences.

NEXT morning the troops on board the *Duchess of Richmond* were disembarked on to lighters which came alongside. The load capacity of these large, flat-bottomed vessels was amazing and the Embarkation Staff Officer from Suez stood at the top of one of the trooper's gangways as part of the Battalion filed on to a lighter. When it seemed to the men just out from England that the vessel was full, there was a shout from the E.S.O., "All right, move up there, we can manage another hundred yet." And somehow or other, another hundred men were loaded on. They were packed like sheep on the deck of the lighter, and as the ungainly looking craft pulled away from the troopship, a chorus of " Baa-Baa" floated back across the water.

On shore the vehicles of a South African troop-carrying company waited to take the Battalion to Qassasin Camp on the Sweet Water Canal, about twenty miles west of Ismailia. Qassasin was only a staging camp but whilst the Battalion was stationed there the troops had their first introduction to a few of the things which had become a part of the Middle East service. There was the camp cinema, run by a fat, prosperous looking Egyptian, with its hard seats which were suffered gladly for the sake of the British and American films. The N.A.A.F.I. stocked a pleasing abundance of many of the commodities which had been short in England, especially eggs and cigarettes, and the troops could relax there after a hard day training. After the voyage from England it was a novelty to live in this great self-contained camp of hundreds of tents which was in effect a small town in the middle of the desert, complete with its own services.

Meanwhile, the higher strategy of the Middle East campaign was shaping. Greece and Crete—after a heroic resistance by British Commonwealth and Greek troops—had fallen and the Axis hold on the Mediterranean had been strengthened. It was considered likely that the Germans would attempt an invasion of Cyprus by air either as a prelude to or simultaneously with a drive through Turkey into Syria. At that time Cyprus was garrisoned only by the 1st Battalion the Sherwood Foresters and a detachment of Coastal Artillery ; as a result, 50 Division was given its first operational role in the Middle East and ordered to strengthen the defences on the island.

The Battalion arrived at Qassasin station early in the morning of July 29th just as the locals were awakening and it was an education—this reveille in an Egyptian village. Most of the inhabitants appeared to have spent the night lying fully clothed on the ground, either outside their hovels or in the streets around the outskirts of the station. Without a doubt, the village of Qassasin was one of the filthiest places visited by the Battalion during the war. Apart from Cairo, Alexandria and a few other large towns, Egypt is a land of dirty native villages inhabited by a disease-ridden population, plagued by flies and smelling to high heaven.

From Qassasin the Battalion went by train to Port Said where the Suez Canal joins the Mediterranean and here ships of the Royal Navy were waiting to embark the 6th and 8th Battalions. The British naval forces in the Mediterranean had recently sustained severe losses by air attack in the evacuations from Greece and Crete, and to diminish the risk of further losses it had been ordered that Cyrpus was to be reinforced at night, so that the ships could be clear of the island by daylight and out of range of Axis bombers. A strict time-table for embarkation was therefore laid down by the Navy and only one hour was allowed for the 8th to embark with all its baggage. Some of the 9th Battalion's baggage was lying on the quayside where it had been left the day before.

The 8th was split into two parts in case of loss by enemy action, with one party embarking on H.M.S. *Latona*, one of the latest class of minelaying cruisers and at that time the fastest vessels of their type in the Navy, whilst the other half of the Battalion went aboard a destroyer. It was indeed a race against time to get the troops and baggage on board the naval vessels within the hour, but a tremendous effort on the part of the Battalion accomplished this and a few extra minutes were stolen from somewhere to get on board the baggage which the 9th Battalion had abandoned.

The crowded warships slipped quietly out of Port Said and after a fast and uneventful crossing—with the *Latona* doing between thirty and thirty-five knots—Famagusta harbour was reached in the early hours of July 30th. The Navy showed their anxiety to get away before dawn by the alarming but effective way in which they unloaded the equipment and stores. Everything was rolled down a gangway on to the quayside and several items of equipment inevitably ended up in the waters of the harbour. At daybreak a fat Cypriot volunteered to dive into the harbour to retrieve the lost stores and equipment. After haggling for some time about payment for his services, he eventually salvaged several boxes of Bren magazines, a Bren gun tripod and an anti-tank rifle. The beaming Cypriot was suitably rewarded and as apparently he put in appearance to retrieve lost property every time troops were disembarked at Famagusta during this period, he had every reason to be grateful to the naval ratings who provided him with this lucrative pastime.

From Famagusta the Battalion went by narrow gauge railway inland to Nicosia, the capital of Cyprus. It was a picturesque little railway system, rather like the Romney, Hythe and Dymchurch Railway in Kent, and a welcome change from the Egyptian State Railways. Slowly but steadily the fussy little engine pulled its heavy load across the hot, dusty plain of Messaria where the only signs of vegetation were occasional palm trees and olive groves. The Battalion detrained at Nicosia and marched from the station to a tented camp which had been pitched among the olive groves on the outskirts of the town.

The task of the 8th Battalion in the Divisional plan for the defence of the island was the occupation and defence of Nicosia airport, about three miles west of the town and the largest aerodrome on the island. After several days of settling in and reconnoitring the battle positions, the Battalion, less B Company and B Echelon, moved out to the airport. Major A. B. S. Clarke commanded a mobile reserve at Waynes House, consisting of B Company, one section of carriers commanded by Lieut. J. Carruthers and a section of mortars. B Echelon remained in Nicosia.

During the settling-in period the Battalion had been able to sample the local brands of liquor and found out in very quick time that there was any amount of cheap alcohol available. Cyprus brandy was only one and six a bottle and the beer drinkers of the 8th made the mistake of drinking this by the half pint in the same way that they disposed of their beer. The results were disastrous and for several nights the Guard Room was never empty. However, after this first burst of enthusiasm the Battalion treated the local poison with a little more respect.

Over at the airport there was plenty of hard work needed on the construction of defences and the Battalion settled down to a routine which was to last for three months. The ground was rocky, pneumatic drills and explosives being needed on all the positions. 505 Field Company, Royal Engineers constructed the pill-boxes and kept the Battalion supplied with all the engineer stores required for work on the platoon positions. As in France in 1940 the large number of miners in the unit proved invaluable ; many were skilled in the handling of pneumatic drills and dynamite and the work proceeded apace, very ably directed by Major R. S. McLaren. The Command Post was hewn out of solid rock and could have withstood all but the heaviest bombs. It was provided with two entrances leading to various rooms for the use of the C.O. and the Signal and Intelligence staffs. The work on the Command Post was carried out by a team of hand-picked miners personally supervised by Major McLaren and was very aptly christened "McLaren's Drift."

It was hard work for the Battalion, a race against time with the ever-present threat of a German airborne invasion, and construction of the defences went on every day, including Sundays. The Battalion also "stood-to" night and morning and there was no easing of the tension during the three months the 8th was on Cyprus. The sweltering heat made it impossible for any work in the afternoon and there was a rest period from after the midday meal until 5 p.m., when a further two hours work was put in on the defences. Fortunately water and grapes were plentiful and somewhat offset the effects of the stifling heat of the plains, which the white population was able to avoid during the summer months by seeking the cooling breezes of Troodos, a town in the hills where a Divisional Rest Camp was established.

Occasionally air raid sirens wailed to disturb the peace of the island when Italian reconnaissance planes flew over at a very high altitude or Italian bombers made a half-hearted attempt to bomb the aerodrome. The bombers did score hits on the airport on two occasions although fortunately there were neither casualties nor damage. R.A.F. Hurricanes of 213 Squadron were based on the airfield and there was a close liaison and friendship between the pilots and ground crews and the Battalion. It was 213 Squadron which shot down the first enemy plane over Cyprus and the event was duly celebrated in the R.A.F. Mess when a wealthy Cypriot presented a cup to the Squadron to mark the occasion.

A familiar landmark on the aerodrome was the R.S.M.'s tent. "Spike" Jennings had acquired a rather antiquated wireless set which would only function properly when an enormous aerial pole was erected. This pole was a constant source of amusement to the fighter pilots, who swooped down low over the aerodrome after a flight to see how close they could get without hitting it. The pole survived to accompany the Battalion throughout the Middle East, and whenever the 8th was in a rest area the swaying pole marked the R.S.M.'s tent.

Although the work on the aerodrome defences was first priority, a certain amount of training was carried out, mostly by B Company at Waynes House, and occasionally it was possible to withdraw one of the other companies from the defence works for a field firing exercise. One C Company exercise ended in tragedy when a grenade exploded prematurely, killing 2/Lieut. A. A. Wood and a private soldier, and wounding Lieut. R. H. Regnart and Sgt. Self. On another occasion a D Company platoon went to Waynes House for field firing and Pte. J. Lobley was killed by a 2″ Mortar bomb.

The Battalion also had to provide ceremonial guards and at frequent intervals one had to be found for Divisional H.Q. As this duty was performed in turn by every unit of the Division stationed on the island there was keen rivalry for the honour of parading the best turned out guard. The Battalion, mainly due to the expert guidance of R.S.M. Jennings, paraded some excellent guards and was complimented several times by the new Divisional Commander, General W. H. C. Ramsden. These compliments were well deserved for the standard of drill and turnout on these occasions was very high considering the conditions under which the men lived and worked. Major Greenwell commanded a guard of honour from B and H.Q. Companies when the retiring Governor General left the island, and on another occasion Captain English did likewise when General Auchinleck, Commander-in-Chief, Middle East, visited the Battalion to inspect the defences. The "Auk," as he was affectionately known throughout the Middle East by the troops under his command, afterwards had tea in the Officers' Mess.

It was nearly all work and no play on Cyprus but it became essential to have some break from the daily routine and other ranks were granted a full day off each week and officers half a day. On these

Lieut-Colonel R. P. Lidwill, D.S.O., commanding from March 21st, 1943 until wounded in the attack at Le Plessis Grimault on August 9th, 1944.

Lieut.-Colonel H. R. D. Oldman, M.C., commanding from August 16th, 1944 until August 26th, 1945.

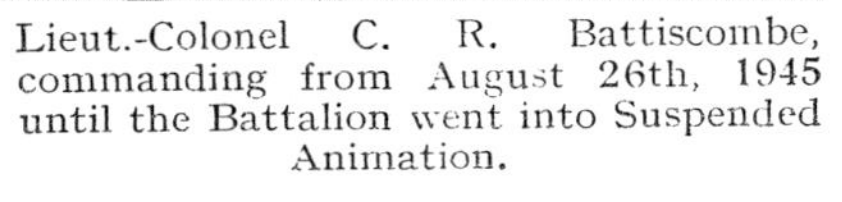

Lieut.-Colonel C. R. Battiscombe, commanding from August 26th, 1945 until the Battalion went into Suspended Animation.

Lieut.-Colonel E. A. Leybourne, T.D., commanding from December 23rd, 1937, until October 20th, 1939.

Lieut.-Colonel C. W. Beart, O.B.E., M.C., commanding from December 21st, 1939 until May 13th, 1942.

Lieut.-Colonel M. L. P. Jackson, D.S.O., commanding from May 13th, 1942 until killed in action at Mareth on March 21st, 1943.

occasions it was possible to get a seat on the local bus, hired to take leave parties to Kyrenia, twenty miles away on the coast. It is a steep and tortuous road which twists and turns over the mountains to Kyrenia and the local Cypriot driver had no respect for the many hairpin bends. He drove his bus with a reckless abandon which never failed to fill his passengers with alarm. However, this hair-raising journey was well worthwhile for the village of Kyrenia, nestling at the foot of the mountain range and looking across the sea towards Turkey, is one of the gems which Cyprus has to offer to the world's tourists in peace time. This beautiful village, with its deep blue waters, crystal clear and very warm, can provide Mediterranean bathing at its best and an afternoon spent there was a welcome change from the daily routine. Suitably refreshed, the leave parties returned to Nicosia at the end of the afternoon, where the night clubs, cafés and restaurants were making small fortunes for the local profiteers.

The men of the mobile reserve at Waynes House were more fortunate as regards amenities than the rest of the Battalion. They were nearer to Nicosia, with its noisy night life, than the companies over at the aerodrome and they also had their own swimming pool in the gardens of Waynes House, which was very popular.

The weather during the first two months had been extremely hot but September brought the first sign of rain. In October there were several heavy showers which soon turned the dry wadis[1] into raging torrents. After one of these downpours, H.Q. Company cookhouse, which had been located in one of the wadis near Battalion H.Q., was washed away by the swirling rainwater. It was a warning sign of a hard winter, and Nissen huts were erected for winter quarters but the Battalion never moved into them. Orders were received that the Division would be relieved on Cyprus by two brigades of 5 Indian Division, and would move to Palestine. Although the period on the island had not been unpleasant, the work on the defences had become very monotonous and the majority of the 8th Battalion felt that it was time the Division moved to fresh fields.

[1]Water course, dry except in the rainy season.

CHAPTER SIX

PALESTINE AND IRAQ

Preparations for a long move—through Baghdad to Iraq—" Fletcher's Rocket "—the second wartime Christmas—bitter weather in a tented camp—good news—1,800 miles in 17 days to join the Desert Army.

WHEN Germany attacked Russia in June 1941, the rapid advance of the Nazi Forces soon made it apparent that a potential threat existed to our security in the Middle East, Iraq and Iran. Consequently there was a certain redeployment of our forces in this theatre and the move of 50 Division via Palestine to Iraq was part of the plan to meet this new German threat.

On November 4th the Battalion left Cyprus and after an uneventful voyage disembarked at Haifa and moved out to a camp at Azzib, a few miles north of the port, where most of the Battalion was able to enjoy the glorious Mediterranean bathing. As usual, the full burden of the coming move fell on the shoulders of the Adjutant, the Q.M. and the M.T. and Carrier Platoons. All the Battalion vehicles had been left in Cyprus for the incoming unit and the 8th took over the transport and some of the equipment of a battalion of 5 Indian Division. The majority of these trucks had clocked at least fifteen thousand miles on their speedometers, miles of hard going. A great deal of maintenance was required before they were fit to tackle the long journey from Palestine to Iraq.

There were several temporary problems which presented difficulties at the time but which were solved before the move. One was how to make the transport desert-worthy and what equipment was required to combat the menace of soft sand. The answer to this problem was to fit the vehicles with sand tracks, lengths of metal about four feet long and a foot wide, which could be placed under the rear wheels if the vehicle stuck. These metal sand tracks were punched with holes and gave the tyres an excellent grip, much in the same way that sacking under the wheels of a car will help in snow. The trucks were also equipped with skid chains, another useful method of combating soft sand. Finally, to make the vehicles completely desert-worthy, condensers were fitted to the radiators. The Carrier Platoon had similar problems but as the carriers were to travel to Iraq on Arab-driven ten-ton lorries in order to save track mileage, they did not present such a problem.

The Battalion with the rest of 151 Brigade moved off on November 12th. The first day's journey was uneventful and the convoy passed through some magnificent country as it crossed the River Jordan and climbed up towards the Palestine–Transjordan frontier. After staging the first night at Mafraq the long line of vehicles moved on again the next day, and the cultivated areas gave place to the Transjordan Desert. The second night was spent in the desert at a point on the oil pipe line known as K.4. The drill of setting up camp for these night halts was always the same with the rifle companies forming the outside walls of a square and protecting Battalion H.Q., H.Q. Company and the M.T. inside the square. The troops slept in 180-pounder tents and after a few days of practice it was surprising how quickly these tents were pitched in the evenings and struck in the morning, although it should be mentioned that R.S.M. Jennings was always in evidence on these occasions in a persuasive capacity. On the fourth day, the convoy reached the end of the made road and took to the desert tracks. The going deteriorated and very soon there was work for the M.T. Platoon ; two of the trucks broke half-shafts and another truck completed the last part of the journey that day with a broken spring. Whilst the Battalion slept, the fitters worked far into the night to repair the damage, and by daybreak they had made two of the trucks roadworthy again. The third one was still not fit to continue the journey and had to be towed.

There was a day's halt at Habbaniya, a welcome break, as arrangements were made with the R.A.F. at the aerodrome for everyone to have a bath. It had been a hot and dusty journey across the desert and the R.A.F. hospitality was well-appreciated. It was a most pleasant feeling to lie back in the cooling water and rinse out the desert sand.

On November 18th the Battalion moved on again and the convoy took the road to Baghdad. As the dust-covered vehicles passed over the Feluga Bridge their occupants were able to see signs, still very much in evidence, of the Iraq Rebellion. The next staging point was at Diltawa, beyond Baghdad. The situation in Iraq at that time was one which called for every possible display of British force and the convoy passed through this city of Arabian Night legends with the Battalion displaying strict discipline. There was no talking allowed and the troops were forbidden to wave to the natives of Baghdad, who looked sullenly but inquiringly as the British vehicles passed through the city. The troops sat stiff-backed in the trucks, looking to the front with their rifles between their knees. It was unpleasantly like a Nazi display of force and a most unusual way for a D.L.I. battalion to pass through a town.

Next morning the news came over the radio that General Auchinleck's offensive in the desert had started. The armoured divisions of the newly-formed Eighth Army had crossed the Egyptian frontier and British, Dominion and Allied troops had been launched on their task of destroying Rommel's Afrika Corps and relieving the hard-pressed garrison of Tobruk. It was good news indeed.

The rest of the journey to the destination of the Battalion at Kirkuk was uneventful. Although the roads were little more than rough tracks they improved as the convoy motored north. It was pouring with rain when the Battalion arrived at the camp at Kirkuk, known as K.I., and as the roads were surfaced with a thick tar by-product of the oil wells, the heavy rain had made them as slippery as an ice rink. Some of the trucks were soon out of control and several careered off the steeply-cambered road to end up in the ditch. It was not much of a welcome to Kirkuk.

The stay at K.I. was shorter than had been expected, and only two weeks after the arrival of the Battalion in the area, orders were received for the 8th to move by march route to a camp at Eski Kellek on the Great Zab River. The Battalion moved off in column of route on December 5th and covered fifteen miles during the first day. It was good going, and companies never covered less in one day; on several occasions during the move the troops marched twenty miles. This excellent training served to toughen up the Battalion. The opportunity was taken of practising march discipline, with quick dispersion in case of air attack, and the routine of striking camp and getting on the move quickly the following morning was brought almost to a fine art. The route lay through the large village of Altun Kopru on the Little Zab River—a tributary of the Great Zab River which runs into the Tigris. Two days later the Battalion passed through the small, picturesque town of Erbil, its narrow streets crowded with pavement bazaars and fruit sellers shrilly shouting their wares. The destination of the Battalion, just south of Eski Kellek, was reached on December 13th after nine days of hard marching. Thankfully the 8th moved into the new camp and for the first three days everyone worked hard to make the area habitable, for Iraq is well known for its hard winters.

At this time petrol was very scarce, but nearby Kirkuk had a plentiful supply of crude oil. Major McLaren invented an ingenious heating system utilising crude oil and water, which was so successful that it was used for all cooking purposes and—most important—to provide steaming hot baths for the Battalion. The baths were the responsibility of Sgt. Fletcher of the Stretcher Bearers and there is no doubt that at Eski Kellek he was one of the most popular men in the Battalion. The heating apparatus was constructed from old petrol tins and this weird, flimsy-looking contraption, which hissed and gurgled and sent up clouds of smoke both day and night, soon earned for itself the nickname of "Fletcher's Rocket." In its own small way it became as famous as the Rocket which bore Stevenson's name, for it gave every man in the Battalion a hot bath once a week and that was a luxury indeed.

The Battalion had only been in the Eski Kellek area a few days when Lieut.-Colonel Beart left to take over temporary command of 151 Brigade from Brigadier Redman who had been posted to the Eighth Army Headquarters as Brigadier General Staff.

Brigadier Redman had commanded the Brigade for just under a year but his quietly efficient though cheerful manner, and his amazing facility for remembering the names of almost everyone in the Brigade after meeting them only once, had made him a popular commander with all ranks. The men of the D.L.I. battalions were sorry to see him go, but they were proud of the fact that their commander had been chosen to fill such an important appointment in the Eighth Army.

The stay in Iraq gave the Battalion an opportunity to put in some hard training which was badly needed after the long weeks in Cyprus, constructing defences under the Mediterranean sun. Tactics were given priority and the troops practised fieldcraft, the use of ground, and section and platoon schemes. The terrain was very suitable for this work, with the training areas close at hand. In the undulating country within a few miles of the camp numerous gazelle ran wild, and gazelle stalks became a popular and most valuable form of training. The objects of the stalks were real live gazelle which could be shot at, and this gave added zest to the training. In fact, keenness was such, that small parties invariably went stalking on Sundays and their efforts were rewarded on one or two occasions with a kill. Back in camp the successful hunters were congratulated, and the gazelle meat made a useful addition to the menus.

There were, however, many who scorned this blood sport. They preferred the good old English game of football and it is probably true to say that more of this was played during the Battalion's stay in Iraq than at any other period during the war. There was keen rivalry between platoons and companies and many exciting games took place which resulted in the Mortar Platoon occupying the position at the top of the table. The Company Championship was won by H.Q. Company which showed its superiority by beating a combined rifle companies team. There were also several keenly fought matches against other units in the Brigade Group and the Battalion never failed to give a good account of itself.

Christmas 1941 was a very festive occasion, considering the conditions under which the Battalion was living. After a break of two or three weeks, N.A.A.F.I. supplies were resumed in time for Christmas and enough crates of beer arrived to ensure at least three bottles for every man in the Battalion, and more for those who could get on the right side of the teetotallers. The official R.A.S.C. Christmas dinner was supplemented by chickens and eggs, purchased by the Battalion from the nearby villages, and in addition the Battalion received a number of parcels from an organisation representing the women of India—a most welcome gift. Each parcel contained cake, biscuits and sweets, and as their distribution was confined to corporals and below, it worked out to one parcel for every three men. These gifts were greatly appreciated and on the whole it was a satisfactorily bilious Christmas with plenty of good food washed down with beer.

Between Christmas and the New Year company leave parties were sent to Mosul, about forty miles away, the nearest town to the camp. It was a welcome change from camp life and the troops made the best of these day visits to Mosul. It was a return to civilisation for a few hours, and many strange purchases ranging from brooches to send home to primus stoves for cooking extra rations in the tents at night, were made in the dingy bazaars and from street traders.

During late December and early January the weather became extremely cold and a mantle of snow, several inches deep, lay over the camp. In this bitter weather, with only the tents for shelter at night, the troops slept huddled together for warmth with mufflers and balaclava helmets over their heads. Boots which had got wet the day before were often frozen stiff in the morning and it was miserable to have to quit the warmth and comfort of a pile of blankets to face the cold, bleak dawn. It was most unpleasant for the British troops, but the men who really suffered hardship were the troops of 6 and 8 Indian Divisions. Many of them, before they experienced this fierce winter in Iraq, had never seen snow, and far from the warmth of their native India they were utterly miserable. They knew nothing of the effect of frost on vehicles, and the bitter cold took a heavy toll of the M.T. in the Indian divisions ; hundreds of trucks were put out of action with cracked cylinder blocks, a serious loss of vehicles at that time. In the 8th Battalion the experiences of the hard winter of 1939–40 in France enabled the Battalion M.T. Platoon to combat the menace and there was only one case of a cracked cylinder block in the unit.

Early in the New Year 69 Infantry Brigade of 50 Division had moved from the Kirkuk area to Syria, and the D.L.I. Brigade followed. The advance parties of 151 Brigade had already left and had arrived at Baalbek in Syria. The rest of the Battalion set off from Eski Kellek on February 5th and, including the troop-carrying lorries, the column numbered more than a hundred vehicles. The carriers were taken across the desert on the ungainly Arab-driven transporters which had brought them from Palestine.

The three months in Iraq had been well spent, and Lieut.-Colonel Beart was right when he said, on his return from Brigade H.Q. to resume command of the Battalion, " The 8th is now more than ready for battle than at any other time during the war."

The journey was uneventful and everything went according to plan. The convoy staged the first night at K.I. near Kirkuk, the second at Tuz Khurmatli and the third at Diltawa. There was a day's halt at Habbaniya on February 9th, where warning was given of the presence of Arab rifle thieves, reputed to be as skilful as the dusky Pathans of the Indian North West Frontier. Special precautions were taken and the sentries carried loaded rifles, for this was no idle warning. The Iraqis were quite capable of stealing into a tent and taking a man's rifle from his hands without disturbing him. In the middle of the night a shot rang out ; a rifle thief had crept into a tent but had been disturbed. As he darted out into the night the sentry fired but did not hit him.

The next stage of the journey from Habbaniya to Mafraq went smoothly, and at the destination good news waited for the Battalion. A fresh infantry division was required in the Eighth Army to relieve 4 Indian Division, which had suffered heavy casualties in the desert. The previous orders for the move to Syria were cancelled, and the Brigade was told to move with all speed through Palestine to Egypt, and then on to the Western Desert to join the Eighth Army. The Battalion left Mafraq in high spirits and the convoy took the route running steeply down the mountains to the Jordan Valley and then turned south to Beitlid.

On February 15th the convoy moved on to Asluj in southern Palestine and the following day covered a hundred and twenty miles to Ismailia in Egypt, speeding along the tarred road which cuts across the Sinai Desert. The Battalion had a day's halt at Ismailia for maintenance which gave the Transport Officer the opportunity of spending a busy day at No. 4 Ordnance Base Depot at Tel El Kebir, trying to obtain spares. This visit to the Ordnance Depot brought home the seriousness of the whole supply position in the Middle East at that time.

The Battalion left Ismailia on February 18th and the convoy sped along the road bordering the Sweet Water Canal and, to the disappointment of everyone, passed straight through Cairo and out on to the Alexandria road. A halt was not called until Halfway House—little more than a map reference in the desert—was reached, too far from either Cairo or Alexandria to make a quick visit possible even had it been allowed. The fleeting glimpse which the troops had of Cairo was to be their last contact with civilisation for five long months.

Next day the convoy took the desert road again and by-passing Alexandria turned westwards along the Mediterranean coastline towards the Eighth Army. The long line of vehicles was soon stretched out along the desert road which ran dead straight for miles on end, its brilliant whiteness throwing back the sun's rays and the blistering heat of the desert. The troops took very little notice as the convoy passed Alamein except perhaps to remark on the wonderful turquoise blue of the sea. At that time Alamein was little more than a map reference and a railway station. Perhaps it was as well that the bitter fighting, destined to rage astride the same road over which the vehicles travelled, was masked by the future. The convoy sped on, with a hundred and twenty yards between trucks ; over the bad, bumpy part of the road which led to the supply base at Daba, and beyond to Mersa Matruh, where Anthony and Cleopatra had enjoyed the glorious Mediterranean bathing in the same way that men of the Eighth Army did whenever they had the opportunity. The convoy left the road at Mersa Matruh and shook out into desert formation. This was the Battalion's first experience of travelling over the Western Desert and the going was very bad indeed. The trucks bumped and lurched over the rough ground, throwing their occupants from side to side like a lot of cattle. Then just as suddenly they would be speeding over perfectly flat desert, their tyres singing on the hard sand. Then back again to the bumps and jolts.

The Battalion halted for one night at Bir el Thalata, the railhead for the offensive the previous November ; by this time the railway had been pushed forward almost to the Egyptian-Cyrenaican frontier. On February 22nd the frontier was crossed and the 8th Battalion camped that night at El Adem in desert which had once been part of Mussolini's Colonial Empire. It was a satisfactory feeling for the troops to know that at last they were on enemy territory. Next day, the 8th and the remainder of 151 Brigade reached its destination, not far from the old desert fort of Acroma, after having travelled eighteen hundred miles in seventeen days with only two full day halts and only one vehicle casualty. On February 25th the 8th moved forward to relieve the desert veterans of the 1/1 Punjab Regiment of 4 Indian Division in the Gazala Line. The men with the blue Durham flash and the T.T. sign on their battledress had joined the Eighth Army.

CHAPTER SEVEN

IN THE GAZALA LINE

Life in the desert—Apat patrols—work for the carriers—the first Battalion half-column.

BEFORE describing the disposition of 50 Division in the Gazala Line it would be as well to break the narrative and give the reader some idea of the Desert, particularly that part of it which was the battlefield of the Allied and Axis armies.

North-east Africa, taken as a whole, is the driest area in the world and the scanty rain supports a thin, drought-resisting vegetation on the hills bordering the Red Sea and along the Mediterranean coast. Inland lies the vast triangle of the Libyan Desert, roughly the size and shape of India. In the north it extends twelve hundred miles westwards from Cairo through Egypt, Cyrenaica and Tripolitania to the hills of Tunisia, and southward it stretches for a thousand miles to the Sudan.

The landscape is one of sharp contrasts and the desert is by no means composed entirely of soft sand. There are grey plateaux of broken stones with boulders the size of footballs, and endless plains of brown pebbles dotted here and there with flat-topped hills of black or white rock. For miles on end the surface is as flat and firm as a billiard table and then, with hardly any warning it gives way to soft sand, which is thrown up by the wheels of vehicles as a screen of choking white dust, visible to aircraft for miles.

There are steep escarpments stretching for a hundred or two hundred miles, when the whole surface of the desert falls away in a series of terraces to a vast depression of shimmering sand dunes reaching out to the farthest horizon. These ranges of rolling dunes and the escarpments are the only barriers in the desert which otherwise allows the same freedom of movement for opposing forces as the oceans of the world.

The climate is harsh and unfriendly. The prevailing northerly wind is mild enough and even in summer the nights are cool, but disturbances frequently cause the wind to rise to storm strength and veer round to one of the other points of the compass. In winter, the Desert Army knew it as a bitter cold wind which whistled through thick battledress, balaclava helmets and greatcoats—penetrating thick, woolly sheepskin jackets. It blew through camps at hurricane force, uprooting tents pegged precariously in the few inches of soft sand which was often all that covered the solid rock underneath. In summer the southerly winds, superheated by the great sands of the interior, are whipped across the desert at such temperatures that they feel like blasts of flame. These are the dreaded Khamsin winds, which drive the dust and sand before them in clouds of unbelievable density.

Communications in the desert are easy to describe. Apart from the centuries-old caravan tracks of the interior such as the Trigh Capuzzo and the Trigh el Abd (the Way of Slaves), there are no roads of any sort apart from the coastal route in the north which skirts the Mediterranean seaboard. Before the war, on the Egyptian side of the frontier with Cyrenaica, a single line railway from Alexandria followed a secondary road for a hundred and fifty miles to Mersa Matruh, and from there onwards there was nothing but a rough track to take the traveller for another hundred and twenty-five miles to the frontier at Sollum. The Italians started to build a road from Sollum to Mersa Matruh after their advance in 1940, and as the battle for Egypt swayed back and forth during the next two years, improvements were made to the road by the engineers of the opposing armies. On the Italian side of the frontier it was a different story. Mussolini's hard-working colonists deserve credit for the excellence of the tarmac road which runs eastward from Sollum along the whole coastline of Libya to Tripoli, a distance of nearly a thousand miles.

The desert can boast of no towns south of the coastal road. The names on the map of Libya represent perhaps an old disused fort, a water-hole—known as a Bir in Arabic—or simply a pile of stones or an empty oil drum marking a caravan route. On the coastal road the towns worthy of the name are few and far between and, after leaving Alexandria, there is no port suitable for the supply of an army until Benghazi is reached in Cyrenaica—three hundred miles beyond the Egyptian frontier.

The general situation in the Gazala area was the result of the fighting which had taken place during the winter. The Eighth Army offensive, Operation Crusader, had been launched on November 14th with the object of engaging and destroying the Axis armour, isolating the immensely strong enemy positions along the Egyptian-Cyrenaican frontier at Sollum and at Bardia, relieving Tobruk and finally sweeping the enemy right out of Cyrenaica.

Operation Crusader had gone well at first but Rommel reacted fiercely on the third day and the British armoured thrust was held by the German Panzers around Sidi Rezegh, south-east of Tobruk. Then followed three weeks of bitter and almost continuous fighting with losses about equally balanced on each side.

The heavy fighting continued until Tobruk was relieved early in December and Rommel carried out a rapid and skilful retreat to the Agedabia area, a hundred miles south of Benghazi, where the pursuit by the Eighth Army was brought to a halt. Most of the British armoured units were then withdrawn for a rest and refit and the newly arrived 1 Armoured Division moved up to the forward area.

Unfortunately the supply problem prevented General Ritchie, the new Eighth Army commander, from maintaining more than the equivalent of one armoured and one infantry brigade in the Agheila position, to which the Axis forces had leisurely withdrawn from Agedabia, and during the first few weeks of the New Year men of the Eighth Army worked tirelessly to open the port of Benghazi for the vital supplies ; but time and the weather were against them. On the other hand, Rommel had received considerable reinforcements during the lull and was ready by the third week in January to join battle with the British forces again. The Germans attacked and, finding the British positions only lightly held, pushed on rapidly to achieve immediate success. By January 25th the situation had deteriorated so much that General Ritchie decided to evacuate Benghazi. There was now no alternative for the British Commander but to retire to positions at Gazala and, although the German advance guard followed hard on the heels of the retreating Eight Army, Rommel did not increase the pressure and temporary equilibrium was reached at Gazala with both sides piling up supplies and reinforcements for the fresh struggle that was to come.

With the position stabilised, the British forces were disposed in the following manner. In the north the Gazala Line was held by 1 South African Division with its right flank resting on the coast. On the left of the South Africans was 50 Division, with all three brigades forward in the line ; the D.L.I. brigade on the right, 69 Brigade in the centre and 150 brigade on the left flank. At the extreme southern end of the Gazala Line, fifty miles inland from the sea, 1 Fighting French Brigade held Bir Hacheim. The Line was continuous only in the sense that a belt of mines had been laid from Gazala to Bir Hacheim, with infantry divisions disposed in brigade localities surrounded by minefields. These positions were known as "boxes." Owing to the shortage of infantry the Gazala Line was not completely covered by fire and there was one gap between 69 and 150 Brigades and another between the left of 150 Brigade and the right flank of the French force.

To the east of the main Gazala Line was a series of strongpoints, surrounded by deep minefields. The most important of these defence areas was around a junction of desert tracks known as Knightsbridge, about seventeen miles west of El Adem. This important position, held by the crack troops of 200 Guards Brigade, was the key to the Gazala position.

The German line did not run parallel to the British. Although Rommel's left flank lay on the coast only a few miles west of Gazala, the line was echeloned back, running southwards to include Mekili. This meant that, whereas there was little room for manouevre in the north, a distance of forty miles separated the rival armies in the south.

The D.L.I. Brigade occupied its own Box, completely surrounded by a minefield through which certain well-marked gaps had been made. Inside this circle of mines lived all the fighting troops of the Brigade Group. There was Brigade H.Q. and the three D.L.I. battalions, the gunners of the 74th Field Regiment, the sappers of 505 Field Company, Royal Engineers, A Company of the 2nd Cheshires with their machine-guns, a battery of the 65th Anti-Tank Regiment, a battery of the 149th Anti-Tank Regiment, a battery of Light Anti-Aircraft guns, and B Company of 149 Field Ambulance.

Brigadier Redman had been succeeded by Brigadier J. S. Nicholls, D.S.O., M.C., known throughout the army as "Crasher," a veteran of the Eritrean campaign and the breakout from El Duda when Tobruk was relieved. He disposed the Brigade with the 9th Battalion on the right, facing north and north-west, the 6th Battalion in the centre and the 8th on the left. Behind the infantry positions, deep pits covered by huge camouflage nets hid the guns of the 74th Field Regiment from prying enemy aircraft. Not far from the gun lines were the dugouts and vehicle pits of the Sappers, and the underground dressing station of the Field Ambulance.

About three miles in front of the Brigade Box each Battalion constructed strong outposts, manned by a rifle platoon, a section of carriers, a Gunner O.P.[1] and a section of Vickers machine-guns from the Cheshires. The 8th established two of these positions, known as Stricklands Post and Petro's Post, named after the two officers who had been given the task of constructing them with their platoons. Only Stricklands was manned, but Petro's was earmarked as an alternative position if withdrawal from the former proved necessary.

Some fifteen miles to the east of the Brigade Box, near a small feature known as Pt. 109, was the Brigade B Echelon area where the Battalion Quartermasters and M.T.Os., had established their H.Q. They quickly settled down and what had once been desert waste soon became a comfortable, well organised area. A visit to B Echelon from the Box was always a very pleasant change from the forward area but, in fairness to the occupants of B Echelon, it must be put on record that they always shared their superior comforts with visitors and many an officer reinforcement to the Battalion can look back gratefully to a night spent at B Echelon with the hospitality of Captains Stray and Blagdon before moving up to the forward area the following day.

At Gazala the troops in the Box lived below ground level. Weapon pits were dug out of the sand and linked together in some cases to form a continuous trench system in a platoon locality. Dugouts were excavated for Battalion and Company H.Q. and the company cookhouses and reserve stores also went below ground level. Some of the dugouts were exceptionally well equipped ; Battalion H.Q. Mess had a table to seat fifteen for meals, a wireless set installed at one end and shelves cut out of the walls for books. Individual weapon pits were as comfortable as their occupants took the trouble to make them and the men of the 8th very quickly adapted themselves to the unusual living conditions of the desert.

The Battalion lived, slept and ate in the slit trenches and dugouts and during the fierce heat of the afternoon, when there was not a man in the unit with the exception of the sentries who did not seek shelter from the burning sun, the only visible sign of the Box was the single strand of wire marking the leading edge of the minefield. Even the few trucks allowed in the forward area were hidden from view, camouflaged with nets and parked in deep pits excavated out of the

[1]Observation Post.

sand. Reserve ammunition, food and water was kept in the section positions, whilst further reserves were buried feet deep in the rear areas of the Box.

Water was one of the main problems at Gazala. The supply of this vital commodity, which had to be brought miles across the desert to the Battalion each day by the R.A.S.C. water-tankers, was very short and rationed to half a gallon per man per day for all purposes. Two pints of this ration was handed in to the company cookhouses where the meals were prepared before being sent out to the platoon areas in containers. Of the remaining two pints, one was for the individual water bottle and the other had to suffice for washing and shaving. The dirty washing water was filtered and added to each day so that it lasted a week or more.

Hot tea being the best thirst-quencher was therefore the most economical way of using the drinking ration, and the early morning midday and evening mugs of tea were looked forward to as eagerly as the mail from home. It is to the credit of the Battalion that only one or two men out of the hundreds in the Box at Gazala ever attempted to supplement their daily ration from the reserve cans in the section trenches although there were several cases in the last days preceding the breakout when men, almost crazed with thirst, drank rusted water from the radiators of vehicles.

The Battalion learned to live on bully and biscuits with tinned foods; contrary to all expectations the men thrived on this diet. There was tinned steak, meat and vegetable, bully beef and processed cheese, supplemented by cans of peaches and pears from the weekly N.A.A.F.I. delivery. Canned American and Canadian beer sometimes came up with the N.A.A.F.I. stores, and this was buried for several days, then dug up after " stand-down " when it was delicious for its coolness. Unfortunately neither the beer nor the tinned fruits ever averaged more than one can per man per week.

The desert was not a very pleasant place but in spite of the heat, sand, flies and the scarcity of water, it was healthy and what little sickness there was confined itself to desert sores. One of the compensations was a free weekly ration of "V" cigarettes. They were not very popular with the Desert Army but at least they were better than the Italian cigarettes smoked by Mussolini's soldiers, and some times they were supplemented by a packet or two of Players from home or the N.A.A.F.I. delivery.

The novelty and glamour of being in the front line in the Western Desert soon began to pall, and the Battalion settled down to a routine every bit as boring as the period on the beaches during the Battle of Britain. The nearest Germans were over thirty miles away, quietly minding their own business, and the main task during the early weeks at Gazala was to organise and strengthen that section of the line which was the responsibility of the 8th. Every day was the same. The Battalion " stood-to " at dawn, and after Lieut.-Colonel Beart had visited the company positions it was time to " stand-down." Then there was P.T. before breakfast followed by the first welcome mug of tea. During the morning and late afternoon the troops worked on the defences, stripped to the waist and to the accompaniment of the jarring noise of the windy picks[1] which had to be brought up to deal with some of the harder desert rock. The Battalion " stood-to " again just before dusk.

However, the Eighth Army was not content to sit back in the Gazala Line waiting for the enemy to attack, and a feature of the Battalion's work between the end of February and the opening of the German offensive on May 27th was the daylight patrols which went out every morning at dawn and returned at sunset. These patrols, known by the code name of Apat, consisted of a section of the Battalion Carrier Platoon, and a section of the Anti-Tank Platoon with two-pounder guns. The Apats, usually commanded by a captain, were completely mobile and their task was to go out fifteen miles ahead of the Brigade Box to maintain observation on a front of five miles. They co-operated closely with the 6th South African Armoured Car Regiment, seasoned veterans of the desert who were acting as reconnaissance unit for 50 Division, and were generally a very useful source of information. Wireless contact was maintained with Brigade H.Q., the patrol commander reporting back every two hours. A Gunner O.P. moving with the Apats was able to call on the guns at Stricklands Post to deal with any emergency.

Most of the observation was carried out during the morning and late afternoon, for the deceptive heat haze which hung over the desert from just before midday until about three p.m. made all movement impossible. The conditions at midday were most unpleasant as by this time the truck and carrier engines were often boiling, and the metal parts of the vehicles which had been exposed to the burning heat of the morning sun were too hot to touch.

As, at this time, the nearest German positions were some thirty miles away, contact was seldom established and the patrols very rarely saw anything of the enemy, although they sometimes had long range glimpses of German armoured cars operating close in to their forward positions. However, these daily sorties enabled some members of the Battalion at least to familiarise themselves with the few landmarks in existence in the desert, and to glean some knowledge of the difficult art of desert navigation—at any rate, it seemed difficult in those early days. The troops fortunate enough to go out on Apats were surprised by the depth and extent of this No Man's Land of apparently limitless desert which stretched away to the west and the German lines.

Constant patrolling of this sort was fine training for the Battalion carrier crews and "Stanley Gap at dawn" became a daily routine order for a section of the platoon. The carrier men with the Apat patrols were able to probe the desert almost at will in their fast vehicles and soon acquired that desert sense which comes from intimate knowledge of its peculiarities. They quickly discovered that the desert is not all alike as it invariably seemed to newcomers ; they

[1]The Durham miners name for a pneumatic drill.

found little differences everywhere and these, together with the more substantial landmarks, became the aids to direction which were invaluable and so necessary in the confusing strangeness of the desert.

At this time the ordnance maps available showed only some of the more outstanding natural features and at Gazala these were few and far between. However, there were some fairly prominent ridges on the Battalion front which made useful observation posts; one of these became known as Heinkel Ridge because of the debris of a wrecked Heinkel bomber scattered about the feature. Not far from Heinkel Ridge was Tank Valley, where fierce fighting had taken place during the British winter offensive of 1941 when a German rearguard turned savagely at bay to overrun a battalion of the Buffs. The debris of the battle had not been cleared away and the blackened hulks of two burned out German tanks, one or two wrecked British ammunition limbers, and several white crosses marking shallow desert graves bore silent witness to the fierceness of the action.

There were many signs of past campaigns to serve as a grim reminder that this period without interference from the enemy was only a prelude to the stern things to come. These landmarks were invaluable and after a time the men of the Carrier Platoon were able to patrol to Sidi Breghisc, a well known feature on high ground to the west of the Gazala Line, without relying on compass navigation. They simply proceeded by way of Stricklands Post, Heinkel Post, an abandoned Italian gun, and a burned out German tank. The Trigh Capuzzo, which ran across the front of the British positions at Gazala, they knew as the Great North Road. The information which the carrier crews brought in was invaluable to the Intelligence Section under Lieut. D. A. Neale, and a map of the Battalion front was started which finally became a most comprehensive record of all available landmarks.

On several occasions the Battalion was called upon to provide elements for columns and half-columns. These hard-hitting formations were known as Jock Columns, after Brigadier Jock Campbell, V.C., an intrepid desert commander who devised a means of utilising the slender resources of the Eighth Army whilst there was a lull in the fighting. The task of these fully mobile columns composed of all arms was to carry out extensive patrolling and to attack specific objectives whenever possible. They were usually made up of a company of infantry, a section of Bren carriers, two detachments of 3" mortars, a battery of twenty-five pounder field guns, a battery of two-pounder anti-tank guns, a platoon of Vickers machine-guns and a troop of Bofors anti-aircraft guns. There were also the usual administrative services and a detachment of the Royal Army Medical Corps.

Early in March the Battalion was ordered to provide infantry, carriers and mortars for a half-column and B Company, commanded by Captain R. I. Pitt, was detailed as the infantry element. Men of the half-column were briefed in an initial lecture by Major J. Barclay of the 65th Anti-Tank Regiment (Norfolk Yeomanry). Major Barclay, who had been in the desert about a year, was a seasoned desert soldier and a very picturesque one in his white shirt, corduroy trousers and suede boots under a long, yellow sheepskin jacket.

A few days later, after the formation and signal procedure had been practised, the first Battalion half-column left the Gazala Line. A plan had been issued showing the position of each vehicle in the formation and, when the half-column was ready to move off from the Box, the navigating truck—carrying a large distinguishing flag—was positioned in front of the minefield wire. One by one the other vehicles passed through the minefield gap and took up their stations from the navigator's truck.

There was a very real danger of air attack at Gazala where the Germans had their fighters and bombers on close call and the column formed up in desert formation—six parallel lines of vehicles with fifty to a hundred yards between each one. The commander, Major Collet-White of the Gunners, travelled in the truck behind the navigator with the commanders of the supporting arms grouped near him, and when all the vehicles were in position he stood up in his truck to raise his arms in a "V" signal and the half-column moved off, heading due west towards the German lines. Each vehicle sent up a cloud of dust and sand as it lurched across the desert, and from out in front the column looked like ships ploughing through a stormy sea with the rear trucks hidden from view by those preceding them.

The column covered thirty miles during the first day and towards evening contacted a patrol of South African armoured cars. Their commander was able to give valuable information about German dispositions, and when plans had been made for the following day the column closed in to laager for the night. All the vehicles drew into a tight compact square with the guns on the outside and the infantry positions disposed around the perimeter. Next morning, before it was light, the column, shaking out into desert formation again, moved forward towards the German positions with the object of reaching the shelter of a conspicuous hillock from where observation of the enemy movements would be possible. The column soon reached this feature and the gunners unlimbered the twenty-five pounders to prepare for action. When in just under an hour a small party of German vehicles appeared at a distance of six thousand yards, the gunners put in some nice shooting, breaking up the convoy and scattering the vehicles in all directions. Lieut. J. Carruthers went after the disorganised enemy trucks with the carriers but was unable to catch them. For the rest of the day the gunners effectively shelled enemy transport, working parties and defensive positions, while the section of carriers guarding the column flank had a grandstand view of the effects of the accurate, concentrated shooting.

Next day the British force moved still further in towards the enemy with a view to getting a line on more substantial targets. Major Collet-White spotted some armoured cars sitting out on a flank and signalling Captain Pitt, the infantry commander, to follow him he wheeled out of the halted column. When the gap had narrowed to less than a hundred yards the armoured cars opened fire at almost point blank range—they were German ! The British drivers turned the trucks round almost in their own length and accelerated back towards the column, snaking their vehicles across the desert and almost overtaking the solid shot from the German turret guns which was bouncing along on both sides of them. The trucks reached the column safely, though their occupants had been badly shaken, and as the armoured cars made off at speed the British gunners gave them several rounds to help them on their way.

After this exciting incident the column moved in closer to the German positions and the gunners went into action against some transport targets on a distant ridge. After about thirty minutes of shooting, a 105-millimetre shell came down with a terrific crump just to the flank of the British gun line. This was followed by several more, the extremely accurate shelling causing some casualties to the gunners. It was difficult to understand how the German counter-battery fire was so accurate unless an enemy O.P. had been established almost on top of the column, and Major Collett-White sent Lieut. Carruthers to locate and eliminate the O.P. The Carrier Section immediately commenced a beat of an area about a thousand yards ahead of the British guns, and about eight hundred yards south-west of the column, Carruthers spotted a white cap in a dense patch of camel thorn. The carriers dashed in towards this ; as they did so an Italian officer and his escort of four Germans jumped into a Volkswagen and made off at high speed. Pte. Foster fired a Bren gun from Carruther's carrier, and hit the Italian officer who was standing up in the car. Shelling of the column stopped at once and switched to the jubilant Carrier Section, but even the unpleasant ten minutes that followed could not damp their spirits and the knowledge of a job well done. They had drawn first blood for the Battalion in the Desert war, and were justly proud of their achievement.[1]

The British troops were full of admiration for the Italian gunner O.P. who had established himself so close to the powerful column in order to direct the fire of his guns. This incident bore out the remarks of Desert veterans that Italian gunners were of much sterner stuff than their infantry.

For the remainder of the day the Carrier Section took up positions controlling the patch of camel thorn which was extensive and provided good cover. On two occasions enemy patrols approached the carriers but were driven off by the deadly and accurate fire of the twenty-five pounders. During the heat of the afternoon the Carrier commander wireless the column, "Enemy infantry again approaching No 1 Section positions." But the heat haze had played a trick on the tired observers of the section and, shortly after the first message,

[1]Lieut. Carruthers was wounded and taken prisoner during the breakout from Gazala some months after this episode. He was sent to a military hospital in Italy, where in the bed next to him was an Italian officer recovering from severe gunshot wounds. One day, proudly showing Carruthers the German Iron Cross which he had recently been awarded, he described how he had won it and been wounded in the action. With the aid of maps and much broken English, French and Italian, he told his story and to Carruthers amazement he realised that this man was the Italian officer who had directed the fire of the German guns at the half-column and then been shot by Pte. Foster.

Carruthers had to signal, "In previous message substitute camels for enemy infantry." It was an amazing feature of the desert war that, whether or not there was fighting, the nomads of the Desert were allowed to move about almost at will and most of them had a complete disregard for the lethal weapons of the opposing armies.

As the light faded the column withdrew to its laager position with the knowledge that the dual mission of harrassing and reconnaissance had been carried out successfully. On the morning of the fourth day the column headed east and made its way back towards the Gazala Line. The men were tired and dishevelled. On the flank a conversation was going on in one of the carriers and a member of the crew raised a laugh with, "I suppose 'Spike' will be waiting for us at Stanley Gap to see if we've got our bloody tin helmets on straight."

For the rest of the month the patrol activity of the Battalion was confined to the Apat patrols which went out every morning from Stanley Gap, and no more calls were made on the 8th for columns or half-columns.

In the Box and at Stricklands Post it was a busy month. There was still plenty of work required on the defences and the changeable weather did not make this an easy task. The wind veered round every five or six days, causing dust storms which swept over the Box, driving every man in the Battalion below ground level. Towards the end of the month the days became noticeably warmer, a foretaste of the really hot, stifling weather of the summer months to come.

CHAPTER EIGHT

THE GAZALA BATTLE OPENS

Rosscol—heat, thirst, and flies—a new C.O.—Rommel closes in—the outpost attacked—commerce raiding—carrier versus tank—a minefield laid across Many Tracks.

EARLY in April the Germans exchanged their previous inactivity for vigorous patrolling in No Man's Land, and it was clear to British Intelligence that Rommel was on the move. The German commander's object was to regain the initiative, which his troops had lost during the patrolling phase, as a prelude to the forthcoming German offensive.

The extent of the reconnaissance by the British daylight patrols was now reduced considerably. Eight miles out from the Box they were shelled by German columns operating in No Man's Land. R.A.F. Hurricanes of the Desert Air Force on their routine tactical reconnaissance flights reported that at El Cheima, nine miles west of the Gazala Line, there was a small force of German armoured vehicles consisting of four tanks and an armoured car. It was essential to regain British supremacy in No Man's Land, and 151 Brigade was ordered to despatch a strong column to carry out a sweep, drive back any German columns, and particularly to deal with the armoured force at El Cheima.

The 8th Battalion was detailed to organise this sweep and at 3 p.m. on April 8th a column, commanded by Major R. S. McLaren, assembled outside the minefield at Stanley Gap. It was composed of D Company of the Battalion, two sections of the Battalion Carrier Platoon, two detachments of the Mortar Platoon, a battery from the 74th Field Regiment, a battery of anti-tank guns from the Cheshire Yeomanry, a platoon of Cheshire Regiment machine-guns, a troop of Bofors light anti-aircraft guns and some sappers from 505 Field Company, Royal Engineers. There were also detachments of R.A.S.C. troop-carriers, an ambulance car section from the Field Ambulance and the usual B Echelon administrative vehicles for ammunition and supplies.

The original orders from Brigade H.Q. were for the column to proceed during the night to El Cherima, ten miles north-west of El Cheima. It was hoped that the presence of the British force in the morning would induce the enemy to retire to avoid encirclement. However, this order was cancelled at 10 p.m. and Rosscol—the code name for the column—was ordered to attack and destroy the German tanks at El Cheima at first light.

When dawn broke on April 9th a thick fog enveloped the desert, a most unusual phenomenon. The British column picked its way carefully through the damp, clinging desert mist towards El Cheima ready to engage the German force when visibility improved. The troops sat huddled in their vehicles, greatcoat collars turned up, scarves or balaclava helmets round their heads and blankets wrapped round their legs.

Visibility did not return to normal until mid-morning, and although no German tanks could be seen there were armoured cars on the skyline to the north, west and south. After the carriers had identified them as Axis vehicles the British gunners shelled them and Rosscol was soon shelled in return. The exchange of gunfire continued for the rest of the morning, but it was some time before the enemy gunners had the range of the British column which was disposed in a hollow in an excellent anti-tank position. Shortly after 1 p.m. the enemy gunners had ranged successfully on Rosscol and were causing casualties. The British gunners, for their part, forced the enemy armoured cars to retire on several occasions, but they appeared again almost immediately on other crests and were obviously acting as observation posts for their artillery.

The intensity of the shelling indicated that the enemy was well supported with artillery, and as their accurate fire was by now causing fairly heavy casualties in the British column Major McLaren gave the order to withdraw, leaving one troop of field guns and a platoon of D. Company on the ground as a covering force. The infantry embussed in the troop-carriers, the guns were limbered up and the main body of Rosscol drew back about three miles to halt clear of shellfire. Major McLaren had just passed a message by wireless for the rearguard to withdraw when an urgent signal came through from one of the British gunner O.Ps. that German tanks had followed up the withdrawal of the column and were preparing to attack. This information was confirmed within a few minutes by the appearance of the troop of guns and the infantry platoon of the rearguard well to the south. They were in "full cry," obviously heading for the Box, and that was the last Rosscol saw of them.

A few seconds later the German tanks appeared, making straight for the column, which prepared to engage and destroy them. The Cheshires opened up at two thousand yards, spraying the tanks with machine-gun fire and forcing the commanders and drivers to close down, considerably limiting the visibility of the tanks. It was later confirmed that this machine-gun fire had, by luck and good shooting, killed one of the German tank commanders in his turret. However, the tanks came on steadily and, eight hundred yards short of the column, pulled out to a semi-broadside position so that the British shells would not have a normal strike, and came to rest.

For a few seconds which seemed like long minutes, the German tanks and Rosscol faced each other—like two boxers in their ringside seats waiting for the bell—and then suddenly there was a commotion in the British column. Due to some unfortunate error which has never been fully explained, the anti-tank gun troop facing east limbered up and withdrew out of the battle area. At the same time, a number of truck drivers seeing this movement, thought that the column had been given the order to disengage and fall back. They started up and followed the troop of guns; they in their turn were followed by most of the remaining vehicles, including the R.A.S.C. troop-carriers, leaving the unfortunate infantry on the ground without transport. Major McLaren at Column H.Q. was horrified to see field guns, anti-aircraft guns, carriers, mortars and all the B Echelon vehicles racing to the rear.

This left Rosscol composed only of two platoons of infantry, one troop of anti-tank guns, one troop of field guns and one Bofors gun and it was indeed a sadly depleted force which stood fast and gave battle. One by one the German tanks opened fire; the British gunners, stripped to the waist, replied shell for shell. At a murderously short range the tanks concentrated their fire on the artillery ammunition limbers and quads[1] which were soon burning fiercely and sending columns of black smoke into the sky. The British gunners hit back and soon three of the German tanks were set on fire. As their crews baled out, the Bren gunners of the two platoons of D Company sent long bursts of fire whipping across the desert and their accurate shooting caught several of the Germans in the open and inflicted casualties. The remaining tanks then switched their fire to the British guns and in a few minutes had put them all out of action, killing or wounding the crews. Whilst this duel was in progress the column was also shelled by German Mark IV tanks which could be seen in the distance. When the last of the British guns had been knocked out a silence fell over the battlefield, broken every now and then by short bursts of Bren gun fire from the British infantry, still shooting at the tank crews.

When the smoke and dust of the battle had cleared away, the men of Rosscol could see two of the eight German tanks retreating towards the west, whilst the three which had been set on fire were still burning furiously and three others stood silent. The lull was broken by odd shells from the Mark IVs in the distance which started to shoot at the column again, but apart from this the field of battle belonged to Rosscol. The battery commander of the field guns, Major G. Fawkes, set off to rally the field and anti-tank gun troops which had withdrawn to the rear, whilst D Company commander, Captain D. Claye, started out with a party of men to destroy the three disabled German tanks which had not been set on fire.

Before either of these tasks could be accomplished another wave of Mark III tanks hesitantly approached the battlefield, halting and machine-gunning as they came. With no field or anti-tank gun support, Rosscol was no match for this new German threat. The breech blocks were removed from the shattered British guns and hastily loaded on to the remaining trucks of the column, together with some of the wounded, the drivers being told to make for the Box. Then the infantry and a few gunners started to march in the direction the trucks had taken, the German tanks following at a distance of about a thousand yards, very slowly and obviously expecting an ambush from the guns of the rest of Rosscol to the rear. The chase

[1] Four-wheel-drive vehicles for towing guns.

went on for half an hour with the British troops stumbling across the desert, until suddenly the Germans plucked up courage and closed the gap. Major McLaren gave the order to scatter and his men hid up in camel thorn or slit trenches. The German tanks passed by and were followed by anti-tank guns which took up action stations a few hundred yards away, cutting McLaren's force off from the rest of the column and the Box.

For a long time nothing happened and silence fell over the desert. Then, as the sun began to set, enemy infantry appeared. Co-operating with the tanks which had now returned, having driven the rest of Rosscol to seek refuge in the Box, they systematically combed the desert and took prisoner about thirty officers and men, who were escorted to the rear. Among those captured were the Column Commander—Major McLaren; the Column Adjutant—Captain T. Preacher; D Company Commander—Captain Claye; two of the infantry platoon commanders, Lieuts. Strickland and Woods; also Lieut. Crofton of the 74th Field Regiment and Lieut. Clover of the Cheshire Yeomanry.

As dusk drew in the German salvage parties arrived. One of the burning tanks was extinguished but the other two were left to burn themselves out. Of the three tanks which had been disabled but not set on fire one was able to leave the battlefield under its own power, one was towed away, and the third was carried off on a tank transporter.

Rosscol in the opinion of many was a failure, but it might have been a very different story had the column stood steady when the anti-tank gun troop pulled out. The wary advance of the second wave of Mark III tanks proved that the Germans had taken a beating and they would probably have left Rosscol in undisputed charge of the battlefield had the column been able to show fight. As it was, a series of unfortunate misunderstandings resulted in a grave loss to the Division of men and equipment which could ill be spared at that time, and a particularly grievous loss to the 8th Battalion of Major McLaren.

Rosscol was a severe blow to the Battalion, but it made the troops realise that the men of Rommel's Afrika Corps were all they were reputed to be—determined fighters who could take the punches where it hurt most and still come back for more. After Rosscol, intelligence reports showed that the German commander had narrowed the gap between the opposing armies by moving the right of his line forward from Mechili to Sidi Breghisc. At the same time the Axis line had been extended southwards to Rotunda Segnali. These moves had been covered by a screen of tanks and it was part of this armoured force which Rosscol had encountered. The enemy line was now only fifteen miles away, thus considerably reducing the Battalion patrol area. Carrier sorties to Breghisc were heavily shelled, confirming the R.A.F. report that this ideal forming up point had been occupied by a strong German force.

The enemy tried to deny observation of his activities by using armoured cars and tanks. The South African armoured cars were gradually edged off of their normal observation posts which the Germans then occupied. Being able to use tanks the Germans were more aggressive and had a distinct advantage for at that time, due to the shortage of British armour, no British tanks were allowed to operate west of the Gazala Line. The Battalion Apat patrols now came into their own and the small mobile columns which went out from Stanley Gap every morning acted as hard-hitting fighting patrols. They had a real job of work to do now, for in the early mornings and evenings the Gunner O.Ps. with the patrols were able to bring down fire on the increased enemy activity. For the rest of the month these bucanneering Apat patrols continued to operate and on several occasions, dodging the German tank screen, they darted in close to Sidi Breghisc so that the British Gunner O.Ps. could get some good shooting at the enemy positions there.

The weather during the month had been getting gradually hotter bringing the accursed desert flies in large numbers. The only peace during the heat of the day from these wretched insects was to sit under a mosquito net from early morning until dusk and as this was quite impracticable the troops came to accept the flies as an evil which could not be conquered. The desert flies were without a doubt by far the most daring and infuriating of their species. Dusk brought respite from them but they returned with breakfast next morning. The danger of dysentery was ever present and the utmost care had to be taken of latrine and cooking arrangements. Every company had its own sanitary man who burned all refuse because it was asking for trouble to bury it in the desert.

Early in May Lieut.-Colonel Beart announced that he was relinquishing command of the 8th on his appointment as brigadier of an East African Brigade. He had been a popular Commanding Officer with all ranks, and the Battalion was indeed sorry to see him go. One of his last gestures before leaving was typical. After Rosscol the Brigadier had made it known that he did not want any of his battalion commanders to take unnecessary risks by accompanying columns or patrols. Nevertheless, the C.O. of the 8th was determined to see the Battalion patrol area before leaving and, ordering a carrier section to be put at his disposal, he then went on a tour of the Battalion front as far as Sidi Breghisc. Every man in that patrol silently wished good luck to an admired commander, these wishes being echoed by the rest of the Battalion.

On May 13th Lieut.-Colonel M. L. P. Jackson, of the Green Howards, came from the 6th D.L.I. where he had been Second-in-Command for a short time, to take over the 8th Battalion. He lost no time in introducing himself, making some unpopular and critical comments about the officers and men of the Territorial Army. There is no doubt that this die-hard regular soldier got off to a bad start with the 8th D.L.I., but underneath his toughness and apparent brusqueness were the very finest qualities of leadership and courage ; the Battalion was soon to forget his early indiscretion and admire him for what he really was—a fine soldier and born leader.

A few days after the arrival of the new C.O., the Second-in-Command attended a conference at Brigade H.Q. when it was announced that a full scale attack against the Eighth Army was likely within a week. This was news indeed and completion of the Battalion defences, both at Stricklands and in the Box, was pushed forward hurriedly.

From the reports of the daily Apat sorties it was obvious that the German offensive was about to be launched. During the afternoon of May 26th a state of readiness order was received from Brigade H.Q. and by 5 p.m. the whole Battalion was on the alert. That same afternoon, Lieut. Dobson, a B Company platoon commander in charge of the outpost, and Captain Stangrome of the Gunners went out from Stricklands to investigate an approaching column. The truck carrying them disappeared from view and nothing more was heard until 1 a.m. the following morning, when Dobson returned to Stricklands on foot and alone. He reported that he and his escort had reached a ridge known as B.13, west of Stricklands Post, where they had been trapped. Dobson managed to escape but he thought the rest of the patrol had been killed or captured. The way in which this patrol had been ambushed was typical of what was happening along the whole length of the Gazala Line. Rommel's forces were closing in.

The Axis attack opened during the early hours of May 27th. Rommel's plan was the well-tried one of turning the open desert flank. Under cover of his air force he planned to pass the whole of the German armour and most of the Italian tanks, together with the infantry formations, round the south of the Gazala Line to engage the British tank formations east of the Line and defeat them on the first day. With this accomplished, a simultaneous infantry attack from the west and an armoured assault from the east was to be launched against the Box positions. The following night the Tobruk perimeter was to be attacked by the whole Axis force, and was to fall by May 30th. Coinciding with the enemy attempt to turn the open desert flank the Italian Brescia and Pavia Divisions were assigned with frontal attack roles on the Gazala Line, designed to hold the British forces in their Boxes.

As a preliminary to the Italian attacks the 69 Brigade outpost at Gabr el Fachri, to the south of the 8th Battalion, and Stricklands Post were heavily shelled during the early hours of May 27th. At first light the small garrison of infantry, anti-tank gunners and machine-gunners at Stricklands under command of Lieut. R. Place watched a battalion of Italian infantry debussing on B. 13 ridge. The British Gunner O.P. at the outpost immediately called for artillery support, and as the enemy formed up to attack, the British gunfire caught them in the open. For a minute or two there was chaos but the enemy force was reorganised and advanced to the attack, two companies coming in from the north-west, one from the south-west and a fourth company moving in reserve. By this time an S.O.S. had been sent for more gun support, and as the Italians advanced across the three thousand yards of desert which separated them from the outpost, the heavy and concentrated fire of the guns in the Box was brought to bear on them. The gunners sent shell after shell whistling over Stricklands to burst among the advancing companies ; it was accurate and concentrated fire and tore large gaps in the enemy lines. As they wavered the Vickers guns of the 2nd Cheshires at the outpost opened fire followed by the Bren guns and rifles of the infantry platoon under Sgt. I. McDermott. The platoon was expertly handled by McDermott and the fire of the three sections played havoc amongst the advancing Italians. He himself showed very little regard for his own safety, and the platoon tackled the task of throwing back the vastly numerically superior Italian force with complete confidence because of McDermott's personal courage and general behaviour under fire. He set a fine example to his men who were outnumbered by at least ten to one.

Eight hundred yards short of Stricklands the attack was halted and the Italians beat a hasty and disorganised retreat, taking their dead and wounded with them. Shortly afterwards the depleted enemy force moved off south-eastwards towards Gabr el Fachri. It was first blood to the Battalion and much of the credit for this successful action against heavy odds must go to Lieut. Place who fought his garrison with great coolness. Disregarding the heavy shellfire he moved about the position and co-ordinated the defences in such a way that the attacking force was met by a series of body blows. Place was awarded the Military Cross for his handling of a dangerous situation and Sgt. McDermott the Military Medal. It will be seen in later pages what a grave loss it would have been to the 8th Battalion if the outpost had been captured that morning.

Just before midday Stricklands was shelled again and soon after the enemy guns started to range on the British artillery in the Box. Then the disturbing news came through that the Italians failing to capture Stricklands were now reinforced and had driven the troops of 69 Brigade out of Gabr el Fachri. In the early afternoon the guns of the 7th Medium Regiment from their positions in the Box shelled the enemy, but the Italians were not to be driven out of their new position so easily ; Gabr el Fachri remained in their hands. As visibility improved towards the evening small numbers of enemy M.T. could easily be seen to the south of Stricklands, moving in a south-easterly direction towards Bir Hacheim. The news which came up with the rations that night was not so good. No further supplies of petrol, water or ammunition could be expected and three-quarter scale rations would come into effect forthwith.

After dusk the first of many foot patrols was sent out by the Battalion. Operating from Stricklands Post, Captain P. H. Bower and Lieut. P. G. Hampson went to the area where the Italian infantry attack had been smashed. No bodies were found but letters and postcards in hastily-dug slit trenches indicated that the Italian troops had been from the Brescia Division. The truck which had carried Lieut. Dobson's ill-fated patrol was also found—abandoned and showing no signs, apart from several bloodstains, of the fate of L/Cpl. " Joss " Little and the rest of the patrol.

Meanwhile the main German attack had not worked out according to plan. After an overnight march from the Rotunda Segnali area the Italian Ariete Division had attacked Bir Hacheim during the early hours of May 27th. The French garrison of Hacheim under the leadership of that gallant Frenchman, General Koenig, reacted furiously to throw back the Italian thrust. However, this setback did not prevent the main Axis column making a detour during the night round Hacheim to strike north behind the French positions at daylight. The German 21 Panzer Division made for Acroma whilst 15 Panzer Division was directed on El Adem. Both these thrusts were

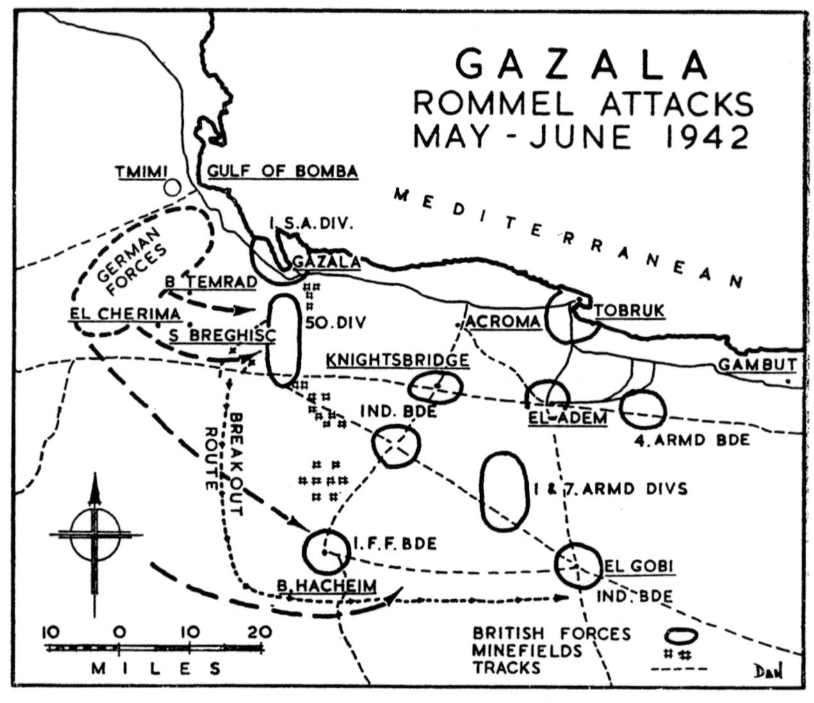

THE WESTERN DESERT. The line-up of the opposing forces at Gazala when Rommel attacked in May 1942, and the break-out route taken by the Battalion a few weeks later, south of Bir Hacheim and back to the frontier

held during the day by the veteran British 7 Armoured Division and 1 Armoured Division. At the same time the Desert Air Force put in heavy and concentrated attacks against the long lines of enemy supply vehicles taking supplies and ammunition forward to the German Panzer Divisions.

These enemy supply columns were using a valley, marked as Many Tracks on the map and known to the Battalion Apat patrols as The Great North Road. When Lieut.-Colonel Jackson received information from one of his carrier sections that large numbers of vulnerable supply vehicles were streaming along this route across the front of the 8th Battalion, he immediately ordered daylight offensive action by fast mobile patrols against this lifeline to Rommel's armour.

On May 28th the Battalion started a period of intense daylight patrol activity, using Stricklands as a base, which was to pay considerable dividends. These operations became known as commerce raiding. At 5 a.m. on May 28th the first patrol, consisting of two sections of carriers, a section of mortars and a section of anti-tank guns left Stricklands Post. Captain I. R. English commanded the patrol and success was immediate. The British force took cover behind a friendly knoll within sight of Many Tracks, and then as a small enemy convoy approached along the tracks, throwing up a tell-tale cloud of dust, one of the carrier sections went into action. It broke cover and raced across the intervening desert to halt the convoy with bursts of Bren gun fire which set one of the trucks ablaze. The astonishment of the enemy drivers, who thought the British were miles away, was almost laughable and, protesting volubly, eight Italian prisoners were loaded on to one of their own five-ton lorries and sent back to Stricklands, escorted by a carrier.

Shortly after the captured truck and carrier escort had disappeared from view Sgt. G. Hill's section of carriers was suddenly confronted by an Italian tank which appeared from behind the shelter of a knoll. The tank could easily have destroyed the whole carrier section, but without hesitation Sgt. Hill ordered his driver to charge the tank. The carrier accelerated and as the gap between the two vehicles was rapidly closed, Hill swept the tank with bursts of Bren gun fire. The Italians showed no fight, most probably because of Hill's ferocious attack, and not a single shot was fired at the carrier. Instead the tank slowed to a halt as the carrier drew level. Sheepishly the Italian crew climbed from the turret and surrendered to Hill who shepherded them back to the main body of the patrol. The sergeant was awarded the Military Medal for this successful attack against heavy odds. The next prize, an Italian lorry carrying a large water tank, was even more welcome. Water bottles at Stricklands were replenished before the vehicle was escorted to the Box. Outpost duty had its compensations for the sweet Derna water from the tanker was a welcome change from the warm, rather sickly liquid which filled the British water bottles. The first day of commerce raiding had undoubtedly been a great success and had provided a rich haul of vehicles, prisoners and mail for identification purposes, urgently wanted by the Intelligence staffs at Division and Corps H.Q. The patrol returned at dusk, well satisfied with the day's work.

In the 8th Battalion Box it had also been a day of excitement. In the late afternoon an Italian fighter was shot down, both C and D companies claiming the credit. About an hour after this the Battalion was ordered to "stand-to" when enemy infantry were reported approaching the positions. It was an Italian ambulance convoy off course. No. 2 Section of the Carrier Platoon brought in this column, a complete Italian medical unit, in spite of the excited protest of a voluble, gesticulating Italian doctor who complained that to take him prisoner was most unfair as he had only been in the desert three weeks.

Just after first light on May 30th the second commerce raiding patrol left Stricklands Post. On Many Tracks the patrol commander, Lieut. R. H. R. Robinson, had a narrow escape when the carrier sections under his command forced a convoy of five German trucks to stop. As the enemy vehicles came to a standstill, a German officer jumped out of the last truck and levelled a sub-machine gun at Robinson and Pte. Cloughton who had left their carrier and were walking towards the truck. Split second thinking by Cloughton saved an ugly situation. As the German was about to shoot, Cloughton fired his Bren gun from the hip and killed him. The captured trucks and the German drivers were then sent back to the outpost under escort while the rest of the patrol lay in wait for the next convoy.

Shortly after midday a line of vehicles was observed approaching along Many Tracks. The Bren carriers, waiting until the enemy trucks were almost level, broke cover and raced towards the convoy, opening fire at a thousand yards. As the convoy drew nearer the carrier crews were horrified to find that it was an Italian ambulance column, and the Bren gunners ceased fire immediately as the patrol closed in. The vehicles were packed with Italian wounded from the Hacheim area and, after a short consultation with an Italian officer, Lieut. Robinson agreed to let the convoy proceed to its destination although he insisted on taking prisoner several wounded Italian officers. They were transferred to a refrigerator truck, which had been travelling with the ambulances, and sent back under escort to Stricklands.

Meanwhile, Pte. Cloughton had caused a sensation with the newly-acquired sub-machine gun which he had taken from the German officer earlier in the morning. He was standing near one of the ambulances whilst Robinson was discussing the fate of the convoy, holding the sub-machine gun at the ready. Unfortunately he was not very conversant with the trigger mechanism and suddenly the gun went off, drilling a neat pattern of holes through the floorboards and sump of the ambulance. Fortunately it did not hit any of the wounded Italians, but it might well have done, for it instantly set up a chorus of wails whilst poor Cloughton tried in vain to explain that he had not meant to open fire. Abuse was hurled at Cloughton who was accused of purposely putting the ambulance out of action so that the occupants would be stranded in the desert to die of thirst. This argument was brought to an abrupt close by the appearance of German armoured cars on the horizon and the carriers made off at speed, leaving the Italians to tell a tale of woe to their allies.

The night of May 30/31st was quiet and at 5.30 a.m. on May 31st the third commerce raiding patrol, under command of Lieut. P. G. Hampson, set out from Stricklands Post. The patrol, accompanied by the official Brigade photographer, consisted of one section of carriers, a section of Battalion anti-tank guns in charge of Lieut. H. C. B. Catford, and a section of 3″ Mortars. The patrol, with Lieut. Hampson travelling in the leading carrier—Sgt. Tennant's—advanced cautiously. Progress was slow and the patrol was not in position at B.13 until about 10 a.m. The British troops settled down in a fold in the ground to wait for victims. It was not long before an enemy truck was sighted about five hundred yards away, making towards B.13, but it suddenly veered off and Hampson ordered his driver to break cover and give chase. The carrier closed in and from about ten yards range the enemy driver was ordered to halt. When he realised his challengers were British, he suddenly accelerated. Although the carrier Bren gunner immediately opened fire and Hampson took a few shots with his pistol, the enemy vehicle got clean away, zigzagging madly across the desert towards the safety of Many Tracks where a continuous line of supply vehicles, escorted by several armoured cars, was moving slowly south-east towards Bir Hacheim. After watching this huge column streaming along Many Tracks for half-an-hour, Hampson decided to advance to B.12, a feature capped by barrels about three miles south-west of B.13 towards the enemy.

Making a wide detour and avoiding Many Tracks the patrol moved cautiously towards B.12, keeping a careful watch for German tanks which were supposed to be protecting the supply line. Before the patrol reached B.12, Hampson spotted from the top of a small nullah six or seven enemy trucks, halted whilst their drivers enjoyed a siesta. A quick plan was worked out and Lieut. Catford positioned the anti-tank guns and mortars whilst Hampson took the carriers round to a flank. The carrier section moved towards the enemy vehicles, using dead ground, and at a given signal they broke cover to accelerate across the three hundred yards of open desert which separated them from the enemy. At the same time the anti-tank guns and mortars opened fire, whilst the Bren gunners in the carriers sent their tracer ammunition into the stationary vehicles. The Italian truck drivers could not surrender quickly enough. They were disarmed and then the carrier crews searched the trucks and found thirty gallons of cool Derna water, the greatest prize of all. The British patrol drank their fill and, suitably refreshed, set out for the Box with seven trucks and forty prisoners.

After a midday meal in the Box, the patrol sallied forth again in the afternoon back to B.12 where they contacted a Gunner O.P. from the 74th Field Regiment and a carrier patrol from the 6th D.L.I., commanded by Captain F. Cole. For some time the patrol commanders watched the ceaseless activity on Many Tracks which the Gunner was shelling from time to time. It was now late afternoon and the columns of enemy vehicles were going west, obviously returning from the main battle area. B.12, a comparatively high feature, was a wonderful vantage point and as the British troops watched, a small convoy came along the tracks, going in the opposite direction to the main columns. The Gunner O.P. ordered two rounds gunfire. It was excellent shooting and the shells landed right amongst the enemy column, knocking out three of the trucks at once. The three vehicles which had not been hit altered course and made straight for the British patrols, obviously not knowing where they were going. The carriers waited until the enemy were within about three hundred yards before breaking cover. Captain Cole's carriers captured two trucks and Hampson's patrol captured the third. It was a good haul and netted thirty prisoners. Deciding not to tempt providence any further the two carrier patrols parted company and made for their separate outposts, taking their spoils with them.

As Hampson's patrol returned to the Box, the C.O. and Intelligence Officer in the Battalion H.Q. dugout were briefing Captain R. I. Pitt of B Company and Lieut. E. Edwards of the Sappers on a mine-laying patrol for that night. The C.O. had decided that an attempt should be made to lay mines across Many Tracks during the hours of darkness to dislocate the enemy supply columns the following day. Speed in laying the mines was essential as there was not much time available between last light and the dawn. This meant that a large party of men would be required to lay the mines with an equally large party for infantry protection. Lieut. R. H. R. Robinson was detailed to take a strong fighting patrol out with the minelayers.

After dark the patrol set off from the outpost—a fairly large and noisy convoy for a night operation of eight trucks—and proceeded cautiously in the direction of Many Tracks. The supply route took a little finding but there was no mistaking Many Tracks when the British vehicles eventually reached it. This desert highway of one broad track and several others running parallel to it was at least four hundred yards wide, and the wheels of the hundreds of supply vehicles which used it every day and the giant caterpillar tracks of the enemy armoured vehicles had churned up the desert into a sea of soft white sand, almost ankle deep.

There was a full moon and the minelaying party quickly set about its task. There was a sense of urgency about the whole operation ; whilst the men worked quietly and steadily laying the rows of mines across the tracks, the infantry sections took up positions to watch for approaching enemy patrols or vehicles. For three hours the work went on under the light of the moon and, when the last mine had been laid, a field five hundred yards wide and fifty yards deep stretched right across Many Tracks. Whilst the work had been proceeding, Captain Pitt noticed two stationary armoured cars some way up the tracks and decided to investigate. He thought they were probably derelicts as this was the area where Rosscol had been trapped.

A quick plan of action was worked out and Pitt detailed Lieut. Robinson and a section of B Company infantry with two Bren guns to accompany him to the armoured cars. The rest of the patrol was embussed in the waiting vehicles and Lieut. Edwards told to take the trucks several hundred yards towards the Box and to wait for the infantry to rejoin them.

As Pitt and Robinson led the section towards the armoured cars a faint sound of throbbing truck engines came to them from the north. The noise grew louder and louder until it was almost a continual roar and the section drew back from Many Tracks and lay down to await developments. As the men watched, a huge convoy of German vehicles came out of the night and moved slowly towards them along Many Tracks. Visibility was so good that the section could see them clearly. There must have been close on a hundred large trucks with escorting armoured cars ahead of them and on the flanks. Nearer and nearer they came to the newly-laid minefield and then, just as it seemed that the leading armoured cars were due to blow up, the whole convoy halted. The section could hear clearly guttural orders shouted in German and whistle blasts as the tailboards of the vehicles were lowered and the troops jumped out for a breather. It was obviously a routine halt and the Germans did not suspect the buried mines only a few yards ahead of them across the tracks.

There was still another hour of darkness left. The two B Company Bren guns which were trained on the convoy opened fire simultaneously, sending a stream of bullets into the massed vehicles, not more than four hundreds yard away. The gunners had no tracer ammunition and it was difficult to judge the accuracy of their shooting but, from the commotion which instantly broke out, the Bren fire was going right in amongst the German vehicles.

Unfortunately one of the Brens jammed and as the gun crew tried frantically to clear it the Germans, coming to life in no uncertain fashion, returned an absolute hail of fire at the British section. The enemy gunners were using tracer and it was like a Brock's firework display in miniature ; the tracer was all colours and every gun in the German convoy was soon firing. Eventually the second Bren was cleared and the British returned the fire. The Germans had only the muzzle flashes of the Brens to aim at, and after each Bren magazine had been exhausted the guns were rushed to a fresh fire position, and most of the German tracer whipped harmlessly over the heads of the British patrol. This dangerous game of hide and seek went on for five minutes until all the Bren ammunition had been used up.

As the section prepared to withdraw, two German armoured cars edged out of the enemy column and advanced warily towards the B Company men, like encircling arms. The British section watched anxiously as one of the armoured cars approached the minefield ; there was a flash as the front wheels of the car touched off a mine and the enemy vehicle lurched to a halt. However, the second car made a wide detour to avoid the minefield and advanced quickly across the tracks towards the section. With no ammunition left the only course open to Pitt and his men was to make for the waiting trucks. They broke all records for a patrol over nearly a quarter of a mile and their language when they found the trucks gone is unprintable. Captain Pitt later discovered that when the German column returned the British fire, the tracer bullets which had whistled harmlessly over the heads of the infantry section had landed amongst the waiting trucks. Lieut. Edwards thought his party had been spotted and had decided to withdraw out of range.

Meanwhile Pitt and his men were scurrying like hunted rabbits from wadi to wadi, playing hide and seek with the German armoured car. The section edged gradually away from Many Tracks in the direction of the Box and, to their relief, the enemy vehicle finally giving up the chase returned to the column.

It was an eight mile walk back to Stricklands and dawn had broken long before the patrol arrived. Thankfully the men climbed into a waiting truck and were taken inside the Box where Captain Pitt reported to the C.O. He did not get the reception he had expected—far from it. He was given a long and carefully worded dressing down for not having kept the vehicles more under his control, although in actual fact "Jake" Jackson was very pleased with the success of this audacious B Company night patrol.

CHAPTER NINE

GAZALA SETBACKS AND SUCCESSES

The loss of 150 *Brigade—tanks join the Battalion—a fight for the outpost—night patrolling—three hundred prisoners in one afternoon—the loss of* 14 *Platoon, C Company—last days at Gazala.*

WHILST the Battalion had been commerce raiding from the Box the armoured battle had been raging continuously east of the Gazala Line. There had been bitter fighting with very heavy casualties on both sides. Rommel decided to shorten the German lines of communication and at the same time to provide a way of retreat for his armour if it became necessary. He ordered his commanders to clear two gaps through the British minefield south of the 150 Brigade Box. This was done, the gaps being protected by strong screens of anti-tank guns. As the armoured battle continued, it became obvious to British Intelligence that the Axis forces were suffering from lack of petrol and water, and there is no doubt that the commerce raids from the 151 Brigade Box were responsible for part of the German plight. Contrary to expectations, the German commander did not withdraw his forces but instead he launched heavy and repeated attacks against the 150 Brigade Box. By June 1st, after thirty-six hours of continuous fighting, 150 Brigade, with all its ammunition and supplies exhausted, was overcome but not before it had inflicted considerable casualties on the enemy. The survivors of the three infantry battalions and all the supporting troops in the Box were taken prisoner. With this firm footing astride the Gazala Line, Rommel directed the bulk of his armour and the Italian 20 Corps against the French garrison of Bir Hacheim during the early hours of June 2nd. Preceded by waves of Axis bombers, the German and Italian troops launched a series of full scale attacks but Bir Hacheim held magnificently all through June 2nd, 3rd and 4th and the German attacks were repulsed.

The early days of the month in the D.L.I. Box, whilst the battle with 150 Brigade was being fought and the first attacks launched against Bir Hacheim, were marked by a continuation of the commerce raids which had been started the previous month. Company officers were sent out in charge of these raids to give them valuable experience. Captain C. L. Beattie and Lieut. J. Carruthers led patrols which captured more transport and prisoners, including several officers. By now the Carrier Platoon was expert in this form of warfare, and had taken to the highwaymen activity like ducks to water. Captain English was now able to see concrete results of his tireless efforts to make the Carrier Platoon a real fighting force. They picked off supply lorries and troops from Many Tracks like ripe plums from a tree.

The few enemy trucks which tried to make a break when ordered to stop were brought to a standstill in the approved sea-faring style with a burst of tracer across their bows. The R.S.M. could never understand why so much of his tracer ammunition "disappeared" during the commerce raiding phase. A great and varied bag resulted from these raids ; all kinds of supplies were captured—ammunition, water, Q.M. stores of every sort, and even hot food in containers, which to the disgust of the Battalion patrols usually turned out to be macaroni. Sweet Derna water was, however, most welcome as were the liberal quantities of Vino to be found in every captured vehicle. It was not long before each member of the Carrier Platoon had his own private arsenal of captured enemy weapons and there was not a single man without an oil compass and a pair of Zeiss binoculars.

In the early hours of June 2nd a warning order was received from Brigade H.Q. of possible enemy minelaying activities in the vicinity of Stricklands. There was certainly a great deal of movement on the Battalion front and a small reconnaissance patrol taken out by Sgt. Pattinson that night reported a column of enemy field guns at the head of a wadi between B.13 and B.15 ridges. The enemy appeared to be closing in on the British line, possibly to put a stop to the damaging commerce raids which were taking such a heavy toll of the German and Italian convoys on Many Tracks.

At seven o'clock that morning the garrison at Stricklands watched three enemy armoured cars and a company of infantry deploy southeast along B.13 ridge, that very useful hideout for the commerce raiding patrols. The Gunner O.P. at Stricklands called for artillery support to shell the ridge, but although the enemy were undoubtedly in the area they were making good use of cover and no further movement was seen that day.

Meanwhile, with the French at Bir Hacheim successfully beating back the German assaults and Rommel's supply line along Many Tracks dangerously exposed, it seemed that the initiative was beginning to swing round to the Eighth Army. Three courses were open to General Ritchie. The first was a drive west into the enemy's rear by 1 South African and 50 Divisions to disrupt communications. The second was to send 5 Indian Division south of Bir Hacheim to take in the rear the Axis forces attacking that position, and the third course was an attack to eliminate the German bulge in the area of the gaps which the enemy had made in the British minefield, now known as the Cauldron Area. The third course was finally adopted and the 9th D.L.I. was detailed as part of the attacking force. (Unfortunately, the attack was a failure when it was launched three days later). As a consequence of the withdrawal of the 9th Battalion, the 6th Battalion moved to the right to take over part of the 9th Battalion area and the 8th took over the left forward company positions of the 6th Battalion. The 8th D.L.I. was now responsible for the defence of another minefield gap—Auckland Gap.

These moves had barely been completed when a violent dust-storm swept over the desert and for the best part of two hours the rival armies were at the mercy of the common enemy. It was one of the dreaded Khamsin winds from the hot wastes of the Sahara, and it whipped the loose sand from the surface of the desert to drive it forward as an impenetratable wall of swirling, stinging sand. With hardly any warning the Khamsin swept over the Box ; the sun was obscured and a cloak of darkness drawn over the desert. The crews of tanks and armoured cars, both British and German, hastily closed down their turrets and buried themselves under a pile of blankets inside their vehicles. Dust caked on the skin and clothes of men who were unfortunate enough to be caught out in the open. They staggered blindly into minefield wire, fell into slit trenches or dugouts, for they could not see more than a yard ahead. It was the second time the Battalion had experienced the ferocity of one of these storms, and very soon this desert fog of dust and sand had halted all movement. Drivers jumped out of their cabs to seek shelter under the vehicles or in slit trenches, whilst the troops in the company battle positions lay face downward in the bottom of their fire trenches, faces muffled with balaclava helmets and scarves and their heads covered with great-coats. Then, as quickly as it had come, the hot breath of the Khamsin wind passed away.

Out of Stricklands the outpost platoon watched four figures staggering towards the gap in the minefield surrounding the positions. As the men drew nearer the British troops could see that they were German. These unfortunate men had been caught in the open desert by the dust storm which had prevented them from regaining the comparative shelter of their vehicle. Dressed only in shirt and shorts, they had no means of sheltering from the storm and lay huddled on the face of the desert whilst the swirling sand whipped them unmercifully. Then, when the Khamsin had gone, they dragged themselves to their feet and staggered in the direction of the British lines. Parched with thirst, their eyes red-rimmed, and exhausted almost to the point of total collapse, they were helped into Stricklands by the men of the outpost platoon. This was the way in which the desert showed its complete superiority over man.

Two nights later Lieut.-Colonel Jackson sent out a foot patrol to Gabr el Fachri—the 69 Brigade outpost which had been captured on May 27th—to test the enemy defences there. The patrol, commanded by Lieut. R. Place—a pre-war Grimsby policeman who always carried a truncheon on night operations—found no enemy in Fachri and the C.O. decided to send a mixed force of tanks, South African armoured cars, and Battalion carriers to find out exactly what was happening in the Fachri area, and to reconnoitre a feature known as Pt.169, south of Fachri. The tanks—Valentines and Crusaders under command of Major Drury, M.C.—had been detached from their unit and placed under command of the 8th Battalion to reinforce the commerce raids as it was now permissible for British armour to operate in front of the Gazala Line. At 7.30 a.m. the armoured force moved towards Fachri whilst the 7th Medium Regiment, a South African Medium Regiment and the whole of the 74th Field Regiment stood by in the

Box to give artillery support if required. The composite force reached its objective without incident and found no enemy in occupation of the outpost, but immediately came under very heavy artillery fire from enemy field guns located in a small depression near Pt. 169. The tanks made a sortie to the east and south, but when returning to Fachri one of the Valentines was hit in the tracks by shellfire and slewed round to a standstill while another came to a halt with engine failure. An S.O.S. was sent back by the Gunner O.P. for smoke and a determined effort made to get the disabled tanks on the move, but the attempt was unsuccessful and it was decided to abandon the two tanks until nightfall. The remainder of the force returned to the outpost, leaving a Gunner O.P. and a section of carriers in Fachri where they remained for the rest of the day whilst the enemy guns shelled the area intermittently.

At dusk a platoon of infantry was moved to Fachri to protect a recovery party and the two tanks were towed back to the outpost without incident. Whilst they were being recovered, enemy troops moved into position facing the outpost and the fact that they wanted to keep this move secret probably accounted for the lack of interest shown in the noisy tank recovery patrol. They established a defensive flank in front of the outpost as a protection for the vital convoys on Many Tracks. For some time the enemy High Command had been aware of the audacious raids carried out from Stricklands against his convoys.

Next day a determined effort was made by the enemy to stop the commerce raiding by the Battalion. In the early hours of July 5th Captain English led a strong patrol out from the Box to Stricklands Post consisting of four carriers, two sections of mortars, a section of anti-tank guns, a section of twenty-five pounder field guns and two rifle sections from B Company commanded by Lieut. P. J. Lewis, a newly-arrived officer who had joined the Battalion from the Infantry Base Depot at Geneifa. Captain English was ordered to establish the patrol astride the B.13 feature. A troop of South African armoured cars had been detailed to accompany the patrol to B.13 and then to reconnoitre ahead of the main body. The small force arrived at Stricklands just after first light and, as dawn broke, the minefield gap was cleared to allow the vehicle to pass through. As they moved forward out into the desert a runner from the Cheshire machine-gun platoon intercepted the trucks to report that enemy movement had been seen close to Stricklands Post. The patrol was halted while Captain English made a quick reconnaissance. He saw that enemy positions had indeed been established in Derelict Vehicle Got, an area of broken ground due west of Stricklands with a number of derelict vehicles. The enemy effectively covered the exit from Stricklands but did not appear to be in much strength.

Captain English decided to put in an immediate attack to clear the area and sent two of the carriers, under Lieut. Lewis, to move down south-east of the enemy positions to the shelter of a ridge from where they could give covering fire to the other two carriers and a rifle section under Sgt. McDermott when they attacked from a flank. As the covering force was moving into position the South African armoured cars, which had taken a long cast to the right from the outpost, advanced towards Derelict Vehicle Got from the west. When they fired a few rounds and hastily withdrew, it was obvious that their commander had spotted some anti-tank weapons.

The position was in fact held in some force and Captain English decided to lead the flank attack himself. As the two carriers and the riflemen advanced they were met by heavy and accurate small arms fire, and whilst moving the infantry section to a better fire position English was wounded, and one of the B Company men also became a casualty. However, English managed to get back to Stricklands Post in the infantry section truck which had not gone forward with the attack. Exhausted and weak from loss of blood he was able to tell Major A. B. S. Clarke, who had just arrived from the Box to find out what was going on, that any further attack would have to be supported by artillery fire. Sgt. McDermott's section remained where Captain English had left it, while the two carriers returned to Stricklands.

Major Clarke made a quick plan to put in an attack supported by artillery, mortar and machine-gun fire from the outpost area with a force made up of the four carriers and the remaining section of infantry under Lieut. Lewis. The plan was for the carriers to attack in two waves with the infantry section riding on the two rear vehicles. Zero hour was fixed for 9.15 a.m., with supporting fire on the enemy positions from a minute before until a minute after zero.

The small attacking force moved up behind cover to a start line and the carriers waited for the signal to go. Owing to some error in timing, the supporting fire started a minute late, and although Major Clarke tried to hold back the attack for one minute, Lieut. Lewis thought he was waving him to go on and led the first two carriers from behind cover at zero plus one. The mortars and machine-guns immediately stopped firing but the artillery continued, and consequently the leading carriers ran into the shellfire. It was well they did for they arrived in the enemy positions whilst the shells were still falling and, to their amazement, found themselves amongst two enemy companies. For a minute or two it was like a wild west film as the two leading carriers weaved in and out among the enemy trenches shooting at everything in sight, whilst the other two carriers raced up with the section of infantry. Most of the Italians were scared stiff by this quick attack before the shellfire had finished and the carriers caught them cowering in their slit trenches, but the position looked distinctly ugly when some enemy anti-tank gunners tried to get their gun into action. Lieut. Lewis's carrier charged them whilst the sweating Italians worked madly to swing the gun round to fire. Sgt. Cairns sprayed the Italians with his Tommy gun as the swaying carrier closed the gap, and although the Italians made a valiant effort to get their gun into action they were just too late and the carrier went right over the gun, killing or wounding the crew.

This seemed to be the signal for full scale surrender and white handkerchiefs appeared in large numbers as dozens of Italians jumped out of their slit trenches with hands upraised. The carriers and the B Company men were joined by the South African armoured cars, and the Italians were shepherded in fours back to Stricklands. There were ten officers and two hundred and ten other ranks—mostly Italians with a few German N.C.Os.—and, as the dejected-looking prisoners started to march back to Stricklands, enemy artillery ranged on the area and machine-guns opened fire. The rear ranks, anxious to get away from the bursting shells, stampeded the rest of the column and the two hundred odd prisoners broke into a run, doubling the rest of the way to Stricklands. The carriers and armoured cars motored slowly along on the flanks, their crews delighted with this spectacle of Mussolini's Empire builders being chased by their own gunfire.

It was an amazing sight as the long column of prisoners, having formed up under cover of Stricklands, trudged back along the sandy tracks from the outpost to the Box at Stanley Gap, creating a cloud of dust. Owing to the enemy shellfire the carriers and armoured cars had not been able to stay and scavenge the area of the action, but nevertheless they collected three anti-tank guns, two German anti-tank rifles, four heavy machine-guns and five light machine-guns which were taken back to the Box in triumph. Our own casualties in the final attack were very light in comparison with the number of prisoners taken. One of the B Company men had been killed by a shell splinter as the rear two carriers ran into the last few seconds of the barrage. It was very bad luck but, if this error in timing had not been made and the enemy given an opportunity to recover after the supporting fire, it is most probable that the small attacking force would have been wiped out. As it was, the attempt to seal the Battalion exit from Stricklands Post had been thoroughly smashed. Lieut. Lewis was awarded the Military Cross and Sgt. Cairns the Distinguished Conduct Medal for their part in the action.

Immediately after this successful action Captain A. E. Jones arrived at the outpost to take over command of the patrol and left at once with a troop of South African armoured cars to reconnoitre the front, leaving the remainder of the patrol at Stricklands. Just before midday the outpost was attacked by Italian fighters. The pilots were spectacular if nothing else and gave a most impressive display of aerobatics in between their attacks. However, they could not miss the concentration of vehicles and, swooping down low, set on fire one of the anti-tank gun portees[1] and a truck. The gun on the portee was completely destroyed and the vehicles soon burned themselves out. Fortunately there were no casualties to the men at the outpost who replied with Bren gun fire, but scored no hits.

Not long after this incident Captain Jones returned to Stricklands having intercepted six enemy vehicles which were so badly damaged that they could not be salvaged. He brought back with him two Italian officers and twenty-eight men and they had only just arrived

[1] A vehicle for carrying or towing an anti-tank gun.

at the outpost when another low level attack was made by enemy fighters. This time the turret gunners in the armoured cars fired back as the planes came down low to strafe. The Italians sought cover in the slit trenches and one of them took a flying leap on top of a member of the outpost platoon whose protests were turned to laughter when the Italian, letting out a shriek of pain, jumped out of the trench clutching the fleshy part of his posteria which had been neatly grooved by a machine-gun bullet. An Italian officer was killed by gunfire from one of the planes as he took shelter in another slit trench, and the rest of the Italians were glad to leave Stricklands for the comparative safety of the Prisoner of War cage in the Box.

Later in the afternoon when visibility had cleared, the armoured cars went out again to intercept four enemy trucks in the B.12 area, setting one of them on fire and badly damaging the others. As the burning truck sent up a column of black smoke, the armoured cars turned for home and made for the outpost with five more prisoners. On the whole, it had been a good day for the Battalion.

That night 2/Lieut. R. Place took out a fighting patrol of two infantry sections and some sappers with the task of locating enemy field guns in an area some two miles south-east of Fachri, destroying the guns with explosives and killing the crews. It was an unenviable assignment but the sort of patrol which the D.L.I. battalions had to send out every night on the Brigade front.

Much has been written about the daylight patrols and the lightning swoops against Many Tracks but the night patrols must not be overlooked. It was an eerie business leaving the safety of Stricklands or Petro's Post and striking out into the desert. More often than not it was a pitch black night, and only those who have been on a night patrol in No Man's Land can know what it feels like with the ceaseless anxiety which accompanies every minute.

Patrol orders used to originate from the Orderly Room every evening at 5 p.m. when the officer or N.C.O. chosen to command the patrol was ordered to report to Battalion H.Q. After being briefed by the Adjutant and the Intelligence Officer with all the latest information about enemy movements, the patrol commander returned to the company area to select his men. He in his turn briefed the patrol and while the C.S.M. arranged the issue of patrol boots—thick suede boots with rubber soles—and the checking of weapons and ammunition, the commander had to arrange details about transport and liaison with the outpost platoon and flanking units. There were a hundred and one things to do ; many of them seemed unimportant but welded together they made a picture of a successful or an unsuccessful patrol. At last light the patrol was taken out to Stricklands in 15 cwt. trucks, which bumped and lurched as they ploughed their way through the sandy track from Stanley Gap to the outpost.

From Stricklands, some of the patrols went out on foot and others were driven to within two or three miles of their destination. They all had one thing in common ; once they left Stricklands Post they were on their own and their lives depended on their own quick-thinking and decisions. The safety of the Box—sometimes not more than a mile or two behind them—might as well have been a hundred miles away if the patrol fell foul of an enemy ambush. Navigation was by compass and the North Star. When the patrols had completed their tasks they returned thankfully to Stricklands and the Box in time for breakfast and a well-earned sleep.

The night patrol which Place took out left Petro's just before dusk and, arriving at Fachri in darkness, pushed on for two miles in the direction of the enemy guns—advancing warily and stopping at fifty yard intervals to listen. When they reached a landmark—a cairn of stones—Place set his compass on a bearing of 248 degrees which he reckoned would bring the patrol to the enemy positions. The men had gone about three quarters of a mile on this new course when Place almost fell over a low wire and he ordered his men to fall back from this and to take up fire positions. With one man he went first left and then right, and discovered that the wire extended well beyond one hundred paces either side of the patrol. Meanwhile, the rest of the party stretched prone near the wire had heard the sound of voices to the left and also the noise of truck engines. A lorry seemed to be approaching and Place decided to tackle it. Leaving the sappers and one section of infantry near the wire he crossed with the remaining section.

As the men moved silently forward, wondering anxiously whether they had stepped into a minefield and expecting an explosion with every step, the sound of digging came to them over the still night air and one of them whispered to Place that he could see dim figures about a hundred yards to the south. By this time, the noise of the truck engine being very loud, Place ordered his men to take up fire positions. He planned to ambush the approaching truck and then turn the fire of his section on to the enemy working party which was obviously pacing out a minefield, afterwards returning to the main body of the patrol near the wire. The men waited tensely. Suddenly the sound of the digging stopped and the lorry, which was almost on top of the British troops, turned about practically in its own length and made off at high speed. The patrol had obviously been spotted and within three minutes enemy guns opened fire from the south. This artillery fire which lasted nearly half an hour, effectively covered the whole area including the route over which the patrol had come. It was a most unpleasant thirty minutes.

Then, as suddenly as it had started, the firing stopped and, after waiting a minute or two, Place rallied his section and moved back to join the remainder of the patrol near the wire. As they started to cross the wire enemy machine-guns opened fire from the south, sending a stream of tracer whipping along the line of the wire. Place and his men, throwing themselves flat, crawled the rest of the way to join the main body of the patrol. Fortunately neither the shellfire nor the machine-gun fire had caused any casualties and, having decided that there was now little chance of finding the enemy gun positions, Place took the patrol back to Fachri where it arrived at 2.40 a.m. Although it had not accomplished its original intention the sortie had established, from the sound of voices, truck engines and the heavy machine-gun and artillery fire, that the enemy positions immediately south of the Battalion were held in some strength.

The morning of June 6th was fairly quiet although the centre company area at Stanley Gap was shelled intermittently. Shortly after midday an enemy plane flew low over the outpost, weaving and sideslippping violently from side to side, obviously in difficulties. Two miles west of Stricklands the machine crashed. There was a dull boom as the petrol tanks exploded, sending a dense column of black smoke slowly into the sky. The South African armoured cars brought in the wounded pilot.

In the early hours of the next morning a report was received from Brigade H.Q. that the enemy had laid an extensive minefield across the B.15 ridge, and that patrols from the 6th Battalion had spent the night lifting a thousand yards of mines at the southern end. The enemy was certainly doing all he could to restrict the movements of the roving daylight patrols.

However, this did not stop the Battalion activities. There was still a gap on the B.13 ridge, and while this was open Lieut.-Colonel Jackson intended to send his tanks and carriers through to shoot up everything in sight on Many Tracks and to create panic in the enemy supply columns. At 7 a.m., bright and early for a Divisional Commander, General W. H. C. Ramsden visited Stricklands where he met and congratulated some of the officers and men who had taken part in the day and night patrols. His visit was followed by a message of congratulation from the Army Commander, who was well pleased with the Battalion patrol activities.

That night a C Company officer, 2/Lieut. T. I. Bulpin, took a reconnaisance patrol of two sections of infantry to find out if the B12 and B.13 areas were held, to watch for enemy working parties and to mark the position of newly-erected wire. No enemy was seen. However, not long after the patrol had returned, enemy infantry moved into a wadi between B.13 and B.15 ridges and were spotted from the outpost at first light. They must have occupied B.13 on the heels of Bulpin's departing patrol and the C.O. decided to send out a strong tank column under command of Major A. Lindsay, 8th R.T.R., to mop up the enemy position. Soon after midday information was received that the enemy, having established a strongpoint in the wadi, were holding it with fifty Italian infantry and two anti-tank guns.

The tank force left Stricklands almost immediately and at 1 p.m. the artillery at the outpost, which had been reinforced by a further troop, opened fire. For ten minutes the enemy positions were bombarded with smoke and high explosives as the two troops of tanks moved up the valley in line, with two of the Battalion carriers and a platoon of South African infantry some three hundred yards to the rear. Leading the tanks as navigator was Lieut. R. H. R. Robinson in a third carrier and, as the British shelling ceased, the tanks lumbered forward into the smoke with the tiny carrier racing ahead. The enemy strength had been sadly underestimated and the carrier and tanks ran into a hail of anti-tank and machine-gun fire. Within a matter of seconds the carrier was hit by an armour-piercing shell which ripped clean through the thin shield of armour plating killing Robinson instantly where he sat next to the driver, and also L/Cpl. Keeble of the Carrier Platoon.

As the carrier slowed to a standstill the Valentines and Crusaders drew level and advanced towards the first line of defences, raking what enemy positions they could see with long bursts of machine gun fire. The Italians did not attempt to fight back but took cover in the bottom of their slit trenches as the tanks lumbered through the positions and went on towards the second line of defences. Then the enemy, manning their guns again, sent bursts of machine-gun and anti-tank gun fire towards the remaining two Battalion carriers which had stopped two hundred yards short of the position. Both the carriers were hit and their crews jumped out to take up fire positions to a flank whilst the remainder of the patrol raced up from the rear.

For five minutes or so the carrier crews fought a violent action with the enemy, and the two hundred yards of open desert between them and the Italians was raked by machine-gun cross fire. Suddenly the Italian fire ceased and the carrier crews saw in the distance the British tanks returning from the enemy second line of defences, driving a motley collection of prisoners ahead of them. As the Valentines and Crusaders drew level with the first line of defences, dozens of Italians jumped out of slit trenches and gun positions, waving white handkerchief and pieces of white rag as they ran ahead of the tanks to surrender. When the platoon of South African infantry arrived, it took over from the tank crews the task of rounding up the prisoners. Through the heat haze of that blazing June afternoon ten Italian officers and over three hundred other ranks were herded back to Stricklands Post, from whence they continued their journey to captivity, stumbling through the flaky sand which marked the track from the outpost to Stanley Gap.

Another attempt to close the gap on the Battalion front had failed but at heavy cost to the Battalion. In addition to Lieut. Robinson, the first officer of the 8th to be killed in action, and L/Cpl. Keeble, one other rank had been killed and four more wounded and a Battalion mortar carrier and a South African armoured car had been blown up on an enemy minefield on the B.13 ridge. The desert war was getting tougher and that evening, as the men of the 8th discussed the action in the Box, they realised that they were right in it at last.

Just before midnight a minelifting patrol under Captain R. I. Pitt left the Box for Stricklands with the task of locating the enemy minefield which had blown up the mortar carrier and armoured car, and to pick up and disarm as many of the mines as possible. Captain Pitt had with him two sections of infantry for minelifting, two sections for protection and several sappers. The Sapper corporal had been out that day with the tank patrol but had only a rough idea of where the carrier and armoured car had been blown up. There was no moon and for hours the patrol wandered about in total darkness without finding any trace of the vehicles. Towards morning the patrol heard what sounded like an enemy minelaying party at work, and the unmistakable chugging of an Italian truck engine. Pitt sent 2/Lieut. P. Worley and a section of infantry forward to a low ridge with orders to fire on the enemy. Having reached the ridge, the section opened fire with their Bren in the pitch darkness in the direction of the working party, hoping to force the enemy to reveal his positions. However, there was no answering fire, only the sounds of hasty movement as the Italians threw down their picks and shovels and clambered aboard their truck. The vehicle was then driven off at high speed, the driver crashing the gears in his anxiety to get clear, and as the sound of the truck engine died away in the distance, Worley withdrew his section to rejoin the remainder of the patrol. The whole party returned to the outpost at 5 a.m.

In the heat haze of the following afternoon Cheshire Regiment machine-guns were sent to Fachri with the task of harassing the enemy positions to the south during the night, and Lieut. P. G. Hampson was warned to stand by with a platoon of C Company until nightfall, when he was to take the platoon and two detachments of Battalion mortars to Fachri to assist the machine-guns. The harassing fire from Fachri that night certainly had the effect of keeping the enemy at a distance. The Cheshires opened up with their machine-guns from time to time and the mortar detachment fired more than forty-five bombs. Truck engines were started, there was a great deal of shouting and generally the patrol, before it withdrew just before first light, gave the impression that Fachri was held in some strength by the British.

Whilst the mortars and machine-guns had been firing, Major Drury of the 8th R.T.R. with L/Cpl. Oates of the Battalion Intelligence Section slipped quietly out of Stricklands Post and made for Fachri to establish an O.P. in the area for the purpose of observing enemy movement to the south next day. Drury and Oates spent the rest of the night camouflaging and preparing a hideout, and for the whole of the following day they lay out in the desert under the burning sun whilst Drury watched the enemy movement through a telescope and Oates noted his observations. The information which these two brought back to the Box at dusk was to prove invaluable at a later stage of the battle.

Meanwhile, Captain Pitt had taken another minelifting patrol out in search of the minefield which had wrecked the carrier and armoured car. This time the patrol left Stricklands with definite information about the position of the derelicts which had been accurately plotted on the map during daylight. As an additional guide a troop of guns from the 74th Field Regiment had been laid on to fire at the derelicts so that the patrol had only to walk in the direction of the flash from the exploding shells. The guns had orders to continue firing until it was judged that the men had reached the area, when they were to lift their fire a thousand yards forward to quieten enemy fighting patrols which might attempt to interfere with the minelifting operations.

At 11 p.m. the patrol debussed at B.13 and advanced on foot. It was an eerie experience for the men as they trudged along silently in the darkness, listening to the whine of the shells as they passed overhead to explode with a roar and a flash in the target area. As the patrol drew near to the derelicts one of the shells fell short, landing within a hundred yards. The men went flat whilst odd pieces of shrapnel whipped viciously over their heads ; it was an unpleasant experience but fortunately there were no casualties.

The sappers quickly located the mines which had obviously been laid in a hurry and were not buried. Swiftly the minelifting sections disarmed and stacked them under the supervision of the sappers whilst the British guns continued to fire overhead. Working in the pitch darkness, which increased the danger tenfold of handling the mines, they disarmed at least two hundred and fifty, making a gap in the minefield about three hundred yards wide, extending on either side of the derelicts. The transport which had been brought forward from B.13 was loaded with mines, and having salvaged a mortar from the wrecked carrier, the patrol set off for Stricklands as day was breaking, with one hundred and sixty mines—as many as they could carry. It had been a good night's work.

June 10th was a quiet day in the Box and at Stricklands, except for shelling of the Battalion area during the morning when two other ranks were wounded. That night, patrols were sent to locate enemy positions south-west and south-east of B.13 and a third minelifting patrol went out to continue lifting the enemy minefield which had been located the previous night. The Intelligence Officer, Lieut. D. A. Neale, and L/Cpl. A. Bark of the Intelligence Section penetrated deeper than any patrol had gone before at night, and brought back invaluable information. The two men left Stricklands at 9 p.m., their faces blackened by burnt cork, with the object of crossing Many Tracks to observe the enemy supply columns for a whole day and to return the following night.

Moving on a compass bearing of 245 degrees they reached the area of the battle on June 8th where Lieut. Robinson had been killed. The Italian positions were still unoccupied but a great deal of equipment had been abandoned and, after rummaging about for a while, Lieut. Neale and L/Cpl. Bark went forward another two hundred yards until a double black telephone wire was found which they tried unsuccessfully to cut. Whilst they were hacking at the wire the noisy chatter of Italian troops came to them across a mile or so of desert from the B.12 area and shouted orders from west of B.15.

The two men moved on cautiously, stopping every fifty yards to listen ; when they had gone a further eight hundred yards they could hear the sound of Italian voices not more than six or seven hundred yards ahead. They crept forward another three hundred yards and lay down to listen and observe. For half an hour they remained motionless in the darkness. Due south they could hear men moving about, sounds of digging and picking to the south-west, and further north a violent argument in Italian which was finally brought to a finish by the bull-like roar of someone in authority. The two men were forced to move back when they heard footsteps coming in the direction of their listening post, and withdrew three hundred yards to wait anxiously until the sound of the footsteps died away in the distance. As time was getting on and it appeared that the Italians had dug positions covering the approaches to many Tracks, Lieut. Neale decided to start the long trek back to Stricklands. After an uneventful journey of several hours, but footsore and weary, he and L/Cpl. Bark arrived at the outpost and climbed thankfully into a truck which took them back to the Box. Their two-man patrol, deep into enemy territory, had resulted in some useful information and their report that B.12 was permanently held was to prove of great value later in the battle.

L/Cpl. Bark was awarded the Military Medal for his work with the patrols which went out from the Gazala Line. It was he who successfully navigated back to the Box the main body of Captain Pitt's minelaying patrol on May 31st, when Captain Pitt and Lieut. Robinson had nearly been captured by German armoured cars. Due to Bark's faultless navigation the unwieldy column reached the Box safely with no casualties to men or vehicles. Good navigators were worth their weight in gold in the Western Desert. They carried a heavy responsibility on their shoulders ; the lives of their comrades, sometimes only a handful of men and sometimes as many as thirty or forty, depended entirely on the navigators' accuracy. Bark navigated fighting and reconnaissance patrols into the heart of the enemy lines on no less than five consecutive occasions and each night the patrols returned safely to the Box without casualties.

The minelifting patrol under Lieut. W. Nesham—which included eight men from the Battalion Pioneer Platoon—was very successful. Accompanied by the tireless Sapper corporal who had gone with both the previous patrols Nesham led his men out from Stricklands and soon found the minefield. Working silently and swiftly they cleared six hundred yards of the field and disarmed a hundred and sixty mines before the approach of dawn forced them to return to the outpost.

Meanwhile, in the south the Axis attack on Bir Hacheim had been continued all through June 6th, 7th and 8th, and by June 9th it was impossible to get supplies through to the hard-pressed French garrison. In these circumstances General Ritchie had no alternative but to order the garrison to withdraw during the night of June 10th/11th. The gallant defence of this vital hinge of the Gazala defences was therefore of no avail, but it had deeper and more far-reaching effects. The magnificent conduct of the small garrison of Bir Hacheim stirred the heart of every free-thinking Frenchman and sowed the seeds of French military revival. Nevertheless, the withdrawal was probably the turning point of the battle. Rommel was now able to concentrate his troops, and reinforced by the Italian Littorio Armoured Division, the whole weight of the Axis forces was directed north to the El Adem-Acroma area where a fresh tank battle was soon raging. However, the South African and 50 Divisions still held the northern sector of the Gazala Line and continued to strike whenever possible at the enemy on their fronts.

On June 12th a plan was made for a tank attack against the positions south of Stricklands Post which enemy troops occupied just before dawn every day. Three troops of South African armoured cars, three troops of tanks, two sections of Battalion carriers—which had been patched up since the June 8th action—and two platoons of C Company under 2/Lieut. A. W. Gaze were detailed as the attacking force. In support of the operation was the whole of the Cheshire machine-gun platoon at Stricklands, all the guns of the 74th Field Regiment, and the whole of the 7th Medium Regiment. The object of this formidable force, led by Major Lindsay of the 8th R.T.R., was to test the enemy defence line and to destroy any small points of opposition.

At 1.30 p.m. the combined gunfire of the 7th Medium Regiment and the 74th Field Regiment was brought to bear on the enemy positions and shortly afterwards the tanks—which had formed up north of the outpost—crossed a start line at Stricklands in two waves of five tanks. The South African armoured cars moved on the right flank with No. 14 Platoon of C Company following the second wave of tanks on 15 cwt. trucks. The second C Company platoon was in reserve.

The men at the outpost, watching the armoured vehicles and infantry advance slowly towards the enemy positions, suddenly saw little puffs of sand and dust jump up around the leading tanks and armoured cars. The crash of enemy gunfire was joined with that of the British guns as a barrage came down in front of the enemy positions. One of the armoured cars was hit almost immediately and Sgt. Cairns of the Carrier Platoon was wounded when a burst of enemy machine-gun fire straddled his carrier. As the shelling became heavier the tanks turned sharply left towards the Box with the exception of one tank, out of wireless touch with the remainder, which carried straight on into the enemy lines, firing its turret and machine-guns.

The armoured cars and the carriers followed the main body of the tanks but to the amazement of the watchers at Stricklands No. 14 Platoon of C Company debussed, and one section started to round up prisoners from the forward positions. The most probable explanation is that, during the noise and confusion of the firing and because of the dust thrown up by the bursting shells, the infantry trucks of this platoon followed the one tank which did not turn left towards the Box. This tank—firing its guns to the last—was very soon knocked out, leaving 2/Lieut. Gaze and the men of 14 Platoon on their own with the few prisoners they had rounded up. Observation from Stricklands was very limited and it was not easy from the outpost to see clearly what was happening, but not a single man of the infantry platoon escaped and they were all posted as missing. The remainder of the force returned to Stricklands without further incident.

Soon after dark Lieut. P. G. Hampson took his platoon from D Company to either locate 2/Lieut. Gaze's missing platoon or at least to find out what had happened to it. Having arranged with the outpost commander for a green Verey light to be fired from Stricklands at hourly intervals, the patrol left the outpost in two trucks and headed due south, stopping every fifty yards so that Hampson could shout for any members of the C Company platoon who might be in hiding. The two trucks proceeded in this way for a mile before the patrol debussed, to advance warily towards the scene of the afternoon's action. As it breasted a small rise, the leading section commander spotted a red glow from the direction of the battlefield. It looked like a burning truck, but when Hampson crawled forward to the ridge and focussed his night glasses he saw that it was the South African armoured car which had been hit in the afternoon. Very carefully, expecting to run into an ambush any moment, the D Company platoon advanced towards the smouldering vehicle, and as the leading men drew closer they could hear groans. The main body of the patrol took up covering positions whilst Hampson and several others dragged three South Africans clear of the armoured car. One man was dead, a second dying and a third badly wounded. Hampson sent word back for one of the trucks to come forward with stretchers and then gave the wounded South Africans a swig of whiskey from his hip flask.

It was almost an hour before the truck arrived with the stretchers, a nerve-racking period of waiting for the men around the armoured car. However, it was not until the truck had stopped and the two wounded men were being lifted carefully on to stretchers that the enemy opened fire with a machine-gun from the south-east. They had obviously heard the sound of the engine. The gun had been sited to fire just above ground level and the enemy gunners had probably been waiting for an attempt to rescue the crew of the armoured car. As Hampson and the men of the leading section lifted the two stretchers into the back of the waiting truck, the Bren guns of the rest of the British patrol returned the enemy fire.

Hampson ordered L/Cpl. Archer, the pre-war Stockport footballer to go with the truck and to make for Stricklands on a due north bearing, checking his direction with the next green Verey light signal, due to go up from the outpost in twenty minutes. As the truck set off towards Stricklands the enemy machine-gun fire was intensified and the patrol fired back until all the Bren magazines had been emptied. Then the sections withdrew, making for Stricklands which was reached at 2.30 a.m. Hampson was amazed to find that L/Cpl. Archer's truck had not arrived, and immediately telephoned Stanley Gap to warn the standing patrol there that the truck might be on the way having by-passed the outpost. However, there was still a chance that Archer, having lost his way, was waiting outside Stricklands. For an hour and a half the patrol stayed at the outpost but although four green Verey light signals were fired at twenty-minute intervals, there was no sign of the truck.

Unfortunately L/Cpl. Archer, instead of making for the outpost, had by-passed it and set his course for the Box in order to get the wounded men back quickly. Archer's truck went right through the check minefield between Stricklands and Petro's posts and eventually ran into the main minefield protecting the Box, not far from Auckland Gap. When the truck ran over the minefield wire, the driver made frantic efforts to stop, but it was too late and the truck blew up on a mine. L/Cpl. Archer and the driver were killed and Ptes. Joyce and Anstey, in the back of the truck with the South Africans, were both wounded. The shock killed the dying South African immediately although his companion survived. It was a tragic ending to a gallant night patrol. Only those who have had to find their way in a truck through the pitch darkness of a desert night will understand how easy it was for Archer to make the slight navigation error during the four mile journey which took the truck into the minefield only a few yards from Auckland Gap.

The following night Lieut. P. J. Lewis took out a B Company patrol to the area of the wrecked armoured car to obtain identification from the deserted enemy slit trenches. The patrol left the outpost at 9 p.m. and returned at 5.15 a.m. the following morning, having thoroughly searched the Italian positions. No enemy were found but letters and documents, removed from clothing in the deserted slit trenches, provided valuable information for the Battalion Intelligence Officer. The British artillery and the machine-gun fire from the tanks on June 12th had caused heavy casualties to the Italians in the forward positions, and the piles of bloodstained, discarded clothing told a grim story to the men of the patrol. Some of the slit trenches had been caved in by tank tracks—probably those of the lone tank which had broken through—and several of the enemy had obviously been crushed to death as they sheltered in the trenches. The men of the B Company patrol were not sorry to quit the area and return to the outpost.

This patrol was the last one sent out by the 8th D.L.I. from the Gazala Line. Later that morning to the surprise of every man in the Battalion 50 Division was ordered to withdraw from the Gazala positions that night. Everyone was stunned by this news; things seemed to be going so well for the Division and, in fact, maps had been issued as a prelude to a Brigade attack westwards from the Box to straddle the enemy lines of communication near Chichiban so as to prevent the lateral movement of enemy reserves from Tmimi to Matuba. The morale of the Battalion was high, and the commerce raiding and successful battles to keep open the gap had convinced the men of the 8th that they could hold their sector of the Brigade Box indefinitely. Reserve rations and water were sufficient for fourteen days, even if the Battalion was completely surrounded, and it seemed that the initiative, so fiercely won and held, was to be thrown away.

However, the reason for the withdrawal was a good one and the only course open to the Army Commander, for although the South African and 50 Divisions were still securely holding their sectors of the Gazala Line, the battle behind the Line had gone badly for the Eighth Army. The tank actions which had been raging continuously in the Acroma-El Adem area since the French withdrawal from Bir Hacheim had resulted in very heavy losses to the British armoured divisions. The superiority of the German tank guns became increasingly apparent and the British tanks were knocked out in their dozens without being able, in many cases, to get within range of the German armour so as to inflict comparable losses. As the situation rapidly deteriorated General Ritchie saw that there was considerable danger of the South African and 50 Divisions being surrounded and destroyed piecemeal in their Boxes, as had been the case with 150 Brigade. He therefore ordered the two divisions to withdraw during the night of June 13th/14th.

So the Gazala spell came to an end. It was a period which taught the men of the 8th many invaluable lessons in the art of war. In particular it had seen the development of the Carrier Platoon into a fine desert fighting force. Nobody in the Battalion denied the men of the Carrier Platoon their share of the honours at Gazala, and the troops of the rifle companies were full of admiration for the section leaders, crews and mechanics who had kept the carriers at peak efficiency in spite of sand, dust, grit and rock of the desert.

CHAPTER TEN

THE BREAKOUT FROM GAZALA

A spectacular plan—the Battalion makes a bridgehead—D Company gets through—back to the frontier.

GENERAL RAMSDEN planned a fighting withdrawal for 50 Division. He decided to launch the Division in an attack westwards from the Line to smash a way first through the German and Italian forward positions, then through the enemy lines of communication, creating confusion wherever possible. 50 Division was then to wheel south deep into the desert and, having broken clear of enemy formations, was to turn east to a rallying point at Fort Maddalena on the Egyptian frontier. It was a daring and spectacular plan which deserved to succeed because of its very nature. This was to be no ordinary attack with the infantry going forward on foot supported by artillery and machine-gun fire. It was to be a fully mobile attack with the whole of 50 Division on wheels—hundreds of trucks split up into fighting columns. After the break-out the columns would have to navigated by night and day across one hundred and fifty miles of desert to Fort Maddalena. No operation of this sort could have been planned anywhere but in the desert. In the words of a veteran anti-tank gunner who had been in North Africa when 50 Division was still in England, " I thought I had seen everything in the Western Desert but this is a new one on me."

Both 151 and 69 Brigades were ordered to establish bridgeheads astride the enemy forward positions through which the rest of the brigades and supporting arms, together with some divisional units, could pass. 69 Brigade was ordered to make the eastern bridgehead and 151 Brigade the western. The 8th Battalion had a major part to play in the 151 Brigade operation, and at 11 a.m. on June 14th a conference was summoned at Battalion H.Q. for company commanders and commanders of supporting arms. The C.O. quickly explained that the Battalion had been ordered to seize and hold the western bridgehead, in the area of Point 168 south of Stricklands, which would enable the remainder of the Brigade to pass through. Supporting troops for the operation were 296 Battery of the 74th Field Regiment, No. 10 Platoon of the 2nd Cheshires, one troop of Bofors guns from 274 Light Anti-Aircraft Battery, a squadron of armoured cars from the 6th South African Armoured Car Regiment, and troop-carrying lorries of the R.A.S.C.

The Battalion and supporting arms were to be formed into one main column under the C.O. and two subsidiary columns under Major A. B. S. Clarke and Major H. S. Sell. The formation of the three columns was almost identical; each had a company of infantry, a section or a troop of field guns, a troop of armoured cars, a section of machine-guns (except the main column), four or five carriers, a section or troop of the Battalion Anti-Tank Platoon, two detachments of the Battalion Mortar Platoon and a detachment of R.A.S.C. troop-carriers. The South African armoured cars were later reduced to one troop for the whole Battalion, with orders to operate on the right flank of the right hand subsidiary column.

Infiltration of the vehicles from the Box to an assembly area at Stricklands was to be completed by 8.15 p.m. After that the main axis of the Battalion advance was Stricklands to Point 168, on a compass bearing of 200 degrees for five miles. Surprise was to be achieved by attacking without preliminary artillery fire. With the two flanking columns in position the Battalion main column and the rest of 151 Brigade—less the 9th D.L.I. which had not returned to the Box after the operation of June 5th—was to pass through on the main axis. A Regimental Report Centre would be established at Stricklands and was then to move forward with the main force. Withdrawal of the flanking columns would not take place until the rest of the Brigade and attached units had passed safely through the bridgehead. The signals for the withdrawal were ; (1) The codename " Benghazi" on the wireless (2) A series of red flares (3) Personal word from Major Ferens attached to the last unit—the 6th D.L.I.—for this purpose.

The company commanders returned to their areas about 1 p.m. and for the rest of the afternoon the Battalion prepared for the night attack. Sentries were reduced in the rifle companies and most of the men were able to take some much-needed rest. However, there was plenty of routine preparation necessary such as the cleaning and testing of guns, the checking of ammunition and the issue of battle rations. The company quartermaster sergeants had to supervise the splitting down of the reserve water supplies to sections and, in addition to this, large 35-gallon drums were manhandled into some of the troop-carriers. In the M.T. lines vehicles were checked for petrol, oil and water and, as a minefield was on the axis of the attack, the floors of all the trucks and carriers were reinforced by sandbags. Whilst these preparations were going on a lone enemy reconnaissance plane flew over the Box but fortunately a dust storm—which had been blowing all day—reducing visibility to a hundred yards, served to screen the activity on the ground and the enemy reconnaissance could not have been very successful.

By 6 p.m. the first trucks were ready to leave the Box for Stricklands and very soon a long line of oddly assorted vehicles—15 cwt. trucks, three-ton lorries, quads pulling twenty-five pounders, ambulances, troop-carriers and a few captured enemy vehicles were bumping along the rough track to the outpost. At Stricklands the trucks were directed into their columns and the men stood around in little groups, waiting anxiously for the order to move forward into action.

By this time the dust storm had blown itself out and as visibility improved the enemy artillery ranged on the outpost area where the columns provided an excellent target. However, dusk was closing in rapidly and the gunfire slackened a little as zero hour drew nearer and the men of the 8th Battalion climbed aboard their vehicles. The two leading columns—with the codenames of Clarkecol and Sellcol—crossed the start line just before 9 p.m.

For Clarkecol on the left flank, the first ten minutes were most unpleasant. The long line of vehicles, moving slowly forward in desert formation into the fast closing night, came under accurate and fairly heavy gunfire from enemy batteries away towards the west. With the noise of so many trucks on the move it was difficult to hear the whistle of approaching shells and the only indication that a shell had landed came too late for anyone to do anything about it ; there was a flash and the crash of the explosion, with pieces of shrapnel whipping viciously into the column. It was particularly unpleasant for the officers and N.C.Os. perched high on the driving cabs of vehicles and to them the progress of the column was maddeningly slow. It was a great relief when darkness finally closed in and the gunfire stopped.

Clarkecol continued slowly towards the bare, flat-topped ridge known as Patrol Grove and the barrel which marked Point 168. On the way the column passed over two Italian positions which appeared to have been recently deserted. There were no signs of the enemy troops but rifles and light machine-guns had been left in position. There may have been Italians in the bottom of the slit trenches but Major Clarke's objective was Point 168 and the column motored on through the positions to reach the objective without incident.

The trucks were brought into close laager below the eastern side of the ridge and the troops started to dig in round the stationary vehicles. This was no easy task as the ground was extremely hard and rocky and only a few slit trenches were dug more than a foot deep. However, it was some protection and, as the infantry settled down into battle positions, wild and inaccurate enemy defensive fire whistled harmlessly over the tops of the column vehicles.

Meanwhile Sellcol was having a battle royal. With the carriers out in front and the South African armoured cars protecting the right flank it moved off from Stricklands at the same time as Clarkecol. After going for about a mile the column came under heavy fire from a southerly direction. The bridgehead position which Major Sell intended to occupy was held by three companies of Italians, and the desert was criss-crossed by the tracer from their machine-guns and anti-tank guns. As Sellcol surged forward into the attack, the Italian defensive fire swept across the column for the few brief moments which it took the carriers and armoured cars to reach the enemy positions. Then one by one the Italian guns fell silent as the British armoured vehicles weaved in and out amongst the trenches, shooting at the occupants in the half light.

The British infantry debussed from the troop-carriers and fixed bayonets as they advanced to mop up the positions. Major Sell had a miraculous escape when his truck was hit at almost point blank range by an anti-tank shell. There was a terrific crash as the shell exploded and a cascade of sparks as the truck stopped dead in its tracks. To the surprise of his men, Sell jumped out of the wrecked vehicle, and with his batman Pte. Etherington wielding rifle and bayonet with deadly skill, he joined his men in the thick of the fighting. It was all over in a few minutes ; grenades were tossed into dugouts, bursts of Tommy gun and Bren gun fire raked the slit trenches and when the Italians had taken a beating they came out with their hands high above their heads.

The position consisted of several " pimples " and quickly a defensive layout was prepared against counter-attack with Lieut. Hampson occupying one sector and Major Sell holding the other with the armoured cars and carriers. By this time darkness had fallen. Sell sent a message that his force was firmly established on the right flank of the bridgehead and, with Clarkecol already in position, the withdrawal of 151 Brigade commenced.

Meanwhile, the men of Clarkecol had been watching burning vehicles set alight by enemy gunfire in the 69 Brigade bridgehead area. The blazing vehicles made an excellent target for the enemy gunners and salvo after salvo of shells straddled them. Major Clarke sent out listening and fighting patrols to the south and Lieut. R. Place, carrying an odd assortment of lethal weapons—including his policeman's truncheon—took out some men from his Battalion Battle Patrol. He discovered an Italian company position, including a signal exchange and an officers' mess, only a hundred yards ahead of the column. The trenches and gun positions were deserted but the patrol did not return until it had ransacked the officers' mess for a few of the spoils of war, and in any case a glass of cool Vino was always acceptable even in the middle of the night.

It was an anxious period of waiting for the bridgehead troops and every minute seemed like ten. By this time the Germans and Italians had a very good idea of what was going on, and from all directions the crash of gunfire, the splutter of automatic weapons and the flaming silhouettes of burning vehicles told the men in the 151 Brigade bridgehead that 50 Division was having to fight hard to break out of the Gazala Line. However, neither Sellcol nor Clarkecol was attacked. The enemy infantry were far too busy ; the Germans in trying to stop the mobile columns and the Italians in trying to get out of their way. There were some Italians who, giving themselves up to British columns asked for a lift to Alexandria, and one group of Mussolini's soldiers obligingly informed a British officer who captured them that he could have a General as well if he cared to wait a few minutes.

By 2.30 a.m., the volume of vehicles passing through the bridgehead having decreased considerably, Major Sell on the right flank reckoned that the withdrawal had been completed, although Major Ferens had not reported. Sellcol commander did not know that the last unit—the 6th D.L.I.—had seen the bridgehead battle in its early stages by the light of flares and burning vehicles and the C.O. of the 6th Battalion had decided to break through the enemy defence cordon elsewhere. The 6th D.L.I. had, in fact, taken the Tobruk road. To add to the difficulties of Sellcol the wireless had been put out of action, cutting communications with Battalion H.Q., and the sky was so full of flares that signal recognition—the red flares previously arranged—was out of the question. The column stayed in position until an hour before dawn when Major Sell decided to evacuate the bridgehead as it was by now quite obvious that the withdrawal had been completed. It was not going to be by any means a simple task, for captured Italian prisoners—one of whom made himself understood in Spanish —gave information of a German strongpoint of two companies, which straddled the Sellcol line of withdrawal only a mile or two away to the south. It was certain that by this time the Germans, having reconnoitred the British column, were ready and waiting for it to break out with the dawn.

Major Sell called a conference of the South African armoured car commander, Captain Bower, Lieut. Hampson and Lieut. Carruthers. He realised that the chances of the column breaking out on foot through the German strongpoint were remote and that they would have to throw the Germans off their guard by doing something entirely unexpected. Quickly he outlined a plan for charging the Germans in the darkness and for countering enemy resistance by opening fire on the move with every available weapon, and to continue firing until clear of the strongpoint. It was a daring plan with just a chance that it would succeed.

The small force was formed up with the armoured cars in front, followed by Lieut. Carruthers and the carriers. Captain Bower and Lieut. Hampson brought up the rear with the infantry. After walking round the stationary vehicles to make sure that as many troops as possible knew the plan, Sell climbed into the leading armoured car and the column moved forward. All went well until the Germans, hearing the noise of the approaching truck engines, floodlit the area with flares, turning night into day. The enemy opened up with every available weapon and machine-gun and rifle fire raked the British column. In the ghostly light of flares, which hung in the sky like giant chandeliers, the truck drivers coaxed every ounce of speed out of their vehicles, and as Sellcol made for the German strongpoint, the turret gunners in the armoured cars and the Bren gunners in the carriers replied to the German fire. A German Spandau[1] post loomed up immediately in front of Major Sell's armoured car, firing tracer at point blank range. The German gunners were made of sterner stuff than their Italian comrades ; they continued in action until the armoured car ran them down and left them lying beside the wreckage of their silent gun.

The strongpoint was well and bravely held. The enemy stood his ground and fought back so fiercely that Sgt. Tennant in the last of

1The German machine-gun.

the carriers turned back to tell Lieut. Hampson, who was following with some of the troop-carriers, that there was no hope of getting through. However, Hampson decided to chance it. There was very little the infantry in the troop-carriers could do except hope for the best as their trucks ran the gauntlet of cross-fire. Fortunately the armoured cars and carriers had silenced most of the defenders of the strongpoint otherwise every single one of the unarmoured infantry vehicles would have been destroyed. As it was, taking advantage of the confusion created by the British armoured vehicles, the three-tonners lurched and swayed as their drivers drove through the enemy position at full speed. However, there were still German machine-guns in action and some of the trucks were raked with fire from stem to stern. Their helpless occupants suffered heavy casualties and it was during this action that the Italians who had been captured earlier that night were either killed or wounded by the Germans.

As suddenly as it had started thc firing and shouting died away as Sellcol broke clear of the strong point but the column had paid a heavy price for the breakout. The armoured cars were all intact but only one carrier had got through ; of the other carriers there was no sign. Captain Bower had been killed by machine-gun fire and Lieut. Carruthers was missing. It transpired that Carruthers, returning in his carrier to pick up stragglers, had run into a minefield. The carrier blew up and Carruthers was lifted out unconscious and badly wounded and taken prisoner. It had been a hectic night for D Company of the 8th Battalion and its supporting arms, and the first signs of dawn were in the sky as Sellcol sped on into the desert. Their job completed, the survivors of the bridgehead force, tired out from a night of almost continuous action, relaxed. Major Sell was awarded the Military Cross for his gallant leadership of Sellcol, both when the initial bridgehead was made and later the breakout.

Meanwhile, Clarkecol had experienced a much quieter night on the left flank of the bridgehead. Just after midnight the enemy positions originally located by Lieut. Place came to life and flares were sent up. As one of the South African armoured cars approached to investigate, it received a direct hit from an anti-tank gun and burst into flames. As it burned, enemy mortars and anti-tank guns continued to fire at it from the south-west for the next two hours. Not long after the armoured car had been hit, a party of unusually courageous Italians dragged an anti-tank gun to within range of the column and were about to open fire when they were spotted and chased away by one of Place's energetic fighting patrols. Soon after this incident Clarkecol was ordered to quit the bridgehead.

The column travelled in close formation through the night, for although the stars shone brilliantly, there was no moon. After moving slowly for some time with frequent halts the vehicles went into single file, and it was perhaps better for the peace of mind of the troops that only the column commander and a few others knew that they were passing through a minefield. It was in this minefield that the column became split up when a Gunner quad ran into a slit trench.

Whilst the crew tried frantically to extricate it, the front part of the column carried on and soon disappeared from view.

The quad was eventually coaxed out of the slit trench to the accompaniment of some hearty swearing, and the rear half of the column moved on again with Lieut. H. Catford and Sgt. Bewick in the leading vehicle. For some time the trucks followed the tracks of the first half of the column but, when they lost them, set their own course. It is well that they did for Major Clarke's vehicles had run into another minefield in the area of Many Tracks and it was here that some ration trucks were blown up. The disabled vehicles were abandoned and a party of thirty-seven men under the leadership of R.Q.M.S. Lightfoot set out to walk to safety—a forlorn hope. However, luck was with them and after trudging several miles they caught up with the column again, which had been making very slow progress because of the many slit trenches in the area. For the rest of the night Clarkecol struck south, and when dawn came was well clear of the enemy positions.

Meanwhile Catford had contacted a Brigade H.Q. column and, as by this time they seemed to be clear of the enemy, he and Sgt. Bewick decided to push on with two of the anti-tank guns in seach of Major Clarke. When dawn came, however, they could see no sign of Clarkecol or any other column and were the only occupants of that particular part of the desert where the dawn found them. Catford and Bewick decided to try their hand at desert navigation and, with the aid of a piece of string and a geometry set protractor, they set course for the frontier and Fort Maddalena which they eventually reached quite safely.

Many tales could be told of gallantry during that memorable night of May 31st but unfortunately only a few of them were recorded. The stories of L/Cpl. W. Charlton and Pte. T. M. Swallow will perhaps serve to illustrate some of the dangers and anxieties which were common to all the columns as they motored to safety. Charlton was with a column, part of which ran into an enemy minefield where a Gunner Quad was blown up. Neither the gun nor ammunition limber was damaged and a truck was called for to tow them to safety so that they would not fall into the hands of the enemy. Charlton immediately volunteered and without hesitation drove his vehicle forward into the minefield where he calmly hitched it to the gun and limber. He then towed his dangerous cargo to safety, showing a complete disregard for the mines which might have blown him up at any moment. He was awarded the Military Medal.

Pte. Swallow was leading Clarkecol when his vehicle ran into a minefield and was blown up. At the time the column was under heavy enemy fire and there was not time to find a way round the minefield ; the column would have to go through it. When others showed hesitation at continuing because of the risk of being blown up, Swallow succeeded in getting his engine going again and in his damaged vehicle he started off at the head of the column and unhesitatingly led the way through the minefield. His was a magnificent example and he was awarded the Military Medal.

The main force, commanded by the C.O. with B Company as the infantry element did not fire a shot that night. It was dark when the column moved off from the outpost and the vehicles were closed right up, nose to tail, as they crawled along in bottom gear. By the time the bridgehead area was reached a lane had already been cleared by the flanking columns and the trucks halted whilst the C.O. checked up on the situation. They remained in position astride the bridgehead until about 2 a.m. when a welcome message was received from the Brigade Commander to disengage and continue the advance. The withdrawal of 151 Brigade and divisional units through the bridgehead had been completed and the C.O. sent out the codeword Benghazi to Sellcol—which of course never received it—and to Clarkecol. Then he gave the order to move off south into the desert.

The men had great faith in their C.O.'s luck and as the vehicles weaved about, by-passing abandoned trucks which had been set on fire and giving a wide berth to local skirmishes, most of them felt that somehow they would get through. As one of them said afterwards, " Whether it was Jake's luck or the I.O.'s navigation, we safely rounded Bir Hacheim and turned east towards the Egyptian frontier wire." It had been a night of incredible happenings but one which the 8th Battalion will always remember with pride. For the attack of the Battalion columns and the establishment of the bridgehead was so successful that the remainder of 151 Brigade was able to pass through safely. Much of the credit must go to the C.O. Throughout the whole operation Lieut.-Colonel Jackson set a fine example of personal courage and disregard for danger ; owing to the skill and determination with which he launched his battalion in the attack the success of the operation was assured. It came as no surprise to his officers and men when some weeks later he was awarded the Distinguished Service Order for the bridgehead attack and also for the way in which he had led and fought his battalion during the operations from the Gazala Line. Yet " Jake " Jackson would never acknowledge his award. If ever it was referred to he used to say : " My battalion won it—it belongs to them." It was typical of him.

The dawn following that night of action and suspense gave way to the sort of morning which men like to remember when they talk of the Western Desert. Safetly round Bir Hacheim the 8th Battalion columns and the dozens of other columns of 50 Division which had successfully smashed a way out of the Gazala Line sped eastwards towards the frontier and temporary safety. The sun came up—a great red ball in the east—and its rays brought warmth to the troops huddled in their greatcoats. The morning was crisp and clear and when the columns reached hard going the trucks surged forward and for brief periods their speedometer needles flickered around the mile a minute mark.

For once the flies were beaten. They could not torment whilst the trucks were on the move and when the columns halted for a brief rest they stopped in desert which in all probability had never been crossed by man before ; where there had been no humans there were no flies.

Well south of the battle area the British columns were right out in the vastness of the desert, their only guides the navigators aided by compasses and the sun. It was certainly exhilarating.

As the day wore on the sun's rays became fiercer, beating down mercilessly on the troops in the backs of the open three-ton lorries. Thirty or forty to a truck they sweltered in the heat, leaning over the hot metal sides trying to catch a little of the breeze. When the columns halted the men who were the first to debuss crawled under the vehicles to seek the shade, while others brewed the inevitable can of tea. After a brief rest they motored on again towards the frontier, still part of the Eighth Army but an army which had been severely mauled.

For the whole of that day the columns of 50 Division streamed across the desert and by the evening of June 15th some of them were within striking distance of the frontier. Major Sell's column, arriving late on June 15th at Fort Maddalena, was ordered to push on a further forty miles east to Bir el Thalata. Part of Clarkecol, under Captain Jones, arrived during the morning of June 16th and the remainder and the C.O.'s column arrived during the course of the day. By that evening, all the Battalion columns had passed through the check point at Maddalena.

The night was spent around the old desert fort. The men of the 8th Battalion were dog tired and many of them, throwing a blanket on the ground, dropped down absolutely exhausted. Others slept in the backs of trucks, oblivious to the hard metal floors, and many of the drivers slept sitting up in the cabs of their vehicles. All around the battered fort of Maddalena, whose ruins were silhouetted against the night sky, dozens of trucks of 50 Division stood silent while hundreds of men slept, not knowing or caring very much what the morning would bring.

CHAPTER ELEVEN

THE WITHDRAWAL CONTINUES

A temporary respite—Tobruk falls—a V.C. for the 9th Battalion—a night attack on wheels.

For the time being 50 Division was out of the battle but it was only a temporary respite. Although the Germans had inflicted grievous losses on the Desert Army the fortress of Tobruk, with supplies sufficient to withstand a three month siege, still remained. The troops on the frontier were to be reinforced and General Auchinleck planned to build up a striking force which would eventually advance westwards to join the Tobruk garrison in driving the enemy out of Cyrenaica.

Whilst the withdrawal to the frontier continued of that part of the Desert Army which had not been detailed to the defence of the Tobruk perimeter, the sadly depleted units of 50 Division moved back to Bir el Thalata on the afternoon of June 17th and early on the 18th the remnants of the 8th Battalion assembled in a brigade camp. The day was spent in reorganising and taking a count of the casualties, which had been heavy. As well as the loss of Captain Bower and Lieut. Carruthers, seventy-one other ranks could not be accounted for and, although some of the missing men were to turn up later, the casualty list as it stood on June 18th was, to say the least, depressing.

Rommel was not slow in staging his attack against Tobruk and whilst the remnants of the British formations in the frontier area reorganised during June 19th, he switched his German and Italian divisions to the assault of the port. Early on June 20th a heavy artillery barrage was opened on the El Duda sector of the perimeter. The shelling was followed by concentrated bombing which helped to blow up the protective minefields and was then directed against the infantry forward posts. The R.A.F., which had been driven back beyond effective fighter range, was powerless to intervene and repeated Stuka dive-bombing attacks were made without interference. Enemy sappers then filled in a narrow stretch of the anti-tank ditch on the perimeter and over this bridge an assault was led by two companies of the veteran desert division—the German 90 Light, followed by a large force of tanks with Italian infantry in support. The defenders were overwhelmed and the tanks swept on to run amok in the town, some of them spreading out fanwise to take other sectors of the Tobruk defences in the rear. The British tanks counter-attacked but by late afternoon not a single one was left in action, although the British and Dominion infantry on the perimeter still fought on and many of them continued to do so throughout the night.

To try to disentangle the sequence of events from the terrible confusion which reigned in the breached but still fighting fortress does not come within the scope of this history. Command arrangements broke down and at 7 a.m. on the morning of the 21st the enemy demanded surrender; two and a half hours later the remnants of the garrison received orders to burn all transport and capitulate. Twenty-five thousand men of the Desert Army laid down their arms and thus, within the short space of twenty-four hours, the Eighth Army had lost a large part of its infantry strength and the majority of its remaining tanks.

The fall of Tobruk was a disaster of the first magnitude. Winston Churchill heard the news in the White House where he was visiting President Roosevelt. His only remark when he read the telegram which told him of the capitulation was the magnificent understatement, "Rather disconcerting." He has since revealed that he was in fact "the most miserable Englishman in America since Burgoyne surrendered at Saratoga."

The enemy had captured enormous reserves of supplies, for Tobruk had been the main base for the offensive which originally it had been planned to launch from the Gazala position, and it was one of the salient features of the Middle East campaign that it took at least four months to reinforce the Desert Army, either with men or materials from Britain or the United States. It was indeed fortunate that 44 and 51 Divisions had left England at the end of May and the beginning of June and that many hundreds of the new six-pounder anti-tank gun were on the way as well as shiploads of new tanks. It was fortunate too that there were in other parts of the Middle East reinforcements which could be rushed to the desert to stem the German advance. These included 9 Australian Division, General Freyberg's magnificent New Zealand Division, 18 Indian Infantry Brigade and some armoured elements. It was these units, together with severely mauled formations such as 50 Division which had not been captured at Tobruk, that were to hold Rommel's thrust for Egypt until the seaborne reinforcements arrived. It is no exaggeration to say that the safety of the whole of the Middle East was in their hands and the men of the Eighth Army and their Australian, New Zealand and Indian comrades who were even then being speeded to reinforce them, knew it and rose nobly to the occasion.

The loss of Tobruk together with so many men and so much armour meant that the frontier position was untenable, for it was too easily outflanked to be held by infantry operating without a strong mobile reserve. Consequently General Auchinleck ordered the remnants of the Eighth Army, under cover of a small delaying force, to fall back a hundred and twenty-five miles to Mersa Matruh. At the same time Auchinleck decided that Matruh was also untenable because its defences had been designed for infantry supported by armour operating on a flank, and with hardly any armour available the defence of the Matruh escarpment might well prove to be a trap. Nevertheless it was suitable for a rearguard action, so from the frontier the Desert Army withdrew to Matruh.

On a Sunday morning, the day after the capitulation of Tobruk, the 8th Battalion was ordered to fall back from Bir el Thalata. During a church parade, with the men of the Battalion drawn up in a square listening to an address by Padre Nesbitt, news came through that enemy armoured cars were operating only a few miles away. This rather disturbing news was quickly followed by an order for the Battalion to withdraw to the Matruh area with the remainder of 50 Division. During the afternoon Lieut.-Colonel Jackson left to command the Brigade when Brigadier Nicholls assumed command of 10 Indian Division. Major Clarke took over the Battalion, and the 8th moved four miles eastwards to a night laager position. The following morning at dawn the 8th went sixty miles farther east and, after a rapid move, arrived during the late afternoon in an area not far from a junction of desert tracks known as Charing Cross. Next day—June 23rd—was spent in getting the Battalion into fighting trim and in carrying out some much needed maintenance on the vehicles.

During the early morning of the 24th Captain C. L. Beattie and company representatives left to reconnoitre a battalion area, and at 10 a.m. the remainder of the Battalion followed to take up defensive positions some five miles south-east of Mersa Matruh.

Meanwhile, Rommel was driving his troops forward beyond the frontier. The Germans and Italians advanced in parallel columns—astride the coast road, along the lines of the railway and edge of the escarpment, and farther south in the desert. Rommel drove them hard and was determined to strike again whilst the going was good. He had available two German armoured divisions, the Italian Ariete Division, the newly arrived 133 Littorio Armoured Division, the German 90 Light Division, and an Italian motorised division in the van. Two days after the fall of Tobruk four more Italian infantry divisions became available.

The British force consisted of an advanced screen formed by 7 Motor Brigade, an improvised armoured car brigade, 3 Indian Motor Brigade, a battalion of the King's Royal Rifle Corps and 29 Indian Infantry Brigade. Behind this screen, in Mersa Matruh, was 10 Indian Division and 50 Division consisting of 151 Brigade, 69 Brigade and a South African Brigade. By this time the Germans had christened 50 Division "The Gazala Gazelles," a taunt which the men of the Division were to pay back with interest. To the south of Matruh was 5 Indian Division, Freyberg's New Zealand Division and an improvised armoured car brigade made up of the remnants of 4 and 22 Armoured Brigades. The odds weighed heavily in favour of Rommel but the British force held fast and prepared for battle.

In line with the overall defence policy the 8th Battalion received orders during the evening of June 25th to move yet again—this time to positions in wadis due south of Matruh, about three miles west of the present positions. The battalion went forward that night and in the new area the troops worked with picks and shovels until the dawn, digging section positions and laying a minefield Lieut.-Colonel

Jackson returned to resume command of the Battalion and all through the next morning, with the sun beating down, the companies continued to strengthen the positions. At noon the sort of thing happened which made the troops curse everyone from a lance-corporal upwards. The Battalion was ordered to move again. An advance party made up of units in the brigade was sent to reconnoitre positions some ten miles to the south, which were to be held with a rearguard action if necessary, to allow 10 Indian Division to withdraw from Matruh.

Late that afternoon the Battalion was embussed in the troop-carriers and taken forward to the new area, on top of a steep escarpment some hundred feet high, running parallel to the coast at this point. The defences were sited on a line of telegraph poles which went through the battalion area direct to the coast. Orders were given for a minefield to be laid during the night to link up with the 9th D.L.I. which had moved into position on the left flank and to the south, having recently rejoined the Brigade. However, the minefield could not be laid because all the mines had been used in the previous positions and no others were available. As darkness was closing in enemy posts were located some three miles to the south-west. Rommel's forces had caught up again with " The Gazala Gazelles."

In fact, by the morning of that day, Rommel had already swung his divisions into position facing the middle of the main Matruh defences. His German troops were some eighteen miles to the south-west of the village, his Italian armour astride the track which runs from Matruh southwards to Siwa Oasis, and Italian infantry had come up on the coast, south-west of Matruh. The German commander wanted a second Tobruk and was quite confident it would be so.

The 8th "stood-to" at first light on June 27th. The Battalion was widely dispersed with each company at least a thousand yards from Battalion H.Q. Although the 8th was not in action it was a memorable day in many ways. Shortly after daybreak anti-tank guns with advanced enemy formations opened fire on a group of vehicles laagered in the Battalion area, belonging to the 11th R.H.A. They were soon scattered by the anti-tank gunfire and departed in all directions for the shelter of the low ground to the east and below the top of the escarpment.

In B Company area Captain R. I. Pitt, the company commander, was inspecting one of his platoon positions. As he stood talking to Lieut. F. Bulman, the platoon commander, he saw a large column of vehicles not more than two thousand yards away to the south-west. Bulman said it was the first he had seen of them and that they must have come up in the night. Most of the vehicles seemed to be British but there was a possibility that they had been captured at Tobruk and were in fact driven by Germans. Pitt and Bulman were not long left in doubt. As they watched through binoculars, a British truck drove past the column towards the B Company positions followed by a British despatch rider, both going very fast. Suddenly there was a long burst of machine-gun fire, easily recognisable as Spandau, from the direction of the column, and the British truck pulled up in flames, short of the B Company positions. There was no doubt that the column was enemy and it was the first of many German and Italian supply convoys to use this route across the front of B Company during the course of the day. Pitt called Battalion H.Q. on the wireless and the artillery supporting 151 Brigade soon ranged on this excellent target. At intervals, a cloud of smoke indicated that one of the enemy trucks had been hit and set on fire.

Soon after this the Germans launched a fierce frontal attack against the 9th D.L.I. on the left flank of the 8th Battalion and, simultaneously, German 88-milimetre anti-tank guns engaged a squadron of Honey tanks, moving down the line of telegraph wires immediately behind Captain Pitt's company area. One tank was hit and, as the crew baled out and ran past the infantry company H.Q., a tank corps colonel shouted to Pitt, " Keep an eye on my tank, old man. I'll be back for it." He never returned and when, a few minutes later, a Bren carrier with the tanks was drilled amidships the Honeys made off.

For the next two or three hours a battle raged furiously for the 9th Battalion positions and slowly but surely the ferocity of the repeated German attacks wore down the resistance of the D.L.I. Battalion.

It was during this fierce action that Pte. Adam Herbert Wakenshaw of the 9th Battalion the Durham L. I. won the Victoria Cross and we are privileged to have the opportunity of printing the story of this gallant action in the pages of the 8th Battalion History.

Pte. Wakenshaw was a member of the crew of a 9th Battalion 2-pounder anti-tank gun that was sited on a forward slope in front of the infantry position. When the enemy attacked, one of their tracked vehicles towing a light gun was brought to within short range of the position. The D.L.I. crew opened fire and succeeded in putting a round through the engine, immobilising the enemy vehicle.

Another mobile gun then came into action. All members of the crew manning the 2-pounder, including Private Wakenshaw, were killed or seriously wounded and the 2-pounder was silenced. In this respite the enemy moved forward towards the damaged tractor in order to get the light gun into action against our infantry.

Realising the danger to his comrades, under intense mortar and artillery fire which swept the gun site, Pte. Wakenshaw crawled back to his gun. Although his left arm was blown off above the elbow, he loaded the gun with one arm and fired five more rounds. These succeeded in setting the tractor on fire, and damaged the light gun. A near miss then killed the gun aimer and blew Pte. Wakenshaw away from the gun, giving him further severe wounds. Undeterred he slowly dragged himself back to the gun, placed a round in the breech, and was preparing to fire when a direct hit on the ammunition killed him and destroyed the gun.

In the evening after the action, the body of Pte. Wakenshaw was found stretched out at the back of the breech block beside the ammunition box.

The ferocity of the assault against the 9th D.L.I. positions and the fact that the Germans were suffering and accepting heavy casualties in their daylight attack indicated that at all costs the enemy had determined to wipe out the Battalion. Eventually the 9th D.L.I. was overrun and the survivors were herded together into a long column and marched away out of sight of the 8th Battalion positions.

The loss of the 9th D.L.I. was a heavy blow as it left the southern flank of the 8th Battalion dangerously exposed. However, the Germans had paid dearly for the capture of the 9th D.L.I. They did not exploit their success by switching their assault troops against the 8th D.L.I. positions and there was a lull in the battle.

During this lull a British armoured car of a G.H.Q. Reconnaissance Unit, searching for information of the battle, nosed its way cautiously up a wadi to Captain Pitt's Company H.Q. A young officer wearing the badge of one of our more illustrious cavalry regiments leaned out of the turret. " What's going on here?" he inquired of Captain Pitt, who gave him a detailed account of the situation as he knew it and the cavalryman then called up his headquarters on the wireless and proceeded to give a running commentary, rather on the lines of Raymond Glendenning of the B.B.C., as if he was the originator of the information. Warm congratulations came back to him over the air and everyone was obviously well pleased. Cigarettes were exchanged while Pitt and the armoured car commander chatted about the merits or otherwise of their respective jobs. The man from the Reconnaissance Regiment seemed rather surprised to have found British infantry and his parting words were, " It has been so nice meeting somebody one can talk to. They usually give these jobs to black men." With that he tapped his driver on the shoulder and Pitt's indignant answer was drowned by the roar of the engine as the armoured car moved away.

The rest of the day on the Battalion front was fairly quiet although enemy shelling, which was becoming more intense, caused some casualties in the company areas ; one man was killed and several others wounded. By the middle of the afternoon the German columns had moved round out of sight to the south and were presumably continuing eastwards. This was in fact the case and, whilst the Italians closed in on Matruh along the coast road from the west, the Germans continued to by-pass Matruh and collected in the Mingar Qa'aim area some eight miles to the south of the 8th Battalion positions where they were well placed to strike northwards into Matruh, at the same time taking some of the British forces in the rear. It may well be the case that the 9th D.L.I. had been cleared out of the way with such thrust and determination to facilitate the operation of this proposed German assault.

At this stage of the battle General Ritchie decided to launch an attack with 50 Division and 5 Indian Division against the Germans in the Mingar Qa'aim area that night. The two divisions were ordered to carry out a raid in transport with the object of cutting and disorganising the enemy lines of communication. Command of 151

Imperial War Museum

The morning after the D.L.I. Brigade had fought its way out of the Gazala Line. A cheerful group of 8th Battalion men—most of them from the M.T. Platoon—at a Report Centre. Cpl. T. Young and Sgt. J. R. Hannah are leaning on the cab of the truck with Pte. J. Anderson, Cpl. W. Miller, Cpl. C. Stead, Cpl. J. McFarlane and Pte. T. Proudfoot behind them.

Brigade had now been assumed by Colonel Dewing of the Royal Artillery and during the afternoon he gave out orders at Brigade H.Q. With the 9th Battalion out of the battle only the 6th and 8th were available and Colonel Dewing directed the 6th Battalion on the left and the 8th Battalion on the right of the 151 Brigade attack.

At 4 p.m. the 8th Battalion company commanders were summoned to Battalion H.Q. where they waited until eventually Lieut.-Colonel Jackson returned from Brigade H.Q. to give out his orders. The Battalion, less C Company which was to be detached, was to form up at last light in a tight column on the right flank of the brigade and was then to drive south through the German lines and the enemy columns moving eastwards to Mingar Qa'aim. Every German laager and group of vehicles was to be attacked and destroyed, and having reached an assembly area, there was a possibility that the Battalion would then have to return to Matruh. It sounded a crazy plan—another attack on wheels with all its disadvantages—but the successful action of the Division at Gazala had apparently convinced the Army Commander that the " Gazala Gazelles" could succeed with a repeat performance.

At last light the Battalion column formed up in good order under light shellfire from a German 105-millimetre gun which had obviously been positioned to harass the D.L.I. Brigade. Then a slight setback occurred. It had been arranged that a wave of Honey tanks would precede the Battalion column. However, an error was made in the timing arrangements. The Honeys started off before they should have done and ran into heavy anti-tank fire. They wheeled about and the men of the 8th Battalion first saw the tanks which were supposed to support them as they raced back over the desert towards the Battalion. Somebody shouted that they were German and within a matter of seconds several machine-guns and Brens were firing at the Honeys. No damage was done but the tank commander quite rightly objected to this unfriendly reception and the tanks disappeared, leaving the Battalion without their support for the operation.

There was a full moon and as the 8th Battalion column moved south and passed through the area where the battle with the 9th Battalion had taken place, it was possible to pick out the shapes of abandoned vehicles, knocked out by the German gunfire. Some, having burned themselves out, were just piles of charred wreckage. The column moved cautiously towards a ridge over which enemy convoys had been passing all day. The Bren carriers were in front with orders to charge and open fire at any vehicles which came into sight. It was an eerie experience, travelling in this column with dark, moving shapes on the flanks. Suddenly the carriers came upon a small group of German trucks and opened fire. The rattle of the Bren guns was soon joined by the stutter of Vickers guns which had been mounted in the open backs of 15 cwt trucks. However, the Germans taking evasive action, got away to the south.

By this time the 6th D.L.I. column and the several columns of 69

Brigade and 5 Indian Division had contacted groups of enemy and there were minor skirmishes going on to the north, south, east and west. It was a glorious " free for all," nobody being sure who was friend or foe. After the 8th Battalion column had travelled four miles, a halt was called in the area of the first objective to allow vehicles which had fallen into slit trenches to be extricated and whilst the column was stationary it was engaged by enemy anti-tank guns. British anti-tank guns, the new six-pounders, returned the fire until the engagement had to be broken off because a column—thought to be the 6th Battalion—came into the line of fire. Whilst the 8th was still stationary a German eight-wheeled armoured car, its driver obviously unaware that the vehicles were British, glided quietly into the middle of the column and parked alongside one of the Battalion two-pounder anti-tank guns which was on its portee. The N.C.O. in charge of the gun could hardly believe his luck. After taking a second look at the black cross on the turret of the armoured car he put a round through the enemy vehicle at five yards range to knock it out.

Soon after this incident the 8th moved on again, continuing towards the second and final objective in the face of sporadic enemy fire. Three enemy trucks suddenly came into view, moving across the path of the column, and the Bren Carriers went into action again but two of the trucks turned off to the south and escaped. The third vehicle—a captured British gun tractor—was intercepted, although the driver managed to get away in the darkness.

Shortly after this a large column of vehicles, thought to be from 5 Indian Division, was seen moving away to the west, but before contact could be made the vehicles drove off at high speed and voices in Italian were heard. The whole operation was rapidly becoming equally confusing to both sides and Captain Pitt with B Company had an amusing experience which will serve to illustrate the chaotic state of affairs. His truck drove for several hundred yards alongside a three-tonner before Pitt, glancing sideways, noticed that the driver was wearing a German cap. The German saw Pitt at the same time and turned his truck round by swerving it violently to flee from the British column. This was no isolated incident. That night held many similar experiences in store for the men of 50 and 5 Indian Divisions. British columns mingled with enemy supply convoys made up of captured British vehicles, and it was impossible to identify friend from foe without driving alongside a suspicious vehicle to take a good look at the driver.

The Brigade H.Q. column with Colonel Dewing leading suddenly came upon a laager of seven or eight German supply lorries. A 15 cwt truck with a machine-gun mounted on the back was manoeuvred into position as the unsuspecting drivers of the German vehicles sat around the cab of one of the lorries, singing to the accompaniment of a guitar. A whispered word of command and the machine-gunners opened fire to rake the enemy vehicles and group of drivers. It was all over in a few seconds and those Germans who had not been killed outright were taken prisoner. There were many such incidents and there is no doubt that the drive south by 5 and 50 Divisions took the enemy by surprise, and threw at least some of his night laagers into confusion.

Meanwhile the 8th Battalion was still under sporadic fire as it neared the final objective—the limit set for the column's penetration. It was an eerie experience as the vehicles advanced towards blue and white enemy anti-tank tracer shells which appeared to bounce fifty to sixty feet at a time as they came towards the column. When the Battalion reached the objective, the whole area where the units of 50 Division were operating presented a confused appearance with both sides firing tracer in all directions without much apparent result. To add to the effect of a large scale fireworks display R.A.F. bombers appeared on the scene and, after lighting the area with flares to try to find out what was going on, proceeded systematically to bomb both sides without discrimination.

The Battalion column waited on the final objective until ordered by Brigade H.Q. to return to its original positions outside Matruh and the trucks formed up facing north. The return journey was much quieter despite the fact that the whole Battalion passed right through the centre of an Italian laager. It was reminiscent of the old Red Indian days. As the vehicles accelerated and drove through the groups of Italian lorries and bivouacs, passengers sitting next to the drivers propped rifles and Bren guns on the truck doors and fired into the laager. The column soon broke clear and as it sped on the shouting of the Italians grew fainter. The Battalion reached its original positions on the telegraph lines just as day was breaking. Although the attack by the two divisions had obviously caused a lot of confusion in the enemy lines of communication, there were many in the 8th Battalion who felt that the operation had disorganised the British forces as much as it had the Germans. For it had not been carried out without casualties, and trucks and men were missing when a count was taken just after daybreak. However, the worst part of the battle of Mersa Matruh was yet to come.

CHAPTER TWELVE

THE FIGHTING AT MATRUH

Rommel's forces close in—a tank attack repulsed—the breakout from Matruh—trapped in a wadi—retreat to El Alamein.

To the east of Mersa Matruh there is a flat coastal strip which extends inland for about a mile and then rises sharply to a high rocky escarpment. Previously the Battalion had been on top of the escarpment but was now ordered to move down to a rest area on the coastal strip. The column vehicles, including the supporting arms, wound their way down the steep slope to the new area where breakfast was prepared. The D.L.I. Brigade was deployed in a box formation in the rest area as a protection against tank attack but, although the enemy confined himself only to slight shelling from the east, it was difficult for the troops to get much rest because of the fierce heat and almost complete lack of cover.

Whilst the Battalion and the other units of 50 Division, which had also returned to Matruh after the night operation, spent the morning reorganising, cleaning weapons, checking ammunition and servicing vehicles, the Germans in the Mingar Qa'aim area launched their attack northwards towards Matruh. They were met and held by General Freyberg's New Zealanders and the tanks of the Queen's Bays. Five times during the course of the day the cream of the German assault troops was hurled against the New Zealand Division and the British armour ; five times they were sent reeling back, the New Zealanders yielding not an inch to tanks or infantry. It was a magnificent stand, but Freyberg's men could not hold the German advance indefinitely, and by midday it had become clear to the Army Commander that the New Zealanders would have to withdraw that night, leaving 50 Division in a precarious position in the exposed rest area below the escarpment. The Division was therefore ordered to break out through the German lines that night and to withdraw some thirty-five miles eastwards to the neighbourhood of Fuka, an R.A.F. landing ground close to the coastal road. It was to be another breakout on the Gazala scale and this time the Germans would be ready and waiting for just such a move.

During the afternoon the company commanders and commanders of the supporting arms were summoned to Battalion H.Q. Lieut.-Colonel Jackson confirmed their worst fears by telling them that the German columns which had by-passed Matruh the previous day had swept round to the south and then northwards to cut the coastal road a few miles to the east of the Battalion positions. Furthermore, although the New Zealanders were holding the main thrust, German tanks were closing in from the south and would soon be overlooking the rest area from the edge of the escarpment. It was gloomy news indeed ; with the coastal road cut to the east the only alternative for 50 Division was to wait until dark, then climb the escarpment and break through the German screen, afterwards sweeping east towards Fuka. Each battalion in the Division, with its supporting arms, was to be formed into a single column and Battalion commanders were responsible for having routes reconnoitred over the escarpment.

The C.O. was still issuing his orders when Major Bogue, commanding the battery of 65th Anti-Tank Regiment in support of the 8th Battalion, drove up in his truck to the edge of the small depression where the C.O. was holding his conference. He leaned out of the driving cab : " Major Fawkes reports a tank attack developing from the west." This rather startling news was confirmed almost immediately by the appearance of enemy tanks, some three or four thousand yards away towards the escarpment. The Germans, using captured Honey tanks supported by eight-wheeled armoured cars, were endeavouring to come down the escarpment with the object of destroying some of the tightly packed and vulnerable maintenance vehicles of the Division parked on the coastal strip.

The conference broke up immediately and the C.O.'s parting words were, " Whatever happens, the Fuka outpost will be held." The company commanders hurried back to their areas and as the riflemen could not take a very important part in the action that was to follow, they sat back and watched the Battalion anti-tank guns go into action. Lieut. Catford, who with Sgt. Bewick—his troop sergeant—had represented the anti-tank platoon at the conference, ran with Bewick two hundred yards to his troop of guns. Quickly the two-pounders were manhandled off their portees and dragged into position on a forward slope. There was no cover of any description but the ground was thick with camel thorn, and Catford reckoned that until the troop opened fire the guns would be difficult to locate from a distance once the portees were out of the way.

The Battalion two-pounders, sighted roughly in line with about twenty-five yards between each, were commanded respectively by Cpl. T. Fenwick, L/Cpl. F. Rimmer and L/Cpl. B. C. Warren. The fourth gun, having developed a mechanical defect during the withdrawal from the Gazala Line, remained on its portee. Meanwhile the German tanks had come down the escarpment to open fire on some of the vehicles and for a moment it looked as though there would be a stampede of trucks. Then there was a sharp crack as the first of Catford's guns opened fire at 1300 yards—a long range for two-pounders—to be followed by the other two guns. In spite of the range the shooting was very accurate, especially that of the gun commanded by Cpl. Fenwick. Within the space of a few moments an ugly situation was reversed and three of the Honey tanks were hit and burst into flames. Catford's troop was using American manufactured ammunition issued to the Battalion only a few weeks previously, which had a somewhat larger charge than the ammunition normally used and gave better penetration. Two of the German armoured cars were then knocked out, by which time several South African guns had backed into position farther up the slope behind the two-pounders and had opened fire from portees.

Another group of German tanks, in position on the escarpment to the south, was firing solid shot at Catford's guns, a number of shells falling among the portees, kicking up small clouds of dust as they ricocheted away towards the sea. Two more tanks were then put out of action by the combined fire of the Battalion anti-tank guns and the South Africans, forcing the remainder of the enemy tanks to withdraw. It had been a most successful action with five tanks and two enemy armoured cars destroyed at no loss to the 8th Battalion.

Meanwhile, on the escarpment to the south enemy infantry had appeared and were forming up to attack from the high ground. Their ranks were broken by the heavy and accurate fire from the machine-guns of the Cheshires and the shelling of the 11th R.H.A. The enemy formed up repeatedly only to be scattered by the British machine-gun and shellfire, which finally forced them to give up the attempt and the attack was called off. For the time being the 8th Battalion had held the German thrust, and as darkness closed in there was a lull marked chiefly by the arrival of Lieut. R. Place from Mersa Matruh with a truckload of beer. Place, who had been sent down to Matruh earlier in the day to collect ammunition, had picked up the beer at the bulk N.A.A.F.I. where the staff were only too pleased to get rid of it. As there was no means of moving the beer back to Egypt it would either have to be destroyed or allowed to fall into the hands of the Germans and Italians. The welcome beverage was promptly distributed to the companies and it improved morale considerably for the forthcoming night operation.

The Battalion was formed into two columns ; No. 9 column, with B Company as the infantry element, was commanded by the C.O., and No. 10 column, with D Company as the infantry element, was commanded by Major H. Sell. Captain C. L. Beattie of the Support Company, who had been sent to locate C Company in the wadi where it had stayed when the Battalion attacked the lines of communication the night before, reported that there was no sign of the company. The Battalion had to go into action without C Company which, however, was to turn up later.

Lieut. J. Parker, the 8th Battalion guide, had reconnoitred the route over the escarpment and at 9 p.m. the Battalion was ready to move off. Parker in his vehicle at the head of No. 9 column led the way up the escarpment by way of a rough track which passed a wrecked Hurricane. The track and the wadis leading upwards were very narrow and in the gathering darkness the vehicles wound slowly up the escarpment in single file. The men of the 8th Battalion did not know what sort of reception they would get but they feared the worst and their fears were not unfounded.

As the column entered a wadi, still climbing the escarpment, several enemy tanks and a convoy of enemy transport could just be distinguished at the far end of the wadi, moving across the Battalion axis of advance. The C.O. and Lieut. Parker, at the head of No. 9 column, made frantic efforts to find a suitable detour which would by-pass the enemy and at the same time take the two Battalion columns over the top of the escarpment, which was very steep at this point. It was too late ; the Germans had already seen the British trucks and there was a single warning rifle shot from a German sentry. Up went a dozen or more Verey lights which immediately turned night into day, and when about twenty vehicles at the head of No. 9 column reached the top of the escarpment the enemy opened fire. At this stage the rear part of No. 10 column parted company with the rest of the Battalion as it was obvious that the C.O.'s column and the leading vehicles of No. 10 column had run into a trap. Orders were shouted from truck to truck, " Every man for himself."

As soon as the enemy guns started shooting, the head of No. 9 column turned away from the German fire and ran off the escarpment into a narrow, steep-sided wadi. It would have been better for the British vehicles had they run the gauntlet of fire and made a break for it across the escarpment, for the Germans were not slow to grasp this heaven-sent opportunity of trapping the leading vehicles of the Battalion. Dragging their anti-tank guns into position on the lip of the wadi they opened a murderous fire on the vehicles massed nose to tail below them. Troop-carriers burst into flames as their occupants scrambled out with Bren guns to return the German fire.

The wadi was almost a cul de sac, with a very steep slope at the end of it leading on to the escarpment. One man afterwards described the slope as being " like the side of a house." Although quite a number of vehicles had succeeded in getting over the top, a three-tonner had stalled its engine below the crest and, until it was able to move on, the rest of the trucks in the bed of the wadi could not get forward.

The troops in the three-tonner having debussed were making superhuman efforts to push the heavy vehicle over the top. At last they succeeded and as the lorry accelerated on to the escarpment the rest of the vehicles in the wadi started to move forward. One by one the trucks which had not been hit went over the top, and as they breasted the rise on to the skyline they ran the gauntlet of German fire, for the enemy had sited a machine-gun to sweep the escarpment at this exit from the wadi. Once safely over the top they set their course independently for Fuka, as by now the Battalion had been well broken up. The C.O. with his Adjutant, Captain G. P. Chambers, stood on top of the escarpment, the two of them acting as traffic policemen whilst just below them on the slope, several riflemen had taken up positions amongst the hard rocks and were trying to reply to the fierce fire which still swept the wadi.

By this time some semblance of order had been restored in the bed of the wadi, mainly by R.S.M. A. Jennings and Pte. G. R. Fearon. In the midst of the chaos when the Germans first opened fire the

R.S.M. had quickly taken control of the situation. He positioned Bren guns to reply to the German fire and himself mounted a 2″ Mortar in the bed of the wadi to send bomb after bomb arcing upwards to fall with amazing accuracy on top of the escarpment, where the German gun crews were out in the open, unable to dig in because of the rocky ground. He personally observed the fire of the 2″ Mortar and the Brens and in doing so was almost continually exposed to heavy fire. Screams and shouts soon told Jennings that the shrapnel from his bursting mortar bombs was having good effect, and he scored a direct hit on a German machine-gun post, killing the crew. This considerably eased the situation in the bed of the wadi although the exit over the skyline was still under fire.

One of the Battalion Bren guns, manned by Pte. Fearon, was taking a heavy toll of the enemy. Fearon jumped out of his truck and placed the gun in position as soon as the column was fired on. He then kept the gun in action for an hour, the whole time under heavy machine-gun fire at very close range from the enemy who were only a hundred yards or so away. Magazine after magazine was fired at the Germans on top of the escarpment ; the steady, accurate shooting must have caused many casualties. There is no doubt that the R.S.M. and Pte. Fearon were responsible for a large number of men and vehicles getting out of the wadi safely, and R.S.M. Jennings was awarded the Distinguished Conduct Medal and Pte. Fearon the Military Medal.

Meanwhile, at the head of the wadi, Captain Pitt's truck went over the top with Pitt and his batman pushing at the back, and then a three-ton lorry came along. Swinging hard over to the right, it's driver accelerated fiercely to tackle the slope. There was a burst of German fire which ripped through the driver's cab sending the truck plunging out of control into the bed of the wadi again. Then a Sapper's truck tackled the climb but the engine stalled just below the crest ; the truck came to a halt in an almost perpendicular position. The small party of 8th Battalion men crouching on the slope could hear the groans of a wounded man coming from the back of the truck. Then the Germans opened fire on the stranded vehicle and two 8th Battalion men crawled forward across the rocky ground, one of them to cut the straps which secured the tarpaulin flaps at the back of the truck. As the Germans continued to fire, the wounded man—a Sapper—was dragged out of the back of the truck and carried to safety. He was taken half a mile across the escarpment and put aboard a three-tonner which had halted to check its bearings.

Fortunately the Sapper's truck had not blocked the exit and the flow of vehicles over the top continued until the bed of the wadi was almost clear. The only vehicles remaining were the heavy troop-carrying lorries which had been knocked out during those first few minutes of chaos. Another truck which also stalled before reaching the crest, was the subject of a rather amusing incident. When the truck stopped, the passengers—a Brigade liaison officer and his batman—jumped out to push from behind as the driver revved the engine. Eventually the truck surged forward and that was the last the officer and batman saw of the truck or driver for the next three days.

Due to the R.S.M. getting the 2″ mortar and also the Bren guns into action, most of No. 9 column eventually got clear of the wadi but the troop-carriers of No. 10 column at the German end of the wadi —which had caught the full force of the enemy fire at the start of the attack—had nearly all been wrecked and most of D Company were either killed or taken prisoner.

However, Lieut. P. Hampson of D Company got away in a Bren carrier. When the Germans opened fire Hampson decided to make a break for it across the escarpment instead of following the other vehicles into the wadi. An enemy machine-gun—with a British ambulance blazing beside it—opened fire at almost point blank range as the carrier set off. As the British vehicle swept by, Hampson leaned over to fire his revolver and hit one of the machine-gun crew in the stomach. The German could be seen quite plainly in the glow from the burning ambulance as he doubled up beside the gun. The carrier passed two German tanks and, a hundred yards farther on, the crew of a German 88-millimetre anti-tank gun shouted for it to stop. Hampson did stop but not before he had covered another sixty yards when he halted the carrier in a small hollow.

With Sgt. Tennant he crept back and saw the Germans standing around the gun. Hampson whispered to Tennant, "Go back and get the Bren. This is the best target I ever had." Tennant was gone only a few minutes. When he returned with the Bren and a pouch of magazines, the sergeant positioned the gun and pressed the trigger; nothing happened. He cleared the gun and tried again but still the Bren would not fire. It had sand in the mechanism. There were no grenades in the carrier and only one rifle, so reluctantly Hampson and Tennant climbed aboard and started off again. As the carrier moved forward, Captain Beattie came out of the darkness and flung himself aboard. His truck had been hit and gone up in flames. The carrier then picked up an Indian and a Senussi corporal and with this heavy load aboard eventually caught up with the C.O. and Captain Chambers who by this time had left the exit to the wadi. Not all the trucks which made the break across the escarpment instead of going down into the wadi had such an exciting journey as Hampson's carrier. Most of them had a much quieter night as they raced for safety across the uneven surface of the desert.

The nature of the breakout meant that everybody in the Battalion had to run a gauntlet of some sort to get through the enemy lines. When trucks of the Battalion B Echelon group were swept by heavy machine-gun fire, several were put out of action and their occupants killed or wounded. It was then that Pte. B. Holmes of the 8th Battalion won the Military Medal. Although under heavy fire he went to the assistance of some wounded men, dressed their wounds and then brought them out of danger. By leaving his own truck he risked being stranded in the enemy position but calmly accepted this risk, and in so doing saved the lives of several of his comrades who would otherwise probably have died of their wounds through lack of attention.

When another group of trucks came under heavy machine-gun fire and shelling Pte. J. W. Wood went out into the open when the German fire was at its heaviest to attend to the wounded. Under almost constant machine-gun fire he collected the wounded, bandaged them and then placed them in his own truck which was safely evacuated. Soon after this his truck was also damaged, and Pte. Wood transferred the wounded to another vehicle which eventually reached safety. To help his comrades he had not only risked his life but had left the security of his own vehicle in enemy territory. He was awarded the Military Medal.

Once clear of the death trap in the wadi the 8th Battalion columns, which now numbered a dozen or more instead of the original two, set course for Fuka. The rest of 50 Division, having by this time been considerably dispersed, consisted of dozens of small columns. All night they raced across the desert at speeds up to sixty miles an hour which meant a nasty accident for any trucks which were unfortunate enough to run into slit trenches, and there were many narrow escapes as the columns drove through German and Italian laagers. One 8th Battalion column ran parallel to a German supply convoy for several miles, gradually dropping behind the enemy vehicles to eventually break away unmolested. A lone three-tonner with a courageous 8th Battalion corporal on the roof of the driving cab drove alongside a German Mercedes Benz staff car and the corporal calmly tossed a hand grenade into the back of the open car as the three-tonner wheeled away.

Just before dawn on the 29th a thick mist descended over the desert which persisted when daylight came, very efficiently hiding the many 50 Division columns from marauding German tank forces. By this time hundreds of vehicles had almost reached Fuka, and when the mist lifted, the columns increased their speed, eventually contacting a screen of British tanks and forward troops. Fuka was already in German hands and the men of 50 Division were advised to make for the El Alamein Line—some forty-five miles to the east. One or two columns, not being warned, made for Fuka where they were trapped by the Germans. It was here that Major Sell of D Company was taken prisoner.

As the Battalion groups pushed on towards Alamein two or three of them would join forces to form a larger group and stragglers were also rejoining the columns. Whereas at first it had seemed as though most of the 8th Battalion had been wiped out in the breakout from Matruh, things were by this time beginning to look much brighter. During June 29th the various groups of 50 Division travelled fast all day and air observers saw an amazing sight as the columns moved towards the safety of the Alamein Line, each one throwing up its own tell-tale cloud of dust. It looked like a sea of moving vehicles.

Most of the 8th Battalion trucks arrived at the single trip wire which marked the forward limits of the Line late that evening. An Indian Division was in the area and the Battalion spent the night outside the minefield not far from the Indian laagers. The men who had driven the trucks throughout that nightmare journey from Mersa Matruh just switched off their engines and fell asleep over the driving wheels. The men inside the trucks tumbled out on to the hard ground to stretch themselves full length under the stars. For the time being they were out of danger and truly thankful.

Early the following morning—June 30th—the 8th Battalion groups passed through a minefield gap in the Line. There was considerable activity as anti-tank guns were being manoeuvred into position. South African and Indian infantry sweated as they dug trenches. Concrete pillboxes were being manned and minefields reinforced. It was most reassuring, and reasonable to suppose that here at last Rommel would be halted.

The Battalion transport vehicles were now breaking down in increasing numbers. Some of them looked as though they were returning from a Brighton outing, with men from trucks which had been abandoned clinging precariously to the sides of those which were still running. By this time most of the vehicles in the Battalion had covered something like thirty or forty thousand miles, under shocking conditions of wear and tear since they had left the factory. It was no wonder that some of them broke down.

After a short rest two miles east of the line, where the remnants of the Battalion re-formed to some extent, the 8th was directed to a Divisional Rest Area at El Hamman, twenty miles to the east of the Alamein Line. The missing company—C Company—rejoined the Battalion here and there were some happy reunions as, during the rest of the afternoon and evening, vehicles of all sorts trickled into the Battalion lines. However, the Matruh breakout had been an expensive action. Casualties had been heavy and no less than seventeen three-ton troop-carrying lorries were lost, many of them in the wadi. As one of the surviving R.A.S.C. drivers put it, " There's never a dull moment when we're carrying the Durhams."

CHAPTER THIRTEEN

BEHIND THE ALAMEIN LINE

Rest area at Mariopolis—leave in " Alex."—B Company is lost in an abortive attack.

ROMMEL had followed hard on the heels of the retreating Eighth Army during June 29th and 30th and his forward elements arrived in front of the Alamein positions early in the afternoon of the second day. It was along the length of the Alamein Line, not forty miles from Alexandria, that the Axis forces were halted. Largely due to General Auchinleck's foresight a great deal of work had been carried out on the Alamein defences and, in addition to this, both flanks of the Line had natural protection. On the northern flank was the Mediterranean with the British Navy and, on the southern, the impassable Qattara Depression—forty miles to the south.

There was no way in which an army could outflank the Line and the German commander knew that his best chance of success was to attack immediately, forcing a breach before the Eighth Army could settle down after its long and difficult retreat and before the arrival of reinforcements. On July 1st the German 90 Light Division, supported by the Italian Trento Division and twenty tanks, launched repeated attacks against the South Africans in the northern sector but, although these attacks were supported by Stuka dive-bombers, the South Africans held their ground. Further south, the sector held by 18 Indian Infantry Brigade on the western end of the Ruweisat Ridge was also heavily attacked. The Indian brigade kept the enemy at bay during the day but the positions were overwhelmed that night and thus a key position in the Alamein Line was lost. The next three days were extremely critical but 50 Division took no part in the fierce fighting which raged between the British and Dominion troops and the Germans and Italians who had gained a footing in the Line. The Division was in no fit state to take any part in this battle and on July 1st—the day Rommel attacked—50 Division left El Hamman for Mariopolis Camp, Amyria, not more than an hour by truck from Alexandria.

It does not come within the scope of this history to describe in detail the fighting which took place between July 1st and July 3rd. Sufficient to say that under the brilliant leadership of " the Auk " —who by this time had taken over direct command of the Desert Army—British and Dominion infantry with British armoured formations fought the enemy to a standstill and closed the gap. By the evening of July 3rd the Line was safe and the British commander had regained the initiative which had been Rommel's since the fall of Bir Hacheim.

July 3rd found the 8th Battalion in the fly-ridden camp of Mariopolis. After the tension and uncertainty of the Gazala and Matruh operations it was pleasant to relax whilst the D.L.I. Brigade re-formed but the camp itself—a collection of tents, corrugated cook-houses and wash-houses—was most depressing. The landing grounds of the Desert Air Force were close by and squadrons of fighters and medium bombers, operating an almost continuous shuttle service over the Alamein Line during the day, were responsible for the permanent dust curtain which enveloped the Mariopolis area, making it more unpleasant than ever. Every time a plane took off or taxied in after landing it created a miniature sandstorm.

The Battalion was willing to put up with the frequent dust storms and the flies—much worse than they had been at Gazala—for Alexandria was within easy distance, and " Alex," as it was affectionately known by the men of the Desert Army, was well worth visiting for a variety of reasons. The Battalion three-tonners left Mariopolis about mid-morning after the Adjutant and R.S.M. had inspected the leave parties and within an hour the trucks were parked in Alexandria. Unlike Cairo the city is fairly clean and the sea breezes which blow in from the Mediterranean give it an air of freshness which is entirely lacking in Cairo. Within the space of a few hours the troops became civilised again. They took cooling baths which rinsed the sand out of their hair and cleansed the pores of their bodies ; they lay back in the barber's chairs while Egyptian barbers shaved them and they had their boots polished to a mirror-like finish by the tousle-headed shoeshine boys. They wandered round the shops buying presents for the people at home who had not yet heard that they were safe. When the lights began to twinkle in "Alex," and the strains of dance music came to them from the cabarets, they had to go back to the dust and dirt of Mariopolis camp. But they were thankful for small mercies and a day in " Alex " reassured them that there was another world apart from the desert—still sane and civilised.

Most of the men in 50 Division spent more than a few hours in Alexandria. A Divisional Leave Camp was opened on the outskirts of the city at Sidi Bishir—just as pleasant as it sounds—and the large majority of the troops spent at least a week here whilst the Division was out of the line. This free and easy camp was run by Captain H. Iris, the Divisional Provost Marshal, and the Commandant and his Adjutant did not mind very much whether a man on leave came in at night through the main gate or under the perimeter wire. The food, under the expert supervision of the Divisional Catering Officer was excellent, but even this was not enough to induce the troops to stay in camp for their meals. They were off to Alexandria directly after breakfast and most of them did not return until late in the evening. The food which was not eaten each day would have fed two infantry companies. Shortly after a new leave party arrived, General Nicholls inspected the camp and, although it was almost deserted, he found five or six men eating a cold lunch of salads and pressed beef in one of the mess tents. The Divisional Commander was very much impressed by the quality and quantity of the food and turned to one of the men : "Well anyway," he said, "you feed well in this rest camp." Back came the reply : "We ought to sir. We're the cooks."

At Mariopolis camp during the early part of July the remnants of the Battalion were re-organised and reinforced. The twenty-six surviving members of D Company were split up between the other rifle companies and a draft of forty-six other ranks joined the Battalion. Even with this new draft the 8th was well below War Establishment, a state of affairs which persisted in most of the divisional units.

On July 8th Major Clarke went to command the 9th Battalion. He had been with the 8th since pre-war days as peacetime Adjutant at Gilesgate. The battalion was sorry to see him go but his promotion was well deserved and he was to make an excellent commanding officer. Major G. Lance of the Somerset Light Infantry came from the Middle East Training Centre as Second-in-Command of the 8th Battalion and Captain G. P. Chambers, who had been Adjutant, was promoted Major and given command of S Company. Captain J. Parker became Adjutant. The other company commanders were Captain R. I. Pitt (B Company) and Captain A. A. E. Jones (C Company).

A and D Companies were not formed at Mariopolis and, with the Battalion so much reduced in numbers, it was difficult to plan any ambitious training programmes. A number of vacancies for courses at the Middle East Training Centre were alloted to the Battalion and several officers—including the C.O.—left Mariopolis on July 24th for Palestine and the comforts of the M.E.T.C., not far from Tel Aviv. In those days the citizens of Tel Aviv were not so hostile towards British troops and it was a good spot in which to spend a week-end.

The day after the party of officers left for Palestine a warning order was received from Brigade H.Q. that one rifle company was to be provided by the 8th Battalion for operations with the 6th D.L.I. under command of Lieut.-Colonel C. L. Battiscombe. The Battalion had been so denuded to provide officers and men for the rest camp, for various courses, and a digging party in the Alamein Line that there was only one company which could be sent to the 6th D.L.I. This was B Company, in splendid isolation at Mariopolis Camp and commanded by Captain Pitt with only one other officer—Captain B. Lindsay.

When Pitt was called to a conference at Brigade H.Q. he learned that a composite D.L.I. Battalion was required for a special digging job in the Alamein Line. The battalion was to consist of three rifle companies ; one from the 6th Battalion, one from the 8th and a third from the 9th battalion. The digging job was not specified at the conference.

The composite battalion, however, had been given a much more unpleasant task than digging reserve positions in the Alamein Line. Since July 5th Rommel had accepted the check at Alamein and set up an anti-tank screen of infantry and 88-millimetre guns, running from north-east to south-west. However, the British commander was not content to sit back and wait for Rommel to strike. In the northern sector the whole of the newly-arrived 9 Australian Division, with the South African Division, launched a big attack on July 9th and both divisions reached their objectives, holding them against counter-attacks. An attempt by British tank forces to exploit the success failed and a position of virtual equilibrium was reached which was to last until Rommel launched his big offensive on August 30th.

Neither side was very willing to accept this stalemate and there were some fierce battles for position. Three substantial British attacks were delivered. The first two were costly failures and the general result of their actions was disappointing. The third attack, planned for the night of July 26th/27th, involved the composite battalion and it was for this task that the battalion had been formed and not for any digging operation. The attack, planned to capture Sanyet el Miteiriya in the central sector and the ridge running north-west from it, would also clear a passage for the British armour through the minefield east of Deir el Dhil. In the centre of the line a feint attack was to hold the enemy. The general plan was for the composite battalion from 151 Brigade and a battalion from 69 Brigade to attack in the south whilst 24 Australian Brigade advanced in the north. Both these assaults were to be strongly supported with artillery and tanks.

B Company of the 8th battalion left Mariopolis Camp soon after dawn on July 26th and, having joined up with the rest of the composite battalion, started the eighty-mile journey up to the Alamein Line. The battalion arrived east of Alamein Station just after midday. During the afternoon Lieut.-Colonel Battiscombe called a conference to explain the plan. The battalion objective was a prominent ridge, known locally as " Ruin Ridge " because of numerous attacks which had previously been launched against it without success. Running roughly east and west and jutting out like a bastion in the enemy defence line, it was strongly held by German and Italian infantry. From their well dug-in positions on the slopes they covered the thick minefield which had been laid all round the foot of the ridge.

The composite battalion had been ordered to attack the south-eastern slopes of " Ruin Ridge " whilst a battalion of Australians captured the north-eastern slopes. Considerable artillery support was available and the C.O. impressed on the officers at his conference that big developments depended on the success of the operation. If the ridge could be captured and held until the arrival of British armoured formations, it might well mean a break-through for the Eighth Army with " Benghazi first stop."

South African engineers had been detailed to clear a gap through the minefield at the foot of the ridge on the composite battalion front and to mark it with shielded lights. The C.O. put two companies forward—the 6th Battalion company commanded by Captain R. Cummings, and Captain Pitt's company. He ordered the 9th D.L.I. company, commanded by Captain A. Hartnell, to move in reserve.

At 8 p.m., under a full moon, B Company of the 8th D.L.I. waited in transport to move off down the track to Alamein Station. The men watched a seemingly endless procession of guns moving forward to positions from which they were going to cover the attack. Morale was high and jokes were cracked as the vehicles rolled by, for it was good to be on the attacking side again after so many weeks of " tip and run."

At last the trucks moved off and, turning south at the station, passed through a gap in the British minefield and then westwards towards the enemy. The vehicles followed a route marked by lights for about a mile and the troops then debussed under cover of a low ridge and went forward silently on foot to the start line. The companies were soon in position, the troops settling down to wait for zero hour. As the battalion was early, the men had to lie there for almost an hour, becoming colder and more nervous as the minutes ticked by. All was quiet and the desert was at peace except for the occasional bark of a German gun, firing at the Australian sector of the line on the right flank.

Then without any warning the British artillery went into action. It was a terrific barrage and the troops on the start line had never heard such heavy gunfire. One by one the batteries joined in until the thunder of the barrage was continuous, and the D.L.I. troops felt heartily glad that they were not at the receiving end. For fifteen minutes shells whistled overhead as the guns bombarded the German and Italian positions on the ridge. When the firing died away the Australian infantry could be heard cheering as they stormed their sector of the ridge. Unfortunately the D.L.I. battalion did not go forward simultaneously with the Australians. The start time was delayed for a further thirty minutes and, although no one in the battalion knew the reason at the time, it may have been because consecutive attacks on each side of the ridge instead of simultaneous ones were considered more disconcerting to the enemy. What happened in effect was that the D.L.I. battalion lost all the "shock" advantage of the barrage and the enemy infantry came out of their holes in the ground after the gunfire had stopped, to man their positions before the battalion attacked.

When at last the D.L.I. companies moved off in open formation to advance down the thousand yard slope to the enemy minefield, like a ghost battalion in the moonlight, the enemy was ready waiting and the battalion came under long-range and inaccurate fire which became uncomfortably accurate as the range decreased. When the leading companies reached the forward edge of the enemy minefield, the point sections found that no gap had been cleared. The party of South African sappers detailed to lift the mines was pinned to the ground by a hail of fire from the enemy automatics. The only course open to maintain the momentum of the attack was to walk through the minefield. The forward companies, after pausing only long enough to regroup, advanced across the minefield towards the enemy. By now the defensive fire was intense and the noise terrific.

Men went down on all sides like ninepins and nobody had much time to wonder whether the minefield was " live " or not. It may well have been a " dummy " for it was the fierce defensive fire and not exploding mines which tore gaps in the ranks of the advancing companies. Somehow the men kept going until they were less than two hundred yards from the enemy and then, firing rifles, Tommy guns and Bren guns from the hip and cheering and shouting they closed in. The defensive fire died down and the British troops let out another cheer when they saw the enemy in the moonlight, running back up the slopes of the ridge. The 6th D.L.I. company went after them and took a considerable number of prisoners.

Meanwhile, B Company pressed on towards its objective, a track running north and south along the top of the ridge. The enemy positions were, however, in some depth and the company was still under fairly heavy fire, particularly from the flanks. As B Company advanced, men dropped out of line, killed or wounded, when the German fire found its mark.

Eventually the company reached the objective and started to dig in with entrenching tools and the few picks and shovels which had survived the journey. Captain Pitt, making a quick check of his platoons, counted only thirty-five men. The strength on the start line had been ninety-seven and B Company had suffered sixty per cent casualties. Some men of the 9th Battalion then arrived on the positions to increase the company strength to between sixty and seventy. There were six Bren guns with very few magazines, one 2″ Mortar and one anti-tank rifle ; certainly not a formidable force by any means but the troops were confident that they could hold the position until the arrival of the British tanks at daylight.

Lieut.-Colonel Battiscombe was now anxious to bring forward the reserve company to strengthen the position but the Signal Officer, Lieut. Butler, informed him that wireless communication with this company had broken down. Butler was sent back on foot to guide the reserve company forward but, after a long wait, there was no sign of the reinforcements and another officer was sent back. Neither of these officers nor the reinforcements returned.

Just as dawn was breaking two German half-track vehicles advanced towards B Company and opened fire with their automatics. One well aimed shot from the anti-tank rifle went clean through the gun shield on one of the half-tracks and the crew abandoned it. The Germans went to ground behind a ridge two hundred yards away, and C.S.M. Leggett scored a direct hit with the 2″ mortar, killing two of the enemy and wounding the rest of the crew. The second half-track turned away and, as it drove off, the B Company gunners gave it several long bursts and had the satisfaction of seeing it go up in flames.

In spite of the fact that the reserve company had not arrived, this successful action with the half-tracks had the effect of raising morale, although there was still no sign of the British tanks. Instead, the British artillery from their positions in the Alamein Line put down a heavy barrage which landed all round the B Company positions. They may have been firing at the burning half-track but this was no consolation to the men of B Company who had a most unpleasant half hour, with their faces pressed into the sand as British shells exploded all round them.

When the shelling stopped, a captured British truck appeared on the scene and drove quietly up to the derelict half-track. Two Germans got out to examine it, apparently with a view to towing it away. Two hundred yards is a short range for Bren guns with a standing target and the two Germans were shot. The unfortunate men had obviously not spotted the British troops and it looked as though the company positions were unknown to the enemy.

By this time, 9.30 a.m., it was becoming unpleasantly hot. B Company had no water or food and very little ammunition, and there was still no sign of the tanks. Away to the right German tanks and anti-tank guns were in action against the Australians who had captured their objective but had then been cut off and forced to withdraw under cover of tanks of the 50th R.T.R. The Australian and tank casualties had been heavy and it was due to this setback that tank support had not been sent forward to the composite battalion.

As the B Company men watched the battle in the Australian sector, a captured British jeep driven by a German officer came racing towards the company, but stopped just under four hundred yards away. Had he seen the British troops? B Company opened fire but unfortunately this did not prevent the German from jumping unscathed into the jeep and driving away in a cloud of dust. The B Company positions had been discovered and the troops waited anxiously for the next move.

They had not long to wait. Twenty minutes later a group of German tanks moved across the company front and started a long circular sweep which brought them up behind the positions. They closed in gradually and the British troops—who had nothing to hit back with—flattened themselves into the sand hoping the tank crews would not see them. Two of the tanks—Mark IIIs.—then closed in to about a hundred and fifty yards and opened fire. It was a murderously close range and the first bursts of fire killed several men and wounded others. It could not last and after another burst of fire several men jumped up with their hands in the air. There was no alternative but for the rest of the company to surrender, and within a very short time B Company of the 8th Battalion had been rounded up by the tanks and marched away as prisoners.

The remainder of the composite battalion had fared no better and only a few survivors returned to Mariopolis to tell the story of the abortive attack. The loss of B Company was a great shock to the 8th Battalion. Besides the men who had been killed and wounded, sixty B Company men had been taken prisoner as well as Captains Pitt and Lindsay. July had been a bad month for both the Eighth Army and for the 8th D.L.I.

CHAPTER FOURTEEN

ALAMEIN—THE SOUTHERN SECTOR

'Monty' takes over the Eighth Army—the Battalion moves into the Alamein Line—patrolling at Alamein—the Greek Brigade—preparing for the offensive.

DURING August there were drastic changes in the Middle East Command. Early in the month Mr. Churchill visited the Eighth Army and a few days afterwards General Auchinleck was replaced by General Alexander as Commander-in-Chief, Middle East. General "Strafer" Gott, the famous commander of 13 Corps and previously commander of 7 Armoured Division (the original Desert Rats) was given command of the Eighth Army. By some strange trick of fate "Strafer" Gott was killed when two enemy fighters attacked the transport plane in which he was travelling back to Cairo, and as a result of this, Lieut.-General B. L. Montgomery was sent out from England to command the Desert Army at Alamein.

On August 13th Montgomery arrived at the Eighth Army H.Q. That same evening, as the sun was setting over Ruweisat Ridge, he spoke to the H.Q. staff officers and explained the mandate which General Alexander and himself had been given by the Prime Minister—nothing less than the destruction of the Axis forces in North Africa. He said that a new atmosphere would be created in the Eighth Army, that the bad old days were over. The Army had got to stand and fight it out and there would be no withdrawal.

Montgomery then spoke about Rommel and the expected enemy offensive. He would not be very happy if it came within two weeks but if it came after that he would welcome it : "It would be excellent." A great British offensive was to be planned immediately and a corps d'élite formed and trained out of the line, consisting of two armoured divisions and one motorised (New Zealand) division. This was, of course, producing a counterpart to the Afrika Corps.

The gist of this forceful address was communicated to corps commanders and General Montgomery spent the next day or two in touring the whole Army, endeavouring to meet everyone. He spoke to officers whenever he could and told them exactly what was wanted. The result of all this was tremendous and the men of the Desert Army felt that at last they had transferred their weight once again on to the right foot.

The preparations for dealing with Rommel's attack when it came went on with the utmost urgency. The Army Commander carried out a very detailed examination of the whole front to decide how the defensive battle would be fought. He appreciated that the Alam el Halfa ridge, in the rear of the southern sector of the Alamein Line and commanding a large area of desert, was of vital importance. It was undoubtedly a key to the whole defensive system, and any break through by Rommel's forces, followed by a right hook, must capture this feature to be successful.

The days crept by and the dangerous two-week period was nearly over. A clear-cut defensive plan was laid down, the various moves rehearsed and a very close liaison established with the R.A.F. By August 28th the Desert Army was ready to take on the best that Rommel could put in the field, and the German attack was expected with the full moon at the end of the month. Two fresh corps commanders arrived, Lieut.-Generals Leese and Horrocks, both of them chosen by Montgomery. Without a doubt the month of August had seen the rebirth of the Eighth Army.

The preparations for an offensive were also going ahead. The corps d'elite was in process of forming, and the new Sherman tank—a great improvement on the Grant—arrived in large numbers. Self-propelled guns, new transport and shiploads of stores came into Suez and were routed to the desert. Intensive training was carried out to fit the men of the Eighth Army for the new offensive, and particular attention was paid to the problem of how to breach the vast minefield protecting the Axis front. There was also a great deal of night training as by this time Montgomery had decided that the main attack would be launched by moonlight in the northern sector of the line.

At Mariopolis, too far behind the line for a visit by the new Army Commander, the 8th Battalion continued specialist training and the survivors of the B Company operation were drafted to C Company or to one of the specialist platoons. A reinforcement demand was submitted for six officers and a hundred other ranks. On August 22nd the Battalion, consisting of C Company, H.Q. Company and a newly-formed B Company under command of Major R. P. Lidwill of the King's Regiment, who had recently been posted to the Battalion from Cairo, moved ten miles south of Amyria to the area of the main R.A.F. landing grounds. The 8th became part of a mobile reserve in defence of these vital desert landing grounds, with a counter-attack role against enemy parachute landings.

On August 25th the Battalion came under 9 Armoured Brigade and moved south of the landing ground area. In line with the Army Commander's plan the armoured brigade had been given the task of preventing the enemy reaching the airfields should the Alamein Line be breached to the south. It was while the Battalion was in this area that R.S.M. Jennings was commissioned as Lieut. Quartermaster and posted to the transit camp at Abassia, on the outskirts of Cairo. Jennings had been through a lot with the Battalion and although he had always been a stickler for discipline the troops were sorry when they heard that he was to go. The officers gave him a farewell party in the Mess when Lieut.-Colonel Jackson thanked the R.S.M. for what he had done in his service with the Battalion.

Shortly before midnight on August 30/31 Rommel launched his attack against the Alamein Line. There were thrusts in the north, centre and south but the latter was the main one. It came in between the left flank of the New Zealand Division in the extreme south of the line, and an isolated hill bordering the Qattara Depression, known as Qaret el Himeimat. Rommel's forces consisted of 15 and 21 Panzer Divisions, 90 Light Division and 20 Italian Corps which included the Ariete and Littorio Armoured Divisions.

Rommel did exactly as Montgomery had predicted. By the evening of August 31st it was clear that the German forces had turned towards the Alam el Halfa ridge where a hot reception was waiting for them. Montgomery moved the bulk of our armour between the ridge and the New Zealanders, who still held their sector of the Alamein Line. This move, having already been rehearsed, went very smoothly and by midday on September 1st four hundred British tanks had been concentrated in this particular area. The German attacks in the Alam el Halfa area were well and truly smashed and once Montgomery was satisfied that the enemy was fully committed he began to regroup, ready for a counter-stroke. He thinned out 30 Corps in the northern sector of the line and brought up the D.L.I. Brigade of 50 Division (including the 8th Battalion which had by this time left the armoured brigade to rejoin the 6th and 9th Battalions) to take the place of the armour he had moved. Early on September 3rd Rommel called off the attack and the R.A.F. reported three strong enemy columns withdrawing westwards. Rommel's final bid to get through to Cairo had failed.

On the night of September 3/4th the New Zealand Division began an attack southwards from its positions in the Alamein Line. This threatened to close the gap by which Rommel's troops had entered the British positions, and the German withdrawal was considerably speeded up. The Axis forces finally halted and turned about to occupy forward positions in the south, facing the Alamein Line, which now followed the line of Deir el Angar—Deir el Munassib—Himeimat. Thus ended as hort but one of the most decisive defensive battles in the history of the war. It can truly be said that for the British and Dominion forces the Battle of Alam el Halfa was the turning point of the war.

Although 50 Division took no part in the actual fighting, the D.L.I. Brigade had moved in to the Alamein Line on September 4th to take up positions vacated by troops of the New Zealand Division. The 8th Battalion took over a reserve area of the line from the 28th (Maori) New Zealand Battalion late at night, and settled down to the accompaniment of the drone of the R.A.F. bombers overhead and the noise of the battle raging to the south, where the New Zealanders were engaged in heavy fighting with the German rearguards. The troops had hardly stretched themselves out in the slit trenches before there was a terrific explosion. A three-ton lorry had run into the minefield and blown itself up. It was just like old times.

During the next few days, whilst the German withdrawal was completed, the 8th Battalion spent every available hour digging and improving the positions vacated by the Maoris. It was a foul area in every sense of the word, and whilst no one will deny that the Maoris are great fighting troops, the Battalion never at any time of the war had to take over an area which had been so neglected in sanitary and refuse arrangements. Flies were everywhere and the danger of dysentery was increased tenfold by the uncovered heaps of refuse. It took almost as many men to clean up the area as it took to improve the defences.

There was a most unfortunate accident on the evening of September 6th. An 8th Battalion carrier on reconnaissance with several company officers on board, was passing out of the gap in the forward minefield which had been reported clear by sappers, when it blew up on a mine. By some incredible stroke of luck no one on board the carrier was injured although one of the tracks was blown off. A New Zealand battalion commander, a friend of Lieut.-Colonel Jackson, was less fortunate. He ran through the gap towards the wrecked carrier, but had only gone a few yards when there was a second explosion. Another mine, which had only been disturbed but not set off by the carrier, exploded killing him instantly. It was one of the tragedies of war which should never have happened. Before any of the officers or men in the wrecked carrier were allowed to walk back through the gap, it was probed thoroughly with bayonets. Ironically, not one more mine was found.

On September 9th orders were issued for the 8th D.L.I. to move into the south-west corner of the Alamein Line to take over from a battalion of New Zealanders. The Battalion reconnaissance party went forward in the early afternoon and the rest of the Battalion followed at 9 p.m., moving into the new positions under cover of darkness. This precaution was very necessary as the Battalion was soon to find out. Rear parties and G Company of the Green Howards, which had recently been attached to bring the 8th Battalion up to strength, were left behind. There were prepared positions for only two rifle companies, and B and C Companies took over from the friendly New Zealanders during the night. Dawn next morning found the 8th Battalion firmly established in the toe of the Alamein Line.

At "stand-to" the troops were able to take stock of their surroundings. The positions were in the south-western corner of the Line and there were few other British troops between the Battalion, Himeimat and the impassable Qattara Depression. On the left of the 8th D.L.I. the 6th D.L.I. was echeloned back and faced south, whilst on the right the Line was held by a battalion of Royal West Kents from 44 British Division which had only recently arrived from the U.K.

The 8th Battalion was reponsible for a narrow front, and both the company positions were sited on forward slopes, one of them facing south whilst the other one faced south and west. A thick belt of minefields, known as the outer circle, protected the immediate front of these companies and a second belt of minefields, the inner circle, divided them from the reserve company positions and Battalion H.Q. Cheshire Regiment machine-gun sections, sited on the flanks of the forward companies, covered the outer minefield.

In front of the outer circle minefield, mainly opposite the sector occupied by the right-forward company, was a saucer-shaped feature known as the Angar Depression. The nearest enemy troops, mostly Italian, were located on the far side of this depression not more than a thousand yards away from the D.L.I. battalion. The forward company positions were under continual enemy observation during the day, and the New Zealanders had not exaggerated when they warned the incoming troops to move about only at night.

It took the Battalion several days to settle down in the Alamein Line and adjust itself to these unusal conditions In B and C Companies there was practically no movement by day, while in the rest of the Battalion area movement was greatly restricted. Patrolling was carried out only at night. Day patrols were out of the question due to the lack of cover and nearness of the enemy.

After a week or two, when all companies had been in the forward area for a spell, the men of the Battalion were quite at home, living underground by day and doing the routine jobs by night. The positions were shelled every time there was any movement, and several men were killed and others wounded during September. In the same way, the British Gunner O.Ps. with the forward companies shelled the enemy positions every time ration or working parties showed themselves.

There was an Italian sniping gun situated on the front of the right-forward company, so close that the report when the gun fired was followed immediately by a quick whistle and the crash of the shell landing. This all happened within the space of about five seconds, leaving very little time for taking cover. If a man was caught out in the open when the gun fired, it was quite useless trying to reach a slit trench more than ten yards away. Five seconds was all the gun allowed and the only thing to do was to lie flat and hope for the best. The company latrines had been situated some distance from the trenches and there were several amusing occasions when men caught in embarrassing positions had to seek the shelter of a slit trench. The sniping gun was soon nicknamed "Guchi," and the troops who occupied the forward company positions waged a battle of wits with the Italian gun crews and adopted musical chair tactics when they had to move about during the day, always trying to keep within sprinting distance of a slit trench.

The platoon positions in the Battalion area were in most cases continuous trench systems, and reserve ammunition, food and water was kept in the trenches. The troops slept fully clothed and were allowed only to loosen the laces of their boots. Each section had to keep two men on watch during the night, and as the sections were only small it usually meant that sentries did at least one spell of four hours before the dawn. It was a wearying vigil and the troops had great difficulty in keeping awake although there was a severe penalty for any man who fell asleep at his post. Sentries were reduced to one man per section during the day whilst the remainder tried to get some sleep or write letters in the bottom of their trenches, with groundsheets to shield them from the sun's rays.

The supply situation at Alamein was very different to that at

Gazala. In rear of the Battalion sector were several small depressions, typical of many such in the desert, and known as "Gots" (pronounced "Goat" in Arabic). R.Q.M.S. Lightfoot established his H.Q. in a Got behind Battalion H.Q. where men going on leave, and boots, equipment and stores for repair or exchange were collected in what came to be known as the R.Q.'s Goat before being sent to the rear.

Rations and water were brought up every evening from B Echelon to the Got and distributed from there to the companies. The hot evening meal was always taken round by truck to the forward areas after dark, and on many occasions Battalion patrols out in front of the Alamein Line reported that they heard the strident voice of C.Q.M.S. Wardle of B Company shouting, " Left hand down—right hand down—straighten up," or some such instruction to his driver when taking the rations up to B Company at night. When the hot suppers were distributed, rations for breakfast and tiffin (the light midday meal) were also delivered, these rations being cooked the following day in the trenches by the men themselves in brew cans heated over a sand and petrol fire. Water was much more plentiful at Alamein than it had been at Gazala, with a daily allowance of a gallon per man for all purposes. It was the Germans and Italians, at the end of a long supply line, who went short of this vital commodity. As a precaution and to guard against supplies not getting through to the Battalion positions in the event of an attack, three days reserve rations were kept in each company area and dug in below ground level.

The rations were good at Alamein, often supplemented by eggs and tinned fruit which had been purchased in Alexandria or from the N.A.A.F.I. at Burgh el Arab. Breakfast frequently consisted of eggs, sausages, bacon and beans with a pint of tea. It was invariably too hot to eat a heavy midday meal and the next substantial meal was in the evening when the C.Q.M.S. brought up the rations. Supper was usually a tin of Maconochies' meat and vegetables followed by a tin of fruit and a mug of tea. Sometimes there was a tin of canned American beer or a bottle of lukewarm Stella beer to wash down the evening meal. Afterwards the troops sat down under the stars, and most of them found a sheltered spot to smoke a pipe of tobacco or a cigarette. There was another very good reason, apart from the prospects of a good meal, why the evening arrival of the rations was eagerly awaited. The colour-sergeants always brought up the mail, which to the majority was more important than the food. The regular arrival of mail from home never failed to keep the men cheerful; it was a wonderful morale raiser.

The main task of the Battalion during the first month in the Alamein Line was night patrolling, for although there was no large scale fighting during the month, both sides were extremely active. During the lull the Axis forces concerned themselves chiefly with fortifying their positions, and the enemy minefields spread over the desert like oil rings expanding on water. Rommel knew that an attack was to be expected but he was confident of repulsing it. " I have not advanced to Alamein," he said at a Press Conference when he visited

Berlin, "with any intention of being flung back sooner or later. You may rely on our holding fast to what we have got." Montgomery, on the other hand, was not content only with fortifying the British positions. He wanted a continuous supply of information about enemy troops, dispositions and minefields from the British and Dominion divisions holding the Line. Vigorous patrolling was ordered along the whole length of the Alamein Line, and the D.L.I. Brigade took an active part in this plan.

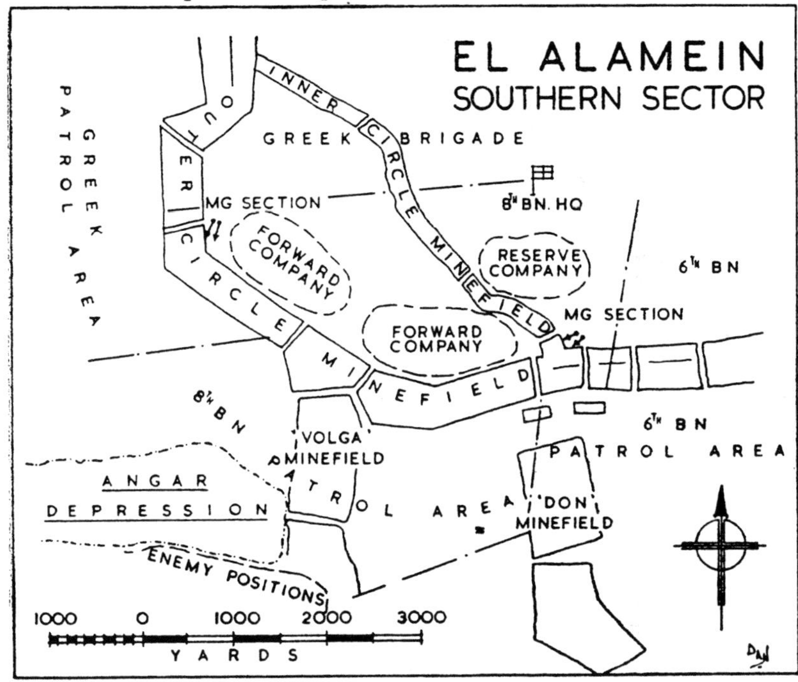

THE WESTERN DESERT. The southern sector of the Alamein Line showing the company localities, minefields and the Angar Depression.

The Brigade was responsible for sending out a patrol every night, and during September the Battalion provided the brigade patrol on no less than twenty-two occasions. In the main, the object of these patrols was to reconnoitre the ground between the forward positions and those of the enemy. Most of them sought information about enemy dispositions in the Angar Depression and the location of enemy minefields, which meant that sappers usually accompanied the infantry to determine the type of mine in the fields. This minefield information, as it came in, was added to the detailed map which Lieut. Neale and the Intelligence Section were preparing at Battalion H.Q.

There was a minefield running due north and south from the toe of the Line, known by the codename "Volga," and the Battalion patrols used the line of the minefield wire on the British side to guide them to a gap running westwards into the Angar Depression. One night, an

Italian patrol kinked the wire just before daybreak so that it took in a part of the minefield, and the following night a 6th Battalion patrol followed the wire into the minefield and suffered heavy casualties. A new route was used after this which took the patrols on a compass bearing to the gap. Contact was not often established with the enemy but this did not make the sorties any the less nerve-racking. The area was strewn with mines and booby traps, the nights were light, and more often than not the Italians were quick to open fire on fixed lines at the slightest pretext with machine-guns and mortars.

The daily communiques usually mentioned patrolling with a sentence on these lines : " There was slight patrol activity in the southern sector of the Alamein Line." A few words, hastily scanned as being unimportant and uninteresting by the readers of the communiques at home. Nevertheless, patrolling to the men of the 8th Battalion, some of whom went out three or four times a week, was very real and unnerving.

The enemy also carried out patrolling but not on such a large scale as did 151 Brigade. However, on one occasion an Italian fighting patrol had some measure of success. At that time the left-forward company position was held by C Company, and Sgt. Anderson with three C Company men was in the listening post on the enemy side of the outer minefield. In the middle of the night the telephone operator at C Company H.Q. was awakened by an urgent buzzing from the outpost extension. By the time he had pulled himself together—far too slowly—and answered the phone he heard the outpost commander whisper that an enemy patrol was approaching the listening post. Before the signaller could give the alarm firing broke out, and as C Company " stood-to," Anderson and his men came running back through the minefield gap. It had been a close call and they had just managed to escape capture. Fortunately the Italians, who were in some strength, did not follow up their success but withdrew, taking with them the greatcoats which Anderson's section had left in the listening post. Although no one had been killed or wounded, this episode had the effect of putting the Battalion on guard and there were no repeat performances by the enemy.

Whilst the night patrolling continued and the new corps was being formed in the greatest secrecy, the front line divisions also carried out extensive training programmes, for the Army Commander was not satisfied with the standard of training in the Eighth Army. The forward troops could do very little, but the reserve companies carried out schemes designed to perfect the infantry in the technique of the night attack and in minefield breaching. This intensive training included early morning P.T., always a firm favourite with General Montgomery. In accordance with the Army Commander's instructions, Lieut.-Colonel Jackson ordered Battalion H.Q. and the reserve company to carry out P.T. every morning. The reserve company had precisely two minutes P.T. on the first morning before it was shelled very accurately, and from that day onwards there was no more P.T. for the 8th Battalion at Alamein. However, the reserve company carried out some particularly energetic schemes in training areas behind the line, and it was one of the consolations of being in the forward company areas that there was no training. Another was that the C.O. very rarely visited these companies during the day, and apart from the shelling it was fairly peaceful, with "very little direction from above."

Late in September a Greek battalion came into the Line on the right of the 8th D.L.I., taking over from the Royal West Kents. The Greeks had no sooner arrived than they proceeded to dominate No Man's Land with their bloodthirsty tactics. One of their favourite pastimes was to lop off the ears of Germans and Italians and bring back these grisly objects as proof that they had in fact encountered the enemy. There were shrieks and yells when the Greeks went into the Angar Depression and they never returned until they had created terror and chaos in the positions held by their hated enemies—the Italians. Neither did they make any distinction in No Man's Land between friend or foe, and after one or two alarming experiences the Brigadier ordered that no D.L.I. patrols were to operate anywhere near the Greek hunting grounds.

The Greeks were almost as dangerous behind the Line as in front of it. On one occasion the reserve company was practising a night attack formation when the route of the advance lay through the Greek artillery gun lines. The Greeks had been warned about the mock attack but one of their sentries panicked when he saw the reserve company advancing towards him in extended order, and opened fire. The bullet from his rifle cut a neat groove in the steel helmet worn by the company second-in-comand, and naturally enough the reserve company went to ground. By this time the Greeks had been roused and an ugly situation was averted by Lieut. Neale, the Intelligence Officer, who walked towards them with Lieut.-Colonel Jackson shouting the one Greek word he had learned—" Audaxi," meaning friend. It had the desired effect, convincing the Greeks that the reserve company was not a German patrol which had breached the Line. There was a great deal of boisterous laughter by the Greeks, who treated the matter as a huge joke, until the C.O. told them what he thought of them in his own inimitable and forceful way, which he did most successfully without using any Greek words.

September passed into October, by which time the British offensive had been planned almost to the last detail. The main attack was to be launched in the north at night, during the full moon, by 30 Corps on a front of four divisions. Two corridors were to be cleared through the minefield, and through these lanes 10 Corps was to pass. In the south 13 Corps was to stage two diversionary attacks with the object of misleading the enemy and containing forces which might otherwise be used against 30 Corps. Both 13 and 30 Corps were to destroy the enemy holding the forward positions, while the final task of 10 Corps was the destruction of the enemy armour. The gun, tank and air support for the Eighth Army was on a scale which the desert troops had never seen before and consisted of nine hundred field guns, well over a thousand anti-tank guns and nearly eleven hundred tanks. The available air strength was five hundred fighters and two hundred bombers, not so many when compared with the later years of the war but at that time a considerable force.

The date fixed for the opening of the battle was October 23rd, and during the early weeks of the month the Eighth Army continued with its preparations for the great offensive. In the south the situation did not change very much. The daily artillery duels continued, causing casualties on several occasions in the 8th Battalion. The sniping gun killed one man in the forward area under particularly tragic circumstances. A party of Cheshires were filling sandbags in the open, having chosen to ignore the shouted warnings from the infantry that their movements would be spotted. Sure enough the Italians had seen the working party, and the first shell landed beside a slit trench where two men—one a Cheshire and the other a Green Howard—were sitting. They were brothers and had just met for the first time since leaving England with their respective units. One of them was killed instantly and the other, although unhurt, had to be evacuated. The Cheshire working party escaped without any further casualties.

The shelling was not confined entirely to the forward area. Battalion H.Q. and H.Q. Company had one or two unpleasant strafes, and the Officers' Mess very nearly received a direct hit one day. The C.O. had banged his head on the roof of the mess tent on so many occasions during the previous month that he ordered the roof to be raised several feet above ground level. This had no sooner been done than the vigilant crew of "Guchi" ranged on this inviting target. Two near misses were sufficient to convince the C.O. that the roof would have to be lowered again and this was done in a fraction of the time it had taken to raise it.

Early in the month G Company of the Green Howards and another Green Howard Company which had joined the Battalion towards the end of September, returned to their own unit and a new A Company arrived. When the Battalion had left Amyria for the landing ground area, Major G. P. Chambers stayed behind to supervise the training of a new company. A hundred reinforcements arrived and this contingent lived with the 6th Green Howards, encamped at Mariopolis. The D.L.I. company was looked after extremely well and Brigadier Cooke-Collis, the commander of 69 Brigade, affectionately known as "Red Ted," visited the troops every day and was most considerate and helpful. The company was commanded by Captain C. L. Beattie, and whereas the new draft had been well trained according to English standards, they had to adjust themselves and their training to the vastly different desert conditions. However, they soon settled down, and in spite of the heat worked hard and cheerfully. When the company arrived at Alamein it was almost ready to take over one of the forward areas. On October 10th everyone in the Battalion was pleased to welcome back Captain I. R. English from hospital and he took over C Company. Two days afterwards Major G. Lance left the Battalion to command the 6th Green Howards, Major R. P. Lidwill

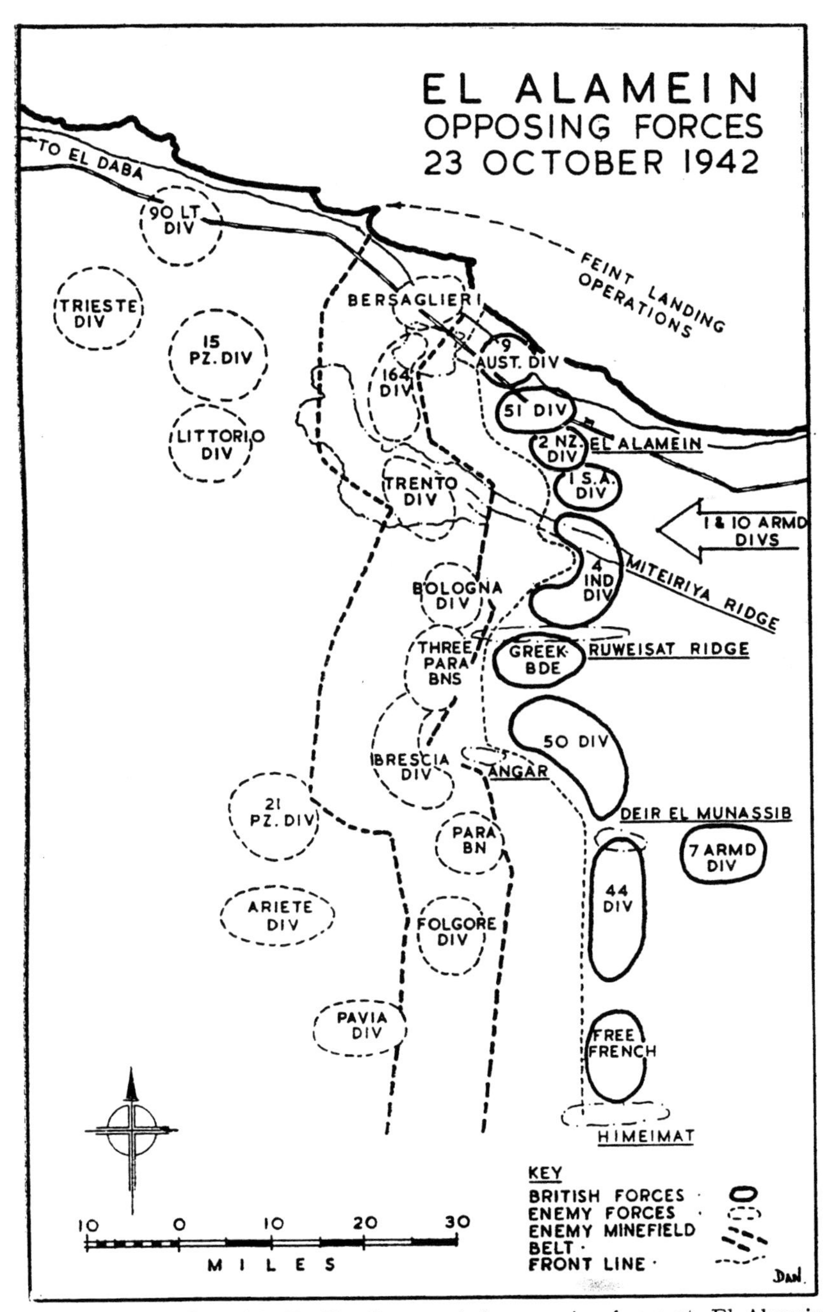

THE WESTERN DESERT. The line-up of the opposing forces at El Alamein just prior to the offensive which was launched by the Eighth Army on the night of October 23rd, 1942. The main attack was in the northern sector.

becoming Second-in-Command.

The patrols continued to operate, probing the approaches to the Angar Depression and plotting the minefields. By this time Lieut. Neale and his staff at Battalion H.Q. had compiled a most detailed map. A great deal of the credit for the patrolling which provided this invaluable information must go to Lieut. R. Hurst, an ex-guardsman who had only joined the Battalion in the Alamein Line. This officer went out almost every other night on minefield reconnaissance and it was a great loss to the Battalion when he was killed in the Angar Depression on October 13th.

Lieut. Hurst, with a sapper corporal and Sgt. Martin of C Company, went into the Depression soon after "stand-down." It was a bright, moonlight night and when the patrol reached the minefield area Hurst warned the N.C.Os. to watch out for trip wires. After probing about for some time searching for mines he moved a short distance away from the rest of the patrol. His body threw a shadow on the ground in front of him, hiding a trip wire which he did not see until too late. His foot broke the slender wire and almost immediately an anti-personnel mine exploded, practically severing the lower part of his body. Martin ran to the side of the mortally wounded officer, but Hurst told him to get back to the Line as the explosion had set off the Italian defensive fire which was sweeping the area. Martin tried to drag Hurst to safety, but the wounded man was in great pain and every movement was agony. He died shortly afterwards. Sgt. Martin and the sapper corporal made their way back to the Line where the forward companies had "stood-to" because of the firing. Several attempts were made by stretcher bearers to reach Hurst but each time they were driven back by the fierce defensive fire and eventually it was given up as a hopeless task. Hurst's death meant a loss to the Battalion of a very gallant officer.

On October 19th and 20th General Montgomery addressed all officers down to Lieut.-Colonel in 30, 13 and 10 Corps. His talks were clear and full of confidence, and the C.O. passed on the gist of them to the officers of the 8th D.L.I. Montgomery had said that he was certain a "dog fight" or "killing match" would take place for perhaps as long as ten days. He gave details of the great strength of the Eighth Army in guns, tanks and ammunition. He drummed in the need never to lose the initiative and how everyone—*everyone*—must be imbued with the burning desire to " kill Germans"; even the padres, " one per week-day and two on Sundays." He had then explained how the battle would be fought, and finished by saying that he was entirely and utterly confident of the result.

The men of the Desert Army, the new boys fresh from home and the veterans, were let into the secret on October 21st and 22nd, from which date no leave was granted. Under Montgomery's leadership there was a tremendous state of enthusiasm in the Eighth Army and morale had never been higher. The men knew they were going to succeed, but few of them could have visualised what far-reaching results the battle would have on the North African campaign and on the whole course of the war.

CHAPTER FIFTEEN

THE BATTLE OF EL ALAMEIN

The attack in the northern sector—Checkmate—the Battalion moves up north—Operation Supercharge—objectives gained at a heavy cost—C Company holds the bridgehead—the New Zealanders take over.

THE battle of El Alamein began at precisely 9.40 p.m. on October 23rd, 1942 with the opening of a mighty British gun concentration on enemy batteries. The weight of artillery support can be appreciated by the fact that in the north there was no less than one gun to every twenty-three yards of front. For twenty minutes the devastating counter-battery fire continued. The British gunners then lifted from this target and started to lay down a creeping barrage, designed to move slowly in front of the attacking infantry.

At 10 o'clock, under a bright full moon, the infantry of 9 Australian, 51 Highland, 2 New Zealand and 1 South African Divisions advanced in the northern sector of the line. By dawn most of the infantry had reached their objectives. But the armoured divisions met considerable opposition in their attempts to move out through the corridors and were halted by mines and anti-tank guns, sited in rear of the main minefield belt ; in the south the attack by 13 Corps was only partially successful.

There followed the period which the Army Commander called the "Dog Fight" or "Killing Match." By a series of carefully co-ordinated attacks on narrow fronts with limited objectives, the Eighth Army infantry gradually crumbled away the main enemy positions and wore down his resistance. The tanks followed through to take up positions west of the main minefield, where they could deal with the enemy's armoured counter-attacks.

However, by October 27th the momentum of the British offensive was already diminishing and the "break-in" area still ringed by a strong screen of anti-tank guns. As a result 10 Corps had been unable to get out into open country and it was now necessary to pause and regroup. First, the New Zealand Division and later 1 Armoured Division were withdrawn into reserve ; then 7 Armoured Division (less 4 Light Armoured Brigade), a brigade of 44 Division and the D.L.I. Brigade of 50 Division were ordered to the northern sector to reinforce the final break-out attack, scheduled for the night of October 31st/November 1st (later postponed for twenty-four hours).

At midday on October 28th the 8th Battalion was ordered to move that night to Beachy Head, a reserve area in the northern sector. Greek infantry who took over the Battalion positions in the early evening were quite oblivious to the necessity for restricting their movements in the forward areas, and one of their cook's lorries arrived at B Company H.Q. in broad daylight. Not even a motor cycle, let alone a large lorry, had ever ventured so far by day, and B Company, waiting resignedly for the enemy guns to open fire, cursed the Greeks roundly for their foolhardiness. The Axis artillery must have been engaged elsewhere for the truck was allowed to unload without interference and return the way it had come. Having handed over to the Greeks, B Company withdrew to the comparative safety of the inner minefield where the troop-carrying lorries waited. As the company marched away in sections, several parties of enthusiastic Greeks walked unconcernedly through the forward minefield towards the Italian lines, carrying only bayonets and presumably in search of ears. By 10 p.m. the 8th Battalion was ready to move off. The convoy of R.A.S.C. troop-carriers, passing through the minefield at Heliopolis Gap, set off across the desert towards Beachy Head. The route was marked by illuminated T.T. signs and the convoy travelled fast, to reach the new area at 5.30 a.m. next morning.

The following two days at Beachy Head were fairly quiet. On October 30th the C.O., Intelligence Officer, and company commanders were called to a Brigade conference, where Brigadier J. O. S. Percy outlined the plan of attack. The appreciation was that, after the severe battering which the German line had received during the last seven days, it would break when subjected to one final heavy assault. The plan, to be known as Operation Supercharge, was for the D.L.I. Brigade on the right and a Scottish brigade from 51 Division on the left to attack along a front of four thousand yards to a depth of five thousand yards, the object being to get astride the Sidi Abd el Rahman track. The infantry were to be supported on their immediate front by the heaviest barrage yet fired in World War II. Thirteen field regiments and three medium regiments had been ordered to stand by—about three hundred and fifty guns in all. Such a large number of guns on so narrow a front was unprecedented. The Brigadier stressed the importance of the infantry keeping close up to the creeping barrage, timed to move forward one hundred yards every two minutes. He went on to say that General Montgomery considered the attack to be vital to the course of operations and that 8 and 9 Armoured Brigades, 1 Armoured Division and the whole of 10 Corps would be waiting to pass through the gap in the enemy lines made by the infantry battalions. The Brigadier planned to attack with the 9th Battalion on the left, the 8th Battalion on the right and the 6th D.L.I. in reserve.

During the night of October 30th/31st the 8th Battalion moved in M.T. up Star Track to an area originally held by 51 Division. The transport lurched along the sandy track almost under the muzzles of British guns putting down a barrage for the Australians in the coastal sector. The night was pierced by the gun flashes, and the truckloads of infantry were silent as an occasional burst of machine gun fire from the direction of the front told them that the main battle had caught up with them again after those hectic days at Gazala and Mersa Matruh.

The Battalion arrived in the new area just after 3.30 a.m. and the troops had no sooner settled down in slit trenches for a few hours rest than a marauding German night bomber flew over the area, which was packed with every kind of transport, and dropped a single bomb. This blew up the office truck and killed the Adjutant—Captain J. Parker—sleeping beside it. The office truck was burned out. Next morning Captain Parker was buried by Padre Nesbitt and a small group of 8th Battalion officers in one of the few open spaces amongst that mass of vehicles, guns and tanks. The commander of the Support Company—Major G. P. Chambers—took over as Adjutant.

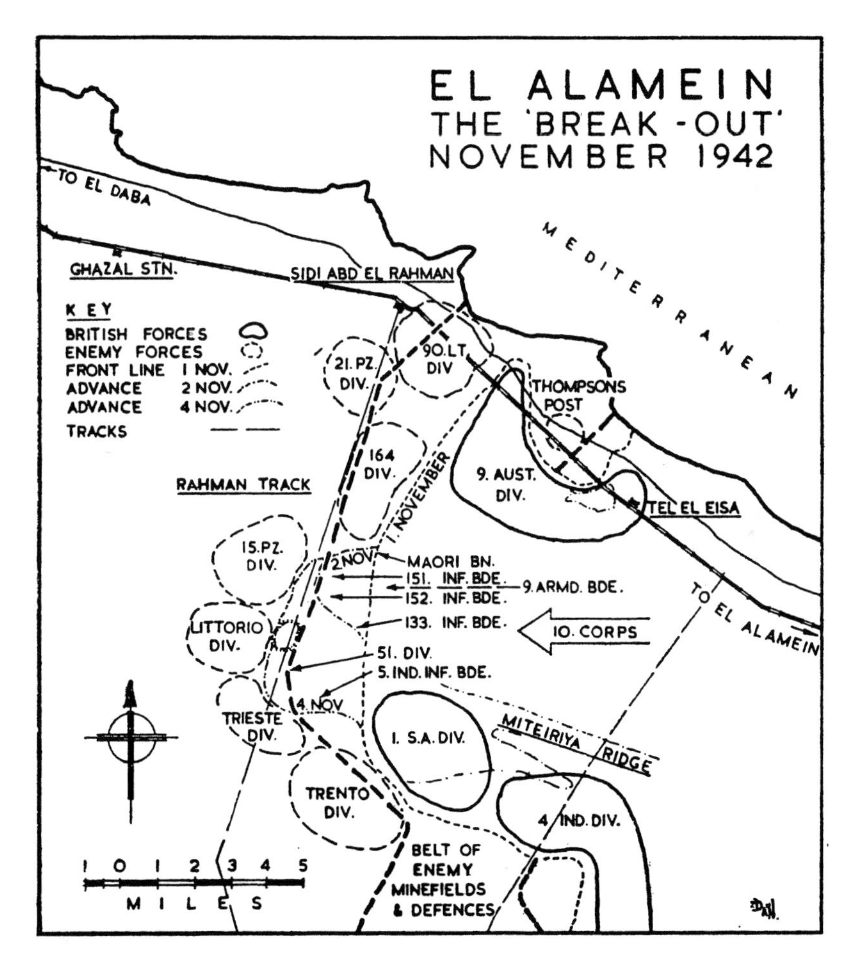

THE WESTERN DESERT. The break-out of the Eighth Army at Alamein which commenced in the early hours of November 2nd with Operation Supercharge, when the D.L.I. Brigade attacked in conjunction with a brigade from 51 Division.

As the attack was timed for that night the C.O. and Intelligence Officer took company commanders forward in the early afternoon to liaise with the Australians in the forward positions. On the way up to the front line the Battalion party saw plenty of evidence of the fierce fighting which had taken place. There were knocked-out tanks, guns and vehicles, including an Australian ambulance which had been machine-gunned from the air. It stood beside the track, its tyres punctured, the body riddled with bullets and the doors at the back swinging on their hinges.

The D.L.I. vehicles parked near Battalion H.Q. of the 22nd Australian Battalion and the company commanders went forward to talk to their opposite numbers as German and British gunners had a violent duel, sending shells whistling overhead. At typically German regular intervals a Spandau sent a burst of fire over the Australian H.Q., and when the Battalion party walked back to the waiting transport an Australian private stopped them. "Are you the coveys who are going in tonight ? " he asked. The C.O. replied in the affirmative. The Aussie pointed in the direction of the German machine-gun. " Well, be sure and fix those bastards," he said, " they think they're there for the duration."

As he spoke, a group of German Stuka dive-bombers suddenly appeared from the direction of the British gun lines with Spitfires on their tails. The planes roared low overhead and the fighters wheeled away as the Stukas swept over the German lines whilst the enemy anti-aircraft guns went into action. There was no doubt that, with the exception of patrolling, the southern sector of the Alamein Line had been a rest area when compared to this. The party finally arrived back in the Battalion area, hot and dusty, to find that the attack had been postponed for twenty-four hours. It was a welcome respite.

The following morning, November 1st, was spent in explaining to the N.C.Os. and men the Army Commander's plan, and in preparing the Battalion for the attack. Lieut.-Colonel Jackson gave out his orders at a conference soon after lunch. The Battalion was to attack with two companies up ; A Company (Captain C. L. Beattie) right and B Company (Captain P. J. Lewis,) on the left. C Company (Captain I. R. English) was to follow in reserve behind A Company. The 28th (Maori) N.Z. Battalion, which had been put under command of 151 Brigade, was to seize a strongpoint on the right of the 8th Battalion, about five hundred yards from the start line. With this secured, C Company was to swing out level with and on the right of A Company.

Three thousand five hundred yards forward of the start line, the leading troops were to halt for thirty minutes on the first objective—the 865 easting grid[1] with the code-name " Cherry." This halt was to give time for the infantry to reorganise whilst the guns lifted for half an hour to pound German positions between the first objective and the final objective—a line two thousand five hundred yards beyond the first objective with the codename " Brandy."

[1]One of a series of numbered lines running from left to right across the map.

The boundaries of each brigade were to be indicated every two minutes by red tracer shells from Bofors guns, firing along the line of advance, and red tracer fired from rifles and Brens was to be used by all British troops as a recognition signal. The 8th had two troops of New Zealand anti-tank guns under command and one platoon of medium machine-guns, with a squadron of Valentine tanks in support.

The C.O. closed by saying that the Axis line on the Battalion front was held by elements of the German 90 Light Division (old acquaintances of the Gazala Gazelles) and the German 164 Infantry Division, with part of the Italian Trieste Division.

At 4.30 p.m. the 8th Battalion marched up to an assembly area west of Tel el Eisa Station, scene of many a bitter struggle, with the company transport following in the rear. The B Echelon vehicles stayed behind in the rest area. It took almost two hours for the Battalion to reach Tel el Eisa and the men were not sorry to see the bullet-riddled signboard, practically all that was left of the station building. As the companies swung off the track, a newsreel cameraman, standing on the roof of a Ford utility, filmed the leading sections staggering along under their heavy loads.

A hot meal arrived at the same time as the Battalion and was dished out immediately. The troops had just settled down in bomb craters and slit trenches to enjoy the meat and vegetable stew when several German planes dived out of the sun to machine-gun the Battalion, and the long column of troops a hundred yards away on the track. Bursts of fire from the planes sent up little spirals of sand but no one in the Battalion was injured and the planes were driven off by anti-aircraft fire. A lance-corporal in B Company had his mug of tea trodden on and upset during the excitement. He looked after the planes, shook his fist, and shouted : " Why the hell can't you wait until seconds out of the ring ? " There was laughter all round and then the serious business of eating and drinking continued.

As the sun went down, the Battalion, led by the Second-in-Command, Major R. P. Lidwill, left Tel el Eisa and joined the seemingly endless line of marching troops, supply vehicles and tanks moving along the Boomerang Track. A Company, followed by B and C Companies in that order, led the long and wearisome march of seven miles to the Forming-up-Place. The sandy track had been churned up by so many lorries and tanks that in some places the powdered sand was well over a foot deep. To the men trudging along silently in column of threes, carrying rifles, Bren guns, grenades, sticky bombs and picks and shovels, it was like walking through snow. Far too frequently convoys passed the marching men, and by the time the 8th had covered three or four miles the troops wore a mantle of powdered sand.

At 11.15 p.m., by the light of a full moon and enemy Verey lights, the companies arrived on the Forming-up-Place where the men, after spacing themselves out along the line of the white tapes, sat down to ease their equipment.

B Company had two platoons up in line, with the company commander positioned between and level with these platoons. He had with him a navigator from the Intelligence Section, his batman and the platoon runners. Main Company H.Q. with the second-in-command, C.S.M., the signallers and stretcher bearers brought up the rear, with the reserve platoon close by. A Company on the right had more or less the same formation, while C Company in reserve also had two platoons forward and one back.

As the Battalion had two hours to wait on the F.U.P. the men tried to get some sleep but it was very cold. They were only wearing khaki shorts, shirts and pullovers. The enemy Verey lights had by this time been joined by aircraft flares which hung in the sky like giant candles as the R.A.F. bombers pounded the Axis gun lines and concentrations of transport. Otherwise the desert was quiet except when an occasional burst of machine-gun fire from the German crew " there for the duration " whistled harmlessly overhead.

At 12.45 a.m.—Monday now—the rum ration came round. It was most welcome and there was plenty of it. Zero hour was at 1.5 a.m., and at 12.55 a.m. the troops got to their feet and took up positions, with the men of A and B Companies spread out along the white tapes. Silently the Battalion fixed bayonets and, as the minutes ticked by, men eased their equipment and shuffled about as they waited anxiously for the guns to open fire. Three—two—one minute to zero hour. It was deathly quiet when suddenly the silence of the night was shattered by the British barrage. In the first few seconds only a dozen or so guns opened fire and then the full weight of the barrage joined in. The infantry looked behind them to see an amazing sight. The whole night to the east was broken by hundreds of gun flashes stabbing into the darkness. The shells whistled overhead to burst with a deafening crash in the target area and from then, until the barrage closed about three hours later, the frightful shattering noise went on continually.

All along the line there were shrill whistle blasts and shouted words of command as the D.L.I. and Scottish battalions moved forward, gradually closing up on the barrage which had been timed to stand on its opening line for twenty minutes. Then several smoke shells were fired to indicate that the barrage was moving forward, and as the guns lifted, A and B Companies of the 8th Battalion went into the smoke and through the dust and muck thrown up by the barrage. The air was heavy with the smell of explosives, the troops coughing and spluttering as they advanced with bayonets fixed. The smoke shells hindered more than they helped and caused a certain amount of confusion.

From somewhere on the left came the skirl of bagpipes as a Scottish battalion went forward and there was the sound of a hunting horn as a 9th D.L.I. company commander led his men, pistol in right hand, hunting horn in the left. Steadily the 8th Battalion advanced, over the Australian wire and into No Man's Land. German Verey lights went up one after the other calling for defensive fire, these frantic S.O.S. signals being answered by artillery and machine-guns which had escaped the terrible counter-battery fire.

Spandaus fired tracer on fixed lines through the smoke and dust into A and B Companies. All along the line men stumbled and fell as they were hit but still the line went forward, close up behind the barrage. Fresh gaps were continually appearing in the ranks of these two forward companies, hardly a minute passing without a call for stretcher bearers. B Company was particularly hard hit, for within a few minutes of crossing the Australian wire the company second-in-command had been mortally wounded, and Lieuts. Cantley and Dudman—the two officer platoon commanders—killed, one of them by a mine which had been placed in the Australian wire.

The noise of battle was terrific. There was the deafening crash of the shells bursting only a hundred yards ahead and the rattle of Brens and Spandaus, interspersed with fierce bursts of fire from German and British Tommy-guns and occasionally the crash of a British hand grenade exploding in a dugout or trench. Immediately in front of B Company, a Verey light went up and a machine-gun opened fire. The gun was obviously firing on fixed lines and its white tracers whipped overhead as several B Company men ran under the tracer and into the post with the bayonet. The Germans were routed and the gun silenced.

The two companies continued across No Man's Land and reached the single line of concertina wire which marked the German main positions. There was no doubt that the barrage had done its work well. The desert had been scarred by dozens of shell holes, many of them only a few feet apart, and it seemed that no one could have lived in that tornado of fire. German and Italian dead and wounded littered the area, some of them in the open where the barrage had caught them and others hunched up in their slit trenches. Many of those who had survived the barrage were morally shattered and almost hysterical as they were taken to the rear under guard.

Some of the Germans, hardened veterans of the Afrika Corps, were made of sterner stuff. A tall, blonde German came out of a dugout with his pistol levelled at B Company commander and was sent crashing back by a burst of Tommy-gun bullets. Another, mortally wounded and with only a few seconds to live, threw a stick grenade after an advancing section.

The forward companies did not pause to consolidate but advanced steadily through the enemy main positions, still keeping up close behind the barrage. Both companies came across deep dugouts which had obviously been a headquarters of some sort and there were several vehicles about, some of which having been hit by shellfire were blazing furiously. C Company reached a big covered in shelter with a red cross flag flying from the top of it. When an officer came out and explained in broken English that he was a doctor and that the tent was a casualty clearing station, he was allowed to carry on.

On the right flank of the Battalion advance, two sheets of flame suddenly sprang into the air as A Company set fire to some German tanks by the simple method of firing Verey lights into the petrol tanks. Beyond A Company, on the extreme right flank, the Maoris advancing well beyond their objective, determined not to be left out of the battle, were wreaking havoc in the German lines. Their war cries could be plainly heard when the noise of battle subsided for a few moments.

In A Company two Military Medals were won, one of them by Sgt. W. Crawford and the other by the company commander's batman, Pte. J. Brown. When Crawford's platoon commander was killed in the early stages of the attack the sergeant immediately reorganised the platoon and carried on towards the objective. He set a fine example, paying no regard to the heavy German fire, and by his fearless leadership inspired complete confidence in his men during the difficult advance. Pte. Brown was continually moving among his comrades, encouraging and urging them on. When all his comrades were either killed or wounded by a grenade thrown from a German defence post, Brown—though slightly wounded himself—charged the post and killed the occupants with his Tommy-gun. He set a magnificent example to all throughout the whole attack.

There was smoke and dust everywhere and the men of the 8th Battalion groped their way through it towards the first objective, stumbling over the shellholes and firing from the hip as Germans appeared suddenly out of the mist, some of them with their hands up to surrender and others determined to fight it out. There was no quarter asked and none given. It was every man for himself and there were dozens of fierce duels between small groups of British and Germans across the whole front of the advance. Considerably reduced in numbers the two forward companies reached the first objective at 2.30 a.m. ; both had suffered very heavy casualties during the three thousand five hundred yard advance, and it was not until they halted on the first objective that their officers and N.C.Os. were able to take a rough count. In the noise and confusion of the battle man after man had become a casualty without it being noticed. The two companies between them had lost five officers killed out of the eight who had crossed the start line and nearly a hundred men had been killed or wounded. In A Company only the company commander and one platoon commander remained alive, and in B Company the only surviving officer was the company commander, Captain Lewis. This officer became a casualty when he was wounded a few minutes after arriving on the objective whilst attempting to reorganise the remnants of his company. This left B Company with no officers and with very few men, and A Company was not much better off. In fact both these companies ceased to function as fighting formations and took no further part in the battle as companies, although isolated sections and groups of men from both A and B continued the advance to the final objective, some of them joining up with other units.

It is at this stage of the battle that the story of the 8th Battalion in Operation Supercharge becomes the story of C Company, which had until now been in reserve. The company had not suffered such heavy casualties as the other two during the advance, and about 2.45 a.m. the leading platoons closed up on the first objective. Captain English, the company commander, sent up the success signal—green over red over green Verey lights—and the troops halted their advance for fifteen minutes, whilst the platoons were reorganised.

At 3 a.m. smoke shells were fired to indicate that the barrage was about to move forward again and the men of C Company got on their feet to advance. There were frequent halts to check direction and to keep the sections together, whilst at the same time the company commander kept his men close up behind the barrage. Enemy opposition was spasmodic and not sufficiently strong to hold up C Company which was doing excellent work with Brens, rifles, bayonets and grenades.

Twenty minutes after leaving the first objective a number of men joined 13 Platoon of C Company on the left flank. They were from A Company and their officer, 2/Lieut. P. Worley, could give no information of the whereabouts of his company commander or the rest of the company. Captain English took these reinforcements under command and they continued the advance on the left of 13 Platoon. Shortly after this a large batch of about fifty Italians were rounded up. After being searched and marshalled by C.S.M. Ranson they were sent to the rear with two walking wounded and a Maori to guard them. The Maori had become separated from his battalion and when C Company found him he was advancing on his own, quite unperturbed, carrying a 2" Mortar.

The company kept going for another fifteen minutes until Pte. Cawley, who had counted every one of the five thousand paces from the start line, told his company commander that by his reckoning they should be on the final objective. C Company continued for another two hundred yards, until the leading troops were very close to the barrage which had halted. This was the objective ; the time 3.40 a.m. The success signal, red—green—red, was sent up by Verey light and the men started to consolidate. They were told to dig as they had never dug before and to get well down before first light when a counter-attack was likely. The consolidation phase of an attack is far more difficult than the actual attack, and after the pent-up excitement of the advance there was not a single man in C Company who had not an intense weariness and desire just to lie down and sleep. However, sleep was the last thing the company could afford to do and the men set to with a will to dig in. At this stage Captain English first noticed that his second-in-command, Captain I. S. Turnbull, was missing. Turnbull, who had been with the rear Company H.Q., was last seen during the advance, making for a German machine-gun post which he intended to destroy. He completely disappeared and no trace of him has ever been found. Captain Turnbull, the son of the Honorary Colonel, was well liked and his loss keenly felt by the Battalion. His war record, although short, was one of which his father can be justly proud.

At 4 a.m. the barrage stopped. The silence which ensued was deathly after the continuous thunder of the guns for the last few hours. It was strangely quiet and the men stopped digging to look around. Some miles behind the forward troops the gunners, who had indeed done a wonderful night's work, flopped down beside their guns to sleep. But there was no sleep for the infantry on the objective and they renewed their digging efforts. Lieut. Roberts and Lieut. Worley went out with patrols to try to contact the 6th Battalion on the right, and A Company on the left. Some time later they returned to report that there was no sign of either the 6th D.L.I. or of A Company. C Company seemed to be absolutely alone on the objective, and as L/Cpl. Simpson had been unable to get through on the wireless to Battalion H.Q. the "fog of war" was complete. The red tracer recognition signals were going up behind the company and on the left flank, but it was difficult to estimate just how far away were these friendly troops. There were two enemy machine-guns still in action behind C Company and the whole situation was confusing. In order to maintain contact and ensure that the platoons and sections kept together, the attacking companies had advanced on a front of only a hundred and fifty yards. Consequently several enemy posts had been missed and not mopped up. Now they were in action again.

Captain English decided to have a look around the area, and taking Pte. Cawley with him walked towards the rear. After a while they swung over to the right until they heard the noise of tank engines quite close. They were British Valentines, allocated to the Battalion, which Lieut.-Colonel Jackson was calmly putting in position. He was walking along with Captain H. Glasper of the Battalion Anti-Tank Platoon, followed by six or seven Valentines. The C.O. seemed in very good spirits but could not give very much news about the battle as his carrier, with the wireless link to Brigade H.Q., had been blown up by a direct hit.

It was largely due to Captain H. Glasper and Pte. C. Beattie that the Battalion S Company and the supporting tanks had been able to get forward at all. Captain Glasper had assumed command of S Company just prior to the attack when the company commander, Major G. P. Chambers, had taken over the duties of Adjutant. During the advance Glasper was wounded but continued to lead the company though suffering considerable pain from wounds in the leg and back. When S Company and the supporting arms were held up by a minefield covered by heavy enemy machine-gun and anti-tank fire it was he who set the example by making a route through the minefield, which had not been cleared of mines. The carrier which led the way was driven by Pte. Beattie who took his vehicle directly through the minefield, all the time under heavy fire, and thus made a safe lane through which the tanks were able to pass in safety. For courage under heavy fire, which enabled the vital supporting arms and tanks to get forward unchecked, Captain Glasper was awarded the Military Cross and Pte. Beattie the Military Medal.

It was now 5.45 a.m. and, leaving the C.O. still positioning the tanks, Captain English and Cawley set off to return to C Company H.Q. It was still dark, and after wandering about for some time over the completely featureless desert without finding the company they decided to wait for the dawn. There was already a faint flush of light

Miss E. T. Turnbull.

Outside the B Company H.Q. dugout in the southern sector of the Alamein Line :—
Captain I. S. Turnbull, 2/Lieut. V. T. Bailey, Major R. P. Lidwill. This photograph was taken during one of the few infrequent periods when this forward company area was not being shelled.

Imperial War Museum

DUST. A Khamsin wind drives an impenetrable wall of swirling, stinging sand towards the Alamein Line. These hot winds from the Sahara were a common enemy, halting all movement and limiting visibility to a few yards.

Captain J. N. Wheatley.

THIRST. All the drinking water at Alamein had to be brought across miles of desert by R.A.S.C. transport. It was limited to eight pints a man per day for all purposes and companies drew their ration in two-gallon cans from the Battalion water-truck.

in the eastern sky.

In effect, the infantry part of Operation Supercharge had gone well, and as survivors of the D.L.I. and Scottish battalions dug in on the final objective the British armour moved forward through the minefield gaps. The desert tracks, which only a few hours before had been crowded with marching infantry, were now jammed with long lines of British tanks, nose to tail. In the opposite direction went the ambulance convoys—vehicle after vehicle—crowded with wounded. There was also another procession moving along the desert tracks to the rear ; the advance guard of the thousands of bedraggled, dejected-looking Axis prisoners who had been taken during the night.

English and Cawley could hear quite plainly the continuous roar of tank engines and tracks. The tired men on the objective, waiting anxiously for the enemy counter-attack, could also hear this heartening sound. As the darkness gradually gave way to daylight the infantry saw the outline of the British tanks moving forward. They were pushing on at a good pace until suddenly there was a flash as the leading tank went up in a mass of flames. Almost in as many seconds three more tanks were hit and soon blazing furiously.

Things became very lively. The tanks opened fire at the German anti-tank guns but the enemy had the advantage of being dug in and put in some very effective shooting. It was obvious that the gap through the German defences was not yet clear and the British tanks had run on to a strong screen of 88-millimetre guns. For half an hour the duel went on, and although some of the German guns were knocked out, no less than twenty tanks were hit and set on fire. On all sides, the burning Grants and Shermans sent up dense clouds of black smoke.

By this time the British twenty-five pounders were in action again, shelling the German anti-tank guns. The 88-millimetre is a devastating weapon and at that period of the war could knock out any British tank—including the new Sherman—at a range of a thousand yards. On the other hand this big, tall gun made a good target in the comparatively flat, featureless desert. The twenty-five pounder detachments were not slow to take advantage of this fact.

Meanwhile Captain English and Cawley had arrived at Battalion H.Q. where English learned that his company was the only one of any strength on the objective. As he was about to leave Battalion H.Q. Lieut. Worley arrived to report that some of the British tanks were machine-gunning C Company, and after pointing this out to the tank C.O., English and Worley with Pte. Cawley set off to get forward to the company. It was not a pleasant journey as enemy shelling of the area had increased considerably, and the three men went from trench to trench, doubling across the open ground.

C Company had settled in well. The platoon localities seemed satisfactory, the men were well dug in, and the fields of fire good. About two hundred yards ahead of the company was a line of telegraph poles on the Sidi Abd el Rahman track and to the right, about a hundred yards away, was a German 88-millimetre, well dug in and sandbagged. On the left of the company area were three burned-out

Grant tanks which the gun had knocked out. At first light the advantage had been with the enemy anti-tank gun crews and, as was always the case, they saw the tanks long before the tank crews spotted them. The 88-millimetres had done some terrible destruction amongst the tanks of 9 Armoured Brigade. However, the German triumph was short-lived. As soon as the 88 opened fire, C Company had engaged it with 2″ Mortars and the German gun crew ran to their slit trenches. C.S.M. Ranson then killed three of them with the Company H.Q. Bren gun and a fourth had been taken prisoner. During the advance Ranson had showed great courage and initiative, and it was to no small extent due to his reorganisation before the attack on the final objective that the operation in the C Company sector had been so successful. He had personally accounted for several of the enemy during the advance, sniping with both Bren gun and rifle. And on the final objective when the company was in an exposed position, his example of steadiness and courage was invaluable to the men of C Company. C.S.M. Ranson was awarded the Military Medal.

C Company was by this time being heavily shelled by enemy field guns, probably directed from Sidi Abd el Rahman. A Sherman came towards the company firing its Besa gun, some of the bursts of fire coming unpleasantly close to Company H.Q. Suddenly the tank went up in a mass of flames. It had been hit by an anti-tank gun away to the left. The driver managed to jump clear of the flames to collapse as soon as he reached the ground but no one else got out of the blazing Sherman. A party from 13 Platoon brought in the tank driver, who had been terribly burned about the hands and face.

By now a number of wounded had been collected round C Company H.Q. and it was difficult to find sufficient slit trenches to accommodate them. It was quite impossible to evacuate these men as nothing could get forward to C Company except an armoured vehicle. Sgt. Moody, Lieut. Worley's platoon sergeant, was one of the wounded with eight or nine others. The condition of these men was pitiful. Some had been hit during the night and it would probably be some hours before they could receive proper medical attention. Their wounds had been roughly bandaged with field dressings, but now that the sun was well up it became unbearably hot. The flies were everywhere and they tormented the poor fellows lying helpless in the slit trenches.

Shortly after 10 a.m. ten German tanks approached the company position. Most of them were Mark IIIs. and Mark IVs. but there was one Mark IV Special, with its immensely long 75-millimetre gun, and also a Mark II commander's tank. Since arriving on the objective L/Cpl. Simpson had got the wireless link working to Battalion H.Q. and the presence of these tanks was reported immediately. They were lying off about a hundred and fifty yards away making no attempt to continue their advance. The C Company platoons, with their 68 grenades ready, could not understand why the tanks remained stationary, but there was a very good reason for their reluctance to advance. The Germans had seen the great concentration of armour massing behind the British infantry. The tanks stayed where they were, and during a lull in the shelling Captain English sent Pte. Davies of the Intelligence Section back to Battalion H.Q. to inform the C.O. of the situation and also to request medical assistance for C Company.

At 11.40 a.m. the Desert Air Force shuttle-bombing service came into operation in front of the company sector. The infantry looked up when they heard the drone of aero engines and saw eighteen light bombers flying in tight formation, their silver fuselages glinting in the sunshine. The troops watched the planes pass overhead and then, on a signal from the formation commander, all their bomb bays opened at once. It was possible to follow the bombs in their course towards the earth. Then the desert in front of C Company was lost in a mass of shattering explosions, the German positions being blotted out in a swirling cloud of dust and debris which rose several hundred feet into the air.

This pattern bombing continued at forty minute intervals and the effect on the enemy was devastating. After three or four hours of it a party of Germans about a hundred and fifty strong got out of their trenches and walked into the 6th D.L.I. lines on the right flank of C Company to surrender.

The Battalion had first seen the light bombers—known throughout the Eighth Army as "The Terrible Eighteen"—in action against the Germans in the southern sector of the Alamein Line. The bombing groups—made up of Bostons, Baltimores or Mitchells—were amazingly accurate. The German infantry and tanks were between two and four hundred yards from the C Company positions yet the bombers dropped their load plumb on the enemy. Only one bomb out of hundreds fell anywhere near C Company during the raids.

The situation in the early afternoon was that, although the enemy morale was obviously breaking, morale in the British units was very good. After the initial heavy tank losses which the Eighth Army had sustained in the early morning, the situation had now improved. German tanks and guns were being knocked out without always being replaced whereas British tank reinforcements were continuously moving forward. However, the Shermans and Grants were still not able to advance against the screen of 88-millimetre guns.

The Germans were attempting to reinforce this screen and replace the guns which had been knocked out, four of them within sight of C Company. The company watched a heavy German half-track vehicle swing off the Sidi Abd el Rahman track, towing an 88-millimetre. It turned left to cross the company front and its position was reported to Battalion H.Q. by wireless. However, C Company were not the only British troops who had seen it, and tanks and field guns opened fire. The half-track kept moving for a minute or two until a twenty-five pounder scored a direct hit, killing most of the gun crew riding in the back.

Soon after 3 p.m. Captain English took stock of the position. As no vehicle of any sort had been able to get forward to C Company since dawn the men had only their battle ration of a packet of biscuits and a tin of bully. This was sufficient to keep the company going for a day or two but ammunition was getting short, especially grenades. Many of the wounded were now in a bad way and it was most necessary to evacuate them.

Soon after this, Pte. Davies arrived from Battalion H.Q. He was out of breath having been shot at repeatedly during the journey. He brought with him orders for C Company to withdraw from its exposed position to conform to the sectors held by the 6th and 9th Battalions. It was going to be a difficult operation as the men would be in full view of the enemy as they withdrew. Captain English ordered 14 Platoon and the A Company troops to pull back first, after which 13 and 15 platoons were to thin out gradually, leaving the Bren teams until last. Lieut. Welch was put in charge of the withdrawal as English had decided to remain until some transport was sent forward to pick up the wounded. Pte. Cawley stayed with him.

C Company pulled back between fifty and sixty strong, leaving English and Cawley on their own with the wounded. There was a possibility that having seen the withdrawal, the German tanks would advance to capture the wounded as well as the company commander and his runner. However, the small group around C Company H.Q. was unmolested and, after waiting anxiously for over an hour and a half, a carrier flying a red cross flag, with Lieut. Greenwood of the Battalion Anti-Tank Platoon, arrived with a jeep driven by a New Zealand sergeant. The wounded men were loaded on the two vehicles with some difficulty, the operation not being made any easier by some of the British tanks which opened fire with their machine guns for some unknown reason. At the same time a Stuka raid took place; ten dive-bombers came over, dropping some of their bombs unpleasantly close. The C Company men were not sorry to leave the area, and the jeep and carrier made for Battalion H.Q. which was eventually reached quite safely.

C Company had fought extremely well and Captain English was awarded the Military Cross for the skilful way in which he had led his men throughout the whole operation. Not only had he personally accounted for several machine-gun posts during the long and difficult advance but his was the only company to reach the final objective. And there, isolated from the rest of the battalion and with no other infantry near, the company under Captain English's leadership had stood steady in an area which provided very little cover from enemy fire, and in close proximity to enemy tanks.

Late in the afternoon the C.O. arrived back from Brigade H.Q. with the news that the 8th Battalion would be relieved that night by the 6th D.L.I., but shortly after 6 p.m. new orders came through. The whole of 151 Brigade was to be relieved before midnight by the New Zealanders.

About an hour and a half before darkness, the remnants of 9 Armoured Brigade began to pull out. Almost immediately the enemy gunners opened fire, putting down the heaviest concentration of shells which the 8th Battalion had ever experienced. It may have been caused by the large numbers of British tanks or it may have been a previously planned barrage but, in any case, the shelling went on for over an hour and not a single man of the 8th Battalion dared move out of his slit trench. There were several direct hits in the C Company area and the dismal call for stretcher bearers went up more frequently during this period of shelling than it had done at any other time during the battle. Sgt. Appleby and several other men were wounded. However, as darkness fell the tanks moved off and the 8th Battalion was not sorry to see them go.

Like the previous night it soon became very cold and the time passed interminably slowly. The New Zealanders were late, not arriving until an hour after midnight. The relief was not completed until just before 2 a.m., and in the early hours of November 3rd the 8th Battalion marched back down Boomerang Track, a collection of tired men whose numbers had been sadly depleted since the Battalion had marched up that same track only twenty-four hours previously. Lieuts. Kidson, Allardice and Cantley, and 2/Lieut. Dudman had been killed, and Major Chambers, Captains Neale and Lewis, Lieuts. Woodruff and Scott and 2/Lieut. Hunter had been wounded. Captain Turnbull was posted as missing. Of the other ranks, sixteen had been killed and seventy-six wounded ; thirty-four men were still missing. It was a heavy casualty list and the 6th and 9th Battalions had suffered just as severely.

The Battalion trudged along for just over an hour before being met by the troop-carriers under R.Q.M.S. Lightfoot. The three-ton lorries were a welcome sight to the tired troops who clambered aboard them as best they could. By 3.30 a.m. the lorries had debussed their loads in the same area which had been occupied by the Battalion before the attack. The slit trenches were still there, and with the exception of a minimum number of sentries for local protection, the men of the 8th slept, exhausted but secure in the knowledge of a job well done.

CHAPTER SIXTEEN

FROM EGYPT TO TUNISIA

The Eighth Army takes up the chase—151 *Brigade in reserve—on the move again—a remarkable Christmas—Gazala revisited—the camp outside Benghazi—nine hundred miles in thirteen days.*

By November 3rd it had become obvious that the enemy was beaten. As a direct result of the success of Operation Supercharge the decisive tank battle of El Aqqaqir had been fought on November 2nd, and although the losses on both sides were heavy they were relatively much greater for the Germans. Planes of the Desert Air Force were up with the dawn on November 3rd and pilots returning to base reported columns of Axis transport, with hundreds of vehicles nose to tail, streaming westwards along the coast road.

It was the beginning of the end for the Axis forces in Africa, but ferocious in defeat the hardened veterans of the Africa Corps fought on. Throughout November 3rd there was still a screen of 88-millimetre guns holding up the tanks of 1 Armoured Division. That night a speedily mounted but most successful attack, which reached the Rahman track south of Tel El Aqqaqir on a front of over four miles, was put in by 51 Division and a brigade of 4 Indian Division. The Germans reeled back and through this breach in the enemy lines the armoured divisions and General Freyberg's New Zealand Division were loosed in pursuit. The battle of El Alamein was over and the chase on.

Meanwhile the two days following the withdrawal of the 8th Battalion from the battle had been spent in reorganisation. A and B Companies were amalgamated to form one strong company, and on November 4th a reinforcement draft of thirty-seven other ranks arrived and was posted to C Company. They were all Welshmen—some of them Territorials—from the Welsh Regiment and Royal Welsh Fusiliers. Naturally, they resented being drafted to a D.L.I. battalion as most of them had hoped for a posting to a Welsh unit. In fact, Welsh came to most of them more easily than English. However, in a matter of weeks they settled down very well in the 8th D.L.I., and by the time the battle of Mareth took place in March they had become as much a part of the Battalion as any Durham lad and were proud to be so. The day the new draft arrived the Brigadier visited the 8th to talk to the officers. He gave them the good news that Rommel was on the run and that the attack by the D.L.I. and Scottish brigades had been instrumental in breaking the last of the enemy resistance.

On November 5th the Battalion was put under command of 9 Australian Division and ordered to march up the railway from Tel El Eisa, mopping up any resistance on the way. However, by this time the last of the German rearguards had pulled out, and after advancing about six miles the Battalion was embussed in Australian troop-carriers. The 8th D.L.I. now became completely mobile and drove on towards El Daba, part of a continuous stream of traffic using both sides of the road and stretching for miles. The Eighth Army columns were composed of every type of vehicle—jeeps, staff cars, water carriers, ammunition lorries and supply vehicles of the Army, Navy and Air Force. In the opposite direction came the Axis prisoners ; Italians in their hundreds—the officers walking along with their men, and Germans by the score. The men of the Eighth Army saw something they had never seen before—German officers walking back to captivity unescorted. In fact, there were very few British soldiers guarding the prisoners. The Germans and Italians all had one thing in common. They were a tired, bedraggled and dispirited crowd and their morale had been absolutely shattered.

The 8th Battalion arrived at El Daba that evening. As the rifle companies moved forward to take up a defensive position, a large body of Italians advanced towards them in the gathering dusk. There was an immediate "stand-to" but the Italians were not looking for a fight. Their transport had been commandeered by the Germans and they were just a small number of the thousands of Italians who had been stranded by their allies in this way. There was never any love lost between the Axis partners, and after the battle of El Alamein practically the whole of the unfortunate Italian infantry was " left on the ground," their transport being taken by the Germans.

On November 6th the D.L.I. Brigade came under command of 51 Division and thus, within the short space of three days, the Brigade had served under three different formation commanders. The Brigadier was informed that his D.L.I. battalions would not take part in the pursuit. This was a bitter disappointment to the troops who had fallen back from Gazala to Alamein and now wanted to taste the fruits of leading the chase. Unfortunately the supply situation only allowed three divisions to take part in the pursuit, and it was another eighteen months before the D.L.I. Brigade took up the chase—in Western Europe.

Late in the afternoon the Battalion moved again, to Bir el Mullah, not far from Ghalal station on the Alexandria-Matruh railway. That night the camp and bivouacs were swamped and the troops soaked to the skin by a torrential rainstorm. This unfortunate break in the weather robbed the Eighth Army of a great prize, for Montgomery had planned to trap the retreating Afrika Corps by cutting the coast road at Fuka and Matruh. However, as 1 Armoured Division and the New Zealanders approached the road a heavy rainstorm turned the desert tracks into a quagmire, bogging down the tanks, armoured cars and vehicles of the supply columns. As a result of this, Rommel's forces slipped out of the trap.

The amazing news came through on November 8th that a large Anglo-American force had landed in Morroco and Algeria. The Allies had gone over to the offensive in no uncertain way and this news, coming so soon after the success of the Alamein operation, resulted in some of the more cautious and seasoned campaigners of the desert war predicting the end of the campaign in Africa within a matter of months. A few days after this welcome news the D.L.I. Brigade, reverting to the command of 50 Division, moved back south-eastward to positions east of the Alamein Line. The Brigade occupied a reserve area a few miles in rear of the sector in the southern part of the line which the Battalion had held before moving up north to take part in Operation Supercharge.

The rest of November and the first weeks of December were leisurely when compared with the months which had passed. The Battalion carried out a training programme, and another reinforcement draft of six officers and two hundred other ranks arrived. The officers included Captain K. Kershaw, who had served with the 1st D.L.I., and Lieuts. R. O'Conor, S. Williamson and A. Richardson—all three recent arrivals in the Middle East. It was now possible to re-form A and B Companies and to make C and S Companies up to strength. A Company was commanded by Captain C. L. Beattie, B Company by Captain K. Kershaw, C Company by Captain I. R. English and S Company by Captain H. Glasper. A most successful N.C.O.'s training cadre was run, and vigorous section and platoon training carried out by companies. The C.O. was applying the maxim that most value is gained from training after a man comes out of battle. Nevertheless, the Battalion found time for games, and R.S.M. Skillen had a football pitch marked out which saw some close matches.

Lieut.-Colonel Jackson organised a visit for some of his officers to the area of the Battalion's old positions in the Alamein Line, partly as a training exercise and partly as a sight-seeing tour. After looking at the front which had been occupied by the 8th the C.O. moved over to the German and Italian lines, and it was most instructive and interesting to see the D.L.I. sector from the point of view of the enemy. After going over the heavily-mined patrolling ground in the Angar Depression the return journey to the British positions was accomplished without incident, although there were several members of the party visibly pleased when they left the mine-infested area.

This period in rear of the Alamein Line would have been quite pleasant if it had not been for the flies and an outbreak of jaundice. There were several cases in the Battalion, a remarkably high proportion being N.C.Os. and, more particularly, officers. It was seriously put forward that drinking whisky and gin was a cause of the disease, but as several of the hardened drinkers in both the Officers' and Sergeants' Messes did not get jaundice this theory was shelved. The high incidence of this unpleasant malady in the Eighth Army was a cause of considerable anxiety to the medical authorities. It invariably meant that when a man went down with jaundice he was away from his unit for several weeks.

The reason for the millions of flies which infested the area was far easier to explain. The Battalion was encamped in a part of the desert which during the last few months had been densely populated by troops. The remains of the camps and dumps attracted the flies in their millions, and they swarmed round the sites of the old cook-houses and latrines, afterwards carrying disease wherever they went. The flies were much worse than they had been at Gazala, or even when the Battalion took over from the Maoris, and the troops had a miserable time. However, the Medical Officer—Captain A. Noble—set to work and produced arsenic fly traps, of which everyone was a little scared at first. With these traps and other gadgets invented by the Pioneer Platoon and the Battalion sanitary squad incredible execution was done to the fly population. Within a very short time this particular piece of desert had become a pleasant place in which to live.

Meanwhile the pendulum of the desert war had swung beyond Tobruk and Gazala to Benghazi, which had been captured on November 20th ; Montgomery's Eighth Army had advanced no less than seven hundred miles in fifteen days. By the 23rd, 7 Armoured Division had forced the enemy out of his positions about Agedabia, and Rommel withdrew to hold the Agheila defences. After the long advance it was necessary to get the administrative services in proper order and December 14th was the earliest date by which the Eighth Army could attack at Agheila.

Although 50 Division was not destined to take any part in the battle, the Division was ordered forward into Libya to Sidi Rezegh, and on December 6th the Battalion, less the carriers which had left for Libya by train on November 30th, moved westwards beyond the Alamein Line to a staging area between Daba and Fuka. Mersa Matruh was reached the following day ; here the Battalion left the road and took to the desert, halting in a staging area some miles inland from the coast.

The route now lay across the desert and, after covering a good average of seventy or eighty miles a day, the 8th arrived in the Divisional Assembly Area on the fifth day to settle down once again in a temporary home. Here, Lieut. H. C. Catford and 2/Lieuts. W. Bailey and W. Nesham rejoined the Battalion from hospital, and on December 15th Major H. Blackden of the South Wales Borderers, who had been serving with the Transjordan Frontier Force, arrived as the Second-in-Command. Major R. P. Lidwill, who had been acting in this capacity, took over B Company once again.

Meanwhile, at Agheila, Eighth Army had broken through and was continuing the chase. Montgomery had planned to annihilate the enemy in his defences but Rommel did not stay to fight, withdrawing his forces before the full weight of the British attack could be launched. Even so, the Afrika Corps only narrowly escaped and the German rearguards were severely mauled by 7 Armoured Division and the New Zealanders.

In 50 Division training started again in earnest. Particular attention was paid to infantry—tank co-operation, and new methods of communication were tried out between tank crews and the infantry on the ground. The use of the armour for carrying rifle sections into battle was also practised and this co-operation with the tanks was by far the most interesting part of the Battalion training programme.

December very quickly drew to a close and Christmas seemed to come out of the blue, almost before anyone was ready for it. However, the Quartermaster (Captain W. G. Stray) and the P.R.I. (Captain Petrocochino) were not caught napping. They put in some very hard work to make this, the second Christmas the Battalion had spent abroad, a great success. Preparations for Christmas Day had involved early and frequent visits to the N.A.A.F.I. at Tobruk, with long standing in queues. The menu was truly remarkable, considering that the Battalion was encamped in the middle of the desert, four hundred miles from the Delta. There was roast turkey and pork with roast potatoes and dried greens, followed by Christmas pudding with rum sauce, and oranges for desert. Every man had a free bottle of beer and there was more available for those who wished to buy it. The dinner was served by the officers and sergeants in the customary manner and the C.O. visited each company. Christmas Day in the 8th Battalion was a great success and a credit to the Q.M. and P.R.I. staff.

A very interesting expedition was carried out not long after Christmas. The C.O. decided to visit the Battalion's old positions in the Gazala Box and took with him several officers and N.C.Os. who had been with the unit at that time. On arrival in the Box the party found everything practically as it had been left six months previously. Cpl. Cutty's watch was hanging up on the tent pole of the Officers' Mess cookhouse exactly where it had been left, and Captain English dug up a pair of his boots which he maintained were "perfectly serviceable," and which he continued to wear until they almost disintegrated at a later stage of the war. A number of stores, including cookers, picks, shovels, tables and tents, were salvaged and loaded on to a three-ton lorry. It was obvious that the Axis troops had never occupied the Battalion positions in the Gazala Line after the break-out, and the only visitors had been the Bedouin who had located and taken away the hidden supplies of food and water. Just before dusk the party left for Sidi Rezegh. It had been a remarkable experience.

The arrival of the New Year could not be celebrated in true North Country style because New Year's Eve found the Battalion packing up and getting ready for a long move to the west. 50 Division was again wanted up forward. Early on New Year's Day the 8th set out in M.T. from Sidi Rezegh along Q Route. The destination was El Agheila, and the desert tracks took the Battalion south of Bir Hacheim where General Koenig's Frenchmen had fought so magnificently. From Hachiem the Battalion set course across the desert for Agedabia and El Agheila. On January 3rd it rained torrents all day, soaking the troops to the skin and bogging down many of the vehicles. These were extricated from the squelching mess of mud and sand by a tow from the front and a hearty push from the rear by a score or so troops. Next day the weather was just as bad, and Brigadier D.M.W. Beake, V.C., D.S.O., M.C., who had taken over from Brigadier Percy after Supercharge, decided to halt the columns for twenty-four hours.

That evening it was learned that the route had been changed for a more northerly one, and next day the Brigade moved on again. The going was as bad as ever, and the columns were only kept moving by a great deal of towing, pushing and digging out of stranded vehicles. Only twenty-one miles were covered that day. The desert was less waterlogged on January 6th and the Battalion, passing through Msus, arrived at Sceledima at 3 p.m. Here, the destination was changed again and that evening saw the column turning north-west towards the coast and the airfield of Benina, a few miles inland from the port of Benghazi.

Next day the C.O. gave the reasons which had necessitated the changes of plan. He pointed out that from El Agheila Rommel had pulled his forces back to Buerat, and Montgomery had planned to attack the Axis troops in these positions with four divisions, one of them 50 Division. It was calculated that the daily tonnage unloaded at Benghazi would be sufficient to maintain an attacking force of this size and also meet the very considerable needs of the Desert Air Force. These hopes were dashed by the torrential storm which raged from January 4th to the 6th, met by the Battalion during the journey across the desert. The storm created havoc in the port of Benghazi. Ships broke loose to career about the harbour, and heavy seas breached the breakwater, sweeping through at flood force into the inner harbour. Four ships were sunk, including one carrying two thousand tons of ammunition, and great damage was done to lighters and tugs. The daily intake dropped from three thousand to one thousand tons a day, forcing Montgomery to change his plans. It was now impossible to maintain the force which had been originally planned for the Buerat attack, and the Army Commander decided to carry out the operation with three divisions of 30 Corps and to use the operational and administrative transport of 10 Corps (50, 4 Indian and 1 Armoured Divisions) to ferry stores forward from Tobruk. The Battalion's part in this scheme was to provide thirty-nine men and nineteen three-ton lorries for the ferry service.

This left the 8th D.L.I. with only a few vehicles, and as Benina was obviously going to be its home for some time, the Battalion settled down to make itself as comfortable as possible. The troops were able to have a look at Benghazi, not that there was a great deal of the town left to see. During two years of war Benghazi had been badly knocked about. Most of the civilian population had left, and gaunt skeletons of buildings were evidence of the havoc wrought by the night bombers of the R.A.F.

Those men of the 8th Battalion fortunate enough to get into Benghazi saw endless columns of tanks on giant transporters, and the heavily loaded supply vehicles rumbling through the almost deserted streets of the town. The Eighth Army was building up for a large scale attack which came not long after the D.L.I. Brigade had moved into the cheerless, tented camp under the Benina escarpment.

On January 15th 30 Corps opened the battle of Buerat, in order to continue the advance on Tripoli. The Germans fought savagely to hold the Eighth Army but by the evening of January 17th the attacking armoured and infantry divisions had almost broken the German resistance. Montgomery drove his troops hard, and in the early hours of January 23rd Tripoli was entered by troops of Eighth Army. The city fell three months to the day after the battle had opened at El Alamein ; the Army had advanced fourteen hundred miles in that time over terrible country, inflicting some seventy-five thousand casualties on the enemy, and destroying not only his armies but also an Empire and many reputations—chief among them Rommel's.

It was obvious that there would have to be a considerable pause before the Eighth Army could tackle its next obstacle, the French-built Mareth Line, some hundred and sixty miles west of Tripoli. Until the port of Tripoli, devastated by the retreating Germans, could be opened up and until reserves of all kinds could be accumulated, nothing but light forces could be sent westwards from Tripoli to cross the border into Tunisia. Work went ahead rapidly to repair extensive demolitions which the enemy had carried out in the harbour. Eighth Army men worked alongside men of the Mediterranean fleet. On February 6th a convoy was accepted, and by the 10th two thousand tons were being handled in a day.

General Montgomery aimed at a methodical advance to gain possession of the principal road centres as well as areas where the R.A.F. could establish airfields from which to support the attack on the Mareth Line. Rain and the very waterloggged nature of the country delayed the Eighth Army's advance into Tunisia, but on February 16th Ben Gardane—just inland from the Mediterranean and twenty-five miles inside Tunisia—was captured. The Eighth Army, pushing on rapidly, closed up on the Mareth Line. Medenine was captured on February 17th, and in the south Foum Tatahoun fell on the following day. The Ben Gardane area was chosen as a forward administrative area and very soon the vast dumps of petrol, ammunition and supplies started to accumulate for the attack.

The end of February was an anxious period for the Eighth Army. The German 15 and 21 Panzer Divisions, partly equipped with the new and formidable Tiger tank, started to concentrate, and Rommel attacked in the Medenine area on March 6th. For the Eighth Army it was another Alam Halfa, a perfectly fought defensive battle. A clear cut defensive plan had been issued and rehearsed, with the result that the Germans completely failed even to penetrate the British positions. After this battle the commander of the Afrika Corps left for Germany and took no further part in the African campaign. Montgomery was now ready to continue with his preparations for fighting the Mareth battle, one in which 50 Division and particularly the D.L.I. Brigade was destined to play a prominent and costly part.

Whilst the Eighth Army had advanced beyond Tripoli to Mareth the bulk of 50 Division remained grounded at Benina. The 8th Battalion spent seven weeks under the escarpment from January 7th until March 1st, a period of fairly intensive training. Individual, section and platoon schemes were soon in full swing and a range and assault course were made. Instruction for all ranks in mines and booby traps was given by 505 Field Company (R.E.) in a valuable series of short courses. Company and Battalion exercises were usually staged in the Jebel Achdar (The Green Hills) and it was mountain warfare in miniature. One scheme, which included an assault by night against positions on the escarpment, was known as Exercise Climber and certainly lived up to its name.

Another interesting form of training, new to the Battalion, was street fighting. Each rifle company marched to Benghazi to spend three days at the 10 Corps Street Fighting School, which had been established in a heavily bombed and uninhabited part of the town. They were three strenuous but most enjoyable days because the troops were allowed to fire all weapons and to toss grenades through the doors and windows of houses as part of their battle training. The schemes were most realistic and on one occasion a team of machine-gunners, supporting a company attack from the roof of a building, not only sprayed the target area but also disturbed the cloistered calm of the Royal Navy H.Q. with a misdirected burst of fire, causing a certain amount of confusion in the naval paymaster's office on the top floor of the building. On another occasion a two-pounder anti-tank shell went through the walls of twenty-two houses before it finally came to rest.

At Benina various reinforcement drafts were received, totalling seven officers and over a hundred other ranks. The officers included Major G. P. Chambers, Captain P. J. Lewis and Lieut. D. A. Neale, all of whom had been wounded at Alamein. Captain P. Lucas joined the Battalion from hospital, and also Lieut. J. Wheatley who had come out to the Middle East with the Battalion and had since been doing a staff job in the Delta. The 8th lost one officer when Captain A. A. E. Jones was posted to the 6th Green Howards.

At Benina the Battalion was visited by Mr. J. Lawson, the M.P. for Chester-le-Street. Mr. Lawson talked to most of the men, especially to those who came from his own constituency. The Battalion was also visited by the commander of 10 Corps, Lieut.-General B. G. Horrocks, who was by this time becoming a familiar and popular figure to the men of 50 Division.

It was not a particularly comfortable camp under the escarpment. It never rained—it poured, and the ground was turned into a quagmire of squelching mud on several occasions. Early morning P.T., when all ranks including the C.O. had to quit the warmth and comfort of their blankets, was one of the penalties of being out of the line. However, the Divisional Concert Party, remarkably well organised by Lieut. "Stringer" Davis, gave some excellent shows from the back of a converted three-ton lorry and never failed to cheer up the troops. On one red letter occasion an E.N.S.A. concert party, which included some very welcome female talent, gave several bright and breezy shows out at the camp and afterwards consumed a large percentage of the Officers' Mess gin and whisky ration.

Soon after the Battalion arrived at Benina the Carrier and Mortar Platoons under Lieut. P. Hampson had been sent off under divisional control to Castel Verde, about eight miles east of Tripoli. Reports filtered back to the Battalion concerning the good time the H.Q. Company men were having in Tripoli, these reports being substantiated when charges from the ever vigilant Military Police reached Battalion H.Q. concerning two members of the Carrier Platoon who had been apprehended in Tripoli. Finally the C.O. decided to send Major Chambers ahead to see what was happening, and on February 25th the commander of H.Q. Company left for Castel Verde. He found the two platoons encamped in a pleasant orchard, a welcome change from the desert. Living conditions, however, were not too good. Food was rather scarce and N.A.A.F.I. supplies non-existent. Cigarettes were at a premium and much easier to obtain at Benina. There was no attraction about Tripoli itself ; the town was dead and the stories about unlimited drink and tobacco had been greatly exaggerated.

However, soon after Major Chambers arrived, the small party was ordered to move forward to the Ben Gardane area which had just been taken by the Eighth Army. The two platoons were carried on tank transporters and it was a slow and tiring journey. The roads were choked with vehicles taking up supplies to the administrative area at Ben Gardane which the Carrier and Mortar Platoons of the D.L.I. Brigade, under command of Major Chambers, had been given the task of defending. It was not going to be a pleasant job by any means, for the area seemed to consist of miles of giant forty-four gallon petrol containers, a wonderful target for the Luftwaffe. Major Chambers reconnoitred possible defensive positions and the 151 Brigade troops then went into laager a mile or two away. Fortunately they did not have to fight from the positions.

Meanwhile the Battalion had left Benina on March 2nd. At 8.30 a.m. the column moved off on its nine-hundred mile journey forward to an assembly area behind the Mareth Line. Unlike the previous move, the route lay along the main coast road for the larger part of the journey, only crossing the desert between Buerat and Homs. The column skirted Benghazi and by 9 o'clock the leading vehicles were speeding westwards along the coast road. The routine for the move was the same each day. The column pulled into a staging area in the early afternoon and left the following morning at 8 a.m. The coast road followed the Gulf of Sirte, and all along the route were signs of the thoroughness with which the Germans had mined the roads and verges. Every few yards there were stacks of disarmed enemy mines, evidence of the hard and dangerous work carried out by the Eighth Army sappers. In Sirte itself was a large notice, " Sirte is dirty with mines and booby traps," and it was asking for trouble to run off the road anywhere along the route where it had not been marked as clear of mines. Where the German rear-guards had fought it out with the British advanced guards, there were abandoned guns and burnt out tanks, with small wooden crosses marking the graves of Panzer

Grenadiers or British troops.

After a seven day journey the Battalion column was within striking distance of Tripoli, and the bare, stony desert gave way to palm trees, irrigation and strips of cultivated land. It was a welcome change and the convoy sped through the type of country which the men of the Battalion had not seen since their last leave in the Egyptian Delta. On March 9th the convoy skirted Tripoli, and to the disappointment of everyone turned left for a staging area in the vicinity of the airfield at Castel Benito. The following day the Battalion pushed on again and kept going fast all day, covering a distance of a hundred and forty miles to cross the Tripolitanian-Tunisian border just as dusk was closing in. The convoy staged that night in the Ben Gardane area where the Eighth Army had by this time built up a network of massive supply dumps. The back of the long journey had been broken and during the early afternoon of March 13th the 8th D.L.I. arrived at its destination, only a few miles behind the forward elements of the Eighth Army. Major Chambers with the Mortar and Carrier Platoons rejoined the Battalion soon after it had pulled into the new area.

CHAPTER SEVENTEEN

THE MARETH LINE

A unique system of defences—50 *Division prepares for the assault—Battalion patrols sound the enemy defences—the* 8*th Battalion Plan.*

BY this time it was obvious to every man in the 8th Battalion that 50 Division was going to play an important part in the Battle of the Mareth Line. This system of defences—quite unique in the African theatre—had originally been constructed by the French to protect Tunisia against attack by the Italians from Libya. The defences stretched approximately twenty-two miles from the sea near Zarat to the Matmata hills in the west.

Except for a few tracks running through narrow passes, these rugged broken hills formed a natural barrier to wheeled transport and at the same time dominated the whole western end of the defence system. In the costal sector the Line had been based on the Wadi Zigzaou, a horrible obstacle, widened and deepened to form a tank trap and covered by enfilade fire along its whole length by a complicated system of concrete and steel pillboxes, gun emplacements and block-houses. The strongpoints, formidable affairs of concrete two or three feet thick, were supported by a well-revetted trench system linked with deep dugouts and funk holes.

Since the Franco-German armistice Italian labour gangs under German supervision had dug an anti-tank ditch twelve feet deep and fifteen feet wide between the Wadi Zigzaou and the defence line, as well as liberally wiring and sowing the whole area with Teller, anti-personnel and shrapnel mines. In addition, a series of well-sited outpost and covering positions had been established forward of the wadi, making it difficult for our advanced elements to reconnoitre the main defences. The Mareth Line was, in fact, a miniature Maginot Line.

The French had always maintained that the Line could not be outflanked but General Montgomery was not prepared to accept this view and as far back as January the Long Range Desert Group had found a way round the Mareth defences. His plan therefore was for 50 Division and 23 Armoured Brigade under 30 Corps to deliver a frontal attack in the coastal sector whilst, at the same time, the New Zealand Corps carried out a wide turning movement to outflank the Line and then to push on to an objective in the Gabes area. This was Montgomery's famous " Left Hook." 10 Corps was to be held in reserve with its two armoured divisions—1 and 7 Armoured—ready to exploit success. Every available bomber and fighter of the Desert Air Force was to be used in support of the operation. The main battle was scheduled to commence at 10.30 p.m. on March 20th.

A preliminary operation was necessary to drive in the remaining outposts covering the approaches to the Wadi Zigzaou. This took place during the night of March 16/17th and was carried out by 69 Brigade of 50 Division, part of 51 Division, and 201 Guards Brigade. The operation was successful except in the case of the Guards who, coming up against a most formidable minefield system, suffered heavy casualties and were forced to withdraw at daylight.

Meanwhile 50 Division was busy preparing for the main assault. The Divisional Commander gave 69 Brigade the task of attacking a series of newly-constructed strongpoints on the British side of the Wadi Zigzaou, whilst the D.L.I. Brigade, on the right flank attacked across the wadi to capture two large forts, Ouerzi and Ksiba Est. The divisional engineers were then to bridge the wadi with causeways so that Valentine tanks of 23 Armoured Brigade could get forward to support the infantry on their final objectives. The artillery plan for the operation was on the same scale as at Alamein.

Meanwhile the L.O.B. personnel under Major R. P. Lidwill had left the Battalion. When a unit is in the forward area it always has a proportion of all ranks "left out of battle" to form the first line reinforcements. They were encamped not far away and Major Lidwill took every opportunity of getting forward to the Battalion for conferences about the coming battle. In this way he kept himself fully in the picture and it was well that he did, for he was to take a very much more active part in the Battle of Mareth than he or anyone else imagined.

On March 18th forward troops of the Eighth Army were within a thousand yards of the notorious Wadi Zigzaou and the defences on its further bank. Two days remained for 50 Division to lay the final plans. It was essential to reconnoitre the wadi, find the best way across, and glean information about the defences. This information could only be gained by night patrols, and during the night of March 18/19th Lieut. Shepherd of A Company 8th D.L.I. took a reconnaissance patrol into the bed of the wadi. The following night Lieut. R. O'Conor of C Company went down to the wadi but neither he nor Shepherd could find any signs of a suspected minefield on the British side of the Zigzaou. However, under the noses and guns of the enemy, they reconnoitred the most suitable crossing places and gained a shrewd idea of the layout of the enemy defences.

The C.O. issued his orders at Battalion H.Q. on the night of March 19th. The Brigadier had given the 9th Battalion the task of capturing Ksiba Ouest on the right flank of the Brigade attack, whilst the 8th Battalion took Ouerzi and a strongpoint to the right of the fort, known as Little Ouerzi. When the two D.L.I. battalions had gained their objectives, Valentine tanks of 50 R.T.R. were to cross the wadi by causeways, followed by the 6th D.L.I. whose task was an attack through the 8th and 9th to extend the depth of the bridgehead.

The enemy dispositions at the time of the battle were interesting. As usual, the Italians held the line with German backing for the important places when it could be spared. The 50 Division attack would meet the Young Fascist Division—the best of the Italian troops —and the German 90 Light Division had been positioned to stop any advance down the main road axis. In reserve, behind the Mareth Line defences, was 15 Panzer Division.

The C.O.'s plan was for C Company on the right to capture Little Ouerzi, whilst A Company took Ouerzi. B Company was to remain in reserve until called forward to support A Company in the Ouerzi locality. A and C Companies were each allocated a Scorpion tank to move ahead of them as far as the near side of the wadi, thrashing the ground with flail chains to explode any mines. It was hoped that the Scorpions would clear a lane through the minefield, and the C.O. explained that, as it would only be narrow, the rifle companies would have to follow the Scorpions in threes. It was an awkward formation for leading troops into battle but the only safe one in the circumstances. The C.O. paused and looked round the officers assembled at Battalion H.Q. " And we shall want someone with a lantern to walk in front of the Scorpions to lead them as far as the wadi when the barrage starts." There was dead silence. It did not need much imagination to realise that it was almost suicide for a man to walk in front of the noisy Scorpions, which would draw the fire of every enemy gun as soon as they started to move forward. On the other hand, without a guide light to follow, the tanks would never reach the wadi, and the infantry would have to cross the minefield without them. The C.O. chose the second-in-command of the Carrier Platoon, Lieut. W. Douglas, for the job, and the laughter which greeted his decision was not so much because of poor Douglas's obvious discomfort but because it was a simple way to show relief.

In addition to the flail tanks, one N.C.O. and three sappers with a mine detector and bangalore torpedoes were to be attached to each company for minefield clearance. The troops supporting the 8th Battalion in the operation were 296 Battery of the 74th Field Regiment, one section of 505 Field Company (R.E.), A Company of the 2nd Cheshires with Vickers machine-guns and 107 Anti-tank Battery, Northumberland Hussars.

The morning of the 20th was bright and clear. Just before midday a sortie of Mitchell medium bombers flew over the Mareth Line, their silver wings glinting in the sunlight. The eighteen planes dropped their bombs, but as they turned for home one of them was hit by the intense German anti-aircraft fire, and a tongue of flame licked the fuselage and tailplane. The Mitchell lost height rapidly, twisting and turning like a leaf as it fell, whilst one by one the crew baled out and their parachutes opened. As the plane crashed, the petrol tanks exploded with a dull boom and the airmen dropped out of sight behind the German positions.

That afternoon the company commanders went forward to have a close look at the wadi and enemy defences. Jeeps took them as far as the H.Q. of 69 Brigade from where they went on foot to Battalion H.Q. of the 5th East Yorks. They crawled forward on their bellies to an East Yorkshire post, within a few hundred yards of the wadi. The section commander was thoroughly fed up. The Divisional Commander, the Brigade Commanders, and the Commanding Officers of the attacking battalions had all reconnitred the Mareth Line from his stretch of trench. There had been some enemy shelling because of the extra movement, and he summed up the situation in a few words. "I don't mind who comes up here," he said, "as long as they keep their heads down, but when Crasher (Major-General Nichols) and Beako (Brigadier Beak) came up here, they bobbed about all over the place and didn't even take the red tabs off their ruddy hats!"

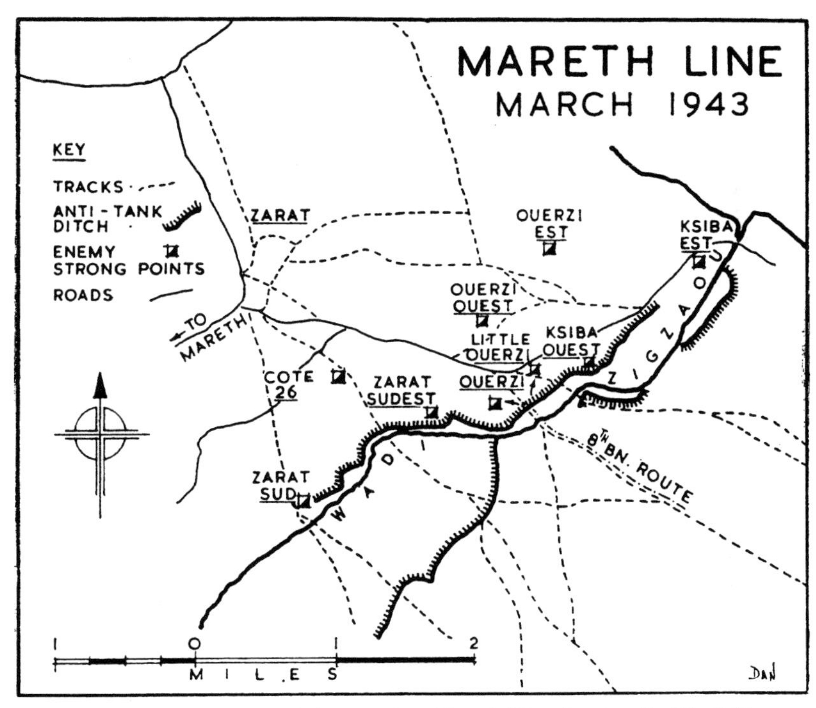

TUNISIA. The eastern end of the notorious Mareth Line showing the Wadi Zigzaou, the anti-tank ditch and the enemy strongpoints which the 8th Battalion attacked just before midnight on March 20th, 1943.

From the trench it was possible to get an excellent view of the Zigzaou and the defences on the far side. The recent rains had swollen the wadi and it looked about thirty yards across with sheer sides. Beyond the Zigzaou, the company commanders could see the anti-tank ditch, and behind it the forts and strongpoints surrounded by wire. On this sunny and peaceful afternoon there was no movement of any sort in the enemy positions. They seemed to be almost deserted. It was uncannily quiet and neither the Axis garrison of the Mareth defences nor the British infantry facing them could have imagined the extent of the frightful carnage and destruction of the night ahead.

CHAPTER EIGHTEEN

THE BATTLE OF MARETH

The Battalion attacks—at grips with the enemy—the loss of the C.O.—B Company moves up—C Company counter-attacked—the bridgehead enlarged—heavy British tank casualties—German Panzers versus the 8th D.L.I.—the Battalion withdraws—a night of fierce fighting—another withdrawal—final victory for the Eighth Army.

At 7.45 p.m., just as dusk was closing in, the 8th Battalion left the assembly area with A Company leading, followed by C and then B Companies. The route lay along fairly recognisable tracks, and when the full moon came up, visibility was very good. However, the men were carrying full scale equipment which slowed down the pace considerably, and the unfortunate members of the rear platoon of B Company were almost doubling. The Second-in-Command, Major H. Blackden, followed the marching troops with a small convoy of jeeps carrying the company 2″ Mortars, wireless sets and hot cocoa in containers. The march from the assembly area, although slow, was not interfered with by the enemy and the only casualties were three men of A Company who were wounded when they walked on to a minefield.

The 8th Battalion reached the Forming-Up-Place at 9.30 p.m. where the Intelligence Officer, Lieut. A. Richardson, met the head of the column and led the troops to their places. The Battalion was laid out in a herringbone formation with the rifle companies, and carrier, mortar and anti-tank platoons on either side of the central axis. The troops settled down, most of them trying to get some sleep as the attack was not scheduled for another two and a quarter hours.

The 8th had not been on the F.U.P. very long when a sapper three-ton lorry carrying scaling ladders and men arrived. The driver raced his engine as the truck was manouevred into position, and the night air must have carried the noise well beyond the Axis positions on the far side of the wadi. Within a few minutes the enemy guns had ranged on the area with harassing fire which was uncomfortably accurate. One of the shells hit the Engineers' truck and it burst into flames, illuminating the whole of the Battalion F.U.P. The shelling immediately became more intense, and as no slit trenches had been dug the men could only lie flat and hope for the best. By some miracle not a single man was killed, although one or two were wounded, and after fifteen minutes of intense shelling the guns fell silent.

Scaling ladders were now collected by A and C Companies and put on the Scorpions for them to carry as far as the British side of the wadi. Everything was all set but there was no sign of the Second-in-

Command with the convoy of jeeps. When it was clear that they could not arrive in time, the C.O. of 296 Battery, Major G. Fawkes, came to the rescue and lent the Battalion two wireless sets which were allotted to A and C Companies and quickly netted in. The Battalion had to do without the 2" Mortars and the hot drinks. "We are kicking off on the wrong foot," said the C.O.

Punctually at 10.30 p.m. the barrage opened in support of 69 Brigade. As the Green Howards and East Yorkshires attacked, the whole weight of the Corps artillery came down on the Mareth defences and there was the continual boom of gunfire, the whistle of shells overhead and the deafening crash as they exploded on the far side of the wadi. Above this noise the waiting D.L.I. battalions could hear the stacatto rattle of the Vickers machine-guns of the 2nd Cheshires in support of 69 Brigade. The noise of this mighty barrage of artillery and machine-guns made it impossible for men to talk to each other without bellowing, but it was most reassuring, especially to those who were soon going in to action for the first time.

Thirty-five minutes after the start of the 69 Brigade operation, A and C Companies of the 8th Battalion fell in and moved off in threes towards the wadi. They followed a white tape laid by the Intelligence Section through an olive grove to the start line. At 11.15 p.m. the two companies crossed this line whilst the giant Scorpions, setting their flails working, began to move forward following the guide light carried by Lieut. Douglas. The infantry let the Scorpions get about a hundred yards ahead before following in threes, led by the respective company commanders and the sapper mine-detecting teams. In the midst of all the noise and confusion there was an amusing incident when the C.O., far from satisfied with the rate of advance of his companies, went forward to C Company and told Captain English to "get a move on and ignore these blasted Scorpions. There aren't any mines on this side of the wadi." He had only just finished the sentence when there was a loud explosion as the Scorpion in front set off a mine.

The companies moved over a ridge and down the slope towards the wadi. It was a strange and eerie sight. The Zigzaou, with muddy water flowing through the middle of it, lay between our troops and the enemy defences like a barrier. On the far side the clumps of palm trees had been frayed by the heavy gunfire, and beyond the palms coloured tracer from the enemy guns whipped towards the wadi on fixed lines. It was quite obvious that the Zigzaou had been well registered.

By this time the flail tanks had ceased to function. The companies paused whilst the scaling ladders were taken off the stationary Scorpions and carried by eight men from each platoon. The troops moved on, and the head of the A and C Company columns was about fifty yards short of the wadi when two shells from a medium gun landed without any warning beside the line of C Company men. Sgts. Martin and Brown, the platoon sergeants of 13 and 14 Platoons, and three other men were badly wounded. This was a heavy and, it seemed, unnecessary blow, for Captain Wakelin, the Gunner officer from 74th Field Regiment with C Company, agreed that they were shells from a British gun. The men's faith in their own barrage was considerably shaken, and after the wounded had been evacuated by the stretcher bearers to the R.A.P. it was with some difficulty that the officers and N.C.Os. got the companies moving again in threes.

The wadi was both deeper and wider than had been expected, and the men struggled through the muddy waters, holding rifles and Bren guns above their heads. There was a short pause on the far bank to see that everyone was present and here Lieut. Shepherd of A Company was wounded. The enemy shelling was becoming much more intense, although the middle of the wadi had not yet been subjected to very heavy fire. The two companies pushed on towards the anti-tank ditch. C Company took the right flank and made for Little Ouerzi whilst A Company carried straight on, heading for Ouerzi.

A Company crossed the minefield with some difficulty. Several men were killed and wounded by mines before the anti-tank ditch was reached. Here Captain Beattie was wounded together with several N.C.Os. and men and Lieut. Wheatley took over command. After the scaling ladders had been placed in position over the ditch, Wheatley led the company across and pressed on towards Ouerzi. Opposition was now stiffening and the advance was met but not halted by artillery and machine-gun fire. Under the covering fire of Bren guns, and using Tommy-guns and grenades, A Company doubled across the last few yards of open ground to close with the enemy of the outer defences, killing some and taking others prisoner.

A Company was fighting well and four members of the company are especially worthy of mention for the parts they played in the closing stages of the advance. C.S.M. G. E. Wood was one of the first to reach the objective. With only one officer remaining it could have been a slow and difficult job getting the company organised as the men were somewhat dispersed. The C.S.M. realised that speed was essential and with a complete disregard for his own safety he moved about on the objective amid heavy machine-gun and mortar fire, doing the work of several and organising the defences of the company position.

During the advance Sgt. W. Crawford was platoon sergeant of a platoon detailed to attack and capture one of the Ouerzi pillboxes. On the approach to the objective, in extremely heavy hostile artillery and machine-gun fire, his platoon commander was blown up on a mine. Sgt. Crawford reorganised the platoon, in which casualties had now occurred, and led it forward in the face of still heavier hostile fire to capture the platoon objective. He then set about clearing three pillboxes and their adjacent trench systems of enemy. One of Crawford's section leaders was Pte. D. D. Michael who led his section through heavy artillery, machine-gun and mortar fire to the assistance of his platoon sergeant. Pte. Michael then joined Sgt. Crawford in clearing the three pillboxes. They were not alone in this task and were soon joined by Pte. W. Higginson, who like Crawford and Michael had kept going steadily during the final assault, and now set about with great zest the task of killing the enemy in the pillboxes.

It was not an easy task to clear the enemy from Ouerzi Fort. The trenches around and leading to and from the fort were very deep which made it difficult to follow their layout. Although A Company partly cleared the area of the Italian garrison, repeated efforts failed to dislodge a handful of intrepid Young Fascists holding out behind steel and concrete in the innermost part of the fort. There was no alternative but for A Company temporarily to share Ouerzi Fort with the Italians, who in some cases were only a few yards away from the British troops.

Meanwhile, on A Company's right, C Company was making good progress. It had originally been planned that on the far side of the wadi the sappers would sweep a path through the minefield in front of the infantry but in practice this was impossible. There was so much noise from the barrage and defensive fire that the sappers could not hear the buzz in the earphones of their detectors when a mine was located ; and in any case there were so many steel shell fragments littering the area between the wadi and anti-tank ditch that the detectors could not discriminate between mines and shell fragments. The only course open to Captain English was to take his men straight through the minefield, treating it as a normal risk of war. The company formed up in threes again and English led the way across the minefield towards the anti-tank ditch. There were surprisingly few casualties, although the sapper lance-corporal and his detector team were killed either by mines or enemy shelling. There were also six or seven C Company men killed and wounded.

It took only a few minutes to bridge the anti-tank ditch with two of the scaling ladders ; the others were not needed. There was a pause of fifteen minutes on the near side of the ditch whilst the barrage hammered away at the pillboxes and strongpoints in the main defences. When it lifted, C Company rushed across the scaling ladders to spread out in open formation, and the change that now came over the company was amazing. The men were full of life and aggressive spirit, whereas before they had been rather nervous and difficult to lead. Threes had been a most unpleasant and uncomfortable formation in which to go into battle and everyone was glad to be finished with it.

Unlike A Company, C Company met with very little opposition. The troops, advancing with fixed bayonets, saw some enemy running off in front, too far away to be engaged. There was heavy Bren gun fire from somewhere on the right flank of C Company where B Company of the 9th Battalion, attacking the fort known as Ksiba Ouest, was obviously meeting stiff resistance. C Company was more fortunate, although enemy shelling caused some casualties, including L/Cpl. Brennan of 13 Platoon. The advance continued steadily, until after covering about five hundred yards the leading platoons came to a road. Captain English decided that this was the objective, if not a little beyond it, and gave orders to dig in. The success signal was sent up by Verey light and confirmed over the wireless set by L/Cpl. Simpson.

The men had no sooner started to consolidate than a great concentration of British artillery fire came down in the area, and C Company had the unpleasant experience of being at the receiving end of a twenty-five pounder barrage. It made them realise what the Germans and Italians had been subjected to at Alamein and again at Mareth. This heavy concentration surprisingly enough resulted in only one casualty. A shell blew Lieut. Johnson several feet into the air. He took no further part in the battle and was eventually evacuated suffering from severe shock and loss of memory.

Meanwhile the Battalion had suffered a grievous casualty. Lieut.-Colonel Jackson had been killed in the wadi. When A and C Companies crossed, he was down at the Zigzaou with the Intelligence Officer and for some time there was no news of the two of them. Then Lieut. Douglas, who led the Scorpions to near the wadi and had then been wounded in the foot, was brought back to Battalion H.Q. His was a miraculous escape. Douglas reported that the C.O. and Richardson had been wounded and were lying helpless on the banks of the Zigzaou. The enemy guns were now shelling the wadi very heavily, and according to Douglas there were a dozen or more wounded men down there, lying in the open at the mercy of the shellfire. A search party was immediately sent out with stretcher bearers but, although the men shouted, there was no reply from either the C.O. or his companion. Neither did they find any trace of the men whom Douglas had last seen alive. The search party returned and no one at Battalion H.Q. doubted that the C.O. and Richardson had died of their wounds. This was, in fact, the case although it could never be established whether they died as a result of their original wounds or whether they had been hit again as they lay in the wadi. It was a terrible shock to the Battalion. Since first taking command of the 8th at Gazala "Jake" Jackson had led the Battalion in three battles. And he led in the true sense of the word. At times he had almost seemed without fear, and his officers and men respected him as a very brave man and a first-class leader. The officer with him—Lieut. Richardson—had only joined the Battalion after Alamein but in that short time this pre-war schoolmaster from Devon had impressed everyone with his cheerfulness and the efficient way in which he dealt with all situations, however difficult.

Meanwhile B Company—the reserve company—was still on the home side of the wadi in the vicinity of the start line. When A and C Companies had moved off, the B Company platoons took up defensive positions on the left flank of the Battalion front, ready to meet any enemy counter-thrust across the Zigzaou. The odd shell fell in the company area, and occasionally machine-gun fire swept over the platoon positions, but most of the enemy defensive fire was falling in the wadi. Nevertheless, it was one of these infrequent bursts of fire which killed a B Company platoon commander—Lieut. W. Bailey. Bailey had been evacuated with a severe attack of jaundice only a few hours before Supercharge, and left hospital to rejoin the Battalion just in time for the move up to the Mareth Line.

Shortly after the platoon runner reported to B Company H.Q. that Lieut. Bailey had been killed, the company commander, Captain P. J. Lewis, met Lieut. Douglas as he was being evacuated. When Lewis heard that the C.O. had been badly wounded, he decided to carry out the original plan and to take his men across the Zigzaou to reinforce A Company on the far side. As B Company had no mine-detecting team, Lewis told his officers and N.C.Os. that the company would have to run the gauntlet and take a chance with the mines. The important thing was to get across the wadi without further delay.

The men moved off in single file with the company commander leading. It was fairly quiet in the wadi, where the enemy gunfire had slackened. The leading sections waded through the muddy waters to reach the far side without incident where Lewis knelt down to speak to Lieut. Shepherd, the A Company officer who had been wounded. Shepherd had scooped out a narrow trench with his hand and this had given some protection but shrapnel had wounded him again as he lay there. He was in a bad way and had been too weak to reply to the shouts of the search party.

As Shepherd with difficulty gave information about the A Company dispositions, there was suddenly a blinding flash and a loud explosion. Lieut. Pentney, the commander of the leading B Company platoon, had stepped on a mine. Pentney was killed instantly and shrapnel from the exploding mine wounded Captain Lewis and killed or wounded most of Advanced Company H.Q. The explosion set off the enemy defensive fire again and a fierce concentration of artillery and mortar fire crashed down in the wadi, causing heavy casualties to B Company. Enemy machine-guns also opened up and the company second-in-command, Lieut. J. F. Gedge, who had just crossed the wadi, was wounded by a burst of fire. As he lay there, in a very exposed position, C.S.M. Brannigan crawled forward to his assistance. He had to face a hail of machine-gun fire which frustrated his first rescue attempt, but undeterred Brannigan tried again and this time he was successful. He reached the wounded officer and dragged him to safety, all the time under heavy fire. The C.S.M. then found that Lieut. Gedge had already died of his wounds. This left B Company with only one officer, Lieut. J. Randall, and whilst C.S.M. Brannigan positioned some Bren guns to answer the enemy fire Randall crawled forward to his company commander, who told him to take what was left of B Company across the anti-tank ditch and up to the A Company objective.

Randall and the C.S.M. collected the platoons together and took them forward, leaving the wounded on the banks of the wadi. These unfortunate men, with very little cover, had a terrifying experience for the next ten minutes. Machine-gun fire swept the crossing place in enfilade whilst the artillery and mortar fire was almost continuous. One of the enemy guns was a 105-millimetre and the wounded men lying in the wadi could hear the shells coming towards them like an express train. Some of them fell in the stream, splattering the wounded with stagnant water and mud. Others crashed down on the banks to kill some of the men and wound others for a second time. This gun did terrible destruction and there were only a few of the wounded B Company men, including the company commander, left alive when this heavy concentration of artillery, mortar and machine-gun fire ended.

With the infantry companies on their objectives, Lieut. P. Hampson marshalled his mortar carriers together, less one of them which had been knocked out by enemy shellfire, and moved down towards the wadi. The leading carrier with Hampson and Sgt. Mitchell edged slowly down the forward slope towards the Zigzaou but had only gone a few yards when it blew up on a mine. Hampson, Mitchell and the crew were not badly hurt although the carrier was wrecked. The time was about 4 a.m. and it was still dark. Hampson decided to unload the carriers and send them back to Battalion H.Q. so as not to risk losing any more on mines. Having done this he went forward on foot with Sgt. Mitchell to cross the wadi and contact the companies. The enemy fire was so intense that the two men had only gone a few yards when they had to take cover in a small ditch where they had to lie for the next two hours, unable to move and with machine-gun fire on fixed lines going over their heads in a steady stream. They eventually crawled on their bellies for a quarter of a mile back to the Battalion H.Q. area.

Meanwhile Major Blackden had assumed command of the Battalion. Having decided to go forward to A and C Companies he crossed the wadi safely but was wounded by shellfire before reaching the anti-tank ditch. He managed to stagger to the ditch where he collapsed, and during a lull in the shelling was dragged in by stretcher bearers with Captain Beattie and the wounded A Company men. The stretcher bearers in the anti-tank ditch were under Cpl. S. Hart, attached to A Company. Many members of the 8th Battalion owe their lives to the sterling work done by this N.C.O. when the infantry companies crossed the wadi and advanced to their objectives. In the early stages of the attack, when A Company had heavy casualties, Cpl. Hart organised and led the work of his stretcher bearers in such a way that although several of his men had been put out of action, he not only arranged the clearance of casualties from A Company but also from B and C Companies who had lost most of their stretcher bearers. On many occasions he went out into the open in the face of heavy fire to rescue 8th Battalion men who were lying wounded and at the mercy of the heavy German shelling. Cpl. Hart saved the lives of a large number of men in this way and for his gallantry was awarded the Military Medal.

Meanwhile the section from 505 Field Company and the Battalion Pioneer Platoon had started work on a crossing place which would carry the weight of tanks and supporting arms. Their gallant attempt was frustrated by intense and accurate machine-gun fire coming from enemy positions on the left of the bridgehead, and by the large number of mines on the banks of the wadi. The Zigzaou had by this time become a veritable death trap.

The rifle companies spent the rest of the night digging in and consolidating their positions. A and B Companies, both considerably reduced in numbers, were able to make use of some of the enemy trenches in the Ouerzi locality, but C Company had to construct new positions. 14 Platoon, now reduced to two N.C.Os. and fourteen men under L/Sgt. Holben, was detailed to dig in on the far side of the road which C Company had reached, with the responsibility of watching the right and right-rear. The ground fell away to the front and right of the company area, and 13 and 15 platoons took up positions covering these forward slopes. Company H.Q. was established on the near side of the road with the Bren guns covering the left-rear. Liason was soon established with B Company of the 9th Battalion on the right. This company, after suffering heavy casualties, had captured Ksiba Ouest, taken some prisoners, and was now astride the same road as Captain English's company.

By this time the command of the 8th Battalion had been taken over by the Adjutant, Captain K. Kershaw. He ordered the machine-gun platoon of A Company, 2nd Cheshires, forward to assist the rifle companies in their consolidation. With little regard for the enemy harassing fire, the Cheshires man-handled their guns across the wadi and anti-tank ditch, afterwards taking up positions near A Company in the Ouerzi locality.

When first light came on March 21st everything was quiet beyond the Zigzaou and there was no sign of an enemy counter-attack. But in the wadi the situation at the proposed crossing places was far from satisfactory. The sappers had laid brushwood fascines as a base for the causeways but their attempts to build these were hampered and frustrated, both by the heavy and accurate enfilade fire from the flank and the great number of anti-tank and anti-personnel mines in the area. However, they gallantly persevered and although they suffered heavy casualties a causeway was built. Three tanks of the 50th R.T.R. got across but the third one unfortunately smashed the fascines, making it impossible for any other vehicle, let alone a tank, to negotiate the crossing. This meant that the whole operation would be delayed and that the remainder of the Valentine tanks, the carriers and anti-tank guns of the 8th and 9th Battalions, and the whole of the 6th Battalion would have to remain east of the wadi. For the infantry beyond the wadi, with no anti-tank gun support, it was a critical situation.

However, although A and B Companies in Ouerzi had only two officers between them—Lieut. Wheatley of A Company and Lieut. Randall of B—and had also lost between a quarter and a third of their strength, both companies had almalgamated and were confident of holding their positions in the trenches of Ouerzi fort. The enemy were equally confident of ousting the two companies and it soon became evident that they had infiltrated back into the positions by means of tunnels, and in fact had re-occupied the three pillboxes which had been cleared the night before as well as parts of the trench system. In some cases sniper and machine-gun posts had been established within grenade range of A and B Companies.

This was an untenable position for the 8th Battalion men, and to Sgt. Crawford, Pte. Higginson and Pte. Michael—the trio who had originally done so well in clearing the positions—must go a great deal of the credit for keeping the persistent enemy infantry at bay. Crawford repeatedly cleared the pillboxes. As soon as he left them, however, more enemy troops moved in and the A Company sergeant, with his frequent sorties, must have killed and wounded dozens of the enemy. He also organised and led attacks on sniper and machine-gun posts which had been established outside his platoon area and succeeded in clearing three of these. Pte. Higginson was responsible for detecting and breaking up several attacks which were launched from the pillboxes and trench system. Due to his presence of mind the attacks were smashed before they could get under way and heavy casualties were inflicted on the enemy and a number captured. Pte. Michael, like Sgt. Crawford, led attacks on the pillboxes and on each occasion killed or wounded a number of the enemy.

It was an incredible situation. The pillboxes could not safely be occupied by A and B Companies but at the same time the enemy had to be kept out of them. If they had not been kept clear of enemy then the two companies would have been forced to withdraw from Ouerzi. The energetic way in which Sgt. Crawford and Ptes. Higginson and Michael set about this task was directly responsible for the maintenance during the battle of a firm left flank to the British positions in Ouerzi. For this and their earlier gallantry in the final stages of the A Company advance, Sgt. Crawford was awarded a bar to the Military Medal he had won at Alamein, and Ptes. Higginson and Michael were each awarded the Military Medal.

Meanwhile, C Company on the right flank was well established and in good heart; the company commander took the opportunity, whilst it was reasonably quiet, to evacuate some of the wounded. He also sent back his second-in-command, Captain H. Welch, to give Battalion H.Q. details of the company positions and to ask for a mortar O.P. and anti-tank guns to strengthen the defensive layout. He knew nothing of the critical situation at the crossing places.

Soon after first light the thudding drone of aero engines in the east heralded the approach of R.A.F. bombers. It was a heartening sight. They flew high overhead, ringed by little black puffs of enemy anti-aircraft fire, and their bombs dropped with a satisfying crump on targets in the enemy rear area. Then they turned slowly and flew back over the Mareth Line.

The enemy was still holding on doggedly to several strongpoints to the front and flank of the D.L.I. Brigade bridgehead. A 20-millimetre high velocity gun, mounted in a strongpoint to the right of C Company, occasionally opened fire without doing much damage. C.S.M. Ranson positioned the Company H.Q. Bren and returned the fire which, although it did not knock out the gun crew, kept the 20-millimetre quiet for several hours.

It was not quiet by any means on the home side of the wadi where Battalion H.Q., with most of the carriers and anti-tank guns parked in the area, had been under heavy shellfire since first light. The enemy guns were right on the target, and together with some heavy mortars caused numerous casualties. In fact, except at night when the shelling and mortars eased up, the area was continually under fire throughout the battle. The drivers of the American Field Service ambulances deserve a special mention. They brought their Dodge ambulances right forward into the area to evacuate the wounded from the R.A.P. which Captain Noble had established near Battalion H.Q.

At 2.30 p.m. Captain Kershaw went to a conference at Brigade H.Q. where Brigadier Beak gave out orders for the night. The 6th Battalion was to pass through the 8th D.L.I. positions and then, aided by a heavy artillery barrage, was to attack with the object of deepening and widening the bridgehead on the left flank. One of the 9th D.L.I. companies and a company of East Yorkshires from 69 Brigade were given the task of broadening the base of the bridgehead. During the night the sappers were to complete the crossing place so that the remainder of the 50th R.T.R. could get over the Zigzaou. After the tanks had crossed, the D.L.I. battalions were to move their supporting arms forward to the infantry. The conference then broke up and Kershaw returned to Battalion H.Q. with Major R. P. Lidwill who, to his obvious delight, had been recalled from the L.O.B. camp by the Brigadier to take over command of the Battalion.

Whilst the conference had been in progress 15 Platoon of C Company (Lieut. R. Roberts) reported Italian infantry forming up on their front. This information was immediately passed to Battalion H.Q. and C Company "stood-to." The Gunner officer with the company, Captain Wakelin, had also seen this enemy movement from the O.P. behind 15 Platoon, and he wirelessed his H.Q. to make it a battery target. This was agreed and a few minutes afterwards the guns went into action. The C.O. of the 74th Field Regiment soon decided to make the enemy troop concentration a regimental target, and the full fire power of the Regiment, thirty-six guns, was brought to bear on the Italians, who appeared to be in about battalion strength. One battery of twenty-five pounders was firing short and their shells landed on C Company, fortunately not causing any casualties.

The remainder of the guns completely smashed the Italian attack. The enemy infantry only advanced a short distance, and when the twenty-five pounders caught them in the open a large number surrendered on the spot, whilst the remainder of the attacking force retreated in some disorder. A section from 15 Platoon and some troops from the 9th Battalion rounded up no less than two hundred and fifty prisoners, the majority of whom were marched into the 9th D.L.I. area. They were Bersaglieri, one of the better Italian regiments, but these men had been morally shattered by the barrage of the previous night and had lost heart in the fight. A number of them carried back British wounded across the wadi to the R.A.P. The gunners of the 74th Field Regiment had done an excellent job of work; the counter-attack had been completely smashed by the twenty-five pounders, and C Company had not fired a single shot. Captain English sent a message over the wireless to the 74th expressing his Company's appreciation of the timely and decisive support, although he tactfully made no mention of the guns which had fired short. The rest of the day passed quietly and no further counter-attacks were put in against the Battalion positions.

That night the attack to extend the bridgehead went in as planned, behind a heavy barrage. By this time the Young Fascists had been backed up by German troops and there was some very stiff fighting. Like the previous night, it seemed that after the barrage had started the noise of battle would never cease. It was obvious that the attacking force was having some difficulty, but no news of the operation reached the forward companies of the 8th Battalion. In any case, A and B Companies had work to do. In the early hours the enemy carried out repeated probing attacks against the positions of these two companies in Ouerzi. They were most probably strong patrols and their task was obviously to sound the Battalion defences in that area. The patrols were held off at long range and none of them succeeded in getting through to the Battalion positions. On the right flank C Company spent a quiet night, deepening their trenches and improving the positions.

News about the attack to extend the bridgehead came through next morning. It had been partially successful and in the wadi the Divisional Engineers, working like blacks and suffering heavy casualties from the persistent enfilade fire, had completed a causeway. At first light the infantry in the forward positions heard the welcome sound of tank engines, and looking behind them saw tanks of the 50th R.T.R. appear from the direction of the wadi. The leading tanks lumbered on to the north-west but were soon held up by a minefield and anti-tank guns. Nevertheless, the armour was across the wadi, and the position in the bridgehead was very much better than it had been twenty-four hours previously. The morale of the forward companies was high and the men felt capable of dealing with anything. At this time the strength of C Company was four officers and sixty-five other ranks whilst A and B Companies, fighting more or less as one company, numbered two officers and eighty or ninety other ranks.

The morning wore on without any sign of the supporting arms, and the men beyond the wadi began to get a little worried. They did not know that the tanks had damaged the causeway so badly that repairs were necessary before it could carry any wheeled traffic. The sappers had hoped to have it ready by midday and had just completed the repairs when there was a cloud burst, which completely wrecked the crossing place. It was a bitter disappointment to the men who had worked unceasingly on the fascines under devastating fire, and a bitter blow to the infantry. It was now absolutely impossible to get wheeled vehicles of any sort across the wrecked causeway, and the men up forward knew what this would mean. They would have to fight without anti-tank gun support and, in fact, not one single anti-tank gun ever crossed the Wadi Zigzaou into the bridgehead. The only anti-tank weapons with the infantry were rifle grenades.

Just after midday a message came through to the Battalion that air reconnaissance had spotted a concentration of seventy-five tanks with infantry of 15 Panzer Division in the neighbourhood of Zarat, and the companies were warned to expect a counter-attack shortly. It later transpired that this attack against 151 Brigade was launched not only by 15 Panzer Division but also by a regiment (equivalent to a British brigade) of 90 Light Division, and the crack Ramcke parachutists. The light bombers of the Desert Air Force had been briefed to smash the counter-attack as it formed up, but unfortunately the rainstorm which wrecked the causeway temporarily grounded the 'planes. This meant that 151 Brigade would have to stand the full force of the German counter-attack, with no supporting weapons except the Valentine tanks, and no air support.

The 8th Battalion received an order from the Brigade Commander, which was passed on to the companies, that the fire of every available weapon was to be used against the tanks. About 1.30 p.m. the shelling of the crossing place in the wadi increased in intensity, and whilst heavy guns pounded the wrecked and useless causeway, concentrations from lighter calibre guns fell on the Battalion positions. The enemy gunfire was very accurate and became even more intense during the next thirty-five to forty minutes, but the companies were very steady under the shelling. When the gunfire was at its heaviest Captain P. J. Lucas, commanding the Carrier Platoon, answered an urgent call from A and B Companies for wireless sets and batteries. Undeterred by the murderous defensive fire sweeping the wadi Lucas went forward in his carrier through a gap in the minefield. He safely crossed the wadi and anti-tank ditch, all the time under heavy fire, and finally reached the forward companies with his valuable cargo. He then returned to Battalion H.Q. the way he had come. Later, under equally difficult conditions, he again undertook the hazardous journey, this time with rations and ammunition. There is no doubt that his actions enabled the forward troops to hold on to their positions and Captain Lucas was awarded the Military Cross.

At 2 p.m. the Germans attacked. They recaptured a position which had been taken by the 6th D.L.I. the previous night, and then news came through that the 9th Battalion had lost one of its positions. About 2.45 p.m. three German tanks—two Mark IV Specials and a Mark III—appeared in the C Company area, but remained out of grenade range. What a pity the anti-tank guns had not got across the wadi. The German tanks made a perfect target.

Fortunately C Company was in very good wireless communication with Battalion H.Q. and the presence of the tanks was reported. L/Cpl. Simpson, the signaller operating the set, behaved as though he was on an exercise, quite undeterred by the heavy shelling of the area. The enemy was using a large calibre gun, probably a 155-millimetre or a 210-millimetre, which was causing casualties in all companies. The only point in the gun's favour was that the troops in the bridgehead could hear the shells coming and were able to take cover. They made a noise like an express train going through a tunnel in the distance and the men christened them " Flying kit bags."

Meanwhile several Valentine tanks of the 50th R.T.R. had been hit by the big guns on the German tanks and were burning fiercely. That afternoon the Valentines fought a gallant action. Only one tank per troop carried a six-pounder gun and the remainder, with their two-pounders, were no match for the 75-millimetre guns on the Mark IV Specials. The Germans sat back out of range, and one after another the British tanks were hit and burst into flames. The Valentines, under the leadership of their gallant commanding officer, Lieut.-Colonel T. Cairns, M.C., fought back doggedly but it was an uneven fight which could only have one outcome. Hopelessly out-gunned, the British tanks were driven off every position they had occupied. Thirty-two Valentines were destroyed and most of their crews killed, including Lieut.-Colonel Cairns. When the last British tank had been knocked out a silence fell over the battlefield. The infantry were alone without supporting arms of any sort.

Presently the German tanks closed in on the Battalion positions and, outflanking Ouerzi, some of them were able to get behind A and B Companies. 15 Platoon of C Company came to the rescue and opened fire with 68 grenades, damaging the track of a Mark IV, whilst 14 platoon opened up with their Brens. The tanks replied with long bursts from their machine-guns which killed or wounded some of the men in the 14 and 15 Platoon positions. Without anti-tank support it was obvious that the infantry could do very little to fight the tanks and Captain English asked for a concentration of artillery fire to be put down on them. Some of the Panzers were so close to C Company that part of the concentration would inevitably fall on the company, but it was a risk which had to be taken. The British guns opened up almost immediately, pounding the company area as well as the tanks, and it was undoubtedly a nerve-racking experience. Evidently the Germans, although they were protected by armour plating, thought so too, and withdrew a hundred yards.

Meanwhile the tanks which had worked round behind Ouerzi had been joined by supporting infantry and were attacking A and B Companies. These two companies, in their maze of trenches and dug-outs fought back with Brens and rifles, neither asking nor giving any quarter. The infantry casualties were heavy on both sides and time and again a German hold on the defences was broken by a desperate counter-attack. In the midst of fierce fighting the only wireless set with the companies was put out of action, cutting off the men in Ouerzi from the rest of the Battalion. They fought on defiantly, holding and beating back the repeated German thrusts, and Ouerzi remained in British hands.

The two companies were fortunate in having with them two such excellent company sergeant-majors. Their conduct from the commencement of the operation had been a source of inspiration to the troops. Under the heaviest fire the two C.S.Ms. had moved about the Ouerzi positions, encouraging the men and giving them the confidence which was so necessary to combat the fierce enemy attempts to recapture the sector. Whenever things looked serious either C.S.M.

Imperial War Museum.

THE MARETH LINE. A concrete and steel pill-box in that part of the Line which was attacked by the 8th Battalion. These strongpoints, formidable affairs with concrete two or three feet thick, were linked up with deep dugouts and a labyrinth of trenches. Enemy snipers were everywhere.

Imperial War Museum

The anti-tank ditch at Mareth, between the Wadi Zigzaou and the main defence line, which Italian labour gangs had excavated. Twelve feet deep and fifteen feet wide, it provided some cover from the heavy enemy artillery and mortar fire during the later stages of the battle. Many wounded were attended to here.

Imperial War Museum.

Wounded being attended to at a D.L.I. Regimental Aid Post on the banks of the notorious Wadi Zigzaou. This horrible obstacle, covered by enfilade fire along its whole length, lay between the infantry battalions of 50 Division and the Axis forces holding the Mareth Line. This wadi was the obstacle which held up the vital anti-tank guns which would have changed the course of the whole battle. Not a single gun was able to cross the wadi.

Wood or C.S.M. Brannigan would appear on the scene to restore the situation. Snipers, mortar artillery or machine-gun fire was all the same to them. They faced every situation calmly and confidently. For their gallantry during the various stages of the Mareth battle the two C.S.Ms. were each awarded the Military Medal.

In the C Company area a runner arrived at H.Q. to report that fifteen men of Lieut. Roberts' platoon were lying wounded. Could they be evacuated? Unfortunately the enemy fire was so intense that nothing could be done. At about 5 p.m. enemy shelling of the company positions increased, and the tanks which had previously been repulsed by the British gunfire lumbered forward again with Panzer Grenadiers advancing behind them. C Company was unable to engage the tanks or infantry because of the concentrated and murderous fire from the tank machine-guns.

One of the Panzers closed in on the positions held by 14 Platoon and started to grind in the slit trenches with its tracks. Sgt. Holben and the remaining eight men of 14 Platoon then surrendered. C.S.M. Ranson and a Bren gunner from 13 Platoon immediately opened fire at the tank commanders. This forced the Germans down inside their turrets and the accurate fire frightened the enemy infantry. The tanks replied by firing their 75-millimetre guns straight at the C Company slit trenches from almost point blank range, a horrible experience for the British troops. Shortly afterwards Ranson was raising his Bren gun to the aim when he received a burst from a tank machine-gun straight through the forehead. So died a very gallant man. He had been an inspiration to the company at Alamein, and in the bridgehead at Mareth his steadiness under fire and continual cheerfulness had been a wonderful example to the younger men.

Afternoon turned to evening and dusk closed in. If only the rifle companies could hold on until darkness fell, the situation might be saved. It was obvious that the Germans could take the Battalion positions if they put in a really determined attack and were prepared to accept heavy casualties. Instead they shouted to the men of the 8th to surrender, saying that the position was hopeless. This invitation was replied to by more Bren and rifle fire.

Since the B Company wireless had been knocked out, C Company was the only sub-unit beyond the wadi still on the air, and Captain English gave a running commentary on the battle as it affected his company. A German tank, with infantry riding on it, which came almost up to the road was met by Bren gun fire and several hand grenades. The accurate fire from one of the Brens, which Pte. Lewis had taken over when the C.S.M. was killed, drove the infantry to seek cover and shortly afterwards the tank sheered off. Its commander evidently called for more artillery support because within a few minutes a really vicious concentration came down on the company area, and it seemed that the end could not be long delayed. The only ammunition remaining with C Company was rifle ammunition and there was very little of it. To make matters worse a shell landed midway between the slit trenches occupied by Captain English and

L/Cpl. Simpson, blowing the wireless set three or four feet into the air. C Company was now out of touch with Battalion H.Q.

Meanwhile, from Brigade H.Q. had come the order for the infantry to withdraw to the anti-tank ditch. A runner got this message through to the remnants of A and B Companies in Ouerzi. These two companies had suffered very heavy casualties during the afternoon of close fighting, but in spite of repeated and vicious enemy attacks had held their ground. The survivors of the gallant garrison were gathered together, and under cover of darkness they went back to the anti-tank ditch. Their withdrawal was covered by Sgt. Crawford assisted by Pte. Michael and his section. The section drew a considerable amount of enemy fire, thus diverting attention from the main body of the two companies which was able to fall back in comparative safety.

On the right flank the order to withdraw did not reach C Company until 7 p.m., by which time darkness had fallen and it appeared that the Germans had pulled back a little. Captain English immediately sent runners to 13 and 15 Platoons telling them to get out of their positions, taking with them as many of the wounded as possible and their weapons. This message never reached 13 Platoon (Lieut. R. O'Conor) and his men did not arrive back at the anti-tank ditch until some time after the rest of the company. When the platoons had rallied under cover of low ground in front of the ditch, the company commander took a count ; all that remained of C Company was four officers and twenty-three men, and at midday the company had totalled sixty-nine other ranks. It had been possible to carry back some of the wounded but unfortunately others were taken prisoner, including L/Cpl. Bainbridge, who had been captured in France in 1940 and had afterwards escaped.

In the anti-tank ditch Major Lidwill was organising the Battalion in its new position. He put the combined A and B Companies, under Lieut. Wheatley, on the right flank where they established contact with troops of the 9th D.L.I. C Company took up positions on the left flank and contacted Major G. Wood's company of the 6th Battalion. The men lost no time in digging themselves into the side of the anti-tank ditch. The Battalion was short of ammunition and for the third time since the start of the battle Captain Lucas answered an S.O.S. and brought ammunition across the wadi in his carrier. He seemed to bear a charmed life. The Battalion had not been there long when Major Lidwill called a conference and explained that an attack was being planned to recapture the ground which had just been given up. The 8th Battalion would assault Ouerzi and the 6th had Ksiba Ouest as their objective. Fortunately this plan was never carried out, for during the early hours of March 23rd General Montgomery cancelled further operations in the coastal sector. He knew the frontal attack, followed by the gallant stand of 50 Division, had forced the enemy to reinforce the coastal sector with German troops, and he appreciated that it would be very costly to persist with this attack. He therefore ordered 50 Division to withdraw east of the Wadi Zigzaou but at the same time deceptive measures were to be taken which would pin down the Germans on the coast by giving the impression that the Eighth Army was reorganising for another attack across the wadi.

Montgomery's primary objective, now that 15 Panzer Division was involved in the coastal sector, was to reinforce the outflanking movement so as to deliver the decisive blow in the Battle of Mareth against the El Hamma-Gabes axis before the enemy could move his reserves to oppose it.

In the anti-tank ditch beyond the Zigzaou that night several German attempts to over-run the ditch were beaten off by the Vickers guns of the Cheshires and the Bren and rifle fire of the three battalions. Some of the fighting was at murderously short range and the Germans suffered heavy casualties as, in waves, they advanced almost to the lip of the anti-tank ditch before they were mown down.

Shortly before dawn the 8th Battalion was ordered to withdraw east of the wadi. This order and the method of carrying it out was passed on to the companies but never reached C Company. A and B Companies and the troops of the 9th Battalion withdrew east of the Zigzaou without much interference, leaving C Company in the anti-tank ditch. However, the company was not alone in this predicament. No message had reached Major Wood's company of the 6th Battalion who, with a section of Cheshires, still held their positions.

Just after first light Captain English walked along the ditch to contact the C.O. and was surprised to find no British troops on C Company's right. A few yards further along the ditch he met a party of five German Panzer Grenadiers. English was the first to open fire and emptied his revolver at the Germans, wounding one of them. The others closed in and after a short struggle C Company commander was taken prisoner. The withdrawal of the Battalion had enabled the Germans to cross the ditch and come in on the flank of the small party of fifty odd men who were still holding out and who knew nothing of the withdrawal of the rest of the Brigade. Their situation was desperate ; in front of them were German infantry and armour, and advancing along the ditch from the right was a column of German Panzer Grenadiers, some of whom had taken Captain English prisoner. On the home side of the ditch the British troops were cut off by Germans and Italians who had worked round behind them, a minefield, and then the Wadi Zigzaou—strewn with mines and without a vestige of cover.

Captain H. Welch, who had taken over command of C Company when Captain English disappeared, gave the order for the company to fix bayonets and charge through the German troops to rejoin the Battalion on the far side of the Zigzaou. The odds seemed hopeless, but the men fixed bayonets and clambered out of the ditch. They fanned out in all directions and the sheer momentum of their charge surprised the enemy, sweeping them aside, but not before several members of this desperate party had been blown up on the anti-personnel mines between the anti-tank ditch and the wadi.

The steep eastern bank of the Zigzaou was unscaleable, apart from two exits, and also under heavy enfilade fire from German tanks. One exit was the route which C Company had taken in the original attack and the second was a small, steep nullah[1], about four hundred yards to the right. As the British troops splashed through the muddy waters they came under fire from machine-guns and light mortars, and on the banks some of them set off the deadly shrapnel mines and were killed instantly or mortally wounded. Half way across, several men, including Lieut. O'Conor, were forced to dive for cover in the muddiest part of the wadi. When they struggled to their feet their clothing was saturated with stagnant mud and water, and it required no mean effort for them to run with the added weight.

On the far side of the wadi both exits were used by the survivors of C Company. Captain Welch with a few of them managed to reach safety, dragging Lieut. Roberts who had been twice wounded in the stomach. "Busty" Roberts was no light weight and the men who had pulled him to safety were only too pleased to lift him on to a waiting jeep which took him back to the R.A.P.

Meanwhile Lieut. O'Conor, after picking himself out of the muddy waters of the wadi, had joined a party of men from the 9th Battalion. Finding the first exit covered by the fire of four German tanks, he led his party along to the nullah. When eventually this was reached there were only six men left—the others had been either killed or wounded and some had dropped from sheer exhaustion. The six ran up the nullah and almost immediately two of them were killed by mines and a third by machine-gun fire. The two leading men reached the crest and safety but O'Conor collapsed some sixty yards short of the crest. Here, Pte. Smith of B Company of the 8th Battalion found him, and after a short rest the two men made several attempts to reach the crest but each time were pinned to the ground by fire from the German side of the wadi. The only course open to O'Conor and Smith was to lie still and pretend to be dead like those around them, and this they did successfully until darkness fell.

Shortly after dark the British artillery put down a heavy barrage on the wadi and anti-tank ditch to assist the withdrawal of any troops of the Brigade who had still not reached the British lines but, unfortunately for O'Conor and Smith as well as others in a similar predicament, the Germans thought the barrage was the prelude to another attack, and replied most vigorously with defensive artillery, mortar and machine-gun fire. The two men were only able to move at their peril—one enemy machine-gun fixed line was only two feet above O'Conor's head—but they were able to get into some dead ground near a track leading to the British lines.

When daylight came the two men found that there was a thousand yards of open ground with no cover of any sort between them and the British troops, making it impossible to get back until darkness fell. They had to lie up for the whole day in a small grove where there was a knocked out mortar carrier, only three hundred yards from the wadi. The carrier had a store of food and water which was indeed welcome as neither man had eaten anything except battle rations for three days. O'Conor and Smith now had the unpleasant experience of being shot

[1]Stream, water course, ravine.

at by their own troops. The carrier hid them from the Germans but the British mistook them for enemy. Every movement brought down heavy shell and mortar fire, and for them it was a thoroughly miserable day. That night their luck changed and they were able to make their way back to the British lines where they ran into a salvage party of the Argyll and Sutherland Highlanders. The two men, who by this time had been given up as lost and posted as missing, eventually rejoined the Battalion after passing through Army H.Q. and the transit camp at Medenine.

After the withdrawal of the D.L.I. Brigade the 8th Battalion was collected behind the original assembly area, and on March 24th the Battalion moved into a Brigade rest area. For 50 Division the Battle of Mareth was over, and in the words of Major General de Guingand, (General Montgomery's chief of staff), " It was sad that that gallant formation (50 Division) had not reaped more tangible signs of the hard fighting but in the big scheme of things they had nobly played their part."

A short time after being captured Captain English was escorted back and he passed over the area where the battle had raged the day before. The fighting had not only been hard but savage in the extreme and casualties in the 8th Battalion had been heavy. It was an ugly sight. The vicinity of every position was littered with British, German and Italian dead, abandoned weapons, damaged wireless sets and equipment. The charred remains of the Valentine tanks were dotted about the battlefield and the whole scene was one of chaos and destruction.

It was the gallant stand north of the Wadi Zigzaou by the north country division against overwhelming odds which drew the German armour out of position and enabled Montgomery to administer the coup de grace with the flanking movement. On March 26th the New Zealanders, now reinforced by 1 Armoured Division, started an attack which took them by first light to within a few miles of El Hamma.

March 27th was a day of hard fighting with the Germans trying desperately to reinforce the El Hamma area. However, by the evening, the defeat of the enemy was complete, and that night the bulk of the New Zealand Corps moved forward towards El Hamma, subsequently by-passing the town and making straight for Gabes. The effect of the success of the El Hamma battle was decisive. The enemy retreated from the Mareth position proper during the night of March 27th/28th, and by the 29th the Eighth Army had captured El Hamma and Gabes, the enemy having withdrawn his depleted and somewhat disorganised forces to man the next obstacle facing the Eighth Army—Wadi Akarit—fifty miles west of the Mareth Line. This natural, fifteen miles wide defile between the sea and the Shott el Fejadj was known as " the Gabes Gap," and to break through this to the open country of Central Tunisia was the next task for the Eighth Army.

CHAPTER NINETEEN

THE END IN NORTH AFRICA

THE end of March found the 8th Battalion in a rest area near Mareth village. Having lost the Commanding Officer, the Second-in-Command, the Intelligence Officer, three company commanders and most of the infantry platoon commanders, the Battalion had to be completely reorganised. This could have been a very slow business but under the able command of Major Lidwill, assisted by the old hands who had survived the battle, the 8th was soon put on its feet again. Reinforcement drafts totalling five officers and ninety other ranks arrived and the Battalion was re-formed—for the first time since Gazala—on the basis of four rifle companies and H.Q. Company. There was a certain amount of company and platoon training and the Battalion also provided salvage parties to recover damaged weapons and equipment from the battle area. Burial parties went down to the Wadi Zigzaou with Padre Nesbitt where they found the C.O. and Lieut. Richardson in an area infested with mines. The task of the burial parties was not made any easier by the enemy who had booby-trapped some of the bodies, and a Battalion stretcher bearer was killed by one of these traps.

Early in the month General Montgomery had regrouped the Eighth Army to deal with the Wadi Akarit defences, and on April 6th three divisions (50, 51 and 4 Indian) attacked the Axis forces holding these positions. The D.L.I. Brigade, in reserve, did not take part in this attack, which was carried out for 50 Division by 69 Brigade. After fierce fighting the three divisions broke the enemy hold on Wadi Akarit, and exhausted and demoralised the Axis troops withdrew during the night of April 6th/7th. The Eighth Army was now in the open and the enemy had no suitable position to hold up the British troops, other than far north at Enfidaville. This meant that the ports of Sfax and Sousse would soon be available for supplying the Eighth Army, which at this time was still being maintained from Tripoli. The Desert Army had every reason to be in good heart and 30 and 10 Corps started chasing the enemy much faster than he wished to go.

Within a few hours of the break-through at Wadi Akarit troops of 10 Corps linked up with the Americans. Four days later the Eighth Army joined up with 9 British Corps of the First Army near Kairouan. The port of Sfax was captured on April 10th and Sousse fell two days later. By the evening of April 13th the leading troops of the Eighth Army were up against the anti-tank defences of the enemy's Enfidaville positions.

The final stages of the North African campaign on the Eighth Army front were entrusted to 10 Corps, which had been reinforced by 4 Indian Division and 50 Division. On April 16th the D.L.I. Brigade moved north in the wake of the Eighth Army and, by the 17th, the 8th Battalion—in the line again—had established a Battalion O.P. to maintain watch on enemy movement east and west of Enfidaville. That day Major A. J. Dunn, joining the Battalion from the 9th D.L.I., was appointed Second-in-Command, and a draft of four officers and forty-five other ranks were posted to the Battalion.

A reconnaissance patrol under a new officer, Lieut. Clark, going out during the night of April 17th/18th found Italian box mines, and during the following night two patrols under officers who had just joined the 8th, Lieuts. A. F. Jackman and R. F. Holloway went out on unsuccessful reconnaissances. It seemed as though the D.L.I. Brigade was going to take part in the Enfidaville battle but on April 20th the C.O. returned from Brigade with the news that 50 Division was being withdrawn from operations with the Eighth Army and would commence the move back to Egypt by road the following day. Nobody in the Battalion knew the reason for this move, but it was rumoured that the Division was required for combined operations training at Kabrit.

It was a pity in many ways that, having come so far and fought so hard, 50 Division could not take part in the final overwhelming defeat of the Germans and Italians in North Africa, which came not so long after the Division had left the Eighth Army. By the end of April the operations at Enfidaville had not been successful in breaking through the enemy's defences, and General Alexander transferred 7 Armoured Division, 4 Indian Division, and 201 Guards Brigade to the First Army. This additional strength made the First Army's offensive irresistible and Tunis and Bizerta fell on May 7th. All resistance by the Germans and Italians had ceased by May 12th and North Africa was ours.

CHAPTER TWENTY

PREPARING FOR AN INVASION

Back to Egypt—Combined Operations training—Full dress rehearsal—50 Division sets sail for Sicily.

IT took 50 Division exactly three weeks to cover the 1,300 miles from Enfidaville in Tunisia to the destination at Sidi Bishr, near Alexandria, in Egypt. Early on April 21st the 8th Battalion column formed up and headed eastwards, covering just over a hundred miles before pulling into an assembly area not far from Sfax. Two days were spent here and the whole Battalion had an opportunity of visiting the town. On April 24th the column moved on again and by dusk on the 26th had covered approximately four hundred miles. That night the vehicles laagered outside Tripoli and next day the men of the 8th Battalion went into the city. It was a pleasant change from the miles of uninhabited desert and the long stretches of coast road. In many ways it resembled Cairo and Alexandria but, unlike the Egyptian cities, the gabardine-coated gentlemen from the Delta had not yet established themselves and it was still the Eighth Army's own city. The men who wandered along the sea front and drank in the few bars wore divisional signs of the Eighth Army on their sleeves. Tripoli represented a way of life which few of them had experienced since their last leave in Alexandria or Cairo, six months previously. The troops had different ideas about how they should enjoy themselves but every man in his own way had a good time, and the Bofors guns—at fifty-yard intervals along the sea front—and the wrecked ships lying in the harbour were the only reminders that there was still a war on.

The following day the 8th Battalion moved on, skirting the city and following the coast road eastwards. In three days of fast motoring, the column covered nearly three hundred and fifty miles, which took it beyond Misurata and Sirte. The only traffic going in the opposite direction was a Free French convoy ; otherwise 50 Division had the coast road to itself. Soon after leaving Sirte a party of officers from the three D.L.I. battalions went on ahead of the main column to join a course at the Combined Operations School, Kabrit. The battalions followed in their wake, round the coast to Benghazi and beyond to Derna. It was some time since Derna had seen any fighting and the small town below the escarpment had regained some of its peacetime beauty. Beyond Derna, at El Adem, the 8th Battalion split up. The unit transport continued the journey along the coastal road but the attached troop-carriers left, and the companies moved into Tobruk transit camp. The following day they entrained at railhead for Sidi

Bishr. The journey took thirty-two hours and was a most uncomfortable one in the train of metal cattle trucks with thirty-five or forty men to a truck, but it was well worth it with Sidi Bishr as the destination. The train arrived there during the late evening of May 10th, and the tired troops thankfully marched to the camp. The following day was spent in tidying up after the long journey, when it was announced that leave would start next day to either Cairo or Alexandria. There was a choice of four days in either city.

By midday on May 12th the T.T. sign with the blue Durham flash was well in evidence in Cairo and Alexandria. By the evening there were plenty of 50 Division parties well under way, and if some of them were rather hectic and caused the Military Police more trouble than at any time during the last six months, it was understandable. In that time Alexandria and Cairo—the fear of war banished—had returned to normal, and Alexandria in particular had become once again almost a pre-war resort. The beaches were gay with bathing parties and the hotels, which a few months previously had been full of R.N., Army and R.A.F. officers, were well booked with civilians. Nevertheless, 50 Division—the first division of the Desert Army to return to Egypt from Tunisia—was not going to adjust itself to Cairo and Alexandria. It was for the Egyptians to do the adjusting and they soon realised it. Within a few hours the night clubs and bars were doing the job they knew so well ; entertaining the men of the Desert Army.

That four days leave was one of the best the men of the 8th Battalion ever had. They alone knew what a welcome change it was after the desert and not an hour was wasted. They wallowed in the luxury of baths—once, twice or three times a day as the fancy took them. They ate and drank well. There were the latest British and American films to see in the cinemas and dancing in the night clubs every evening. Whilst the new arrivals watched, a little puzzled by it all, the old hands spent their accumulated pay and collected their hangovers.

However, all good things eventually come to an end, and on May 22nd the Battalion transport moved by road to Kabrit. The infantry went by train and arrived at Fayid station in the canal zone at the unearthly but perfectly normal military arrival time of one o'clock in the morning. From there, troop-carriers took the Battalion by road to Kabrit, and two days later the troops moved into the Combined Training Centre, where hard work started immediately. The training was entirely new and most interesting. The Royal Naval staff at the C.T.C. gave every possible assistance most willingly, and it was largely due to their efforts that the combined operations course was such a success.

There was so much to learn about the new technique of landing a complete army on enemy-held coast, and so little time in which to do so. Naval officers lectured on the type of naval support available to protect large convoys of troopships. They described the close support which could be given to the assaulting divisions once they had landed, by battleships lying out to sea and fast motor torpedo-boats close inshore. They talked about the many and various types of craft which had been built to carry the army and all its transport and supplies.

The craft at the C.T.C. were Landing Craft Assault, manned by naval ratings and capable of carrying thirty-five men. In these craft the infantry companies practised rapid embarking and later, beach landings. A drill was evolved for taking up a position on the beaches, afterwards breaching a minefield and advancing inland. The M.T. and Carrier Platoons had to learn how to waterproof their vehicles, and the Quartermaster (Captain W. G. Stray) had so many new worries thrust upon him that it would take a separate chapter to describe them all.

When each rifle company had carried out a preliminary invasion scheme, Exercise Dredger took place on May 28th. This gave the Battalion practice in landing on an enemy-held coast, penetrating the wire and minefields defending the enemy forward positions, and advancing inland to capture several strongpoints. The Battalion was able to practise its full invasion drill, and the men tried out their battle order, carrying the full assault scale of weapons and ammunition. The signallers practised intercommunication arrangements, and Battalion H.Q. was established, first of all on board ship and later ashore. Exercise Dredger taught some valuable lessons. It was also excellent training for the supporting arms.

Early in June, Exercise Duchess took place. It was on more or less the same lines as Dredger, but on a brigade level. This completed the training at Kabrit, and at 8.30 a.m. on June 6th the Battalion embarked in Tank Landing Craft for the journey down the canal to Suez, whilst the transport went by road. The troops moved into a tented camp under a most formidable-looking escarpment, which had all facilities for range practices and cliff-climbing exercises, where several days were spent settling in and getting the companies on the ranges. On June 9th the Battalion entrained for Port Tewfik to embark on a British troopship, H.M.T. *Dunera* for a full scale invasion exercise in the Gulf of Akaba.

Two days later the *Dunera*, after a quick journey through the sweltering heat of the Red Sea, anchored in Akaba Bay. The Battalion H.Q. Group and company commanders went ashore on June 12th for a signal exercise, a preliminary to Exercise Bromyard which commenced at 3 a.m. in the morning. Bromyard gave 13 Corps practice in the capture of a port (Akaba) and the establishment of a bridgehead preparatory to further operations. 50 Division and 5 Division were landed in conjunction with a brigade of an airborne division which went in first to secure an important objective. Bromyard was an impressive affair and the Army Commander came down to Akaba to watch it. The enemy was represented by troops firing Bren guns into carefully-sited pits, and previously prepared charges dug into the ground were exploded at intervals to represent the flash and discharge of coastal defence guns. It was as near as any exercise had ever been to the real thing and, because of this, was most valuable training.

Bromyard finished at 10.30 a.m. next morning, and the Battalion marched back to a camp area not far from the beaches. That afternoon the whole camp was enveloped by a Khamsin which raged for two hours, making everybody thoroughly miserable. Later in the day General Montgomery talked to the officers of 5 and 50 Divisions who had taken part in the operation. A large building the size of a cinema had been erected, and after a pep talk fully up to the standard of the Army Commander, the officers came away feeling that one thing was certain about the forthcoming operation ; the defeat of the enemy.

The Battalion left Akaba in the *Dunera* on the 15th and arrived in Suez Bay on the 16th, after a voyage which owing to the fact that the ship was "wet" had not been entirely uneventful. The *Dunera* dropped anchor not far from the ship which was to carry the Battalion in the invasion. She was a Dutch vessel—the *Ruys*—and next morning the Battalion was ferried to her from the *Dunera* in landing craft. For several days the troops remained on board and practised embarking in L.C.P. (Landing Craft Personnel) and L.C.I. (Landing Craft Infantry) by day and night. The 8th Battalion had not been given an assault role in the forthcoming operation, and apart from D Company was going to be carried from the *Ruys* to the enemy shores by L.C.I., American-built ships capable of carrying just over two hundred men.

On the 20th the Battalion disembarked from the *Ruys* and returned to the camp below the escarpment. The training there deserves a special mention. It was tough and, both before and after the seaborne exercise at Akaba, carried out intensively. The escarpment was climbed every morning before breakfast, by no means an easy climb. Its hazardous nature can best be illustrated by the fact that a man from H.Q. Company slipped and fell to his death, and the Medical Officer was kept continually busy with men who sustained injuries—some of them serious—during the climbs. For all this it was invaluable training, and had it not been carried out the Battalion might have fared badly in the invasion.

Brens, rifles, mortars, anti-tank guns and Piat guns were all fired on the ranges, and there was a most liberal allowance of ammunition. The Piat, a new platoon anti-tank weapon just out from the U.K., was responsible for the death of a B Company N.C.O., and on the ranges Lieut. J. E. Johnson, who had rejoined the Battalion after his miraculous escape at Mareth, was killed by a misdirected burst of Bren gun fire.

On June 24th, the officers attended another talk by General Montgomery in the Britannia Cinema in Suez Transit Camp, and the following day he visited the D.L.I. Brigade to speak to the men. They showed their faith in him in no uncertain way, and it was easy to see that the morale of the troops under his command had never been higher. The invasion was imminent. Suez was a sealed camp and no one was allowed into the town.

There were several small Battalion and Brigade exercises, and then on June 27th the new Divisional Commander, Major-General S. C.

Kirkman, O.B.E., M.C., visited the 8th to talk to the officers. Two days later at 7.30 a.m., the 8th Battalion was taken in troop-carriers to Adabia Jetty, and then in landing craft to the *Ruys*. The Dutch ship sailed up the Suez Canal next day, and secrecy regarding the forthcoming operations had been so well kept that not a man in the 8th D.L.I., apart from Lieut.-Colonel Lidwill, knew where the assault had been planned. Even the hardened old Dutch skipper, a character straight from the pages of Punch, did not know. "No one tells me noddings," he complained bitterly. The *Ruys* sailed slowly through the canal, and as she passed Kabrit the hospitable staff of the C.T.C. stood at the end of the jetty and waved their greeting to the men they had trained. The anti-aircraft teams on canal defence thought the convoy of troopships was homeward bound. "You want to get some sand in your shoes before you go back to Blighty," they shouted. And for once the men of the 8th D.L.I. could not shout back an answer.

The ships from Suez carrying 5 and 50 Divisions dropped anchor at Port Said where other ships joined the convoy. There was the continual drone of aero engines overhead as every type of plane to be used in the invasion circled slowly over the ships, to give the troops practice in aircraft recognition. The Divisional Commander came aboard the *Ruys* and talked to all ranks about the vital nature of the forthcoming operation. On July 5th the *Ruys* sailed with the rest of the Suez-based D Day convoy. As the ships took station and set their course westwards through the Mediterranean, the men were told their destination ; the island of Sicily, gateway to the soft underbelly of the Italian mainland.

CHAPTER TWENTY-ONE

THE INVASION OF SICILY

An ambitious plan—through the Mediterranean—rough seas off the invasion beaches—ashore at last.

PLANNING for the invasion of Sicily had started early in April. Originally it had been planned for a western task force of three assaulting divisions plus one airborne division to land in the north-west corner of the island, and an eastern task force (The Eighth Army) of four assaulting divisions plus one airborne division to land on a wide frontage in the south-eastern corner of the island. This plan was not favoured by General Montgomery; his initial reaction was that the landings were too dispersed and that a far more concentrated effort was required if the invading forces were to overcome the resistance which they must expect after their experiences in North Africa. The modified plan which was finally agreed had both task forces, supported by strong naval units, landing in the south-eastern corner of the island, in roughly the same area which was originally to have been the responsibility of the Eighth Army. Prior to the assault the Allied air forces were to intensify their efforts against enemy ships and aircraft, which was no light undertaking for the Axis had concentrated a very formidable air force in the Central Mediterranean area.

The initial objective of the seaborne landing was to capture the port of Syracuse in the Eighth Army sector. The assault was to be preceded by an airborne operation, and once the invading forces had firmly established themselves, operations were to be developed to capture the whole island. During this phase the occupation of the ports of Augusta and Catania, both in the Eighth Army sector, and the vital airfields of the Catania plain were to be given high priority. The western task force, the Seventh American Army of General "Blood and Guts" Patton, after landing in the Gulf of Gela and capturing first the port of Licata and then the airfields of the Comiso group, was to ensure the security of the left flank of the Eighth Army during the advance northwards.

Montgomery planned to attack with two corps. 13 Corps, consisting of 5 and 50 Divisions, airborne troops and commandos, was to land in the Gulf of Noto, south of Syracuse. An hour or two before the seaborne assault, airborne troops were scheduled to drop west of Syracuse with the main object of capturing a most important bridge which would facilitate the quick capture of the port. The commandos had the task of dealing with enemy coastal batteries. 30 Corps, consisting of 51 Division, 231 Brigade from Malta and 1 Canadian Division from the U.K., was to land south of 13 Corps around the point of the

Pachino Peninsular; its next task was to establish contact as quickly as possible with 13 Corps and take over areas captured by that corps. This would allow 13 Corps to pursue its main objective. 30 Corps had also the responsibility of ensuring the early capture of the airfield area on the Pachino Peninsular, as well as to link up with the American Seventh Army.

The enemy garrison of Sicily consisted of two German armoured divisions and five Italian divisions. There were six additional Italian divisions with coastal defence duties, but in spite of the preponderance of Italian formations, it was the strategically placed German divisions inland which were to prove such a tough nut to crack.

Early in the afternoon of the second day at sea Operation Orders were issued and officers briefed. It was a most thorough briefing, and the C.O. spent the whole afternoon carefully detailing the plan on a scale model of the coastal sector where the Battalion was likely to land. This model, complete in every detail, showed buildings, roads, tracks and suspected enemy positions. With this, and the excellent series of photographs taken by Royal Naval submarine reconnaissance parties and the R.A.F., the C.O. had no difficulty putting his officers in the picture more so than they had ever been for any previous operation.

The 50 Division landing, on the left of the 13 Corps front, was to be carried out in three stages. The first was the assault by the D.L.I. Brigade Group on the beaches known as Jig Sector and the capture of a covering position. The second was the landing of the 69 Brigade Group and subsequent reorganisation of the position captured by the D.L.I. Brigade. The final stage was the landing of the remainder of 50 Division, less 168 Brigade Group, and the organisation of the Beach Area. 168 Brigade was to land on the third day.

The assault operation by the D.L.I. Brigade was also divided into three phases.

1. The assault on the beaches by the 6th and 9th Battalions and the capture and mopping up of the beach defences.

2. The establishment of a beachhead position by the two assaulting battalions, to deny the enemy ground from which he could bring effective small arms fire to bear on the beaches.

3. The landing of the 8th Battalion on Jig Green beach and the occupation of a covering position north-west and south-west of the small coastal town of Avola, to deny the enemy high ground from which observation could be obtained on to the Beach Area.

For the landing the 8th Battalion had under command one detachment of 505 Field Company, R.E., one Light Section of 149 Field Ambulance, two machine-gun platoons of the 2nd Cheshires, and in support the 98th Field Regiment with 105-mm. guns on tank chassis, as well as 107 Anti-tank Battery of 102 Anti-tank Regiment, R.A.

After the landing, A Company (Captain C. L. Beattie) and B Company (Captain P. J. Lewis) had been given the task of capturing a covering position north-west of Avola, whilst C Company (Captain H. O. Walmsley) and D Company (Captain P. J. Lucas) were to

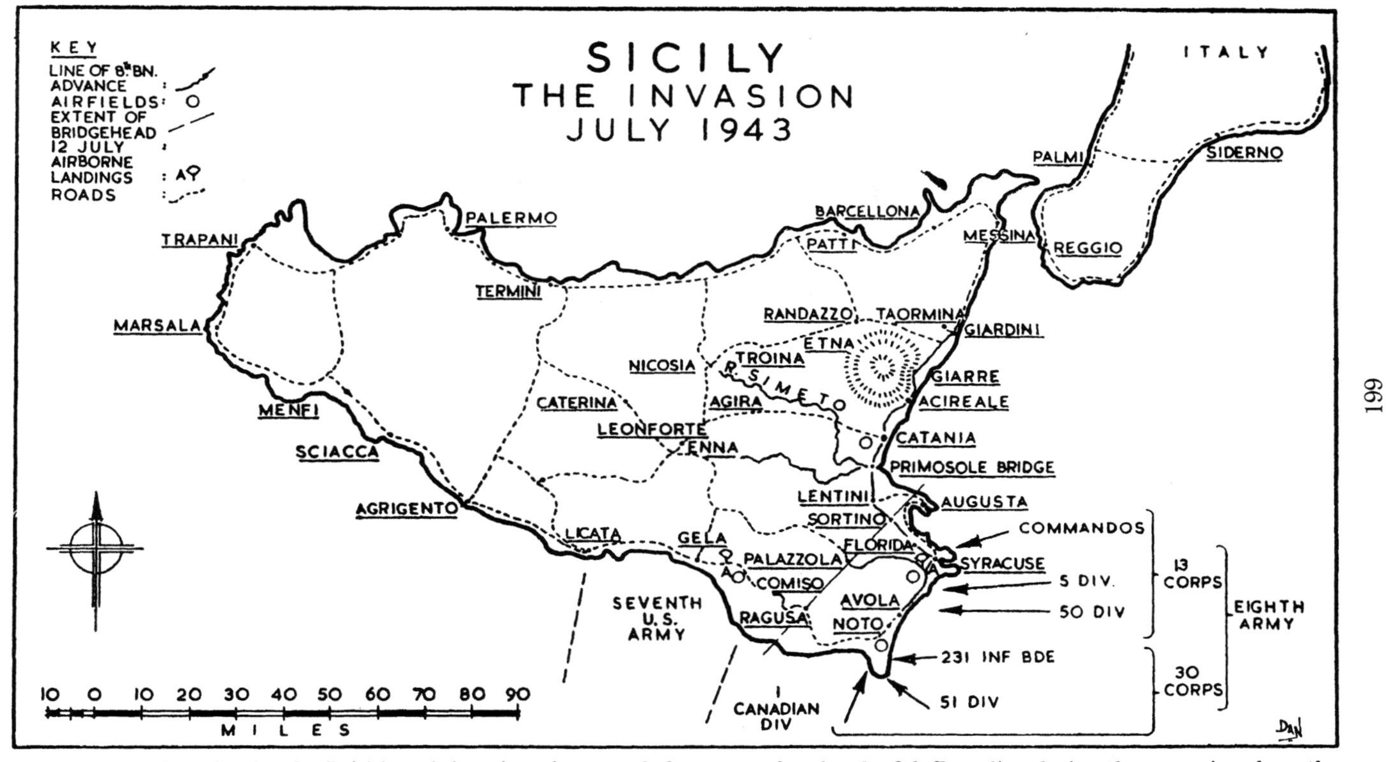

SICILY. The invasion by the British and American forces and the route taken by the 8th Battalion during the campaign, from the Avola landing beaches to Giardini. The Battalion was engaged in heavy fighting south of Catania at Primosole bridge capture the high ground east of Noto, commanding the road approaches to Avola. The C.O. stressed that it was absolutely vital for the companies to gain the high ground before the enemy mobile reserve, whatever the obstacles and however hard the climb. So much for the fighting part of the plan.

The administrative plan was more complicated than it had ever been before. The troops were required to have a general idea of the many and varied points in the plan and a thorough knowledge of most of them. All ranks were to be issued with a forty-eight hour mess tin ration for consumption on D Day and D plus 1, no other food being available for these two days. The few vehicles landing on D Day were to carry two days' rations, but one day was to be kept in reserve for airborne units or commandos operating on the Battalion front. Petrol was so severely rationed that in no circumstances were petrol fires to be used for cooking. The tea situation did not look too good, and in any case there was apparently going to be very little water with which to make tea. Each man was limited to half-a-gallon a day for all purposes.

The initial password had to be learned. The challenge for the Eighth Army was " Desert Rats," with a most appropriate answer, " Kill Italians." The troops had to know what action to take with regard to civilian personnel and property, and which installations in the brigade area had to be kept intact. There were " Do's and Don't's" upon entering a village or town. The Do's included impounding the Mayor and the Chief of Police and guarding wine distilleries. A booklet was issued to each man, " The Soldier's Guide to Sicily," describing the island, its history and the people. Without a doubt the Battalion had never had to learn so much about an operation in such a short time. The troops co-operated to the full, and by the time the evening of the last day at sea drew in, most of them felt that this was one operation at least when it had been possible to brief them thoroughly. As a result their morale was high, and the 8th Battalion fighting fit.

The voyage through the Mediterranean took five full days, during which time everything was done to ensure that not a single man had any doubts as to the Battalion plan. The scale model of the landing area, with the latest intelligence and aerial summaries, was made available to each company in turn. No company commander took less than three hours to brief his company. There was also the inevitable P.T. before breakfast, which was cursed roundly at the time but appreciated to the full soon after the landing. There was so much to talk about and discuss that the time passed quickly, in spite of the fact that the *Ruys* like her companion ships was "dry." Every day the position of the convoy was marked on the naval map on board the trooper, which showed also the location of other convoys sailing from the North African ports, Malta and the United Kingdom.

For the first five days the Port Said convoy was not a large one, consisting mainly of troopers carrying 5 and 50 Divisions with their supporting arms, as well as a number of escort ships. This was changed soon after midday on July 9th—the last day at sea—when the Malta and North African-based convoys made their rendezvous with the ships from Port Said. It was an amazing sight. As far as the eye could see there were hundreds of ships of all shapes and sizes ahead of, astern of, and on either quarter of the *Ruys*. The naval liaison officer with the 8th pointed out to several of the officers a trio of American-built L.C.I. on the starboard beam, pitching and rolling like small rowing boats. " They're yours for the show," he said. " They only crossed the Atlantic a few weeks ago." To the troops on board the *Ruys* the L.C.I. looked most unseaworthy.

Beyond the L.C.I., Tank Landing Craft in company with M.T. ships and Flak ships (anti-aircraft ships) ploughed their way through a sea which had suddenly become angry in the last few hours. Almost on the horizon were the cruisers and battleships which formed the heavy escort, while closer in the destroyers fussed about in and out of the convoy. To look at that vast array of shipping it hardly seemed possible that there was room for it all to lie off the shores of Sicily.

Soon after tea the latest information was chalked up on the blackboard in the forward lounge of the *Ruys*. It was to the effect that American Mustang dive bombers would be operating over the 5 and 50 Division beachheads from first light. There followed some information about the state of the beaches, which had only been obtained by submarine reconnaissance parties the previous night. A page from an illustrated magazine had been pinned below the notices. It showed an attractive girl in a very abbreviated bathing costume. " Come to sunny Sicily for your holidays," had been chalked underneath, and below this someone else had written : " I bet she won't be waiting on Green Beach."

After the evening meal, the men settled down in their troop decks and some of them slept, whilst others read or played cards. The Bren guns, mortars and anti-tank weapons had all been given their last check and were lined up on top of the hatches. There was not long to wait before the assault flights of the 6th and 9th Battalions were due to land, but it seemed an age. At about 1 a.m. a naval lieutenant came into the officers' lounge where most of the occupants were dozing in the comfortable arm-chairs. He rudely awakened them by shouting " You can see the Flak going up over Sicily." Sure enough, over the island there was the flash of bursting anti-aircraft shells, with an occasional brighter flash as a stick of bombs from Allied night bombers found their mark.

The *Ruys* hove to about twelve miles out from the island. Searchlights from Sicily probed the darkness and occasionally a beam dropped to sea level, but fortunately did not settle on any of the troopers lying so silently out at sea. One beam did flash for a second over the *Winchester Castle* to starboard of the *Ruys* but to everyone's relief passed on again almost immediately. A few minutes before 2 a.m. the loud-hailers on board the *Ruys* sent out warning messages to the troop-decks. The first serials were to go ashore in Landing Craft Personnel and the voice of the controller came over the loudspeakers : " Serial No. 45. Get dressed now." The voice repeated this instruction, and then : " Serial No. 45. Move along to your L.C.P. That is all."

Serial No. 45 (part of D Company of the 8th Battalion) moved to the boat deck along a pre-arranged route, and led by the company commander the twenty-three men climbed into the L.C.P. With all the men on board, the assault craft remained suspended at the davits for a short time before being swiftly lowered. She hit the water with a splash, and immediately the boat became remarkably unsteady. The engine was started and the assault craft, moving away from the *Ruys*, began to circle, waiting for the rest of the craft to be lowered.

The same procedure was followed by Serials 46, 47, 48, 49 and 50, until the whole of D Company and most of Battalion H.Q. had been embarked. By this time it had blown up very rough, and as the L.C.P. circled the *Ruys* waiting for the other 8th Battalion Serials to disembark, the watchers on the trooper could see that the small boats were making heavy weather of it. They were being buffeted unmercifully by the rough seas, and some of the men on board were already laid out, too ill to move.

The next serial to disembark was No. 51, with the Second-in-Command and the whole of A and B Companies. One of the American L.C.I. had been allotted to carry this serial and, as she closed with the stationary *Ruys*, the voice of the controller came over the loud hailer : " Serial No. 51. Move along the starboard alleyway to the starboard midships sally port. Your L.C.I. is waiting. That is all." The controller was an optimist, for it was some time before the L.C.I. was eventually in a satisfactory position alongside, and even then the American ship was lifting and falling with the waves in a most alarming fashion. It was quite impossible to keep her steady against the trooper, and to make things worse it was a pitch black night, no lights of any sort were allowed and the men were heavily laden with kit. It took four times as long to get the two hundred odd men aboard the L.C.I. as it had taken during the practices in calm water at Suez, and it was almost a miracle that no one was lost in the surging waters between the ships. Each man went down the side of the *Ruys* by an iron ladder, waited on the last rung until the L.C.I. lifted on the crest of a wave, and then jumped outwards and backwards. The two company commanders, some A and B Company N.C.Os. and members of the American crew of the L.C.I. caught the men and broke their fall as they landed on the iron deck.

Meanwhile, the unfortunate members of Battalion H.Q. and D Company in the L.C.P. were still circling the Ruys, and by this time most of them felt thoroughly ill. No one was more pleased than they when the L.C.I. eventually cast off. She pulled away from the trooper, leaving two more L.C.I. to disembark the rest of the troops scheduled to land on D Day, including C Company of the 8th Battalion. It was now 3 a.m. on July 10th, and the steady drone of aero engines could be heard as the planes carrying the airborne troops approached the island. The noise of the engines increased and became a roar as the transports passed fairly low over the convoy. As the noise receded the thoughts of the 8th Battalion men were with the troops of the 6th and 9th Battalions in the assault craft, crouching down as the tiny

Imperial War Museum.

The invasion of Sicily. Men of an infantry battalion go down the gangway of a landing craft which has grounded on a false beach. Life-jackets take their weight as they wade towards the Beachmaster standing at the water's edge.

vessels swept in towards the beaches. But they did not have much time to think about it, for suddenly the coastal batteries opened up. The invasion of Sicily was no longer a secret.

The L.C.I. with A and B Companies set her course for the island. The run to the beaches took over three hours, and as most of the men were below decks, battened down in the fore and aft holds by the watertight doors, the incessant pitching and rolling of the craft caused many of them to feel very "green." Nevertheless, they were dry, unlike the troops in the L.C.P. A and B Company commanders and the Second-in-Command, Major H. Blackden, stood on the deck of the L.C.I. with several N.C.Os. With the first streaks of dawn it was just possible to see the island, with Mount Etna towering above the morning mist. The mist cleared to reveal the convoys of troopers and cargo ships lying off the shores. Overhead the first daylight Spitfire patrols from Malta circled in the sky above the beachhead, whilst a cruiser level with the L.C.I. to starboard appeared to stand still as she belched a salvo at a coastal gun searching the beaches. Running in close to the shore was a Naval Landing Craft Support, laying a smoke screen and firing at the few enemy strongpoints which still held out.

It seemed that the assault waves had been successful. Crews of L.C.P. returning from the beaches gave the thumbs-up signal as they swept past on their way to pick up more passengers from the troopers. The group on the deck of the L.C.I. studied the island through binoculars and compared the layout with the aerial photographs. They could see the farmhouse on top of the hill which had been shown on the scale model, and beyond it the track which A and B Companies had to reach. It all looked deceptively peaceful in the morning sunlight.

The illusion was soon shattered when three Messerschmitts swooped low over the beaches, raking them with machine-gun fire. As the naval anti-aircraft gunner in the bows of the L.C.I. opened fire, without any success, a flight of Spitfires above the convoy peeled off to dive after the German planes. In another few minutes the L.C.I. would beach. The watertight doors were opened, and the men of A and B companies warned to get ready to land. The naval ratings started the winches which would push the twin gangways over the bows and on to the beach, as a B Company signaller shouted that the 6th Battalion had captured all its objectives. This good news was passed on to the men down below.

During the night the L.C.I. had strayed from her course and was being called in by a beachmaster on a 5 Division beach. An enemy coastal gun ranged on the beach was dropping shells into the water around the landing craft already unloading. A cruiser out to sea was joined by two destroyers as she fired a salvo, but the enemy coastal gun still continued to fire. There was a roar and a sheet of flame as another L.C.I. received a direct hit on the stern just as she was about to beach. She turned lazily round, broadside on, a thin wisp of smoke curling out of the aft troop hatch. A dull boom as the gun fired again; this time, a miss.

By now the L.C.I. from the *Ruys* was almost in, and then—she hit a false beach about thirty yards from the shore. With the coastal gun still firing and some of the shells falling unpleasantly close, the only thing to do was to wade ashore. B Company went down the left-hand gangway and A Company down the right—into six or seven feet of water ! The life jackets took the weight as the men paddled in towards the beach, and naval ratings waded out with long boathooks to tow in some of the smaller men who were having difficulty. There was not a man from the L.C.I. who did not land soaked to the skin.

On dry land a naval beachmaster stood by a loud hailer : " Come along Durhams," he shouted. " That guy's been trying to hit something for an hour now. He's no bloody good ! "

" That last one wasn't too bloody bad," growled one of the B Company runners as he passed by.

The two companies staggered along the beach. The men's equipment was weighty enough anyway, but waterlogged as they were the troops could hardly move. As the leading files turned left into a minefield gap a film cameraman cranked the handle of his cine camera, and the voice of the beachmaster came over the loud hailer : "Through the minefield gap and turn right for the assembly area."

The sun streamed down through the olive groves, and the houses along the road were shuttered and silent; they seemed deserted. A batch of Italian prisoners marched towards the beaches and a British military policeman, wearing his soft-peaked red hat, directed the two companies to the assembly area. If this was Mussolini's so-called fortress, it wasn't so bad.

CHAPTER TWENTY-TWO

INSIDE MUSSOLINI'S FORTRESS

An exhausting climb—on the covering position—the Carriers in action—50 Division answers an S.O.S.

THE assembly area was in some orchards just off the coast road, and apart from an occasional burst of enemy machine-gun fire the European fortress seemed peaceful enough. The troops were not slow to seize the opportunity of resting and drying out their equipment. The Battalion was not yet complete, for C Company, which had disembarked from the *Ruys* after the rest of the Battalion, had been delayed and did not land on the beaches until later in the morning.

Just before 8 a.m. the C.O. called a conference at Battalion H.Q. to pass on information he had just received from the Brigadier, to the effect that the assaulting battalions had captured all their objectives, sustaining very few casualties. The immediate task of the 8th Battalion was to occupy the two covering positions, one north-west of Avola and the other east of Noto. The C.O. stressed the point that although 151 Brigade had met very little opposition on the beaches, the Germans still had to be reckoned with, and it was therefore essential to reach the covering positions before they did.

A few minutes before nine o'clock the 8th Battalion, less C Company, marched out of the assembly area and turned left along the coast road towards Avola. The leading sections had covered a hundred yards or so when a company of men from a battalion of 5 Division trooped down the road, going in the opposite direction.

"Landed in the wrong Div. area," one of them shouted. "Where is this perishing battle anyway?"

He was quite right. Where was the battle? By this time the lone coastal gun and the machine-guns had been silenced, and Sicily could not have been more peaceful. The answer was, of course, that the Italians on the Eighth Army front were determined not to have a battle.

Shortly after this amusing episode the 8th Battalion split up into two columns. D Company continued towards Avola and Noto, whilst A and B Companies and Battalion H.Q. started to climb the lower slopes of the hill towards the right-hand covering position. The going was very bad and the hill much steeper than it had appeared either on the scale model or the photographs. The troops cursed the Sicilian farmers, who had ploughed up every single yard of the hillside, and the plough was divided at thirty or forty yard intervals by four-feet brick walls which had to be climbed. The hillside was in fact a succession of terraces. The signallers, with heavy wireless sets strapped to their backs, were bent almost double. The reason for the intensive P.T. at Suez and on the ships now became apparent, and there were more than a few members of the Battalion who thanked their lucky stars that the invasion ships had been " dry." That early morning climb in Sicily was no time for alcoholic troubles of any sort.

Under the fierce rays of the sun it was a brute of a climb—every minute of it—and by the time the column reached the covering position, after six hours of hard climbing, there was not a single man with sufficient energy to fire at two Messerschmitts which had just completed a beach-strafing mission. The planes, roaring inland towards the Catania airfields, were not more than fifty feet up as they swept over the exhausted companies. However, the troops soon pulled themselves together with the aid of a fresh water well, and by mid-afternoon A and B Companies were in position on the high ground.

D Company under the Second-in-Command, Major H. Blackden, reached their objective after much the same unpleasant climb as the main column. Soon after passing Avola station and turning inland towards the high ground, the company came across dozens of discarded parachutes. They were of all colours and some, with supply canisters attached to them, had caught in the branches of trees. It was evident that a large number of airborne troops, scheduled for the Syracuse area, had been dropped very wide of the mark.

Meanwhile, down on the beaches guns, tanks, carriers and some of the D Day transport had come ashore, and the 8th Battalion carriers joined A and B Companies during the course of the afternoon together with some of the Battalion transport. In the early evening several of the carriers patrolled beyond the A Company positions towards Palazzolo Acreide, and after a short skirmish on the road brought back with them two Italian officers and sixteen other ranks. Apart from this the first day in Sicily ended peacefully. The colour sergeants of both A and B Companies went on scrounging expeditions, and C/Sgt. Foster of B Company drove a small, grey Balila Fiat into the company area just after dusk had fallen. A Company acquired a very smart Lancia Aprilla saloon, and in addition to these vehicles, the Battalion collected an odd assortment of bicycles and carts from the Sicilians. The locals had been given to understand from the Germans and by propaganda broadcasts that the British and American forces would shoot all civilians on sight. Having discovered this to be untrue the Sicilians became surprisingly friendly towards the invading troops, and did not object unduly about the loss of their property.

Next day a platoon of Cheshire Regiment machine-guns arrived in the Battalion area with some of the Battalion anti-tank guns. During the morning Major Blackden's force on the left-hand covering position —having seen no enemy—was relieved by the 9th Battalion, and just after midday Lieut.-Colonel Lidwill sent the anti-tank gun portees and the platoon 15 cwt. trucks to fetch C and D Companies. These two companies were brought back without incident and soon moved into position with the rest of the Battalion.

The men of the Carrier Platoon were out all day, following a report that the Germans held Palazzolo Acreide, and in the early evening a section of carriers was ambushed by anti-tank guns three miles from the town. Two of the carriers were lost. On the credit side the platoon had brought in several prisoners during the day but the loss of two carriers, with no prospect of getting them replaced for some time, was a serious setback for the Battalion.

Shortly before dusk the covering position was taken over by the 1st Gordons of 51 Highland Division, and the 8th Battalion, feeling very much like the Grand Old Duke of York's 10,000 men, marched back down the hillside which had been climbed so laboriously the day before. Darkness rapidly closed in, making the journey through the orchards and over the low walls most unpleasant. To the accompaniment of a certain amount of shouting and cursing, the Battalion eventually arrived in an assembly area just off the coast road and thankfully turned in for the night. C Company commander, Captain H. O. Walmsley, started the descent of the hillside on the back of a commandeered horse, and arrived in the assembly area heartily wishing he had never seen the animal.

Good news reached the Battalion during the night. The invasion of Sicily had been carried out according to plan, although the airborne landings had not been entirely successful. Nevertheless, those airborne forces which were landed in the target area held on doggedly to the important bridge south of Syracuse, their gallant stand enabling troops of 13 Corps to press inland from the beaches and to capture the undamaged port of Syracuse by nightfall on D Day. On the left of the Eighth Army front, in the 30 Corps sector, assaulting divisions had met very little opposition, and by the evening of the first day 30 Corps was in possession of the Pachino Peninsular and airfields. Neither of the British corps had met any Germans, and the Italians—particularly those of the coastal divisions—were only too pleased to give themselves up. The Americans had not been so fortunate. Soon after landing they were counter-attacked by German troops, and there was heavy fighting around Gela. The situation was restored by the dogged fighting of the Americans, by the United States Navy steaming close inshore to give very short range support, and by the courageous leadership of General Patton, who went ashore at the danger point personally to supervise the operations.

With the Eighth Army established on Sicily, General Montgomery's immediate intention was now to secure the main road centres and so restrict enemy movement. The Army Commander ordered 13 Corps to advance northwards beyond Syracuse to take Catania whilst 30 Corps moved by the axis Caltagirone and Enna to the major road centre of Leonforte, west of Catania and Mount Etna. To speed the advance of 13 Corps an airborne attack was planned for the night of July 13th/14th to capture and hold the vitally important Primosole bridge, carrying the main Catania road over the Simeto river some fifteen miles south of the city. The airborne troops were to hold the bridge until the arrival of the leading battalion of 13 Corps.

As one of the two infantry divisions of 13 Corps, 50 Division was soon on the move, and the 8th Battalion left its assembly area at 5 a.m. on July 12th. As yet very little transport had been landed on the island, which meant that the Battalion was carried principally by the portees of the anti-tank platoon and the few platoon and company vehicles which had come ashore on D Day. These vehicles were very crowded and it was fortunate that the Luftwaffe was busy elsewhere. The Battalion column covered fifteen miles during the day, passing through Cassibile and Floridia to Solarino, where the 8th took over from a battalion of Inniskillings of 5 Division. The Battalion was not in contact with the enemy, but the 6th D.L.I. on the left had a sharp and noisy engagement with units of the Italian Napoli Division, knocking out some armoured vehicles. That night practically all the Battalion transport was sent under special orders to 524 Company R.A.S.C. so that the move forward the following afternoon to Sortino was carried out on foot. After a ten mile march the Battalion arrived in the Sortino area late at night and had to take up defensive positions by moonlight.

During the night British airborne troops captured Primosole bridge and disarmed the demolition charges which had been placed in position. Unfortunately many of the troops were landed well away from the target area, and it was only a small force which held back the repeated enemy attacks to recapture and blow up the bridge. By the morning the airborne troops, though sadly reduced in numbers, still held the bridge. It was essential for the infantry of 13 Corps to reach them during the course of the day or at the latest by nightfall. Up to this time the spearhead of the 13 Corps advance had been 69 Brigade of 50 Division, but now the D.L.I. Brigade was ordered to lead the advance.

With very little transport available, it meant a forced march for the three D.L.I. battalions. The 9th Battalion led the way, followed by the 8th, then the 6th. It was hot and dusty, and the officers and N.C.Os. wondered how the men were going to stand up to the longest operational march since the Battle of France in 1940. From Sortino to Primosole is a distance of nearly twenty-five miles. They need not have worried, for the troops knew the desperate plight of the paratroops holding the bridge, and the leading battalion was well over half way to Primosole when the dry heat of the afternoon gave way to the welcome cool of the early evening. The pace quickened, and by dusk an armoured brigade and the 9th Battalion were within a mile of the bridge.

The paratroops met them with bad news. All day the airborne men had fought back repeated counter-attacks, holding the bridge until 7.30 p.m.—only two hours before the arrival of the Shermans and the 9th Battalion—when lack of ammunition forced the sadly depleted force to withdraw in the face of yet another counter-attack. Nevertheless, thanks to the foresight of the airborne troops in removing the demolition charges, the bridge could not be blown by the enemy, and the British paratroops ensured that no one came close enough to plant any more charges.

Needless to say, the enemy troops on the far side of Primosole bridge were not Italians. They were Germans of the 3rd Parachute Regiment, hardened veterans of the Crete invasion and the Russian campaign. This battalion and other paratroop units had been flown from the mainland of Italy with orders to stem the Allied advance northwards.

By the time the situation was clear to the Commander of 151 Brigade darkness had fallen, and for several reasons it was impossible to do anything that night to recapture the bridge. The leading troops of the Brigade were dog-tired after their forced march and little or no reconnaissance had been carried out of possible crossing places over the Simeto. The 8th Battalion, still four hours back along the road, was just as tired as the 9th, and having marched a full twenty-five miles would be in no fit state to fight a battle when it arrived ; the 6th Battalion was even farther back along the road. In view of all this the Brigadier decided that time must be given for reconnaissance and for the troops to rest, and an attack by the 9th Battalion to recapture the bridge was planned for 7.30 a.m. the next morning.

CHAPTER TWENTY-THREE

THE BATTLE OF PRIMOSOLE BRIDGE

The first attack fails—the 8th Battalion captures the bridge—heavy casualties in B and C Companies—a day of continual fighting—the Battalion holds fast—the bridgehead is enlarged—end of a savage battle—back in reserve.

It had turned 2 a.m. by the time the 8th Battalion reached the end of its long and tiring journey, a mile or two in rear of the 9th D.L.I. Thankfully the companies marched off the road to bivouac areas where, with the knowledge that the morning would most certainly bring with it action of some sort, the exhausted infantry stretched themselves out on the hard ground to try and get a few hours' sleep before the dawn. They were unlucky ; at 4 a.m. there was violent automatic fire and frequent explosions from the direction of the 9th D.L.I. positions. The 8th Battalion immediately "stood to," but it was not until next morning that news came through of the short but fierce action fought during the night. The 9th Battalion had been attacked by a section of Italian Marine Armoured Cars which penetrated as far as the Battalion H.Q. area before being halted. The situation was saved by the prompt action of the D.L.I. anti-tank gun crews, and the armoured cars were hit and set on fire. There were very few survivors and the failure of this desperate bid by the Italians to shoot up the 9th Battalion H.Q. was not due to lack of courage on the part of the armoured car crews.

A conference was held at the 8th Battalion H.Q. just before daybreak, when Lieut.-Colonel Lidwill explained that the 9th D.L.I. would be attacking the bridge at 7.30 a.m., supported by the guns of two field regiments. He went on to say that, immediately after an early breakfast, the 8th Battalion was to advance and take over the positions vacated by the attacking battalion.

Soon after 7 a.m. the Priests (self-propelled guns on tank chassis) of one of the field regiments swung off the road into the 8th Battalion area, and took up their positions to support the assault on the bridge. At 7.35 a.m. the Battalion moved off, the companies keeping clear of the road which was being shelled, and after a short march arrived in the 9th Battalion area. From the high ground where the 9th D.L.I. had spent the night it was possible to watch the progress of the attack against the bridge. Although the bridge itself was clearly visible nothing could be seen of the enemy positions north of the river, where the close country offered good concealed positions. On the south side the country was flat and utterly devoid of cover. The attacking companies, advancing in open formation, came under heavy machine-gun fire and suffered a considerable number of casualties before they reached the banks of the river. Only odd platoons succeeded in crossing the Simeto, and they were halted and eventually forced back by German paratroops concealed in the vineyards and lining a sunken road some four or five hundred yards north of the bridge. After fierce hand-to-hand fighting, the precarious hold of the battalion on the north bank of the river was finally broken, and those men who had managed to get across were driven back, leaving their dead and most of the wounded in enemy hands.

The situation at 9.30 a.m. was that the remnants of the 9th Battalion lined the southern bank of the river, whilst the Germans on the far bank prepared to meet another attack. Any movement on the flat ground south of the river immediately brought down heavy German mortar fire, and any approach by British tanks to the bridge was met by the accurate and devastating fire of German 88-millimetre guns firing over open sights down the Catania road. It was quite obvious that the C.O. of the 9th Battalion would not be able to mount another attack for some while, but his men were in such a position that they could prevent the Germans placing charges to blow up the bridge. They did this most successfully, breaking up several enemy attempts during the course of the day.

At 10 a.m. the Divisional Commander ordered 151 Brigade to attack the bridge again, this time with stronger artillery support, and the 8th Battalion was ordered to stand by. Zero hour was tentatively fixed at 4 p.m., and accompanied by the C.O. of the 9th Battalion and the commander of the supporting artillery, Lieut.-Colonel Lidwill reconnoitred the bridge and its approaches from all aspects.

Primosole bridge was four hundred feet long, with a superstructure of iron girders about eight feet above a sluggish river bordered by reeds. North of the bridge were two small farms, one on either side of the road, each consisting of two or three buildings and a barn. The road which could be seen beyond the bridge, running absolutely straight between two lines of poplars, was the main road to Catania. Northwards from the river banks thick vineyards, dotted with olive trees, extended to a depth of some four to five hundred yards. Beyond the vineyards was open country. Nothing could be seen of the enemy positions, nor was the existence of the sunken road, which had played such a large part in breaking up the attack of the 9th Battalion, suspected at this time. The first assault had failed to establish a bridgehead, and a second frontal attack appeared to be suicidal. The prospects looked gloomy indeed for the 8th Battalion.

After returning to Brigade H.Q., where the artillery plan was finalised, Lieut.-Colonel Lidwill made his way back to Battalion H.Q. where the company commanders and commanders of the supporting arms were waiting for him. Battalion H.Q. was situated in a small cave, and the C.O. had just started to outline the plan when a stranger appeared in the entrance. He was unshaven, his khaki shirt and trousers were covered in stains and grime, and he looked dog-tired. He walked over and sat down beside the C.O. " My name's Pearson," he said[1]. " I commanded the paratroops down at the bridge and I

[1]Lieut.-Colonel A. S. Pearson, D.S.O., M.C., Commanding the 1st. Parachute Battalion.

understand you are attacking again this afternoon. I think I can help you."

His information was invaluable. He pointed out that a direct attack on the bridge was out of the question as the Germans had concentrated all their fire power on the approaches. He knew of a place about three hundred yards upstream where it was possible to wade across. "In fact," he said, "I'll show your assault companies the way over to the other side." It was impossible not to feel an intense admiration for this burly Scotsman who, having fought continuously for twenty-four hours with his paratroops to hold the vital bridge, was now offering to lead another attack to capture it, knowing full well that he need take no further part in the battle.

By this time it had been decided that another assault by daylight would be suicidal. Zero hour had been put forward to 2.10 a.m. the following morning, when the attacking battalion would have the advantage of a full moon. The C.O., having revised the times in accordance with the new instructions from Brigade H.Q., gave out his orders. For an hour and twenty minutes prior to zero hour the Gunners were to put down artillery concentrations in the area of the bridge and in the vineyards immediately north of the river, extending for five hundred yards to the left of the bridge. For the last ten minutes every gun was to be concentrated in the area of the bridge. The barrage was to be thickened by a squadron of tanks firing from the low ground south of the river, as well as a machine-gun platoon of the Cheshires, positioned on the high ground overlooking the bridge.

A and D Companies of the 8th were to ford the river at 2.10 a.m. at a point to be indicated by Lieut.-Colonel Pearson, afterwards working their way downstream in an easterly direction, through the vineyards and on to their objective—the bridge. If this was captured intact the rest of the Battalion and supporting arms were to cross the river by the bridge to enlarge the bridgehead. The position north of the Simeto to be consolidated was approximately fifteen hundred yards in depth and some two thousand yards wide. The northward curve of the river on both sides of the bridge would enable the Battalion flanks to rest on the Simeto.

From A Company's position on the high ground there was a good vantage point, and during the late afternoon officers and N.C.Os. were able to carry out a reconnaisance of the country north of the river. There was very little movement beyond the Simeto and no one was able to pick out the line of the enemy defences, although from time to time one or two Germans could be seen walking about. Down by the bridge a Sherman tank edged cautiously forward at intervals to fire at movement around the farm buildings on the northern bank, but apart from this all was quiet. It was the deceptive lull preceding a stiff battle which the old hands in the 8th Battalion knew only too well.

The A Company area had been a Luftwaffe rest camp for German airmen on leave from the airfields on the Catania Plain. A number of tents in the area had comprised the H.Q., Officers' Mess and sleeping quarters of the German pilots. Captain Beattie's Company H.Q. was soon established inside the mess tent, where a half-consumed meal still remained on the table. The Germans had left hurriedly, and a great deal of useful material was picked up in the area by the Battalion, including cameras, air-filled mattresses, German fleece-lined flying coats, and a portable lighting plant which came in very useful later in the campaign. It was only natural that A Company should commandeer a large part of this booty, and for once the Carrier Platoon did not collect a major portion of the spoils.

A hot meal which came up from B Echelon late in the afternoon was most welcome, as was the news that a rum ration would be issued before the attack. At dusk a troop of Shermans from the 44th R.T.R. took up positions about two hundred yards upstream from the bridge, and roughly a hundred yards south of the river, in order to give covering fire for A and D Companies immediately prior to the assault.

During the evening the 6th Battalion moved into the 8th Battalion area, and at 9.40 p.m. the men of A and D Companies formed up in single file in their company areas. It was a clear moonlight night when at 10 p.m. exactly the two assaulting companies left the assembly area and marched to the F.U.P. (Forming-Up-Place) where they met Lieut.-Colonel Pearson and some of his paratroops ; they had gone down at dusk to tape a route from there to the river. Meanwhile, the reserve companies—B and C—with the supporting arms and Battalion H.Q. had moved to their respective assembly areas, east and west of the main road and some thousand yards south of the bridge.

At 12-50 a.m. the barrage opened, and the Cheshire machine-guns went into action. It was a heavy barrage for such a narrow front, and the noise was deafening. For an hour and ten minutes the artillery and machine-guns raked the vineyards beyond the Simeto, and then ten minutes before zero hour the whole weight of the gunfire was directed at the northern end of the bridge. The effect of this artillery and machine-gun fire must have been devastating to the Germans in this area.

At zero hour the British tanks opened fire with their Besa guns, and guided by Lieut.-Colonel Pearson and his men, A and D Companies with the C.O. forded the river in single file at two points about fifty yards apart. They crossed without any great difficulty or serious interference from the enemy. However, although the average depth of the river was four feet, there were several deep holes—possibly caused by shells—and a number of men were completely submerged before they could be rescued.

Under cover of the far bank the two companies formed up rapidly and started to move forward in an easterly direction towards the bridge, with A on the right and D on the left. The vineyards—thick, closely planted and entwined—made movement difficult, and sections and platoons had to shout their numbers to maintain contact. The operation in daylight would have been difficult enough but at night it was doubly so. However, the fact that it was such an unusual form of attack took the enemy by surprise, and most of the defenders of the bridge had withdrawn three or four hundred yards.

There was a certain amount of automatic fire from the left which was ignored, as the main task was to capture the bridge intact, speed being essential. The enemy automatics were using tracer and it was not difficult to dodge the fire. When the two companies reached the area of the bridge only a few enemy were encountered, and to the accompaniment of shouts and cheers these were speedily disposed of with bayonets, grenades or Tommy guns. The heavy artillery fire had accounted for some of the bridge defenders, and the main body had withdrawn.

Having gained the Catania road, C.S.M. S. Wardle established D Company H.Q. in a ditch adjacent to one of the farmhouses, and immediately came under intense mortar fire from the enemy. A Company, after cutting a way through some barbed wire, rushed the pillboxes around the northern end of the bridge and routed the defenders. The company objective lay beyond the Catania road, and as the road was covered by accurate bursts of Spandau machine-gun fire, A Company did not have an easy time getting across. However, most of the company ran the gauntlet safely, and Captain Beattie and his men, after cutting another belt of barbed wire, pushed on to their objective which was in some vineyards about five hundred yards from the road where the river turns sharply northwards. The company commander positioned No. 7 Platoon (Lieut. H. C. Catford) on the left, and Nos. 8 and 9 Platoons (Lieuts. F. Clarke and W. H. Waggott) on the right.

The company dug in quickly with entrenching tools about a hundred yards north of the river banks. A Spandau was constantly sweeping the area from a position over towards the road, and small parties of Germans harassed the company by throwing grenades at close range. The whole area was thickly covered by vines, shrubs and tall grass. There was a fair number of trees, making it difficult for the troops to see what was happening in front of their positions, even when standing up. From the slit trenches, observation was limited to a few yards. It was, without a doubt, the worst defensive position A Company had ever occupied and it required constant vigil to keep the persistent German paratroops out of the area.

With the first phase of the battle successfully carried out the remainder of the 8th Battalion could now cross the bridge. The C.O. had arranged several alternative methods of contacting his Rear H.Q. The first was by 2" Mortar flare, but the mortar and most of the bombs had become separated in the dark, and the one flare which did go up was not seen south of the river. The second method was by wireless, but during the fording of the Simeto both company sets had become "drowned" and would not operate. As a last method of communication the C.O. had ordered the R.E. officer, whose task it was to reconnoitre the bridge for mines, with the 8th Battalion Carrier commander, Captain G. Lohan, to station themselves in a wireless-equipped carrier at the southern end of the bridge When the C.O. went back across the bridge he found that the carrier had received a direct hit, killing both the officers and badly wounding the members of the crew. The wireless set had been put out of action.

The only other possibility, without walking up the road to where the rest of the Battalion waited, was to use one of the Sherman tanks on the southern bank of the river as a link. The C.O. found a tank, and as there was still a lot of firing from the other end of the bridge and the tank engine was running, the only way he could make his presence known was to tap the commander's head where it showed just above the turret. The tank closed down hurriedly and so for the time being this method of communication failed. The Sherman was as firmly sealed as a sardine tin and the crew obviously had no intention of opening up.

By a lucky chance, as Lieut.-Colonel Lidwill walked back to the road wondering how he was going to get the rest of his battalion forward, a War Office observer (Major Wigram) came into view riding a bicycle! He could not have arrived at a more opportune moment, and turning his bicycle round he pedalled back to where the rest of the Battalion waited, with a message for them to move forward immediately.

This unfortunate chapter of events had delayed things considerably, and dawn was not far off when B and C Companies left the assembly area to march in single file down the road towards the bridge. The two companies, with B leading, passed the wrecked carrier and wended their way across the bridge, carefully avoiding the mines which had been laid on the surface. On the far side, as the leading troops drew level with blazing farm buildings on the left of the road, somebody in D Company shouted: "Push on B Company, there's only a few 'Ities' up in front."

The two companies advanced quickly up the Catania road, but as there was by this time a certain amount of enemy small arms fire, Captain P. J. Lewis led B Company into the ditch on the left of the road, whilst C Company took to the ditch on the right of the road. Three hundred yards north of the bridge the first shots were suddenly fired as a prelude to twenty minutes of the fiercest hand-to-hand fighting the 8th Battalion had ever known.

In the darkness and shadows of poplar trees flanking the road, the men of the leading sections got to within a few yards of German machine-guns before the enemy opened up at almost point-blank range. In the first few seconds of firing, the Spandaus cut down the forward sections of B and C Companies before the men realised what had happened. The German fire was murderous and it practically wiped out the leading platoon of B Company, led by Lieut. R. F. Holloway. If it had not been for the ditch there is little doubt that the two companies would have been shot down almost to a man.

As it was the troops recovered remarkably well, and the fire of the Spandaus was returned by B Company Bren guns from the ditch on the left of the road, whilst C Company took to the fields on the right of the road and tried to work round behind the Germans. This move, the fire of the B Company Brens and a gallant charge by a handful of

C Company men, led by Lieut. A. F. Jackman, forced the enemy to withdraw. The small party were shot down almost on top of a German Spandau and Jackman himself was badly wounded.

With C Company in the open country on the right of the road, B Company—with fixed bayonets—went off into the vines on the left of the road in search of the enemy. The paratroops were waiting for them, and within a minute of leaving the road the front half of B Company was engaged with the enemy in a grim game of hide and seek. It was very difficult to distinguish friend from foe in the shadows, and it meant every man for himself with no quarter asked or given on either side. Individual fire fights and hand-to-hand fighting broke out in several places, and C.S.M. M. J. Brannigan, using a bayonet with deadly effect, accounted for several paratroops within the space of a few minutes.

Advancing cautiously through the thick vines some of the B Company men were shot down at point-blank range, whilst others crept up on German paratroops to shoot them where they lay or stood. It seemed as though there was a German behind every tree and vine ; every bush. The situation was unreal, almost fantastic. Both sides fired at trees by mistake, thinking they were men ; both sides threw grenades until it was realised that the exploding bombs were just as likely to kill friend as foe. British and Germans were afraid to use their weapons at a range of more than a yard or two for fear of killing their comrades.

The ultimate result of this close hand-to-hand fighting was that within the space of twenty minutes the two sides fought themselves to a standstill. The front half of B Company and the Germans suffered nearly a hundred per cent casualties, and the only men left in the area where the fighting had taken place were either dead or wounded. It temporarily broke the close contact with the paratroops. True, B Company had gained ground and some of the company, including the company commander, had reached the German positions in the sunken road some four hundred yards north of the bridge, where after a fierce fire fight they were all killed or wounded. Although the paratroops had suffered equally heavy casualties as B Company they still held the sunken road, the key to the whole of their defensive position.

The rear part of the company, little more than forty men under Captain D. A. Neale, was still in the roadside ditch. C.S.M. Brannigan, one of the few men to survive the hand-to-hand fighting, walked back to Neale with the news that the rest of B Company—fifty or sixty men—had ceased to exist as effective fighting troops. At this time Neale had no knowledge of the sunken road, and decided to take the remnants of the company forward to the original objective. B Company broke out of the ditch about sixty yards south of the sunken road and started to move across the fields. As it was still not light there was a lot of shouting to keep direction. The company had only left the shelter of the ditch about forty yards behind, when hand grenades were thrown by the paratroops lining the sunken road. In the face of heavy and accurate automatic fire B Company went to ground amongst the grape vines, although they provided no cover from the enemy machine-guns.

The existence of the sunken road did not become apparent until the first pale glimmers of light were beginning to show in the east. Captain Neale decided that the company could not stay in such an exposed position, neither could it push on towards the original objective which lay beyond the sunken road. Within a few minutes the light was sufficient to see a large embankment, some eight feet high, surrounding a farmhouse to the rear. It was decided to withdraw the company to the shelter of the embankment, but no sooner had the men started to move back in widely extended order than the paratroops emerged from their dug-in positions in the sunken road and put in a short but very effective bayonet charge which completely overran the rearguard under Sgt. F. Mitchinson. The sergeant shammed dead to avoid capture, allowing the enemy to pass him by. One of the paratroops actually kicked Mitchinson to see if he were dead and was apparently satisfied. When the Germans moved on Mitchinson opened fire with his Tommy gun, throwing them into complete confusion and thus allowing the main body of the company to complete the withdrawal.

A gallant action by C.S.M. Brannigan also helped considerably to save this ugly situation. Seizing an automatic weapon as soon as the Germans started to advance, Brannigan stood his ground to give covering fire as the company withdrew. The sergeant-major's shooting was deadly but he was a target which the Germans could not miss. He was killed, still firing his gun, just as B Company reached the outer side of the embankment. His unselfish action had saved the lives of many of his comrades and it was typical of the gallant way in which he had always fought with the 8th Battalion. A way was found round the end of the embankment, and Captain Neale positioned the remnants of B Company, not now more than thirty men, on the north and west side of the embankment, whilst the Germans again withdrew to the sunken road.

C Company was, if anything, even worse off than B Company. It had suffered heavy casualties when the paratroops first opened fire, and the remnants had become very scattered when they took to the fields on the right of the road. Here their numbers were gradually reduced and, by first light, C Company having no officers left was not holding a company position but several scattered localities.

A Company, also on the right of the road but back towards the river, had not experienced such a hectic night as either of the other two, but there had been a certain amount of activity on the company front. Shortly before dawn this activity ceased and the old hands in A Company knew that a German attack was imminent, for the German is always most dangerous when he is silent. Sure enough, as soon as it became light a counter attack developed against the two platoons on the right of the company front. The area was so thick with grapevines and the field of fire so restricted that the paratroopers, experts in the art of stalking, were able to work their way almost up to the A Company positions before coming into the open. They overran the two platoon localities, but only after some fierce fighting at close range amongst the section positions. There was a high proportion of casualties on both sides ; Lieut. Clarke, the commander of No. 8 Platoon, was killed and Sgt. Crawford wounded, after putting up a gallant fight with his Tommy gun to account for several of the enemy. The fighting continued until the numerically superior paratroops drove the two A Company platoons back to the banks of the river, where some of the men swam the Simeto to safety. The position of the third A Company platoon, No. 7 under Lieut. Catford, now became precarious. Captain Beattie ordered this platoon to withdraw to the main battalion position at the northern end of the bridge, and A Company H.Q. pulled back at the same time.

It was during the first night that L/Cpl. F. H. Spink of H.Q. Company won the Military Medal when shells from the heavy British artillery barrage fell short, inflicting serious casualties amongst the Battalion forward troops. In the midst of the resulting confusion L/Cpl. Spink calmly volunteered to contact the Gunner O.P. so as to get the range corrected, although this meant going out into the open where the shelling was heavy. He carried out his mission and his disregard for danger to himself resulted in saving the lives of many of his comrades. Three hours later, aided by three other men, he was bringing in a wounded man who had been lying in the open a considerable time. When the party started to cross the road they were immediately subjected to such a hail of machine-gun fire that Spink's three companions made for cover. The N.C.O. did not abandon the wounded man but stayed with him, then rallied his carrying party and brought his casualty to safety. Throughout the night's operations he showed great resource and leadership in organising the evacuation of wounded men exposed to enemy fire. His gallantry saved many lives.

Six o'clock found the 8th Battalion in close contact with the enemy and lively fire being exchanged at ranges decreasing to as little as twenty yards in some parts of the bridgehead. The Battalion had by this time taken up positions to form a salient three hundred yards in depth and equidistant in width. B Company still lined the embankment opposite the sunken road, and the remnants of C Company had come into position on their left. Beyond C Company, Battalion H.Q. had been established at the junction of the embankment with the Catania road. D Company, the only company which had not suffered heavy casualties, was in position on the other side of the road, level with B and C Companies. The remnants of A Company came into position on the same side of the road as D Company to line a white wall which ran parallel to the Catania road. Captain Beattie's company still having four officers, the C.O. ordered Captain Wheatley, the A Company second-in-command, to take over what was left of C Company.

The men in the bridgehead knew how precarious was their hold on the northern bank and how vital it was to maintain that hold at all

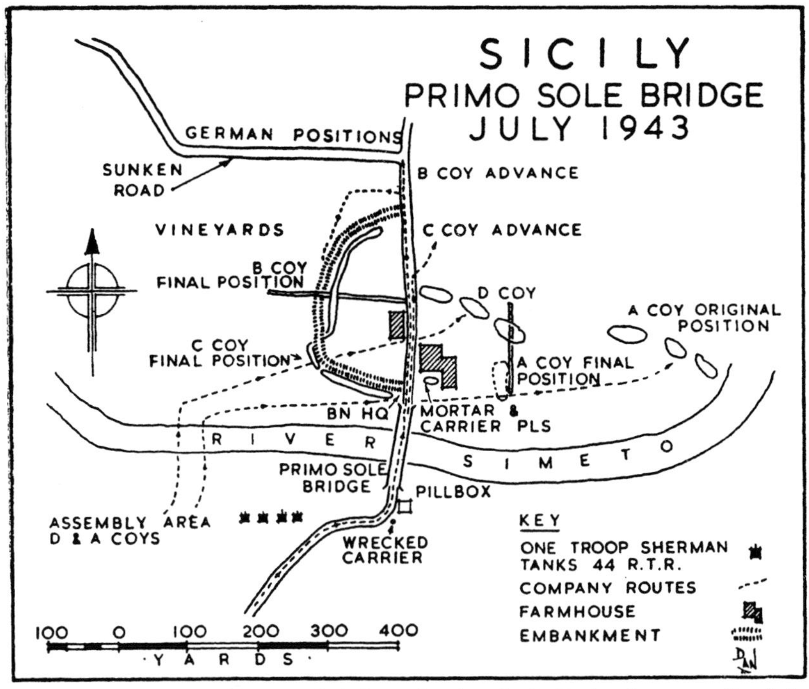

SICILY. The battle of Primosole bridge showing the bridgehead area north of the River Simeto where there was fierce fighting with German paratroops.

costs until the arrival of reinforcements. The C.O. realised the seriousness of the position better than anyone, and no one who was at Primosole will forget the picture of him standing hatless against the group of shattered farm buildings where Battalion H.Q. had been established. Dressed in a dark shirt and a pair of torn slacks, with his pistol slung from a webbing belt, he walked round the Battalion positions inspiring complete confidence in the men under his command, as he had done during the anxious days at Mareth.

Primosole bridge was under constant and accurate small arms fire, and the Brigade Commander, who had crossed it to reach the 8th Battalion H.Q. by dawn, was unable to return to his H.Q. because of the bursts of fire which swept the bridge. However, tanks could still cross, and the men in the bridgehead heard the welcome sound of tracks as two Shermans came over the bridge. The tank commanders had been ordered to deploy their Shermans one left and one right of the road and engage the enemy but, believing the vineyards to be an obstacle to movement, they kept to the road and almost immediately came under fire from a German 88 millimetre gun some eight hundred yards north of the bridge. To the disappointment of the infantry, who felt they could get forward with the help of the tanks, the two Shermans withdrew hurriedly and crossed the bridge to the south side of the river.

It was quite evident that there was a strong force of paratroopers holding the line of the sunken road, and B and C Companies kept up a constant fire fight at short range. At no point on the left of the road were the Germans more than sixty yards away. The B Company Bren gunners fired at the slightest sign of movement from the sunken road but the Brens were jamming constantly. A small group was established at Company H.Q. with the sole object of getting the guns into action again with the least possible delay.

At 6.30 a.m. the Battalion Carrier and Mortar Platoons were ordered forward. In spite of heavy small arms fire, the platoons crossed the bridge in their carriers to take cover behind a farm on the right of the road. Several of the carrier crews crossed the road to help B Company, whilst the remainder organised a precarious supply of ammunition and food across the bridge and assisted in the evacuation of the wounded. The bridge was so well covered by fire that it was suicidal to attempt to cross except in a carrier, in one of which the Brigadier had to make the return journey.

North of the bridge, Lieut. Hampson brought his 3″ Mortars into action at once from behind the farmhouse. Their very effective supporting fire was a great help to the infantry in the bridgehead and, having covered all the company fronts, Hampson ordered his mortar teams to range up and down on either side of the road. The accuracy of their shooting and the fact that it scared the paratroopers considerably can be vouched for by several wounded B Company men, including the company commander, who were being evacuated to a German casualty clearing station at this time.

The Battalion also had excellent support from the Priests in position south of the Simeto. The artillery officers who had accompanied the assault companies established their observation posts on the right of the road not far from the mortars, and they did not need any encouragement to bring down the fire of their guns. The Priests and mortars did excellent work.

The C.O. next called forward two anti-tank guns, which were towed across the bridge by carriers at two-minute intervals. The guns were placed in position at the northern end of the bridge, and shortly afterwards three Sherman tanks crossed the river with orders to deploy in the open country on the right of the road. They kept on the road too long and the German 88-millimetre, waiting until the tanks were sitting targets, opened fire to knock out two of the Shermans in as many minutes. One of them was hit just beyond the Battalion position and caught fire. As the Sherman ran off the road its tracks tangled in some barbed wire which caught the clothing of Lieut. Jackman, the wounded C Company platoon commander who had been lying in the ditch since daybreak. Jackman was dragged along the ground but fortunately the tank soon came to rest. He was eventually picked up by a party of German stretcher bearers and taken to Catania Hospital, where the Germans left him, more dead than alive, when they evacuated the city. Jackman was in a bad way when British troops found him, but eventually recovered from his wounds. In the bridgehead the Priests had got the range of the 88 soon after the tanks were hit, and the Gunners brought down a concentration which knocked out the gun and killed the crew.

The morning wore on, the paratroops keeping up constant and accurate harassing fire with their automatic weapons. A Company in particular had several casualties from sniping, as the enemy in the sunken road could to some extent fire at the rear of the company. It was extremely hot in the sun and most unpleasant for the majority of the A Company men ; because of their position they could not shelter in the shade.

Throughout the day the paratroops attempted to launch counter-attacks against the bridgehead. These attacks were all beaten back by machine-gun, mortar and small arms fire. The Battalion Mortar Platoon fired over six hundred bombs during the Primosole battle and, together with a platoon of Cheshire machine guns in the same area, kept up a constant barrage, breaking up enemy groups as they formed up to attack and making the paratroops pay a high price for any movement.

Lieut. Hampson kept his mortars firing from completely exposed positions. Any target which presented itself was immediately engaged and Hampson himself acted as O.P. for the platoon. He was continually up forward with the infantry, cheering them on and inspiring them by the nonchalant way in which he walked about in the open wherever the fire was heaviest, swinging a fly whisk leisurely from side to side. He spotted many targets from the infantry positions and was responsible for directing his mortars so that their fire broke up at least three enemy counter-attacks. Every effort the enemy made to form up was immediately frustrated. It was largely due to his untiring efforts that the Battalion bridgehead was maintained, and Lieut. Hampson was awarded the Military Cross. He could not have been backed by a better Mortar Platoon one of whom, Cpl. W. D. Scriven, was awarded the Military Medal. Scriven was in the thick of the battle throughout and with his section of mortars must have accounted for dozens of snipers, while all the time he was in an exposed position and being shot at continually. When two of his section were wounded he carried them himself across the shell-swept ground and then over the bridge, thus saving their lives. Towards the close of the bridgehead battle he volunteered to lead a tank against a pillbox which was doing considerable damage. Crouched on top of the tank, under heavy machine-gun fire, Scriven directed the gun from the outside while the commander fired from the inside. The pillbox was destroyed.

At Primosole close support by the guns of the 98th Field Regiment was impossible because of the nearness of the enemy. However, the guns were seldom silent, and judging by the number of German dead found after the battle, their fire was most effective. Two unfortunate incidents occurred during the early afternoon. The British gunners, by an error, brought down a heavy concentration on Battalion H.Q. and B Company. This killed Captain K. H. Kershaw, the Adjutant, as he was speaking to Brigade H.Q. on the wireless, and caused several other casualties at Battalion H.Q. In B Company, five men were killed and several wounded, reducing the company to one officer and twenty men. It was a heavy and unnecessary loss to the Battalion.

The troops in the bridgehead heard with relief, late in the afternoon, that the 6th and 9th Battalions were to enlarge the bridgehead under cover of darkness. Zero hour was to be at 1 a.m. The day's fighting closed as dusk fell. A Sherman tank came down the road towards the bridge, with the commander standing up in the turret waving his arms wildly. It was a captured British tank, and the man in the turret was a German paratrooper. Two hundred yards short of the Battalion positions the tank opened fire with all its guns and then withdrew. The paratroops did not miss a single opportunity of inflicting casualties. They were first-class fighting troops and fanatics to a man.

The artillery barrage for the 6th and 9th Battalions came down as arranged, a heavy weight of gunfire which must have caused considerable casualties, and shortly after 1.30 a.m. the men of the 8th Battalion heard the 6th Battalion crossing their front on the left of the road, whilst the 9th Battalion advanced on the right of the road. Both Battalions, using the route taken by A and D Companies the previous night, had forded the river downstream from the bridge. The Germans were not caught napping. They fought back savagely and the tracer from their Spandaus criss-crossed the Catania road and traversed the grapevines. The paratroops stood and fought it out until they either shot down their enemies or were shot down themselves. Even when the attacking battalions advanced beyond the sunken road, the Germans still held on to their positions there. When dawn broke they were still in the sunken road, and in spite of the fact that they were cut off continued to fire at any movement in the B Company positions.

Some of the 6th and 9th Battalion supporting arms, including carriers and anti-tank guns, were ambushed when they crossed the bridge and tried to get forward via the Catania road to their respective battalions. Watched by some of the 8th Battalion men a fierce fire fight developed, with the D.L.I. anti-tank guns being used at almost point-blank range against the German paratroops.

The attacking battalions did not have things all their own way by any means, and at 6.30 a.m. the C.O. of the 9th Battalion sent an urgent message to the 8th Battalion, for 3″ Mortars to put down a smoke screen and assist one of his companies to withdraw from a position on the right of the road where it was pinned down by heavy Spandau fire. Lieut. Hampson put down a smoke screen, (the only occasion in the war when he used mortars for this purpose) and the 9th Battalion company extricated itself.

Nevertheless the weight of the two-battalion attack had considerably shaken the Germans, and when Sherman tanks crossed the bridge at 7 a.m. the paratroops must have realised the game was up.

The Brigadier met the Shermans north of the bridge and ordered them to deploy left and right of the road, at the same time pointing out to them the enemy positions. The tanks broke through the grapevines, shooting at everything in sight, and the effect of their presence was seen almost at once. The sunken road was quieter than it had been at any time during the last twenty-four hours, and a white handkerchief fluttered from the German position. This was followed by the appearance of an 8th Battalion man who stood up and walked towards B Company followed by several Germans. Some of the B Company men lining the embankment suspected a trick, and shots were fired in the direction of the advancing party. With some difficulty Captain Neale stopped his men from opening fire again, and as soon as the advancing party saw there was no further danger they came on. White handkerchiefs then appeared all along the line of the sunken road and the paratroops gave themselves up in increasing numbers; seventy or eighty surrendered to B Company alone. On the right of the Battalion front the Germans gave themselves up in the same way. The battle for the bridgehead was over, and by mid-morning mopping up operations were complete and all resistance in the area of Primosole bridge had ceased.

The remainder of the day was spent by the Battalion burying the dead, evacuating the wounded and tidying up the area. Men who had experienced the fiercest fighting of the North African campaign at Alamein and Mareth said they had never seen so much slaughter in such a small area. The three D.L.I. battalions between them had lost five hundred men killed, wounded or missing, whilst three hundred German dead were found and another hundred and sixty taken prisoner.

The sunken road—a long dusty cactus-fringed lane—which had been held so fanatically by the paratroops was a shambles of smashed rifles and automatic weapons, torn pieces of British and German equipment, blood-stained clothing, overturned boxes of ammunition and a smashed anti-tank gun at the junction of the Catania road with the sunken road. Along the whole length of the road and in front of and behind it were the bodies of British and German dead. The ditches running along either side of the Catania road were just as much a shambles, and the whole of the bridgehead area was indeed a scene of terrible destruction.

It is doubtful if the Germans had better troops in Sicily than the paratroop battalion which held the bridge. In the words of the London Times of August 27th: "They fought superbly. They were troops of the highest quality, experienced veterans of Crete and Russia: cool and skilful, Nazi zealots to a man and fanatically courageous. To fight against them was an education for any soldier."

To capture and hold the bridge against such opposition had been a fine fighting achievement on the part of the 8th Battalion. Although a fierce fight it had been fairly fought, and as the German battalion commander was being led away to captivity the C.O. of the 9th Battalion, Lieut.-Colonel A. B. S. Clarke, shook him by the hand.

The fierce fighting for possession of Primosole bridge had seen many gallant deeds, a few of which have been described in the preceding pages. There were many others, some of them unfortunately unrecorded, and a number of decorations were won by the Battalion not so much for a specific deed of gallantry but for outstanding leadership and devotion to duty during the whole period of the bridgehead battle. Lieut.-Colonel Lidwill was awarded the Distinguished Service Order, for it was largely due to his resolution and personal courage in the face of heavy enemy opposition that the bridgehead was taken and afterwards held against that fanatical force of German paratroops. His calm, forceful way of fighting the battle and his scorn for the German fire, however heavy, gave his troops that confidence in his leadership which was so necessary at Primosole. Had the 8th Battalion been driven back beyond the Simeto it might have seriously affected the whole course of the Sicilian campaign.

Another officer who distinguished hmself at Primosole was Captain A. Noble, the Medical Officer. During the battle, when his R.A.P. was under continual and heavy fire from enemy artillery, mortars and machine-guns and inundated with wounded, Captain Noble worked untiringly to ensure the best possible treatment for the men in his care. He worked without rest for long periods to ensure speedy evacuation and his sterling efforts must have saved the lives of many 8th Battalion men.

In A Company Captain Beattie won the Military Cross and C.S.M. Hannah the Military Medal. Both were well to the fore when A Company crossed the river in the initial attack. Captain Beattie led the way and was first across and first on the objective, closely followed by his C.S.M. During the battle, when the company was constantly under heavy machine-gun, mortar and shellfire, Captain Beattie was always to be seen where the fire was heaviest, encouraging his men. He was constantly sniped but never showed signs of fatigue. The C.S.M. also showed a complete disregard for his own safety, ignoring the enemy fire to keep the platoons continually supplied with ammunition and water.

Another member of A Company, Pte. R. G. Goodwin, was also awarded the Military Medal. He was a Bren gunner in one of the assault sections, and when A Company crossed the Simeto he covered his section forward by Bren fire from the hip. When the company was forced to withdraw—some of the men across the river—he stayed behind to cover his platoon and only got clear himself by backing away, firing from the hip. When Goodwin eventually rejoined A Company in the bridgehead he accounted for at least four enemy snipers, though continually under heavy machine-gun and sniper's fire.

In B Company Captain Neale was awarded the Military Cross and Sgt. F. Mitchinson and L/Cpl. G. F. Shepherd both won the Military Medal. After the German counter-attack against B Company had been thrown back, largely by the joint action of Mitchinson and C.S.M. Brannigan, the sergeant had rejoined the company. During the remainder of the action he set a fine example to his men, always cool

Captain J. N. Wheatley.

Primosole bridge from the southern side. A wrecked German troop-carrier is in the foreground below the level of the road, and the group of farm buildings on the far side were those cleared of enemy by A and D Companies during the initial attack.

Captain J. N. Wheatley.

The memorial cairn, faced with a white marble plaque, at the junction of the Catania road with the sunken road, in memory of the men of the D.L.I. Brigade who fell during the fierce fighting for the bridge.

Captain J. N. Wheatley.

After the battle for Primosole bridge. Stretcher bearers carry a wounded man along the Catania road and past a wrecked Sherman tank and Bren Carrier. In the foreground stands a German medical pannier, pierced with bullet holes. The whole area was a scene of terrible destruction, and men who had taken part in the fiercest fighting of the North African campaign said they had never seen anything like it.

and steady under very heavy fire, always cheerful however grave the situation. Captain Neale, who had taken over command of B Company when Captain Lewis was wounded, fought the sadly-depleted company most successfully. With no other officers, and his C.S.M. dead, Neale did not have an easy task. Throughout the battle, with his company in close proximity to the paratroops in the sunken road, he set his men a splendid example of courage and cheerfulness which enabled the company to hold this vitally important sector of the 8th Battalion front. He was helped considerably by the Signal Platoon N.C.O. attached to B Company, L/Cpl. Shepherd. During the initial heavy fighting with the paratroops Shepherd had worked his wireless set continually under heavy fire to maintain contact with Battalion H.Q. until the batteries were exhausted. He then organised a system of runners between B Company area and Battalion H.Q., making his reconnaissance over ground swept by machine-gun and rifle fire. When the C.S.M. was killed, Shepherd took over the organisation of supplies to the company, carrying forward food and ammunition himself under very heavy fire. This precarious supply line was personally maintained for two days by Shepherd, during which time he had no rest.

In D Company Captain J. A. Leybourne was awarded the Military Cross and C.S.M. S. Wardle and Sgt. C. W. J. Mackmin were both awarded the Military Medal. When D Company ran into heavy opposition and Captain Lucas the company commander was wounded, Captain Leybourne encouraged his men forward and the objective was gained. Throughout the first day in the bridgehead, when D Company was under intense machine-gun and shellfire and was being constantly sniped, Captain Leybourne moved about the position, regardless of the enemy fire. One German machine-gun post on a flank was particularly troublesome and Leybourne set out to kill the crew himself. Under heavy machine-gun and sniper's fire he stalked the gun until he reached a position from where he was able to silence it with Bren and 2″ Mortar fire. He then returned to the company.

C.S.M. Wardle was one of the first across the river and on to the objective. There he reorganised the company to meet and throw back a heavy counter-attack at first light, and during the course of the bridgehead battle several more counter-attacks were beaten back with severe losses to the enemy. He had the situation completely in hand. Enemy snipers were abundant and D Company was continually harassed. Wardle moved amongst the company, often in the face of heavy enemy fire, and himself accounted for several snipers by setting up a Bren gun in an exposed position and picking off the paratroops one by one. Sgt. Mackmin was platoon sergeant of an assault platoon in the original attack across the river and on the far bank he went looking for trouble, making a special point of being wherever the enemy fire was heaviest to encourage his men. In the bridgehead he took command of the platoon when he learned that the platoon commander had become a casualty, and under heavy fire he put his sections in position. All day he engaged enemy snipers with a Bren gun and at last light, when the paratroops tried to bring up reinforcements in half-tracked vehicles, Mackmin grabbed a mortar and crawled forward. Heavy fire was opened at him by enemy machine-guns but he succeeded in getting close enough to the half-tracks to set one of them on fire with a well-aimed mortar bomb.

Corporal D. J. Richards of the Carrier Platoon also won the Military Medal at Primosole. He was one of the N.C.Os. sent across the bridge to help the infantry companies, where he organised the defence of a ditch, and throughout the days of the the 16th and 17th personally supplied the position with ammunition and water. Under extremely exacting conditions he never relaxed his efforts and was always to the fore, firing a Bren or Tommy gun whenever he had an opportunity. During the second night in the bridgehead he volunteered to take out a patrol—no easy task with the enemy so close—and brought back valuable information.

Although the fighting for the bridge was over, the Germans still tried to destroy it, and by midday the range of Primosole bridge had been registered by the enemy, using one very heavy gun from positions some miles to the north. The shelling was most unpleasant and very accurate, and several men of the 8th, including one of the Anti-Tank Platoon officers, Lieut. W. Nesham, were wounded whilst bathing in the Simeto.

That night 69 and 168 Brigades put in an attack to extend the bridgehead, which was only moderately successful. However, it did have the effect of bringing 151 Brigade into reserve, and during the afternoon of July 18th the 8th Battalion was ordered to withdraw south of the river to a rest area on the high ground where it had been prior to the attack. A Company crossed the bridge without sustaining any casualties, but the troop movement had been seen and heavy long-range shelling of the bridge area commenced almost immediately. Unfortunately for B Company they had left the shelter of the embankment, where the battle had been fought, and were moving in extended order across open ground. One shell landed amongst a section of five men, killing them all, wounding four others and thus reducing B Company to little more than ten men. As the casualties were being evacuated another shell landed and wounded Lieut.-Colonel Lidwill, but fortunately not seriously. The rest of the Battalion forded the river and everyone was well pleased to get away from the bridge.

The story of Primosole bridge closes with a tragic incident. When darkness fell, Captain Neale—with four volunteers—went back to the area beyond the river to bury the men who had been killed by the long-range shelling. C/Sergeant T. Marsden of H.Q.Company, one of the oldest members of the Battalion and a Territorial, joined the party and, whilst the B Company men were being buried, Marsden went down to the river bank to fill some water cans. He had only been gone a few minutes when the enemy long-range gun opened fire, and by some strange trick of fate he was killed by the first shell. Captain Neale and his party returned safely to the rest area.

CHAPTER TWENTY-FOUR

LAST DAYS IN SICILY

In the line again—the capture of Catania—a difficult advance—end of a campaign—50 Division sails for home.

IN spite of the fact that a firm bridgehead had at last been established beyond the Simeto, the Germans had no intention of evacuating Catania and dug themselves in astride the main road, half way between Primosole and the city.

The enemy had recovered his balance since the initial British and American landings, and it was now clear that he was determined to delay as much as possible the Allied advance towards Messina, to give time for the defence of Italy to be organised. He also wanted to deny to the Allies the use of the excellent airfields around Catania. With these objects in view the main enemy defences were established to pivot on the Catania-Mt. Etna position, in perfect defensive country. The lava and close nature of the country made movement off the road almost impossible, and the Allied advance could be held up by frequent and extensive demolitions. In addition to this the excellent observation from Mt. Etna and her foothills was a distinct advantage to the enemy.

With this situation on the 13 Corps front, where the infantry of the corps were tired after many days of continuous fighting in extremely hot and unpleasant weather, General Montgomery decided on July 21st to switch the weight of the Eighth Army attack to the left flank, which meant that 13 Corps assumed for the time being a defensive role. 30 Corps, reinforced by a fresh formation from North Africa—78 Division—continued the attack with the object of advancing round the west side of Etna to threaten the rear of the enemy position. Meanwhile the 8th Battalion had rested for one day south of the Simeto in comparative peace and quiet. Then, on July 20th, the Battalion O Group went forward to the 69 Brigade area where positions held by a battalion of Green Howards were reconnoitred. During the course of the day the Battalion was considerably strengthened by the arrival of four officer and eighty-six other rank reinforcements. Unfortunately Lieut.-Colonel R. P. Lidwill, whose wound was giving trouble, had to be evacuated; as the Second-in-Command, Major H. Blackden, had been wounded during the battle for the bridge, Major G. P. Chambers took over command of the Battalion.

Next day the 8th left the rest area, crossed the Simeto and moved up to relieve the 7th Green Howards. The 69 Brigade troops were holding a forward position west of the Catania road, just ahead of a farmhouse known as Mass della Palma. The country was very open, and nine hundred yards away the Germans had prepared positions in the Fosso Bottaceto. The 8th took over at night when the forward companies moved into a seven foot ditch, a good natural defensive position. The troops had to cut fire steps in the side of the ditch so as to be able to see over the top, and in this way it was reminiscent of trench warfare of the 1914/18 War.

The Battalion spent only three days in the line, and although neither side put in a large scale attack, this short period was enlivened by some patrol activity, intermittent shelling of the Primosole bridge area—only a few miles back—by enemy long-range guns located on the lower slopes of Mt. Etna, and constant mortaring of the 8th Battalion area. In the early morning and at dusk the Germans in the Fosso Bottaceto swept the Battalion positions with sporadic bursts of machine-gun fire, most of which whistled harmlessly overhead.

The Germans were determined to keep 50 Division at bay until the ammunition dumps on the Catania plains had been destroyed, and periodically enormous mushroom-like columns of smoke billowed slowly up into the sky, followed by distant rumblings as one by one the dumps were dynamited.

The 9th Battalion was ordered to take over the 8th Battalion positions, and in the late afternoon of July 23rd the C.O. and Second-in-Command of the 9th arrived at Battalion H.Q. to discuss the relief. They had not been there long when the area was heavily mortared. Lieut.-Colonel Clarke was killed instantly, and his second-in-command Major Robinson was fatally wounded, dying on the way to hospital. It was some small consolation when the 8th Battalion mortars immediately went into action to silence the German guns. In less than half-a-minute the 9th Battalion had lost a fine C.O. and second-in-command, and Lieut.-Colonel Clarke's death was a personal blow to many officers and men of the 8th who had known him so well when he was with the Battalion. This unhappy incident did not hold up the relief by the 9th D.L.I., and next day the 8th moved back into Brigade Reserve.

On July 26th these reserve positions were taken over by the 6th Green Howards. The 8th Battalion moved back across the Simeto to a very pleasant though somewhat mosquito-infested rest area close to the sea-shore, where the Royal Engineers cleared the mines from a stretch of beach so that the troops could enjoy sea-bathing. A and B Echelons were established close by, and the Battalion received 112 reinforcements. The C.O. had by this time returned from hospital, and a new Second-in-Command, Major A. H. Green of the Middlesex Regiment, had arrived. After a short but very welcome rest the Battalion moved forward again on the night of July 30/31 to take over positions held by the 10th Royal Berks of 168 Brigade, north of the Simeto and east of the Catania road. These positions were slightly in rear of the area the Battalion had occupied a few days previously.

Meanwhile 30 Corps had advanced rapidly, capturing Agira on July 28th, Catenanouva on the 30th followed by Centuripe on August 3rd. In the face of this threat from 30 Corps the enemy had no alternative but to withdraw from the Catania sector and 13 Corps immediately went over to the offensive.

At 6 a.m. on August 4th the 8th Battalion—the spear-head of the 13 Corps advance—moved off with Catania as the objective. Led by the carriers the Battalion advanced rapidly and the enemy rearguards were not encountered until 9.30 a.m., when B Company was heavily mortared, one man being killed and seven others wounded. As the Battalion approached the city and moved amongst the outlying houses, enemy snipers opened fire on the advancing companies, and mortars harassed the road, causing casualties to carriers and their crews.

Information was then received that a party of Italians in a wood on the right flank wished to surrender, and C Company (Lieut. R. C. O'Conor) with D Company (Lieut. J. A. Kailofer) went over to investigate. They reached the area to find traces of an H.Q. camp but no Italians, and it was not until the two companies reached the end of the wood overlooking the city that they met the enemy, holding well prepared positions in houses and gardens, determined not to surrender after all. A fierce fight developed and continued throughout the day, with both C and D companies trying to manoeuvre into more favourable positions. Nevertheless there was a considerable number of Italians equally determined to surrender, and the Battalion had taken three officers and 156 other ranks prisoner by midday.

The situation quietened down during the afternoon and evening, although A Company reported enemy tanks on their front at 7 p.m., and an hour later all forward companies reported German infantry assembling with tanks. The enemy was quickly dispersed by very effective artillery and mortar fire. In the city itself several fires were burning, and one terrific explosion as an ammunition dump was blown up at uncomfortably close quarters shook the whole area. The multi coloured lights and sparks were equal to any peace-time firework display.

The 8th Battalion did not have the honour of capturing Catania for at 3 a.m. the Battalion was relieved by the 9th D.L.I. and moved into Brigade Reserve. During the night the enemy withdrew from the city, followed by the 6th and 9th Battalions.

With the fall of Catania a new type of fighting developed which was to continue until the end of the Sicilian campaign, and as far as the 8th Battalion was concerned from August 5th until August 12th. Whereas previously the fighting had been of an open kind, with a certain amount of room to manoeuvre, it was now restricted by the high terraced hillsides covered with grapevines and stone walls. They forced the Battalion, as well as the enemy, to use the solitary coast road north of Catania ; consequently large forces could not be deployed and a hide-and-seek battle developed, involving advance guards with German rearguards.

Casualties were considerable in the infantry companies, for the Germans lay in ambush until the leading platoon was almost level with them before opening fire with automatics at close range. For the men concerned, this type of advance was nerve-racking in the extreme. The coast road was dotted with small towns, each dominated by an ornate church, each with a bridge over a deep, dried-up watercourse, and apparently deserted at first sight. The Germans combined these factors into a fine psychological weapon. The bridges were always blown, usually before the Battalion arrived, but in the town of Magnano after the leading company had crossed. The empty streets, with their barred doors and shuttered windows, offered no cover from ambush and invariably gave the impression of a trap. The churches, occupied as observation posts by both sides because of their commanding view, were used most effectively by the Germans to bring down artillery and mortar fire. After two or three experiences the leading troops of the Battalion knew that somewhere on the route through every town the church bells would suddenly peal out, the signal for a heavy concentration of artillery and mortar fire. These bombardments caused surprisingly few casualties but were nevertheless most demoralising.

Communications were never easy and the story of Pte. C. B. Simpson will serve to illustrate how it was often difficult to maintain the vital links between Battalion H.Q. and the infantry companies.

During the advance A Company was without C.S.M. Hannah, and Pte. Simpson carried out the duties of C.S.M. at the same time doing his own job of company runner. When the company was held up on the northern outskirts of the town of Acireale by intense machine-gun, mortar fire and snipers, the company was without wireless communications with Battalion H.Q. It was essential to get messages back and four times during the day Pte. Simpson returned through the town. On each occasion it meant a journey of three to four miles, part of the way through streets swept by machine-gun fire and in full view of houses which had not been cleared of snipers. Although exhausted he insisted on carrying on and thus maintained the vital communications. He was awarded the Military Medal.

The advance beyond Catania was in every way a most unpleasant phase of operations, and three officers are especially worthy of mention. There was the C.O., Lieut.-Colonel Lidwill, always at hand when trouble was brewing. There was the Brigade Commander, Brigadier R. H. Senior, blatantly displaying his red hat and getting up to the forward companies whenever he could to encourage them. Last but not least there was Padre G. Nesbitt ; having been trained in Rome he was able to converse freely with the Sicilians, and obtained valuable information from them about the enemy. The Padre seemed to have second sight so far as casualties were concerned, for no sooner had they occurred than he was up with the wounded, giving first-aid and making the men comfortable until the arrival of the stretcher bearers.

The 8th fought its last battle in the Sicilian campaign on August 11th, the seventh day of the advance beyond Catania. With D Company on the right and C Company on the left the Battalion entered the town of Giarre, 16 miles north of Catania. D Company was successful in reaching the river north of the town, due very largely to the efforts of Sgt. Mackmin, who took a patrol forward and cleared a way for the company. Captain Wheatley with C Company was less fortunate and, as the leading platoon was crossing the only bridge over the river, the Germans opened fire over open sights with light artillery and Spandaus. Lieut. Godwin, a newly-arrived officer, and a number of his men were killed instantly as they gallantly tried to rush the bridge, and Captain Wheatley was forced to withdraw his company from the area. The casualties in wounded and missing were heavy and A and D Companies took over the C Company responsibility. For the 8th Battalion this was the end of the fighting in the Sicilian campaign, and the following night the Battalion was relieved by the 6th Green Howards of 69 Brigade and moved back in transport to the area of Stazzo.

By this time it was plain that the days of the Axis in Sicily were numbered, and the closing stages of the campaign became a race for Messina by the Eighth Army and General Patton's American Seventh Army. The Americans were advancing rapidly along the northern coast, speeded by a most successful seaborne landing behind the enemy, whereas the Eighth Army was not moving quite so quickly. On August 15th the leading British troops occupied Taormina, but the going was very bad. Extensive demolitions had been carried out which meant that bridges had to be built every few hundred yards. In order to speed the advance General Montgomery ordered a seaborne landing to be carried out in rear of the enemy at Ali, on the night of August 15/16. It was too late, for the enemy had withdrawn. The Americans won the race, capturing Messina on the 16th ; some of the Eighth Army troops, who had landed at Ali, joined up with them within a few hours.

The Battalion spent only a few days at Stazzo before moving to Giardini, a small town on the coast below the rocks of beautiful Taormina. Bivouaced in the lemon groves it was a pleasant change from the strain of recent weeks, and the Battalion took a well-earned rest. The troops relaxed, bathed and wrote letters home, each preparing in his own way for the invasion of Metropolitan Italy, the inevitable next step for the Desert Army.

At Giardini, with the Battalion more concentrated than at any time since landing on the island, a more social atmosphere was encouraged, and the men had an opportunity of getting to know each other. There had been many new arrivals since the *Ruys* had set sail from Suez. The Signal Officer, Lieut. L. Barton, organised two very successful concerts, and at the first one a certain "Scats" Wilson asked several members of the audience to " do something." Few people who were there will forget Captain Neale singing " Chatanugah Chu-Chu," Padre Nesbitt's " Ganning along the Tunis Road," or Pte. Franklin's violent protests at being asked at all. The second Barton concert—this time for the whole Battalion—featured a bass from the Milan Opera, whose rendering of songs from Figaro brought the house down, and Pte. Smith who produced some remarkable illusions with the aid of bottles and pieces of string. Considerable applause went to the energetic producer, who compered the concert in a most lively fashion, dressed in a pale pink blouse, corduroy trousers and desert boots.

On August 30th General Montgomery visited the D.L.I. Brigade. The Army Commander's open tourer was driven into the centre of the hollow square formed by the Brigade. As the car drew to a stop the man who had broken the Afrika Corps stood up on the rear seat, and ordered the solid files to " break ranks, come nearer, sit down and smoke if you want to."

When the men had settled down, their Commander summed up the Sicilian campaign, making the whole operation seem almost a personal affair. He congratulated the Brigade on its successes and generally made the men feel quite proud of themselves. He went on to say that the Brigade had travelled many thousands of miles ; it had fought as many battles as any other comparable formation in the Eighth Army, and in spite of numerous reinforcements was tired and needed a rest.

The troops expected him to say next that 50 Division would be returning to the U.K., but instead, he described in detail the preparations for the invasion of Italy, and closed with a sentence which will long be remembered as a promise of trust and respect, but which at the time seemed almost a threat. "And never forget ! Wherever I go, I shall send for my 50th Division."

The D.L.I. Brigade was clearly disappointed, and the general uncontrollable murmur caused by this statement was silenced only by Montgomery's own action when he held out his hands and exclaimed : " But wait ! I may be going to England." The troops laughed but did not believe him. Nevertheless, as he drove away in his car they let him know that although he had not given them the good news they would have liked, he was still their popular Commander.

September was a busy month, with an extensive training programme. Lessons learnt during the Sicilian campaign were brought out in company schemes, and for the first time the Battalion trained in mountain warfare. In fact, each company took a mule on the strength. It seemed obvious to all ranks that once more the Division was to take part in the assault, and although no briefing conferences had been held the men were mentally prepared for the task ahead of them. The continuous stream of artillery along the Messina road indicated that the proposed landing on the " Toe of Italy " at Reggio was likely to be supported by a barrage comparable with Alamein. Nevertheless it was not all work and no play. E.N.S.A. parties, with George Formby and Gracie Fields, visited the area and there was a Brigade sports meeting when the Battalion won a shield, as well as several football matches.

Towards the close of the month Captain Wheatley took a party of eleven men to the site of the Primosole battle. Assisted by some sappers they erected a memorial to all those men of the D.L.I. Brigade who had been killed in the fighting for the bridge. A simple cairn faced with a white marble plaque was set up at the junction of the sunken road and the Catania road. They built it in two days with stones taken from the rubble of smashed German pillboxes, and although it was not possible to arrange an unveiling ceremony, Brigadier R. H. Senior, who wrote the memorial inscription, travelled specially to see the cairn completed. He was accompanied by Lieut.-Colonel R. P. Lidwill, Lieut.-Colonel H. R. Woods—the new C.O. of the 9th D.L.I.—and Padre G. Nesbitt of the 8th Battalion.

Training continued in the early part of October, and then the almost unbelievable good news came through that the whole of 50 Division was returning to the U.K. within a matter of weeks. Training stopped, the invasion of Italy and everything to do with the war was forgotten. The days dragged by until the Battalion packed up for the long move, and after an uncomfortable journey by cattle-truck arrived at Port Augusta. In many ways the veterans and some of the newcomers were sorry to be leaving the happy family of the Eighth Army, but nothing could conceal their pleasure at returning to the U.K. On a dull day in October 1943 the D.L.I. Brigade embarked on a Dutch ship, the *Sibajak,* and sailed in convoy out of Augusta Harbour for Algiers, Gibraltar and home.

CHAPTER TWENTY-FIVE

PLANNING OPERATION OVERLORD

Welcome home—four weeks leave—training at Haverhill and Southwold—Exercise Fabius—sealed in the invasion camp—the great plan unfolds—the armada sails.

IN the early hours of November 5th the *Sibajak* arrived in the Clyde. Two days later, with all the irritating but necessary formalities completed, the 8th Battalion disembarked at Gourock. At the railway station the band of the Cameronians played while the W.V.S. handed out tea and buns. The arrival of the convoy was meant to be secret but the magnificent welcome given to the Battalion by the Scottish people as the train sped towards Glasgow made it quite obvious that they knew a division of the Desert Army had arrived home.

The route from Gourock to Glasgow was gay with flags, and messages of greeting had been chalked or painted on walls and hoardings. People in the country lanes and others working in the fields stopped to wave and cheer when the occupants of carriages leaned out, with German steel helmets, enemy flags and other souvenirs held at arms length. The sight of the fields, woods, villages and people of Britain once more after such a long time had an amazing effect on everyone and a real holiday spirit developed.

South of Glasgow, to the disappointment of all, the special train carrying the Battalion passed through Newcastle and Durham. Its destination was the small Suffolk town of Haverhill which had been chosen as the H.Q. of the 8th Battalion. The train arrived there at three o'clock in the morning, when the Battalion was met by a reception party from Eastern Command who had a hot meal waiting for the troops.

A few days after the arrival of the Battalion at Haverhill, parties of men were sent off on disembarkation leave, varying from fourteen to twenty-eight days, depending on length of service overseas. By the beginning of December most of the Battalion had returned from leave, and companies settled down to the serious business of preparing for war. At Haverhill the aim of the strenuous training programme was to make the Battalion a hundred per cent physically fit and at the same time to ensure that every man was fighting fit—skilled in the handling of all infantry weapons. There was of course that old friend early morning P.T., as well as another form of training which has always been unpopular with the footsloggers—long route marches in full equipment.

There were no large scale exercises at Haverhill, for the most important task of the C.O. and his officers was to fuse together the old with the new blood—the veterans with the new recruits—and to ensure that the Battalion *esprit de corps* was increased to the fullest extent in the short time available.

Despite all this hard work the social side was not neglected. The billets were good and the local people went out of their way to be friendly. There was a free cinema show at which every man was given ten cigarettes, and a number of dances were financed and run by the hospitable townspeople. Many of them invited members of the Battalion to their houses and, as the weeks passed, many good friendships were made.

At Haverhill numerous people visited the Battalion including Lieut.-Colonel E. A. Leybourne, who had commanded the 8th at the outbreak of war. He was most welcome and spent several days with his old friends. The Honorary Colonel of the Regiment—Colonel C. L. Matthews—was another welcome visitor, and then on February 15th General Montgomery inspected the Durham Brigade on Haverhill football ground. Afterwards he spoke to the men of the three D.L.I. Battalions who gathered round him. Having praised 151 Brigade and 50 Division for their fine record in the past, he then announced that he had decided to give the Division a leading place in the forthcoming operations which were being planned. To those who had recently had a glorious reunion with their families, this statement was received with no great enthusiasm. Many of the men, well aware of the fact that there were in England several divisions which had never been in action, saw no reason why 50 Division should lead the assault against Hitler's Atlantic Wall. During the next few weeks, however, they were to learn that every effort had been made by the Higher Command to ensure the success of this great operation, and when the time came to set sail for France they were proud to be with 50 Division in the forefront of the assault.

Not long after General Montgomery's visit, His Majesty the King inspected the Battalion and spoke to several of the men. He may have wondered, as he walked slowly along the motionless ranks, how many remained of the Battalion which he had inspected on that bitterly cold winter's day of January 16th, 1940 at Chipping Norton.

On March 12th the 8th Battalion left Haverhill, having enjoyed the generous hospitality of the townspeople for just over three months. The Battalion went to Southwold on the East Coast, where the change in atmosphere was most marked. The town itself had suffered considerable damage from bombing, and as the majority of the inhabitants had been evacuated there was an air of desolation about the place. The few bright spots were very soon found by the troops and patronised to capacity.

At Southwold the training was intensified and became more realistic. Scale models were produced, and the best methods of attacking strongpoints and coastal defences were discussed. Later these ideas were put into practice on the ground in Exercise Bullshead when for the first time the men of the 8th were allowed to see some of the new and still secret weapons which were coming into use. The mine-exploding Scorpion tank, which had been seen by the Battalion for the first time in the Battle of the Mareth Line and had since been considerably improved, was on show. It was now known as the Crab but apparently the Higher Command had some objection to the use of this word in connection with a tank and it later became known as the Flail tank. The Battalion also saw flame-throwers and amphibious tanks, together with block-busters which had been designed to deal with the heavily fortified pillboxes and blockhouses of Hitler's Fortress. The fact that the troops were able to see these new secret weapons considerably helped morale.

When stores began to arrive in large quantities to make up deficiencies, and reinforcements were posted to the Battalion in large numbers, it indicated that the 8th would very soon be taking part in more ambitious training programmes. About this time the Battalion was issued with a number of weird-looking machines, described in Army language as " Bicycles Airborne." No one seemed to know the exact function of these uncomfortable mounts, but those members of the Battalion who had to ride them swore they were an ancient method of torture which had somehow survived from feudal times.

Early in April 50 Division left Southwold and moved to a concentration area in the neighbourhood of Romsey, Hampshire where the 8th Battalion took over Toothill Camp and went under canvas in a lovely dense oak wood. In this area, on the fringe of the New Forest, the Battalion completed its preparations for the strenuous task which lay ahead.

General Montgomery was continually seeking to improve the standard of training in the divisions which made up 21 Army Group. He gave them no respite ; formations like 50 Division, with years of battle experience, put in long, hard days of training alongside divisions which had not been overseas. On April 17th the 8th Battalion took part in Exercise Smash, which had been designed primarily to test the naval plan for the landing and handling of the Beach Groups. The infantry did not go aboard the landing craft but were guided by men of the Beach Groups through dummy minefields on the Dorset coast and so to an assembly area inland, near to Swanage. There followed a long, strenuous advance when the marching troops of 50 Division were driven really hard as they had been in North Africa and Sicily. Several mock battles were fought and the exercise was watched by General Montgomery and the senior Naval and Air Commanders, who seemed pleased with what they saw and the many lessons which had been learned.

The 8th Battalion took part in another large-scale combined operations exercise at the beginning of May. This was the final full-dress rehearsal before D Day, and known as Exercise Fabius had been designed to test the complex machinery which the planning staffs had worked out so methodically for the movement and embarkation of the vast invasion army and its stores. The Battalion was taken down to the Hards at Southampton where the infantry companies went aboard American L.C.I. (Landing Craft Infantry) while the unit vehicles were driven on to L.C.T. (Landing Craft Tank).

These were the ships allotted to the Battalion for the invasion and the Durhams were soon on good terms with their easy-going and likeable American crews. It was an excellent opportunity of getting to know the men on whom so much would depend on D Day. In spite of slight differences in outlook and—very markedly—in speech, a good liaison was quickly established and cemented after the exercise when the 8th Battalion officers were invited to lunch on the ships. In return, Lieut.-Colonel R. P. Lidwill gave a dinner in Southampton for the American officers.

The L.C.I. were the same type as those used for the Sicily invasion and held approximately two hundred and forty men, the equivalent of two companies. The Battalion lived on board for three days but it was too much to expect even a brief rest from the interminable training. There were route marches and P.T. in the dock area, although it is only fair to put on record that a Royal Marine band played for the men during one afternoon. A member of the 8th Battalion did remark, however, that " It was a wonder we didn't have to do P.T. to the music of the band."

During the night of May 3rd the landing craft put to sea. In the darkness they headed out past the Isle of Wight into the English Channel, and the first streaks of dawn revealed the ships sailing in convoy towards Hayling Island, a few miles east of Southampton. About an hour later the beaches were sighted and soon the hulls of the invasion craft touched bottom. The ramps went down and the companies filed off into water, waist high. As the men waded ashore the Battalion vehicles protected by their ugly waterproofing equipment were driven off L.C.T. through shallow water to the beach. On dry land the Battalion moved inland to an assembly area in Leigh Park. This was virtually the end of the exercise although in the assembly area signal communications—so vital in battle—were tried out throughout the Battalion. Next day the 8th moved back to Toothill Camp.

Soon after the Hayling Island exercise, F Echelon (the rifle companies and S Company) moved to Camp C. 17 in Nightingale Wood, on the opposite side of the main Romsey-Southampton road. The Q.M. with B Echelon and the M.T. remained in Toothill Camp. There was no slackening of the training tempo and Lieut.-Colonel Lidwill did not miss any opportunities of making his Battalion a hundred per cent fighting fit. He organised and directed company and battalion schemes which in their own small way were just as strenuous as the Divisional and Corps exercises. The companies spent hours on the ranges with rifles, Brens, Piats and mortars, or took part in realistic field-firing exercises. It can be said truthfully that not a minute was wasted in the 8th Battalion.

During the brief intervals between training, the Q.M. and his staff with the company quartermaster sergeants and the company officers checked and rechecked that every man and section in the Battalion was fully and properly equipped ; the soldier with his full scale of personal clothing and equipment—the section with its weapons, ammunition and stores. They worked all hours of the night and day to ensure that the 8th was fully prepared with the multitudinous stores of every description with which an infantry battalion goes into action.

In the midst of all this bustle and preparation there was a lighter side to the life of the Battalion. Dances were organised and a camp cinema showed films every night of the week. The Battalion also ran an inter-company drill competition as well as a most successful sports day. The C.O. well knew the value of the competitive spirit and his keenness was matched by the troops. The enthusiasm throughout the Battalion made the drill competition a great success and the Brigade Commander, Brigadier R. H. Senior, with his Brigade Major judged D Company to be the winners by a narrow margin. Encouraged by their success the men of D Company went on to score top points in the sports meeting, one of the most popular and amusing ever organised in the Battalion.

However, these were merely pleasant diversions from the stern work which everyone knew lay ahead. On May 13th the Supreme Commander of the Allied Expeditionary Force—General Dwight D. Eisenhower—inspected the D.L.I. Brigade. Afterwards he gave a most inspiring talk on the great task which the Allies had to undertake, stressing the vital necessity of close Anglo-American co-operation and understanding, so as to ensure the successful outcome. His simple, direct manner of speaking and his strong personality undoubtedly impressed the Durhams

As the hot May days wore on, the whole world waited, knowing the day of invasion could not be long delayed. In England this period of suspense began to oppress not only the servicemen but the civilians as well. Those who knew nothing of the great strength of the Allies regarded the operation with considerable misgivings. There was an atmosphere of tension throughout the country, particularly in southern England. This tension was heightened by the very stringent security precautions which were in force. In April every unit had been given an Army Post Office number, and no place names of locations could be mentioned in the address. A visitors' ban was imposed on the coastal areas where the assaulting divisions waited and this extended inland to a depth of ten miles. Nevertheless, although the people of southern England saw little of the invasion troops, they did see the ever-active Allied air forces. Day after day they watched Fortresses and Liberators, Marauders and Spitfires drone overhead towards France ; at night they listened as the Lancasters of Bomber Command flew out over the Channel to blast key targets on the French coast and inland.

The civilians would undoubtedly have been happier about the vast invasion project if they could have seen the detailed planning which at that time was being carried out at all levels down to Battalion H.Q. In the 8th the C.O., the Second-in-Command—Major A. H. Dunn, the Adjutant—Captain J. G. Walker and the Intelligence Officer—Lieut. P.M. Laws worked out in great detail the part the Battalion was to play in the assault. The Orderly Room became the planning room and no one was allowed near it except under instructions from the C.O. ; even then, those who were permitted to enter did so only after all maps had been carefully covered. The Intelligence Sergeant, Sgt. A. W. Bark, was busy making a scale model of the landing beaches which was topographically correct, but on which the place names of the French towns and villages had been altered. This model was later used to brief the companies.

May wore on into June and still there was no word of the news for which everyone was waiting. However, during the last week of May the thousands of Allied troops in southern England had been sealed in their invasion camps. High barbed wire fences were erected round each camp and after the orders for sealing had been issued no one was allowed in or out without a special pass.

The day following the sealing of the 8th Battalion camp, the company commanders and specialist platoon commanders who at this time were Major C. L. Beattie, M.C. (A Company), Major T. L. A. Clapton (B Company), Major J. A. Leybourne, M.C. (C Company), Captain I. R. English, M.C. (D Company), Major G. P. Chambers (S Company), Captain W. Woodruff (Carriers), Captain R. C. O'Conor (Mortars), Captain H. E. C. B. Catford (Anti-tank) were taken by Lieut.-Colonel Lidwill to Brigade H.Q. for briefing by the Brigadier. First the Brigade Intelligence Officer, Captain W. Teggin, described the enemy defences and dispositions, then Brigadier Senior outlined his plan, followed by each of the commanding officers who explained in detail the task which his battalion had been allotted.

The German strength in France, Belgium and Holland amounted to sixty divisions, including ten Panzer divisions. In the immediate area of the Normandy assault the German Seventh Army disposed nine infantry divisions and three Panzer divisions ; the very strong coastal defences were manned by Lower Establishment divisions, often made up of a large proportion of foreign nationals who had been pressed into service. Inland the real fighting strength of the enemy was held in reserve ; infantry and armoured divisions composed of battle-tried troops and formations of a very different calibre to those manning the coast defences.

The Supreme Commander's plan was for an assault on the Normandy coast between St. Laurent on the Cotentin peninsular on the right, and Ouistreham near the month of the River Orne on the left by five divisions—three British and two American—with two follow-up divisions. In addition, the Americans on the right were to be assisted by the dropping of two airborne divisions in the vicinity of St. Mere Eglise, and on the left 6 British Airborne Division was to seize the vital crossings over the Caen Canal and the Orne river between Caen and the sea. The British divisions of the Second Army taking part were 50 Division of 30 Corps on the right, 3 Canadian Division in the centre and 3 British Division on the left, both of 1 Corps.

The Brigadier explained the details of the joint fire plan which embodied the resources of all three services with the object of assisting the Army to get ashore. The assault on Hitler's European Fortress was to be opened the night before D Day by Bomber Command, in great strength, pounding the most important coastal batteries. As the Lancasters and Halifaxes returned to base, medium bombers and naval forces in the Channel were to continue the bombardment. Half an hour before H Hour[1] every available plane of the American 8th and 9th Air Forces was to attack the enemy coastal defence artillery and beach defences, bombing and then strafing at low level with cannon, rocket and machine-gun fire. At H Hour, as the assault craft ran into the beaches, they were to be covered by the fire of light naval forces and also the fire of twenty-five pounders and tanks in L.C.T.

When the listening officers heard the details of this plan and the weight of bombs, shells and rockets which were to be dropped on enemy strongpoints on the divisional front, their morale was raised immensely; in fact some felt almost sorry for the Germans who manned these positions. With such a devastating fire plan the reason for the great optimism of the higher commanders was apparent, and in a few minutes the officers of 151 Brigade were sharing that optimism.

For the landing operation 50 Division had been reinforced to a strength of four infantry brigades and one armoured brigade, making it the strongest division in the Second Army. The Divisional Commander's plan was for 231 Brigade on the right and 69 Brigade on the left to carry out the initial assault on what was known as Gold Beach, between La Rivière and Arromanche, while 56 Brigade (right) and 151 Brigade (left) would be the follow-up brigades. In accordance with this plan Brigadier Senior gave out that 151 Brigade would land with two battalions up, the 6th D.L.I. on the right and the 9th D.L.I. left, with the 8th Battalion in reserve. The Brigadier closed with a brief description of the great artificial harbour, known by the code name Mulberry, which was to be towed across the Channel and anchored off the shore at Arromanche and through which the Army and Air Force units would be maintained until a major port had been captured.

During the next few days the briefing of the lower ranks went on, and by stages the platoon commanders, N.C.Os and men were let into the secrets of this great plan. However, they were not told the locality in which the landings were scheduled to take place. This piece of information did not go below company commanders until after the ships had sailed.

The excellent models both at Brigade and Battalion H.Q. were studied in detail, and a large series of air photographs covering the beaches and the country a few miles inland were examined. All this ensured that everyone knew what the Normandy countryside looked like before they left England. As the details of this plan were unfolded to the men the effect on their morale was even greater than it had been on that of the officers. This was welcome, for the lack of enthusiasm and signs of indiscipline amongst the formations which had been brought back from the Mediterranean was a constant source of worry to the authorities. There had been a very high incidence of

[1]H Hour was the time laid down for the leading troops to land.

absence without leave in 21 Army Group, mostly in the divisions which had been engaged in North Africa and Sicily. This was largely due to the fact that published announcements about leaves in England could not be carried out owing to the pressure of events.

It was also said of the battle-tried formations that the field training and manner in which they carried out the exercises was not up to the standard of the divisions which had been training in England since Dunkirk. The 8th D.L.I. was not exempt from these criticisms, but this lethargy and apparent lack of enthusiasm for the cause had disappeared in part after the talk by General Eisenhower, and dissolved completely when the details of the plan for the invasion of Europe were given out. The men who had been absent returned and a remarkable change came over the unit ; the troops were intensely eager to get the job started and finish off the war as quickly as possible. This subtle change of outlook was to be borne out when the Durhams first went into action after the landing. Their morale was immeasurably higher than that of the enemy opposite them, and the experience of the old soldiers who had been through it all before stood them in good stead, so that they were able to help the newer recruits through their first few actions.

At last, on June 3rd, came the order to get ready. Emergency rations and sea-sick pills were issued, together with life-jackets, waders, tommy-cookers and all the paraphenalia so necessary for a modern seaborne landing. Equipped to full scale the Battalion boarded the transport vehicles which moved slowly down to the docks. The unit was divided up into small parties, each serially numbered, to ensure quick embarkation in the landing craft. Before the 8th went aboard the L.C.T. a party of notables, including Mr. Churchill, Field Marshall Smuts, Mr. Eden and Mr. Bevin, walked slowly down the line of troops. Although no cheer was given and there was no outward sign of emotion, the men appreciated this friendly visit from the nation's political leaders.

The L.C.I. were moored three or four abreast alongside the quay, and with over two hundred men on each ship there was very little room to move about. On another quay the carriers and anti-tank guns went aboard L.C.T. Next day it was given out that the operation had been postponed twenty-four hours because of the weather. During that and the following day the men were allowed on to the quay, but no further. A temporary rest camp had been organised in a large shed on the quayside, and here the men could read or lounge in easy chairs, listening to the wireless.

During the evening of June 4th General Eisenhower, in the face of unfavourable weather forecasts, made a memorable decision. He said : " We will sail tomorrow." So, at 8.30 p.m. on Monday June 5th, 1944 the landing craft cast off, and in the twilight joined others in formation ; the great armada slipped silently from Southampton Water under the watchful eyes of the Royal Navy and R.A.F. The results of all the months of training and preparation would now be seen. Another step was being taken to put an end to the war, with the 8th D.L.I. as a part of the greatest seaborne invasion ever—Operation Overlord.

CHAPTER TWENTY-SIX

THE INVASION OF NORMANDY

A rough crossing—unopposed landing—The Battalion captures St. Pierre—the first counter-attack beaten off—a second counter-attack fails—end of a gallant struggle.

As soon as the convoy was under way the O.C. Troops in the various ships gathered all the men together to read out the Special Orders of the Day, which had been sent out by General Eisenhower, General Montgomery and Major-General Graham, the Commander of 50 Division. Maps which had been kept in sealed containers were issued down to platoon sergeants. This time there were no bogus names; they showed the invasion beaches and the immediate hinterland. Names like Bayeux, Caen, Villers Bocage, Arromanche and Tilly-sur-Seulles were printed on them; names which were to mean much to the 8th in the days to come. Handbooks with useful information about France were also given out to each man.

The order on board the L.C.I. was that the decks should be kept clear of troops, and having taken one last look at the shores of England the men went down below to try to get some sleep. It was not easy, for the troops' quarters in the fore and aft holds were crowded with all the weapons and equipment which had to be carried. The atmosphere was not improved by the way in which the landing craft started to roll as they set their course for France.

H Hour in Gold Sector was 7.25 a.m. but the 8th Battalion in reserve did not expect to land until 11 a.m. The L.C.I. ploughed their way through an angry sea, and at daybreak the sky was overcast with the sea distinctly rough. The flat bottomed craft pitched and rolled in a most alarming fashion. Very few of the landlubbers in the vast invasion armada had any breakfast that morning as most of them were very seasick, in spite of the two anti-seasick pills which had been issued to each man before sailing.

Many troops recovered from their sickness before landing but others were so weak that they had to be carried ashore. Nevertheless, the bad weather was a blessing in disguise for it enabled the Allies to take the enemy almost completely by surprise. The Germans considered a landing in such rough seas impossible and neither the High Command nor the infantry manning the beach defences expected the invasion fleet to set sail from England. The enemy surface craft had been driven into port by the bad weather, and many of the troops manning the coast defences were not fully alert.

The coast of France was sighted at 8 a.m., indistinct at first and then clearer in outline as the ships carrying the 8th Battalion altered course slightly. The American and British officers on the decks, muffled with scarves against the bitter wind, asked themselves the same questions. " How are we getting on ? Has the initial assault been successful ? " They heard the dull boom of heavy gunfire and saw the flash of naval guns as battleships and cruisers of the British Navy, standing off the French coast, fought a duel with the few enemy strongpoints still holding out in rear of the beaches on the 50 Division sector. They stared in amazement as the convoy approached the tremendous concourse of shipping, stationary a mile or two out from the beaches. It seemed incredible that such an armada could lie off the coast of France, almost with impunity. As far as the eye could see there were ships and still more were coming from England.

Destroyers and gunboats weaved in and out amongst the warships, fussing around L.S.T. (Landing Ships Tank) and L.S.I. (Landing Ships Infantry) from which the infantry had been lowered into their assault craft. Hundreds of smaller craft, L.C.I., L.C.T. and support ships, pitched and tossed on the angry waves. On the beaches lay the landing craft which had carried 69 and 231 Brigades, some broken by the waves or beach obstacles and others well on to the beach, their ramps down. It seemed that the assault, at any rate in the 50 Division sector, had been successful.

At 11 a.m. the order to get dressed was given. However, the flotilla of L.C.I. did not go in to land immediately but circled round for some time, gradually closing with the beaches. As the ships drew nearer the men on deck could see details of the shore and roads leading down to it. The whole area was exactly as they had studied it on the scale model in England, and with the aid of the air photographs the officers were able to pick out the routes leading inland from the beaches. There was no doubt that the 8th Battalion was being landed in the right place. On shore it seemed comparatively quiet, though occasional flares and tracer bullets could be seen.

At last, a minute or two after 11.30 a.m., the Battalion H.Q. ship ran in towards King Beach closely followed by the L.C.I. carrying A and B Companies. The two landing craft were unable to run right on to the beaches because of wrecked assault craft and partly submerged amphibious tanks which blocked the way. As the ramps touched down, Lieut.-Colonel Lidwill led the way ashore through a very rough and choppy sea. The men followed, wading up to the waist with rifles and Brens held high above their heads. They landed fairly dry thanks to the long, waterproof anti-gas trousers with which each man had been issued after Exercise Fabius.

C and D Companies were not so fortunate. Their L.C.I. avoided the wrecked assault craft and tanks to run in towards the beaches but grounded out of a man's depth. The ship slowly backed out ; then the powerful motors drove her forward and again she grounded. It was still deep water but the ramps were lowered and Major Leybourne was first into the water. He was soon out of his depth and had to swim. As he struck out towards the beach an American sailor swam ashore with a life-line, which he fixed in position so that the troops could pull themselves ashore with it. However, when the leading sections from each company went down the ramps, the water ran in over the top of their anti-gas waders, which instead of being a help became a trap. It was a struggle to get ashore through the buffetting waves and some men, especially those carrying bicycles or heavy weapons, were nearly drowned. Captain English, commanding D Company, immediately ordered the men of both companies to remove their waders. By means of the life-line and helped by the men of the Beach Groups, C and D Companies then waded ashore successfully. The men were soaked to the skin ; the only dry part about them was their steel helmets.

The whole Battalion had landed without any opposition from the Germans. Indeed there seemed to have been little fighting on or around King Beach. The body of a Green Howard soldier of 69 Brigade was the only sign that the initial landing had been opposed. One D Company man, standing dripping wet on the beach, echoed the sentiments of at least his own company when he ruefully said, " It's a good thing there are no Germans about. We're so wet we couldn't even argue with them, let alone fight them."

When the rifle companies were complete they moved quickly through the minefield gaps on to a track leading to the village of Ver-sur-Mer. Here the Battalion saw signs of the havoc wrought by the Allied bombers. Large craters, particularly round a coastal battery set in massive concrete positions, were evidence of " softening up " by the R.A.F. and U.S. Air Force. Within an hour of landing on the beaches the 8th Battalion was complete in an assembly area in a cornfield to the west of Ver-sur-Mer, the S Company platoons having had a better landing than the rifle companies. The men dumped their assault respirators, issued before the landing, and D Company (the cycle-borne company which had been trained for use in a mobile role) collected its airborne cycles from the other companies. The men dried out their clothing and equipment, particularly the unfortunate members of C and D Companies who looked like drowned rats.

At 1.45 p.m. the 8th Battalion was ordered to continue the advance —inland towards the town of Bayeux. As the companies formed up preparatory to moving off, the Battalion received its first casualties in the Western Europe campaign. A high-velocity shell fell in the area, seriously wounding the Medical Officer, Captain N. Thornton, and an orderly. The Regimental Aid Post was temporarily left in the capable hands of Sgt. S. Hart and L/Cpl. A. Glendinning.

By 2 p.m. the Battalion was on the move with A Company, as the advance guard company, leading. The route lay through the village of Meuvaines to the Forward Assembly Area at Sommervieu. By the evening, A, B and C Companies had taken up positions in the orchards round the village, while D Company was sent forward to a road and track junction about a mile to the south-east. Apart from eight German bombers which flew over low on their way to bomb the beaches, the night was quiet and uneventful. So passed the first day in France.

Little sleep was possible due to the necessity of " standing-to " a few

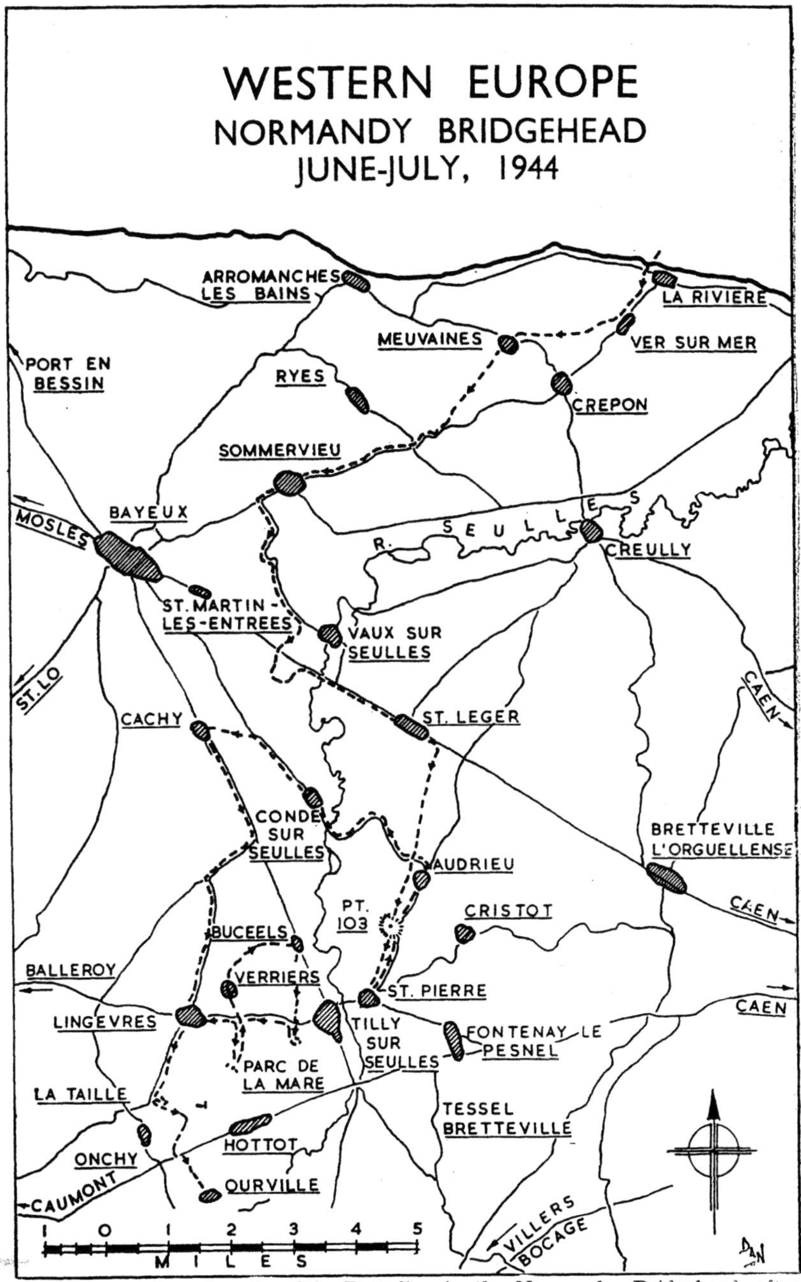

The route taken by the 8th Battalion in the Normandy Bridgehead after landing west of La Riviere on D. Day.

minutes before dusk at about 11 p.m. and again when dawn broke at 4 a.m. At 7 a.m. on June 7th the Battalion moved forward to take up positions astride the main Caen-Bayeux road, D Company putting out an outpost platoon under Lieut. E. Y. Cousins in the village of St. Martin-les-Entrées to watch the south-west exits from Bayeux. Small patrols were sent out to round up snipers and to search woods and other hiding places ; an A Company patrol brought in one officer and fifty-five other ranks as prisoners. During the day Brigadier R. H. Senior and his liaison officer were wounded when their jeep ran into a German ambush ; they only avoided capture because of the timely appearance of some Bren carriers. Lieut.-Colonel Lidwill took command of the Brigade, the 8th now coming under the Second-in-Command, Major A. H. Dunn.

That night B Company sent a patrol to reconnoitre the line of the River Seulles on the left flank of the Battalion, and the remainder of the night was without incident. Early next morning the Battalion was ordered to form a joint post with 69 Brigade of a rifle platoon and a section of anti-tank guns under the command of Captain J. A. Kailofer, second-in-command of D Company. Once again the Battalion was fortunate in having another quiet day.

During the evening Lieut.-Colonel Lidwill, as acting Brigade Commander, and the C.O. of the 24th Lancers visited Battalion H.Q. to explain to Major Dunn the plan for operations on the next day. The 8th D.L.I. was to come under command of 8 Armoured Brigade (the armoured brigade in 50 Division) whose orders were to advance from the area of St. Leger to seize and hold the Tessel-Bretteville feature, some six miles to the south—and east of the River Seulles—thus threatening the important road centre of Villers Bocage. That night companies concentrated in the area of Battalion H.Q. ready for an early start the next morning.

At 6.50 a.m. on June 9th the 8th Battalion moved off south-eastwards along the Bayeux-Caen road to a point about a mile beyond St. Leger. Here, orders were issued and the companies " married up " with tanks of the 24th Lancers. The column, consisting of armoured cars, infantry, tanks, 147 Field Regiment with self-propelled guns, and a troop of Northumberland Hussars (Anti-tank gunners), moved off at 9.30 a.m. with A, B and C Companies riding on the tanks of their respective squadrons. D Company brought up the rear on their bicycles, or it would be more accurate to say pushing their bicycles. As the column did not keep to the roads but moved over the undulating cornfields the going was too bad for bicycles, and the exasperated D Company men had to push them most of the way. This caused some ribald amusement amongst the other companies who had up to this time rather envied D Company in their mobile role. After advancing for approximately two miles the armoured cars reported enemy holding the village of Audrieu ; it was decided to by-pass this pocket of resistance and push on as far as Point 103, an important feature overlooking the village of St. Pierre which was held by the enemy in some strength.

When the column reached the area of Point 103, Major Dunn in conjunction with the C.O. of the 24th Lancers and the C.O. of 147 Field Regiment worked out a plan of attack against St. Pierre, as it would be necessary to capture the village before the advance could be continued towards Tessel-Bretteville. The village was surrounded by very thick hedgerows and bushy trees but it was possible to see a little of St. Pierre from Point 103, and when Major Dunn had carried out a reconnaissance he gave out his orders from an orchard on the feature. The plan was to attack with C and D Companies forward. On reaching the village C Company was to swing right-handed to take up a position round the church and the bridge over the River Seulles, covering the western exits. D Company was to push through the village and hold a position astride the road leading to Fontenay-le-Pesnel ; this was to be the limit of advance. A and B Companies were to be called forward when the leading companies had reached their objectives. The 24th Lancers would protect the open left flank. Concentrations on the village would be fired by 147 Field Regiment for fifteen minutes before the advance commenced.

At 5.45 p.m. C Company moved off behind a rather ineffectual smoke screen, closely followed by D Company. In St. Pierre the Germans waited until the two companies were almost into the village before they opened fire with Spandaus and mortars. In the first minute or two of firing C Company had several casualties, including Sgt. Ogden. Meanwhile D Company had come up and the two companies lost no time in getting to grips with the Germans. Fierce fighting broke out in the back gardens and orchards of cottages, Brens and Sten guns being used at close range. After a short but fierce fight the two companies broke the German hold on St. Pierre, drove the enemy from the village and gained their objectives. The rest of the Battalion saw the red and green Verey lights—the success signal—go up and Major Dunn immediately ordered A and B Companies forward[1].

During the next two hours the 8th Battalion dug in while Major Dunn visited each company in turn to co-ordinate the defences. Although the Germans had been driven out of the village they stubbornly kept up steady and accurate mortar fire, and one or two of their machine-gun posts, still holding out in front of C and D Companies, made it extremely dangerous to move about in these two company areas.

In the fight for the village C Company had suffered heavy casualties, particularly in officers. Major Dunn arrived at Company H.Q. to find

[1]An 8th Battalion officer, Captain W. S. Williamson, who visited St. Pierre in 1948 was told by a Frenchwoman of an incident which occurred shortly after the Battalion entered the village. She described how four British soldiers came to her house and then withdrew into the orchard. Shortly afterwards a German officer with eight men arrived to ask whether she had seen any British troops. She answered "No" and as she closed the door the Germans started to walk along the road. Almost at once, shooting started. When the Frenchwoman peered cautiously out of her window she saw the German officer, bleeding profusely from several wounds, limping along the road. In the road, not far from her house, were the bodies of four Germans and Pte. D. Cropper of the D.L.I. " I am sure," she said, " that he came from the orchard to shoot these Boches. He was a very brave man to fight with nine of them."

that the company commander, Major J. A. Leybourne, and Lieut. J. R. Hannah had been wounded. Lieuts. J. D. Mould and G. Galvin were both missing. It later transpired that Mould had been killed and Galvin very badly wounded.

On the left flank of the Battalion front D Company had also suffered casualties during the short but vicious action, and now very accurate Spandau fire prevented 18 Platoon of D Company moving up to its positions. Every time the platoon tried to get forward the Germans halted the sections with long bursts of fire ; several men of 18 Platoon were killed or wounded including Lieut. P. Lawn, commanding 16 Platoon, who subsequently died of his wounds. The Germans had excellent observation on to the village and surrounding country, and one or two of the tanks with the 8th Battalion were hit and set on fire by long-range anti-tank gun fire from the direction of Fontenay-le-Pesnel. When darkness fell the Battalion had strengthened its hold on St. Pierre but the Germans were far from beaten ; on the outskirts of the village they waited patiently for an opportunity to recapture it. During the night Lieut. S. C. Rood of A Company took a reconnaissance patrol down to the bridge over the Seulles, lying between St. Pierre and Tilly-sur-Seulles. He found it intact and strongly held by the enemy.

Next morning at 6.15 a.m., a few minutes after the companies had "stood down" and were thinking about cooking breakfast, German artillery and mortars bombarded the Battalion positions, straddling the village and company areas with heavy concentrations. It was the prelude to a strong counter-attack which was launched, first of all, against C Company, already much reduced in numbers and now commanded by Captain J. Wheatley. The thrust and determination of the German attack swept aside the forward platoons of the company, which were quickly overrun, and soon A Company in rear of C reported enemy infantry approaching its positions. About this time Lieut. H. Waggott of A Company was killed.

Lieut. P. M. Laws, the Battalion Intelligence Officer, went forward and took command of the remnants of C Company. He quickly reorganised them and the situation was temporarily restored. When the sadly-depleted company had to make a further withdrawal Lieut. Laws stayed behind to give them covering fire, and used a Bren gun most effectively against the enemy at very short range. He was wounded in the groin and though unable to carry the Bren gun continued to use a rifle. He did not withdraw until C Company was firmly established in its new position.

Meanwhile D Company of the 8th Battalion was engaged in fierce fighting with German infantry and tanks which had come from Fontenay-le-Pesnel. Concentrated defensive fire temporarily halted the enemy but, reorganising quickly, the Germans—veteran S.S. troops—came on again to drive a wedge between 17 Platoon and the rest of the company. The platoon suffered heavy casualties and was forced to withdraw. This exposed 18 Platoon dangerously on the left, and the company commander, Captain English, was obliged to withdraw the platoon and the anti-tank gun crews to a mutually supporting position with the rest of the company. As D Company took up its new positions more German infantry and tanks worked round to the left of the village to advance towards the B Company sector.

The German tanks came on, some of them partially overunning the infantry company. One section came under particularly heavy enemy tank and machine-gun fire, and all but Pte. F. Protano were either killed or wounded. Protano refused to withdraw, although other sections started to pull back, and remained at his post shooting at the tanks with a Bren gun he had taken from a wounded man. When eventually the enemy tanks were driven off the men of B Company who moved forward to re-occupy their positions found Protano still at his post, busy dressing the wounded men of his section. He was awarded the Military Medal.

Major Dunn, at Battalion H.Q., sent an urgent message for the 24th Lancers to move down from Point 103 to support the Battalion in the village. The call was answered very promptly but the first tank to enter St. Pierre was hit and set on fire at about the narrowest point of the village street. Blazing fiercely it completely blocked the road. Some of the remaining tanks deployed to the north of St. Pierre while others skirted the village on the left flank and moved out into open country, where they came under immediate and very accurate anti-tank gun fire. Two tanks were knocked out in as many minutes and the others withdrew to the hedgerows and orchards near St. Pierre. The few tanks which attempted to get into the village were shot up by the Germans and destroyed.

In St. Pierre the noise of battle was deafening as the fighting reached its climax ; the crash of the bursting shells and mortar bombs mingled with the stacatto rattle of machine-guns and Sten guns. The fierce German artillery and mortar fire was exacting a heavy toll on the men of the 8th and wounded were coming into the Regimental Aid Post faster than they could be dealt with. A mortar bomb landed midway between Captain Wheatley and Captain English, Wheatley receiving the full blast of the explosion. He was taken away on a stretcher but died soon afterwards. It was a sad end to an officer who had nobly played his part at Mareth and in the heavy fighting for Primosole bridge.

In another part of the village Lieut. Laws, in spite of his wound, was moving from house to house, garden to garden—pausing for a few minutes to snipe at any German who showed himself. Then he moved on again. Laws was a good shot ; taking careful aim and apparently oblivious of the noise of battle around him he picked off several of the enemy. Captain English found him sniping most successfully from the top floor of a house. By this time Laws had propped himself up and was very weak from loss of blood. Captain English had him evacuated immediately and for his gallantry during this morning of heavy fighting Laws was awarded the Military Cross.

Meanwhile the enemy was putting in a very strong attack on the right of the Battalion positions, against A Company and Battalion

H.Q. They made several determined rushes, the last of which was only stopped by the concentrated fire of every officer and man in the area. Runners, clerks and batmen were firing their rifles alongside the men of A Company. Captain Walker, the Adjutant, jumped on to a tank which was parked near Battalion H.Q. and, shouting and waving his arms, he directed the fire of its Besa right into the ranks of the on-coming Germans. They broke in the face of this determined defence, and that was the nearest they ever reached to Battalion H.Q. While this fight was in progress three enemy tanks advanced in single file down one of the narrow streets of the village, driving some cows before them. L/Sgt. S. P. Wallbanks of 17 Platoon of D Company rapidly restored the situation. The No.1 on the Piat gun was killed but in spite of the heavy German machine-gun fire and bursting shrapnel from the enemy artillery and mortars, Wallbanks threw himself down behind the Piat and fired three shots in quick succession. One bomb skidded between the startled cows and under the tracks of the leading tank. This put a stop to the German advance. The sergeant had saved a critical situation and he was awarded the Military Medal.

Towards midday the noise of battle died down and it seemed the German attack had been held, at any rate for the moment. It was now possible to take stock of the position and reorganise the Battalion. Many casualties in both officers and men had been suffered and the 8th had been forced to give up its forward positions round the church and astride the St. Pierre—Fontenay-le-Pesnel road. However, the Battalion was still in possession of most of the village and confident of staying there. Major Dunn ordered the remains of C Company to come under command of Major Beattie, commanding A Company. B Company stayed in its original positions while D Company was pulled back, so that two of its platoons could occupy houses at the northern end of the village. 16 Platoon, now under command of L/Sgt. R. Richmond, remained on B Company's right.

During the afternoon Major Dunn took a platoon of A Company and a troop of tanks into the village to shoot up a number of enemy who had been withdrawn slightly from the positions they had reached during their attack. This patrol included some men of the Anti-tank Platoon who recovered two guns and their carriers. A few hours later Captain Stray—the Quartermaster, and Captain Williamson—the M.T.O., reported B Echelon in position behind Point 103. A hot meal, which came up after dark, was excellent and did everyone a lot of good. Meanwhile Lieut.-Colonel Lidwill had returned from Brigade H.Q. to take over command of the Battalion once more. Apart from occasional enemy shelling, the night passed uneventfully. The following morning, June 11th, tanks of the Sherwood Rangers relieved the 24th Lancers who had lost a considerable number of tanks in the severe fighting of the previous day. Shortly after this, however, the C.O., Adjutant, Intelligence Officer and the Signal Officer of the Sherwood Rangers were standing together in a farmyard when a shell landed between them, killing all four officers.

Brigadier B. B. Walton, the new commander of 151 Brigade, and

Captain Teggin, the Brigade Intelligence Officer, visited the Battalion during the afternoon with news of the fighting in other sectors. The initial landings and subsequent actions had been very successful, except on the left of the American sector where the assaulting troops met very heavy opposition on the beaches. By dint of the most gallant resistance this situation had been overcome, and the bridgehead was now continuous throughout the invasion frontage. However, enemy resistance was stiffening everywhere and there was fierce fighting just north of Caen. Shortly after the Brigadier's visit elements of 7 Armoured Division were reported in Tilly-sur-Seulles. This was good news, but unfortunately they were soon driven out by a heavy counter-attack.

About 7 p.m. a second attack was launched against the 8th Battalion in St. Pierre, this time mainly by tanks. Again, artillery and mortar fire swept the village and continued as the German armour—Tigers, Panthers and Mark IVs—approached from the east and south-east, some by-passing the village to make for Point 103 and thus for a time completely surrounding the 8th in St. Pierre. It so happened that the C.O. was away at a conference at H.Q. 8 Armoured Brigade when the attack started and was unable to get back until it was nearly dark.

The tanks of the Sherwood Rangers took a severe hammering from the Tigers and Mark IVs which, with their superior gun power, were able to lie back out of range and pick off the British tanks one by one. After a while they advanced beyond the disabled and burning British tanks to close in on St. Pierre down the road from Cristot. They were soon able to enfilade B Company in its positions along the hedgerows, and immediately swept the B Company platoons with murderous bursts of machine-gun fire at close range. There were heavy casualties, including the company commander, Major Clapton. Major Dunn, the Battalion Second-in-Command, was also wounded. The latter was brought in to the Regimental Aid Post that night, but Major Clapton was not found until the next morning, by which time his condition had deteriorated to such an extent that he died soon afterwards. Meanwhile other tanks were shelling St. Pierre, including the barn where the Regimental Aid Post was established. This made the task of the overworked doctor and medical orderlies almost impossible.

It was during this attack that Pte. J. Cawley of D Company won the Military Medal. After the fighting had been going on for almost an hour it was found that the crew of an anti-tank gun had not reached their position. The German tank threat was serious and it was essential to man the gun. Pte. Cawley led the crew forward, crawling over ground which was continually being swept by burst of fire from the tank machine-guns. The small party eventually reached the position where Cawley then helped to fire the gun at the German tanks, only two hundred and fifty yards away. Crouched behind the gun shield the crew were unable to see the tanks so Cawley stood up in full view of the enemy and directed the fire of the gun. The Germans were kept at bay but had the gun not been manned it would have been a very different story.

In A Company Cpl. D. D. Michael, who had won his Military Medal at Mareth, was awarded a bar to it. He was with A Company when it was ordered to restore the situation on the right flank. Cpl. Michael's platoon commander was dead, his platoon sergeant missing. He immediately took over command and under extremely heavy machine-gun and artillery fire led his platoon forward. Twice German fire swept across the platoon and forced the men to take cover, and on each occasion Michael found another route until finally the objective was reached. Here he immediately organised a defensive position, defying every German attempt to oust his platoon.

In spite of the determined and ferocious German attack the 8th Battalion refused to give way. Stubbornly the companies held their positions, and when darkness fell the Germans withdrew from the battered village, leaving the tired defenders confident in the knowledge that they had smashed another German attack. On his return from Brigade, Lieut.-Colonel Lidwill moved A Company into B Company's positions, to strengthen the left flank, and pulled back D Company into the old A Company area. Apart from intermittent enemy shelling the night passed quietly, and at dawn next morning the expected enemy attack did not develop. It seemed that the Germans had, for the time being at any rate, given up the fight for the village and withdrawn. In order to confirm this a patrol under Lieut. E. Y. Cousins moved forward and established a post around the road junction in the south-eastern end of the village. At midday this section was relieved by another under Lieut. W. H. W. Jalland. During the morning six prisoners of war were captured and identified as Panzer Grenadiers of the Panzer Lehr Division. It was learned subsequently that both this division and 12 S.S. Panzer Division were engaged in the fighting in the St. Pierre area.

In the preceding pages the story has been told of some of the acts of gallantry which took place during the fighting for the village. There were many others; Cpl. S. L. Brydges, the Battalion medical orderley, worked in the R.A.P. throughout the whole action and night and day the aid post was under fire from enemy artillery. Twice it was surrounded and swept by bursts of fire from enemy tanks, sniped by enemy infantry. Although the house where the R.A.P. had been set up was hit by mortar and shellfire and was continually under machine-gun fire, Cpl. Brydges disregarded his own safety to tend the wounded. He saved the lives of many of his comrades and was awarded the Military Medal.

L/Sgt. R. Richmond, a D Company N.C.O., also won the Military Medal at St. Pierre. During the original attack his platoon commander and platoon sergeant were both wounded. He at once took over the platoon and led them forward to rout the enemy and capture the objective. Throughout the advance and during consolidation the platoon was under heavy shellfire but Richmond kept his men together and successfully held his objective. On one occasion enemy tanks got to within twenty yards of the platoon but under Richmond's orders the tanks were engaged with every available weapon until they withdrew.

In St. Pierre Cpl. W. Higginson of A Company won a bar to the Military Medal he was awarded at Mareth. He was commanding a section during the original attack on June 9th when just short of the objective, whilst crossing some open ground, his platoon was heavily mortared and several men were wounded. Nothing can demoralise a body of men more quickly than accurate mortar fire but as far as Higginson was concerned there might never have been a single bomb. He was completely calm under the heavy barrage. His steadiness restored the situation and the platoon continued to the objective. Later in the battle he volunteered for a patrol to find out whether the bridge at Tilly-sur-Seulles was blown. Although sniped and mortared for most of the way to the bridge he would not be deterred and brought back the valuable information.

Cpl. B. Thomas of A Company also won the Military Medal. When his section came under very heavy mortar, artillery and sniper fire the corporal decided to put a stop to the snipers if nothing else. Seizing a Bren gun he jumped out of his slit trench and ran across to the nearest tree which he then climbed whilst German small arms fire whistled around him. In the branches of the tree he kept a lookout for enemy snipers and at intervals there was a burst of fire from his Bren gun. He killed three German snipers before he eventually climbed down the tree to rejoin his section. He then reorganised his men, encouraged and steadied them, and when his platoon sergeant was hit he took charge.

During June 12th 8 Armoured Brigade and the 8th D.L.I. were ordered to withdraw from St. Pierre. Everyone was now extremely tired, and the effective strength of the Battalion was only about half of what it had been three days previously when the 8th first entered St. Pierre. The casualties numbered twelve officers and nearly two hundred other ranks, so naturally a short rest out of the line sounded very attractive. On the other hand, to give up the village after such a gallant struggle seemed poor recompense for the effort and great sacrifice which had been made in order to hold it. Apparently the Higher Command realised that the Tessel Bretteville feature could not be captured without committing a completely fresh division. Also, the advance of 7 Armoured Division on the other side of the Seulle had been held. This left the 8th D.L.I. in a dangerous salient. So it was decided to regroup. The Battalion was to withdraw, and reverting to the command of 151 Brigade was to move back into Brigade Reserve in the area of Cachy. Nevertheless it was a great shame that the village had to be evacuated, for some days later when the 10th D.L.I., part of 70 Brigade of 49 Division, had to attack the village they only captured it after a stiff fight.

Shortly after the orders for withdrawal had been issued two other ranks of C Company reported in to Battalion H.Q. They had been cut off from the company when the Battalion first entered St. Pierre, and with Germans blocking their escape route they hid under some wine barrels in the cellar of a house. The Germans then occupied the house and for two days the two men remained hunched up under the barrels, while German troops moved about within a few feet of them. A cough or sneeze would have given them away. They pinched each other to keep awake, for to have slept and snored would have been disastrous. At last the Germans withdrew from the house and that night the two men climbed out, stretched themselves painfully, then made their way back to the 8th Battalion positions.

At 11.15 p.m. the Battalion moved out of St. Pierre and back to Point 103, which was now held by the 5th East Yorks of 69 Brigade. After marching about a mile beyond the East Yorks positions the men were picked up by troop-carrying vehicles and taken to the village of Cachy, about three miles south of Bayeux, arriving at dawn on June 13th. Here a hot meal was waiting which was eagerly consumed.

The men were utterly exhausted from days of hard fighting. Their meal finished, they slept as only men can do who have fought and beaten a ruthless enemy. After this, their first battle of the Western Europe campaign, the men of the 8th Battalion knew they were a match for the Germans in Europe as they had been in North Africa and Sicily. It was an encouraging thought.

CHAPTER TWENTY-SEVEN

IN THE NORMANDY BOCAGE

Reinforcements arrive—back in the line—heavy casualties from shellfire —B Company "bags" the first tank—life in the Bocage—17 Platoon holds Ourville—the first rest in fifty-six days.

For two days after the St. Pierre battle the men rested while the Battalion was reorganised and re-equipped. Reinforcements of eleven officers and one hundred and ninety other ranks were drafted to the 8th D.L.I. and all companies made up to strength. C Company was re-formed and commanded by a newly-arrived regular officer, Captain A. St. George, with Lieut. H. Welch, a fairly old member of the Battalion who was also a reinforcement, as his second-in-command.

Unfortunately the period out of the line was all too short. On June 13th the 6th and 9th D.L.I. had attacked the villages of Verrière and Lingèvres, the latter being on the Tilly-Balleroy road. Both Battalions had heavy casualties, especially the 9th D.L.I. who lost their very popular C.O., Lieut.-Colonel H. Woods, but Lingèvres was taken and held against a determined German counter-attack with tanks.

The 9th Battalion had been relieved by the 2nd Gloucester Regiment of 56 Brigade, and the 8th Battalion was now ordered to take over from the Glosters. At 9.30 a.m. on June 15th the Battalion moved off from Cachy and by midday had completed the relief in the Lingèvres area. A and D Companies, as the two forward companies, took up positions south of the main road while B and C Companies were in reserve, about four hundred yards to the rear. On the right of the 8th Battalion the 6th Green Howards of 69 Brigade moved into position while the 6th D.L.I. came in on the left flank.

During the first night in the Lingèvres area a German patrol approached the D Company positions. A sentry in one of the forward section posts heard suspicious noises and his shouted challenge was answered by a single shot. Meanwhile the remainder of the section had "stood-to"; the section commander sent a burst of Bren gun fire in the direction of the shot while L/Sgt. Wallbanks fired parachute flare bombs from the platoon 2″ Mortar. Not a single flare lighted; they had all been soaked on D Day. As the D Company men peered into the darkness the Germans made off in haste, leaving behind them Spandau machine-guns and equipment. A dead man found next morning in front of the company positions was identified as belonging to 2 Panzer Lehr Division. If the parachute flares had gone off the whole patrol might have been caught.

Next day the 8th Battalion mortars supported a 6th Battalion attack. Determined German resistance held up the 6th D.L.I. as they tried to reach their objective—Tilly-sur-Seulles—and during the attack the Brigade Commander, Brigadier Walton, was wounded. For the second time since landing in Normandy Lieut.-Colonel Lidwill took over command of the Brigade ; Major Chambers became acting C.O. of the 8th Battalion. It was about this time that old friends of the Battalion—the 74th Field Regiment—moved into position to support the D.L.I. Brigade. The Regiment, having landed only recently in Normandy, had not yet seen any action. Major P. Wakelin, who had been well known to the 8th in the desert and on Sicily, was now commanding 296 Battery, which had often worked with the Battalion in the past.

Early on June 18th the 8th Battalion was ordered to move forward to occupy the Parc de la Mare area about a mile to the south-east of Lingèvres ; this time there was to be no artillery support, companies infiltrating silently into their positions. The route lay along the Lingèvres-Tilly road for about three-quarters of a mile, then south along a minor road to Parc de la Mare. B Company was to lead the advance, followed by C Company. When they were in position A and D Companies were to move in behind them.

B Company moved off at 7.30 a.m. with Captain H. Crossley as the artillery forward observation officer. All went well until, about four hundred yards south of Parc de la Mare, the leading sections of B Company came suddenly upon a party of Germans in a field. The enemy, taken completely by surprise, was in no position to fight it out and B Company, using Brens and Sten guns at short range, killed or wounded a dozen or more Germans and sent the rest scurrying for the shelter of a large house known as the Chateau du Cordillon. However, the enemy was not slow in hitting back. Quickly, German mortars ranged on the B Company platoons and followed up with a short but vicious bombardment of the area which caused several casualties, including C.S.M. B. Moscow. C Company now moved into a position in rear and slightly to the right of B Company. About this time the presence of enemy armoured fighting vehicles was reported, and Captain Catford's anti-tank guns were hurriedly brought up. It later transpired that the armoured fighting vehicles were German half-tracks retiring southwards.

During the afternoon A Company took up positions on B Company's left, becoming left forward company, while D Company moved in behind them. The rest of the day was spent digging in, all the time under heavy and accurate mortar and Spandau fire. This caused many casualties, particularly in B Company where the men could not move about much during daylight.

In the evening a sharp and vicious German artillery "stonk"[1] burst in the trees directly above Battalion H.Q., killing the Adjutant—Captain Walker, and wounding Lieut. Barton—the Signals Officer, Lieut. Gibbon—the Carrier Platoon Commander, and some signallers. Owing to the area being so thickly wooded, the casualties from artillery and mortar fire were considerable, many of the shells and mortar bombs exploding in the trees, and the shrapnel bursting down-

[1]Heavy concentration of shellfire.

Imperial War Museum.

German Panther tanks lying by the roadside at Lingèvres. They had been knocked out in the fierce tank battle for possession of the village when the 6th and 9th Battalions had heavy casualties.

Imperial War Museum.

D DAY IN NORMANDY. A landing craft, hove to off the beaches, with three infantrymen wading ashore through a rough sea, up to their necks in water.

wards to kill or wound men in their slit trenches where they were normally immune from anything but a direct hit. That evening Lieut.-Colonel Lidwill returned to take over command of the Battalion. Captain Ridealgh of A Company was made acting Adjutant and Lieut. Cousins, Signal Officer.

June 19th was very wet and it rained hard until the early evening. In the afternoon 231 Brigade launched an attack south from the Parc de la Mare area with the object of capturing Hottot, a village on high ground on the Caumont-Fontenay-le-Pesnel road. As was soon to be learned the Germans were very sensitive about any British advance in this sector, and 231 Brigade had to make three heavy and costly attacks before Hottot was eventually captured on July 18th.

The first attack was supported by the Corps Artillery, including that of 49 Division on the left. Unfortunately the fire plan was not co-ordinated very well, or else the gunners were unaware of the 8th D.L.I. position, because the barrage started in rear of the Battalion and advanced step by step through the line occupied by Battalion H.Q., then on to the reserve companies and finally on to the forward companies. As Captain Catford said : " The shells came down so fast that the explosions made a sort of drumming sound on the ground ; " at least everyone knew now what the Germans had to put up with. Though it was most unpleasant it did not cause any casualties to the 8th D.L.I., but it landed amongst the 1st Hampshires on their start line, causing considerable casualties before the attack started ; this naturally upset them and they never really recovered. When the Hampshires finally advanced, it was to reach a line only a few hundred yards in front of the positions held by A and B Companies of the 8th D.L.I. The 2nd Devons got into Hottot but were driven out again. The Germans reacted violently with both defensive artillery and mortar fire, also with tanks.

This heavy counter-shelling had its effect on the 8th Battalion. A shell landed in the trees above C Company H.Q., killing both the company commander—Captain St. George, and his second-in-command—Lieut. Welch ; other casualties were Lieut. England of D Company and Lieut. Robertson of A Company, both wounded. In the evening, when the rations were being brought up by the colour sergeants, the enemy started shelling the Battalion area with nebbelwerfers or "moaning minnies" as the troops called them because of the noise the bombs made in the air. These six-barrelled weapons could lay down quite a heavy concentration in one area and a bomb from a nebbelwerfer killed Colour Sergeant Barron, the D Company Quartermaster Sergeant. Barron, an old D Company Territorial, since becoming the Company Quartermaster Sergeant had made quite certain that his company never went short of anything. Whatever the situation Barron never failed to get forward with the rations. In his own way, largely on the administrative side, he contributed a great deal to the fighting efficiency of the company. When he was killed D Company lost an excellent quartermaster sergeant.

On the evening of the same day the Battalion knocked out its first

J

enemy tank in the Western Europe campaign. A string of Hawkins anti-tank grenades had been drawn across the road by men of Lieut. Jalland's platoon of B Company. The tank came down the road from Chateau du Cordillon towards Parc de la Mare and the B Company platoon watched it run over the grenades. There was a loud explosion which blew off one of the tracks and the tank slewed round to a standstill. As the crew baled out they were captured by the elated members of Jalland's platoon.

In the Parc de la Mare area, largely as a result of casualties, various changes took place amongst the officers of the Battalion. Captain Kailofer, who had been second-in-command of D Company, took over C Company. Lieut. J. Collingwood was promoted to the rank of captain and sent to C Company as second-in-command. Captain English was promoted to the rank of major. At the same time reinforcements of seven officers and eighty-nine other ranks were drafted to the 8th ; these included Major W. T. Woodruffe, a regular officer who arrived as the new Second-in-Command, and four Canadian Officers—Lieuts. Stuart, F. E. Morrison, H. Niznick and G. H. Luffman—on loan to the British Army under the Canloan Scheme. These Canadians quickly settled down in the Battalion : efficient, friendly and excellent in every way, they got on very well with the Durhams.

During the next few days the Battalion remained in its positions in the vicinity of Parc de la Mare, and as these days were typical of many during the latter part of June and July, it is perhaps opportune to describe the routine of an infantry battalion in the Bocage country and how that country influenced the method of fighting.

There is no doubt that, for the first week or ten days, the men of 50 Division found the close country of the Bocage very strange after the Desert and Sicilian campaigns. The whole country was a maze of small fields divided by thick, tall hedges and sunken lanes. Even the main roads were enclosed by steep banks and hedges. The men could rarely see more than two hundred yards and very often not as far. This was ideal terrain for the sniper and the mortar. When the Durhams got to know it they realised it was first class infantry country and began to make use of the cover instead of being frightened of it. Everyone lived in slit trenches, avoiding the houses which were apt to become artillery targets and were frequently booby-trapped.

The close nature of the Bocage had its effect on the handling of the supporting weapons of the Battalion. The Carrier Platoon could not operate as it was meant to do and was virtually grounded. The men were used as an extra rifle platoon, and it was not until the pursuit through France was begun that the Carrier Platoon really came into its own. Similarly, the Anti-tank Platoon had to be content with short fields of fire. Since no serious tank attack developed against the Battalion after St. Pierre, the platoon could do no shooting as the 6-pounder anti-tank gun is entirely a defensive weapon. So, during the weeks in the Bocage, Captain Catford's problems were mainly administrative. In the Bocage the Durhams learnt what an excellent weapon was the Piat, both as a short range weapon against tanks and for use against infantry in hedgerows.

On the other hand it is probably true to say that the Mortar Platoon fired more rounds against the enemy than any other platoon in the Battalion during the campaign in Western Europe. Like the rest of the unit Captain O'Conor's men found the closeness of the country difficult at first, especially in the establishment of observation posts with any but a limited field of view. They therefore developed artillery methods of firing off the map. O'Conor and his detachment commanders, Sgts. Martin, Allen and Baxter and Cpl. Heslington, made a point of examining their targets after an advance and so learnt of any discrepancy between mortar and map range. After a time real accuracy was obtained off the map and this method was used even for targets which were visible, because they could be engaged at once without ranging. It gave the enemy no warning and prisoners testified to the devastating effect British mortar fire had on the German troops.

A characteristic feature of the Normandy fighting was the awful destruction of cows. This part of France, a rich agricultural area, has always been noted for the large number of dairy cows. Unfortunately many of these poor beasts were killed in the fighting and the horrible, rotting smell of their bloated carcases became all too familiar to the men of the 8th Battalion. In the rear areas it was sometimes possible to use bulldozers to bury the carcases but nearer the enemy they were quite a problem. Even when men could be spared to bury them, there was a risk of the digging parties drawing enemy fire. Attempts to burn the carcases after they had been soaked in petrol usually brought down heavy artillery and mortar fire. Consequently all but the most offensive of the dead animals had to be left alone, the infantry nearest to them having to put up with the stench.

The daily routine in the Bocage was always more or less the same. The Battalion "stood-to" from 4.30 a.m. to 5.30 a.m. after which everyone would try to snatch an hour's sleep. In the mornings the company quartermaster sergeants brought up the breakfast and the food for the light midday meal, usually biscuits, margarine and jam. Tea was also issued and brewed in the platoon areas. Then followed a day of hard work. Ammunition had to be checked, weapons cleaned, sentries changed and the defensive positions improved. All this went on amid fairly regular shelling, mortar and Spandau fire. During the day, patrols were briefed and prepared for their night task. A regular system for the preparation and sending out of patrols was evolved. A battalion patrol officer was appointed, usually the Second-in-Command. In the morning he would detail the officer and company to provide the patrol. Air photos of the Bocage were found to be invaluable. Owing to the close country it was almost impossible for the patrol leader to get to a position where he could see the ground over which he was to operate, but with an air photo he could see at a glance exactly what the country was like.

The evening meal came up at about 8 p.m. and with it the mail; consequently this visit of the company quartermaster sergeants was to most men the most popular event of the day. The Battalion "stood-to" from 10 p.m. until 11 p.m., and after "stand-down" there were very few nights which were not disturbed by scares and reports of German patrols approaching the company positions. Almost every night 8th Battalion patrols went into No Man's Land, their objective usually the Chateau du Cordillon. This old French chateau, surrounded by a high wall, was used by the enemy from time to time as a lying up area for tanks and infantry. The Chateau and surrounding grounds had been booby-trapped and sown liberally with anti-personnel mines. It was a death trap for the unwary. All the patrolling during this time was done at night and much valuable information of enemy dispositions and movements was obtained. Later the value of the day patrol was appreciated, these being usually carried out by the sniper section.

This, then, was life in the Bocage—day after day of not knowing where or when the enemy would strike next or what the days and nights would bring in the form of patrols or sorties. Casualties in the eight days since the Battalion had taken over from the Glosters at Lingèvres had been ten officers and ninety other ranks. On June 23rd the 8th was relieved by the 1st Battalion the Hampshire Regiment and moved back as reserve battalion of the D.L.I. Brigade to an area south of Buceels.

These spells out of the line as reserve battalion were always very busy. The counter-attack role had to be practised, and deficiencies of clothing and other stores indented for and made up, but there was no patrolling and sentries could be reduced. A system was started about this time for sending four to six men per company every day to B Echelon for a bath, change of clothing and a good night's sleep. This was very well run by the Quartermaster, Captain Stray, and was greatly appreciated by all ranks. Later a Corps Rest Camp was started on the coast near Arromanche ; men went there for three days and were very well fed and looked after. Bathing, riding, cinema shows and entertainment parties were arranged. A visit to these rest camps certainly did everyone a lot of good.

The Battalion moved back into the line on the night of July 2nd/3rd, to take over positions south-west of Tilly-sur-Seulles from the 6th D.L.I. Included in the defence plan was a platoon of medium machine guns from C Company of the 2nd Cheshires and a troop of guns from 107 Anti-tank Battery, Northumberland Hussars. The artillery support came as usual from 296 Battery, 74th Field Regiment. While in this area constant patrol activity was maintained, information being brought in of enemy locations in the houses and farms on and to the south of the main road. The sniper section, which had been recently formed and trained under Lieut. W. H. W. Jalland, did some very good work on this front and had several Germans to their credit.

On the night of July 5th/6th Lieut. S. C. Rood led a raid against an enemy strongpoint in a house overlooking C Company's position, with the object of obtaining prisoners. Great importance was attached to this raid by the new Brigade Commander, Brigadier D. S. Gordon, D.S.O. and it was carefully rehearsed by the men taking part. As it was thought that the house was held by, at the most, a platoon, the strength of Rood's party was only thirteen men, but the raid was supported by the fire of two field regiments and one medium battery. The result of this support was disappointing ; when the party got near the house they were met by intense machine-gun and mortar fire, which killed one man and wounded three others, while the remainder were pinned to the ground. It was quite clear that the raid had failed. The Brigade Commander was somewhat displeased with this, and sought to attribute the blame to Lieut.-Colonel Lidwill. When a week or two later this house was attacked by two companies of the 10th D.L.I., who had over fifty casualties before it was captured, the true strength of the place was revealed to Higher Command.

About this time the Battalion suffered a great blow. Padre Nesbitt was killed by a stray shell while burying the dead just behind the 9th D.L.I. positions. He had been with the 8th since the end of 1940 and was well loved by all ranks, whether of Roman Catholic faith or not. His quiet manner, yet very strong personality, impressed all those who came in contact with him. Always cheerful and willing to help anyone in trouble, he was regarded as a personal friend by many. He was a great example of courage and fortitude and his death deeply affected all members of the Battalion. All the old officers of the 8th, headed by the C.O., went back to attend the funeral at 149 Field Ambulance.

On July 8th the Battalion once more went into reserve, being relieved by the 10th D.L.I. of 70 Brigade, 49 Division. This time the rest only lasted two days. On July 10th positions about a mile south of Lingèvres were taken over from the 7th Green Howards of 69 Brigade. During the relief Lieut. Bridgeman was wounded. Two days later a local attack on a farm known as La Taille was carried out by a platoon of A Company. Several booby traps and mines were encountered, one of which killed Lieut. O. A. Davies the platoon commander and wounded his sergeant, so the attack was called off by the C.O.

While the unit was in this area the Panzer Lehr Division was relieved by the German 276 Division, recent arrivals from the south of France. Owing to the magnificent work of the Maquis and the attention of the Allied air forces it had taken a month for this division to reach the Normandy front. The 8th quickly realised that it was a low quality division, very different from the Panzer grenadiers.

In the area of La Taille the respective British and German positions were only thirty-five yards apart, and the slightest move on the part of the enemy brought down heavy Bren and Piat fire. Lieut. B. Wyatt of D Company fixed up the Piat as a mortar and periodically dropped bombs into the yard of La Taille farm. After several days of this the enemy became extremely "bomb happy" and several deserters came over to the British lines ; some were Poles who had been impressed into Hitler's army but most of them were Germans. They spoke of a fanatical N.C.O. who stood over them with a pistol in his hand and made them shoot. They said the whole unit was ready to desert but that the men feared they would be shot by the " filthy

English." Such is the power of propaganda. In the hope that more deserters would come in, measures were taken to persuade them. Propaganda shells were fired which, on bursting, scattered leaflets offering a safe conduct for anyone who came into the British lines. A British officer who spoke German fairly fluently called on the enemy to surrender with the aid of a megaphone. Next day a Psychological Warfare Unit arrived with a van and a loud speaker ; an hour's truce was called in which it was arranged that no firing would take place. Unfortunately no one told Captain O'Conor about this, and the broadcast had only been going a few minutes when the Mortars started one of their "hates." O'Conor's men were somewhat puzzled when told to stop firing. However, no deserters came in that day. Just before the truce was due to finish, Lieut. Niznick, the Canadian officer with C Company, went out to investigate ; a German threw a stick grenade but Niznick killed him with a burst from his Sten. So the war started again.

July 13th was memorable because on that day the 8th D.L.I. had its first issue of bread since landing in Normandy. The Battalion had lived on compo rations since D Day—excellent in every way, especially the plum puddings—but the compo packs included biscuits, and after six weeks the men were thoroughly tired of biscuits three times a day ; they longed for a loaf of good, white bread. The bread issue when it came was one of many indications of the efficient way in which the British supply organisation was already working in Western Europe. It was possible in the Normandy Bocage to supplement the compo rations with occasional purchases of Camembert and cream cheeses. The local drinks were also sampled by some of the men. The cider was rough, sour stuff—an excellent laxative, and calvados was anything from a good liqueur to fire water.

Good news came through on July 18th ; the enemy was withdrawing. In spite of reinforcements he had been able to obtain from other parts of France, he was beginning to feel the strain of the repeated Allied thrusts. General Montgomery's plan had been to retain the initiative by a succession of attacks which the German Commander could only stop by throwing in his armour to plug the breaches in the line. Six weeks of this type of fighting had worn down the enemy strength along the whole of the Allied front. In the middle of July the American First Army had launched a heavy attack, which resulted in the capture of St. Lo, and was now poised to break out to the south. On the left of the British Second Army an offensive started on July 18th aimed to capture Caen.

In the face of these thrusts on the flanks the Germans now withdrew slightly in the centre. The D.L.I. Brigade was quick to follow up the move and D Company led the Battalion advance past the farm at La Taille, down over the main Caumont-Fontenay-le-Pesnel road a mile west of Hottot, and up on to a small ridge overlooking the River Seulles. Further progress was then halted by enemy holding the small village of Ourville.

The Battalion was in contact with the 9th D.L.I. on the left and the

7th Green Howards on the right, round the Orbois Chateau. Two days later a small infantry and tank attack was put in against a group of houses known as Le Vesque, C Company succeeding in occupying this place ; at the same time D Company established a platoon in Ourville. On July 27th the enemy attempted to retake Ourville, which was important because of the good view it commanded of the surrounding country. For thirty minutes prior to the attack German guns ranged on the village, systematically straddling Ourville with heavy concentrations of fire. Then two platoons of German infantry attacked. 17 Platoon of D Company under Lieut. Wyatt stood firm and the enemy was halted by accurate defensive fire. The Germans wavered, then retreated leaving the village still in British hands.

During the next few days the rifle companies patrolled down into the valley and into the village of Sermentot. They found many mines and booby traps, and on one of these a Canadian officer, Lieut. Luffman was killed ; next day three A Company men were killed and five wounded on "S" mines. The Pioneer Platoon under Lieut. J. Pugh had a difficult task locating, disarming and lifting the deadly mines.

By August 3rd 59 Division in its progress down the right bank of the Seulles had come across the front of 50 Division, and 151 Brigade was the first to be " squeezed out." Gradually the front became quiet. Men could relax and safely walk about in the open, and for the first time since D Day they could sleep outside their slit trenches. Except for the short spells in Brigade Reserve the 8th Battalion had been in the front line almost continuously since D Day—fifty-six days of living and fighting in close proximity to a determined enemy. In the Bocage hardly a day had passed without casualties, and the strain and lack of sleep, the constant patrolling and necessity of being ever alert in the company positions had slowly begun to tell. During the last few days the whole division had undoubtedly been suffering from battle weariness, and it was a great relief to get away from the fighting. Nevertheless it was amazing what a quick recovery was made during the next four days. Morale went up by leaps and bounds and this was important in view of the forthcoming battle of Le Plessis Grimault.

Out of the line the new Corps Commander, Lieut.-General Sir Brian Horrocks, C.B., D.S.O., M.C., visited the 8th D.L.I. ; several officers had met the General before on more than one occasion when the Battalion was in 10 and 13 Corps, which he commanded in the desert. He gave a most interesting and amusing talk on the way the Normandy campaign had been conducted and the plans for the future. General Horrocks had a very pleasant manner and an easy and lucid way of putting everything across. He was a man of great personality and enormous enthusiasm, which he passed on to everyone who listened to him. It was difficult to believe, having heard him speak, that the eventual outcome of the Western Europe campaign would be anything but victory for the Allied Armies.

CHAPTER TWENTY-EIGHT

GERMAN RESISTANCE BREAKS

On the move again—the Battalion attacks near Le Plessis Grimault—Lieut.-Colonel Lidwill seriously wounded—a most successful action—the Carriers help the 9th D.L.I.—a message of appreciation.

IN the afternoon of August 7th the Battalion moved through Feuguerolles-sur-Seulles and Villers-Bocage to Aunay-sur-Odon. Of the two latter places there was literally nothing left except rubble. They had been very heavily bombed by a large force of Lancasters of Bomber Command in order to prevent the movement of German vehicles through them. Alan Moorehead in his book " Eclipse " says, " When we got into Villers-Bocage there was nothing you could really recognise any more. The bulldozers arrived and drove new roads through the twenty-foot deep rubble. It was like an archaeological excavation into a lost world." Aunay-sur-Odon was worse. It was generally agreed that this was just useless destruction, for it did not prevent the movement of German vehicles—they simply went round instead of through the towns.

The next day was characterised by a succession of different plans and orders which were cancelled soon after their issue. First, the Battalion was to act as advance guard to the Brigade, moving initially to Roucamps, a village about three miles south of Aunay, then supported by tanks to advance on Condé-sur-Noireau. This was cancelled as opposition to 7 Armoured Division was heavier than expected, and the Battalion was warned for a night attack on the hamlet of La Rivière, two miles south of Mont Pinçon. In the evening the 8th moved to a place a mile west of Roucamps, but shortly after arriving there the night attack was called off. The night passed fairly quietly.

Early on August 9th the C.O. was called to Brigade H.Q. where the general situation was explained and orders issued for an attack south of Mont Pinçon. Since the end of July the American First and Third Armies had swept south past Avranche into Brittany, then eastwards towards the River Seine. They had captured Le Mans and Alençon, and one corps was pushing north for Argentan to meet the Canadian Army attacking south from Caen towards Falaise. It was these movements which formed what has been called the " Falaise Pocket." On the right of the Canadians the British Second Army was pushing south in order to annihilate the remains of the German Seventh Army in the pocket ; 50 Division was to take part in this by capturing Condé-sur-Noireau, through which all German forces moving out of the "pocket" had to pass. Condé was some ten miles south of Mt. Pinçon, the highest, most important feature in the whole of Normandy, which had recently been captured by 43 Division after a fierce battle. The enemy formation holding the Condé sector of the front was 276 Infantry Division which was known to be of poor quality. Behind them was 21 Panzer Division.

The Brigade Commander's plan was to attack southwards from Le Plessis Grimault—a village at the foot of Mont Pinçon—astride the road to Condé, with the 8th D.L.I. right and the 6th D.L.I. left ; the 9th D.L.I. in reserve was to hold Le Plessis Grimault as a firm base. Each battalion had in support a squadron of 13/18 Hussars and the attack was to go in behind a barrage provided by five field regiments. The objective was the La Rivière feature, which meant an advance of four and a half miles, and on reaching the objective 69 Brigade was to be passed through followed next day by 231 Brigade through 69 Brigade ; this was designed to keep the enemy off balance and allow him no time to recover.

When Lieut.-Colonel Lidwill had explained this plan he took his O Group (company commanders and Support Company platoon commanders) to reconnoitre the start line for the attack at Le Plessis Grimault. At this time the group consisted of Major C. L. Beattie (A Company), Captain J. H. Maier—a regular officer newly-joined from the Northamptonshire Regiment (B Company), Major J. A. Kailofer (C Company), Major I. R. English (D Company), Major G. P. Chambers (S Company), Captain H. C. Catford, Anti-tank Platoon ; and Captain R. C. O'Conor, Mortar Platoon.

The road to the village led over the top of Mont Pinçon ; from the crest it was possible, for the first time since D Day, to look down over the bridgehead and out across the Loire valley. No one had much time to admire this view because the road over the top was in full view of the enemy and was being consistently and very accurately shelled. On reaching Le Plessis Grimault the jeeps were parked and the party went on foot to a sunken track on the far side of the village, which was to be the start line. The C.O.'s plan was a simple one. C Company right and D Company left were to be the forward companies with A and B Companies in reserve. Each company was to have a troop of tanks in support and zero hour was at midday exactly. The C.O. finished his orders by stressing the importance of keeping close to the barrage.

Meanwhile the Battalion had been ordered forward and the O Group returned to the village, expecting to find the companies waiting there. There was, however, no sign of them and it was not until just after 11.30 a.m. that the party of 8th Battalion officers, waiting anxiously in Le Plessis Grimault, saw the 6th D.L.I. appear down the road from Mont Pinçon. The Germans had now spotted the considerable movement of men and vehicles over the crest and were shelling both the road and village very heavily. The men of the 6th D.L.I. were, not unnaturally, taking shelter in the ditches whenever the shelling became particularly heavy. Unfortunately the 6th Battalion did not move on again quickly enough. Lieut.-Colonel Lidwill, from where he stood, saw all this and realised that if the 6th D.L.I. did not speed up their advance the 8th Battalion would be late on the start line when the barrage commenced at midday. Ordering the O Group to wait, the C.O. with Sergeant A. W. Bark, his Intelligence Sergeant, went up the hill in full view of the enemy, ordering and coaxing the 6th D.L.I. to keep on the move. In this he was successful, and as soon as C Company of his own battalion appeared, the C.O. led them on as fast as he could until the leading men were met by Major Kailofer. The company was then taken forward to the start line, followed by D, B and A Companies in that order.

The men were hurried through the village, not only because of the time factor but also because the German guns were pounding Le Plessis Grimault unmercifully with heavy concentrations of shellfire. At the crossroads the marching infantry saw a knocked-out King Tiger tank, one of the first—if not the first—to fall into British hands. C and D Companies arrived on the start line only just in time, and there is no doubt that the Battalion would have been late if the C.O. had not urged on the 6th D.L.I. and then led his own battalion forward.

On the start line there was very little time to liaise with the tank crews. The D Company plan was for the tanks, one with each leading platoon, to advance slightly ahead of the infantry, spraying the near and far hedges of the fields with their Besa machine-guns. Two rifle sections from each platoon were to advance in single file down the sides of the fields, most of which were very small, keeping as close to the barrage and Besa fire as possible. The third rifle section and Platoon H.Q., spread out in extended formation across the fields, was to follow the tanks. The C Company plan was similar to this.

Precisely at midday the barrage started with the usual whine and crash of shells. There was no time for platoon and section commanders to pause and pick up their bearings. However, the men soon settled down and the advance got under way very quickly. C Company had not gone very far when Major Kailofer was badly wounded. He was lying beside a track, waiting to be picked up by stretcher bearers when he was hit again and killed. This was a very sad blow as he was very popular with everyone and an excellent company commander.

Lieut.-Colonel Lidwill had his Tactical H.Q. right up between the leading companies, and was a great inspiration in the advance, encouraging and exhorting his men to keep close behind the barrage. At first, enemy reaction was slight, then a certain amount of defensive artillery and mortar fire came down, which landed amongst the reserve platoons of the forward companies and the reserve companies. Captain J. Collingwood and Lieut. I. T. Hanson of C Company, and Lieut. Morrison, the Canadian officer in D Company, were wounded, and there were casualties amongst the men of C Company and 18 Platoon of D Company. Just before the half-way mark was reached two Germans jumped out of a ditch close to Lieut.-Colonel Lidwill shouting " Kamerad " ; as the C.O. moved forward to disarm them, several German shells fell very near, wounding him, the two Germans and a runner. The C.O. had a most serious stomach wound ; although he was evacuated immediately it was only just in time to save his life.

Imperial War Museum.

Men of the Durham Light Infantry (thought to be C Company of the 8th Battalion) moving up for the attack at Le Plessis Grimault. The road, leading over the top of Mt. Pinçon, was under heavy enemy mortar and shell fire.

Imperial War Museum.

A Lloyd Carrier and a jeep pass a knocked-out German King Tiger tank at a cross-roads in Le Plessis Grimault. This was believed to be one of the first, if not actually the first, of this improved type of Tiger tank to fall into British hands.

The Second-in-Command, Major W. T. Woodruffe, automatically took command. C Company, having lost all its officers and some of the senior N.C.Os. began to lose momentum, so Captain Maier moved B Company up and brought the remainder of C Company under his command. The co-operation between the infantry and tanks was working well and the fire of the Besa machine-guns kept down the heads of the German infantry. The leading companies, keeping close up to the barrage, often found the Germans completely dazed. The first positions were mopped up fairly quickly and a number of prisoners taken and sent to the rear without escort ; they seemed glad to be out of the battle, after days of almost continual shelling.

If everything was going according to plan with the forward companies the same could not be said for Battalion H.Q., which had been established in an orchard on the southern outskirts of the village. By this time, being fully aware of what was happening, the enemy brought down the very heaviest defensive fire on the southern edge of Le Plessis Grimault in the hope of stopping the advance. The men at Battalion H.Q., not having had time to dig slit trenches, were caught in the open by this formidable shelling, which caused several casualties. As Major Wakelin of the 74th Field Regiment said : " This is quite the worst shelling I have had since Mareth."

During the last two thousand yards of the advance enemy resistance stiffened and was only broken by the determined use at close quarters of Stens, grenades, and Brens fired from the hip. The men of the rifle companies, in a very aggressive mood, were fighting well. It felt better to be advancing again after the last few weeks of comparatively static warfare round Parc de la Mare. As a result all opposition was quickly overcome, and the momentum of the Battalion advance was never checked.

The objective, the road running west from the Le Plessis—Condé-sur-Noireau road, was reached with a few minutes to spare according to the timetable, and the companies began to dig in ; B Company on the right, and D Company on the left, in touch with Major Galloway's company of the 6th D.L.I. Major Woodruffe came up to co-ordinate the defence and brought C Company back into reserve near A Company. The tanks of 13/18 Hussars, whose support during the attack had been most effective besides having a very good morale effect on the men of the rifle companies, stayed in the company areas until the anti-tank guns were in position. Captain Catford had difficulty in bringing these up because, having sighted his guns, he could not get in touch with his platoon owing to the wireless sets being out of order, as happened frequently after a battle. It was only just before dark that the anti-tank guns were in position.

At 4 p.m. the 6th Green Howards of 69 Brigade passed through, and most of their objectives had been won before darkness fell. In the evening, shelling of the Battalion H.Q. area continued with hardly a pause. More casualties were inflicted. mostly on the Mortar Platoon which had a total of ten including Sgt. Martin, Cpl. Heslington and Pte. Harris. Fortunately darkness brought some relief from this. The next day was spent in cleaning up the battlefield, burying the dead and collecting British and enemy equipment.

The attack at Le Plessis Grimault was one of the most successful attacks ever undertaken by the Battalion ; one hundred and twenty prisoners had been captured and many Germans killed. In contrast, the Battalion casualties had not been heavy, and it bore out the truth of the C.O.'s conviction—that infantry are reasonably safe provided they keep right up with the barrage. There were two features of this battle, one of them the way in which the Battalion settled down and gave a very good account of itself after a harassing approach march and a rush to reach the start line in time. The other was the very good mutual co-operation between the tanks and infantry, even though the two units had never worked together before and had no knowledge of each other's ways.

Two men did a great deal towards ensuring the success of this attack ; one of them was Major I. R. English, commanding D Company, and the other C.S.M. J. E. Ineson of B Company. Whilst moving up to the start line Major English's company was heavily shelled but English moved about in the open amongst his men, disregarding the enemy fire, and got them to the start line. Throughout the whole advance he was in front, leading his men through heavy artillery and mortar fire which caused considerable casualties. When C Company on the left flank lost all its officers Major English pushed relentlessly on, mopping up on the way and taking over fifty prisoners. He was first on the objective where the enemy was quickly disposed of and then he reorganised his company under very heavy fire. He was awarded a second bar to the M.C. he had won at Alamein[1].

C.S.M. Ineson was with B Company and when the company moved up to take over the C Company responsibility it came under intense mortar and shellfire. The C.S.M. immediately gathered together a small party of men and leading them in the van of the company he so inspired the remainder that the impetus of the attack was fully maintained. On two occasions he rushed enemy positions under fire without waiting for the assistance of the supporting tanks. He personally forced out of their fire positions at least fourteen of the enemy and the fact that B Company reached the final objective was in no small way due to the fine example of C.S.M. Ineson who was awarded the Military Medal.

During the next two days 231 Brigade continued the attacks on the high ground near the village of St. Pierre la Vieille. On August 11th the 9th D.L.I. was ordered to capture two prominent features, Point 249 and Point 262, but this operation was postponed 24 hours ; the Carrier Platoon of the 8th D.L.I. was warned that it would be required to assist the 9th Battalion when the attack was eventually carried out. Since June 18th, when Lieut. Gibbon was wounded, there had been no officer commanding this platoon. Major Woodruffe now decided to appoint Captain P. G. Hampson, who had been second-in-command of B Company, to command the Carrier Platoon.

[1] The first bar was awarded for his leadership of the Carrier Platoon at Gazala, when so much damage was done to the German transport using the route across the Battalion front.

The C.O. of the 9th, Lieut.-Colonel J. Mogg, planned to attack Points 249 and 262 with tanks of 13/18 Hussars as the leading wave, closely followed by the two carrier platoons ; the latter to take on with their 2" Mortars and Brens any anti-tank guns which were holding up the tanks. When they reached the objective, the rifle companies were to follow up as quickly as possible to occupy the position.

When the British artillery barrage started the Germans replied by heavily shelling a crossroads, which was the start line for the attack. Lieut. D. Hurst, the 9th D.L.I. Carrier Platoon commander, was killed and three of his carriers hit. Meanwhile Captain Hampson was in radio communication with the squadron leader of the tanks who reported that they were engaged in a battle and had knocked out two German Panthers. Eventually the tanks moved on, the carriers following fairly closely. Behind them were the rifle platoons of the 9th D.L.I., advancing steadily in spite of heavy shell and Spandau fire.

The first objective, Point 249, was soon reached and thirty Germans surrendered. After a pause to allow the 9th to come up and take over the feature, Captain Hampson's carriers pushed on to Point 262. The second stage of the advance encountered less opposition. Concealing the carriers in some scrub the men advanced on foot and took up positions with magnificent fields of fire in every direction. They remained there until it was almost dark, when Major K. Wood of the 6th Battalion arrived with his company to relieve them.

Later, the Brigade Commander, Brigadier D. S. Gordon, thanked the platoon personally, saying it had been a very well executed and successful attack.

On the same day, August 12th, the 8th Battalion received orders to move back to a rest area north of Mont Pinçon. The men marched, arriving in the early hours of the 13th. During the day a small re-inforcement draft arrived including a new C.O., Lieut.-Colonel C. F. Hutchinson, D.S.O., who had been wounded on D Day when commanding an East Yorkshire battalion in 3 Division ; however, he had only been with the Battalion two days when he had to be evacuated sick on the 15th. The following day Lieut.-Colonel H. R. D. Oldman, M.C., who had been second-in-command of the 7th Green Howards in 69 Brigade, arrived to take command. Another new officer, Major C. Riley of the East Yorkshire Regiment, took over B Company, Captain Maier becoming the Adjutant, and Captain Ridealgh going to B Company as second-in-command.

The five days in the rest area were spent, first of all in rest and recuperation, then in smartening up, reorganisation and physical training. It was at this time that news was received of the Allied landing in the south of France, Operation Anvil. The news was as welcome to the 8th as it must have been discouraging to the Germans. Meanwhile the enemy front in the "Falaise Pocket" was rapidly breaking up, and the Allied armies were preparing to close up on the Seine. The long days of hard, slogging warfare in the Normandy Bocage were now being left behind, and 50 Division was to take part in the pursuit, the end of which it was difficult to foresee.

General Horrocks, in a message of appreciation to all ranks of 50 Division on the "Falaise Pocket" battle, said: "I cannot give you higher praise than by saying that the most experienced battle-fighting division in the British Army has once more lived up to its high reputation."

CHAPTER TWENTY-NINE

THE PURSUIT TO BRUSSELS

The Battalion takes up the chase—through the desolation of the Falaise Gap—champagne in Beaufour—across the Seine—skirmish in Picquiny—memories of 1940—welcome to Brussels.

THE advance of the Second Army to the Seine was to be led by 30 Corps on the right and 12 Corps on the left. The role of 50 Division was to protect the flank of 11 Armoured Division as it drove forward to the river. On August 18th the 8th Battalion commenced an advance which was only to end at the Albert Canal in Belgium, three weeks later.

The usual method of moving was a queer mixture of peace and war; of a quiet administrative move and a tactical advance. Soon after daybreak each morning the Battalion advance party, consisting of one N.C.O. per company under Major Chambers, reported to a Brigade rendezvous and was then directed to the new Battalion area. The advance party led the main body of the battalion and moved more or less unprotected. Its task was to lay out the new area so that the Battalion could harbour immediately on arrival. The situation was often extremely vague; the 8th Battalion men knew that 11 Armoured Division was somewhere in front, but reliable information about the enemy was usually lacking. On several occasions the advance party—being the first British unit in a particular area—was overwhelmed with reports as to the whereabouts of "Les Salles Boches" the numbers of whom would vary from a dozen to a hundred. The strength of Major Chambers' party was six men and he had to explain carefully to the local inhabitants, who usually included several Resistance men armed with a varied assortment of weapons, that the rest of the Battalion would be following shortly. After the arrival of the main body in the afternoon the C.O. would often order small patrols, consisting of a section of carriers and a rifle platoon, to search places in the neighbourhood. Quite a number of German stragglers were captured in this way.

During the first four days the Battalion advanced in this manner through Condé-sur-Noireau, Putanges, and Cuie near the main Falaise-Argentan road. In the Cuie-Chambois area the men of the 8th Battalion were able to see for the first time with their own eyes the havoc which the Allied air forces had inflicted on the fleeing enemy. Both sides and often the middle of the roads were jammed with wrecked lorries, guns, horses and tanks; dead men and horses lay about in grotesque attitudes, and here and there a truck or gun limber which had been set on fire was still smouldering. Abandoned staff cars and many other vehicles were packed with loot ; field glasses, typewriters, pistols and small arms by the hundred, cases of wine and boxes of ladies' clothing. Many of the vehicles were untouched and could have been driven away but no one had the time.

On August 22nd the Battalion was ordered to clear the Foret de Gouffern. This had been used as an Army H.Q. and it was thought that the Army Commander was still hiding in the area. Lieut.-Colonel Oldman's plan was to divide this large forest into three areas, making each rifle company responsible for one. The chief difficulty was to keep control and direction. Only nine Germans were found and the operation was useful chiefly as a signal exercise.

The following day the Battalion, with a squadron of 13/18 Hussars and a section of 505 Field Company, Royal Engineers under command, moved through Laigle to Beaufour, a village near the town of Bourth. Shortly after arriving in the new area the Brigade Commander ordered the 8th Battalion to sweep the southern portion of the Foret de Breteuil. Although not so large as the Foret de Gouffern, it was densely wooded and the going was very difficult. The whole operation was carried out in pouring rain ; this, and the fact that no Germans were found, did not improve the good humour of the troops. However, on returning to the village the men were pleased to find that the C.O. had arranged with the villagers for most of the troops to be billeted in barns.

There was no move the next day and everyone enjoyed the welcome rest. In the evening the Mayor, ably assisted by the Chef de Resistance and some of his men, gave a party for the 8th Battalion officers to celebrate the liberation of Paris. Champagne, brandy, and an assortment of wines flowed freely, and the Mayor made a speech of welcome in which he said : "During four long years the people of Beaufour have waited for the Liberation. We have passed through hard times under the Germans, but we never lost hope that some day the English would return." Lieut.-Colonel Oldman replied in French on behalf of the Battalion. Numerous bouquets of flowers were then presented to every officer present and the party was fittingly concluded by four brothers stepping forward, cornets in hand, to play the Marseillaise. This was the first time the villagers had heard it in public since 1940. When it was over the Mayor regretted that the musicians were not able to play " God Save the King." However, the officers had great pleasure in singing the National Anthem unaccompanied.

On the following night, at a Battalion party for the villagers, the Brigadier presented to the Mayor a plaque bearing the Regimental Crest and the following inscription : " To the people of Beaufour and Bourth to commemorate the liberation of Paris, 23rd August, 1944, and as a pledge of lasting fellowship between Great Britain and France." The men of the 8th Battalion are not likely to forget the marvellous welcome they received in that small French village.

At 5.15 a.m. on August 26th the Battalion moved on about forty miles to a point near Vernons on the River Seine. The Corps plan was for 43 Division to force a crossing of the river at Vernons and establish a bridgehead. Through this 11 Armoured, Guards Armoured and 50 Divisions were to pass. During the three days' halt, when the Brigade was waiting for the bridgehead to be established, news was received that Sgt. A. W. Bark had been awarded an immediate commission. He was appointed Intelligence Officer. To his friends this promotion seemed long overdue. Bark, who had joined the 8th Battalion at Charlbury in 1939 with the King's Own Scottish Borderers draft, had been the Intelligence Sergeant since 1943, and had been acting Intelligence Officer since Lieut. Laws was wounded at St. Pierre.

Before crossing the Seine all units in the Division were ordered to surrender their captured enemy vehicles. In the Falaise Pocket most units had come into possession of numerous abandoned trucks, and it had been discovered that single infantry battalions were occupying almost as much road space as complete brigades. Most of this surplus transport was formed into what became known as a Captured Enemy Vehicle Supply Column, and was used to run supplies into Paris for the civilians.

By August 28th the 43 Division bridgehead was firmly established and 11 Armoured Division had crossed the river ; 50 Division followed next day and at 6.30 p.m. on August 29th the 8th Battalion crossed the Seine by the pontoon bridge. The plan was for 30 Corps, now reinforced by the Guards Armoured Division, to establish itself in the area of Arras and Amiens, regardless of the forces on its flanks, then to cut the communications of the enemy forces in the coastal belt and eliminate the flying bomb sites in the Pas de Calais, from which the V.I.s were being launched on London and the south coast. This role was popular with all ranks, many of whom had their families in southern England.

The advance went well and the Battalion moved quickly through Gisors to occupy positions near Morgny on the road to Gournay-en-Bray. Next day, very early in the morning, the 8th Battalion was again on the move and just before midday, during a short halt, was ordered to push on to Amiens to relieve units of 11 Armoured Division which had captured a bridge over the Somme, after a brilliant drive through the night. By early evening A Company was in position around the bridge with the other companies deployed to cover the western approaches to the city.

Next morning, September 1st, the Brigade Commander arrived at Battalion H.Q. with orders that the 8th Battalion, having been relieved in its positions by the 9th D.L.I., was to move immediately to Picquiny, a town on the Somme to the north of Amiens, and there to capture the bridge over the river. The Carrier Platoon, under Captain Hampson, was sent off at once with instructions to capture the bridge intact if possible and, failing that, to find out the enemy dispositions with a view to the capture of the town by the rest of the Battalion. The carriers were met on the outskirts by the Mayor who reported that the Germans were still holding the place. Captain Hampson, Sgt. Cairns and Pte. Crighton went in on foot, and seeing that the Germans were preparing to leave, called up the carriers which came dashing into the town and made for the bridge. As the leading vehicle was only twenty yards from it the bridge was blown up.

Shortly afterwards D Company and some self-propelled anti-tank guns all under the Second-in-Command, Major Woodruffe, arrived. D Company commander, Major English, had the advantage of knowing the town, which had been a favourite spot for an evening's recreation when the Carrier Platoon was attached to D Company at Fourdrinoy in 1940. The enemy started to shell and mortar the place heavily, presumably to cover his withdrawal, and Major Woodruffe, Major English and Captain Hampson were pinned to the ground near the river by very accurate machine gun fire when they moved forward to reconnoitre the banks. The town itself was the scene of the most amazing contrasts. In the street near the bridge, men moved warily and kept under cover because of German fire, while just around the corner in the big market place, crowds of townspeople were laughing, dancing and singing—celebrating the liberation of the town by drinking to the health of the Allied armies.

Lieut. Pugh, the Pioneer Platoon commander, and Major English were able to cross the river by a lock gate, and the latter was preparing to move his company over when the leading elements of 12 Corps—armoured cars of the Royals—arrived in Picquiny. Apparently the Battalion was operating outside the corps boundary, and was obliged to leave the town to others. While waiting to be relieved, the Battalion did some excellent shooting with 3″ Mortars and anti-tank guns on the enemy pulling out of farms and buildings on the opposite bank. The high ground on the southern side overlooked the low lying fields on the north bank and afforded an excellent view. 296 Battery of the 74th Field Regiment set up an observation post and successfully shot up German transport, while machine-gunners of the 2nd Cheshires and the self-propelled anti-tank guns joined in with some extremely accurate fire, playing havoc with the Germans withdrawing over the open ground. In the afternoon the 8th Battalion moved back to the village of Ferrières on the Amiens road.

That evening Majors Chambers, Beattie and English, all of whom had been with the 8th in 1940, visited the villages where the Battalion had been billeted. At Oissy they were recognised by the people, who remembered even the numbers of the unit vehicles. In those days the tactical number was TT.16 and the Battalion was known to the French as the 16th Durhams. They had a good memory for names and asked after Commandant Raine, the Padre Duggan and Captain Walton.

After this short skirmish at Picquiny the 8th D.L.I., with the rest of 50 Division, was ordered to advance as quickly as possible to the industrial area of Lens. At 5.45 a.m. on September 2nd the Battalion moved off to a position about three miles north of Doullens, which was reached at 9.30 a.m. From here, a patrol consisting of A Company, with a section of carriers and a troop of self-propelled anti-tank guns, spent the day searching the villages of Humberchamp and Gouy-en-Artois, but no enemy was found. The only Germans seen were those working under members of the Maquis, digging holes to bury dead horses which were still being encountered at intervals along the tree-lined French roads. That evening a draft of reinforcements arrived, mostly from the 10th D.L.I. of 70 Brigade which had been recently broken up. Lieut. J. Hannah, who had been wounded at St. Pierre with C Company, was included in the draft. With this increase in strength the C.O. decided to re-form C Company under the command of Captain J. H. Maier.

September 3rd, the fifth anniversary of the outbreak of the war, will always be remembered as the day on which Brussels was liberated by the Guards Armoured Division, after a magnificent dash from the Belgian frontier ; 11 Armoured Division entered Antwerp on the following day. The 8th Battalion, with the rest of 50 Division, was some way behind the armoured divisions, playing a less spectacular but no less important role in the race through Flanders. The speed of the advance (30 Corps covered two hundred and fifty miles in six days) by-passed many centres of resistance, and on the flanks numerous enemy groups, though considerably disorganised, were still capable of fighting. 50 Division was ordered to face north to protect the left flank of 30 Corps by covering the approaches from the north and north-west, between Tournai and Lens.

The advance of the Battalion was continued with a move to the north of Arras. Vimy Ridge, with its memories of the fighting at Petit Vimy and Givenchy in 1940, was seen on the right and in the evening the built-up area was reached. The progress on this and subsequent days will long be remembered by those who took part in these operations. The route was lined by cheering crowds, most of them waving flags ; as soon as the column halted, the vehicles were besieged by people who wanted to shake hands with " Les Anglais," by girls who wanted to kiss the dusty, grimy faces of jeep and truck drivers, and by people who offered great loads of fruit to the troops.

At 7.30 a.m. on September 4th the Battalion came under command of 8 Armoured Brigade and the C.O. went to that Brigade H.Q. for orders. As the column was now halted only three miles from Gondecourt, Majors Beattie, Chambers and English thought that this was an excellent opportunity to visit their old 1940 billets, and to look up old friends. They went into the estaminet owned by Monsieur Couvelard, who had been Mayor in 1940. He was still Mayor and overjoyed to see his English friends. After opening a special bottle for the great occasion he took Major Chambers upstairs to his attic where he proudly produced some of the Battalion's band instruments, which it had been necessary to leave behind in 1940. He had been able to hide some, though the Germans had removed most of them. They were in good condition and the Mayor had risked his life hiding them during the four years of occupation. As it was, Monsieur Couvelard had been imprisoned by the Germans for some time because of his non-co-operation. The old billets were visited and the ladies immediately set about preparing lunch for their unexpected English guests ; unfortunately, orders were received to move on again to the Belgian frontier, much to the sorrow of the people of Gondecourt and the old members of the Battalion.

During the day the Battalion occupied positions astride the Franco-Belgian frontier in the villages of Sainghin, Cherens and Willems, in order to prevent any withdrawal from Lille, which was supposed to be an enemy straggler's post. As the Battalion frontage was about five miles, platoons were extremely widely dispersed. Reports of five thousand S.S. troops in Lille kept coming in, but Majors Woodruffe, Chambers and English, who went into the city that afternoon, saw no signs of them. The rest of the day and all the next was spent in patrolling the area, but only odd stragglers were captured.

The day's halt was very welcome to the Battalion B Echelon and the supply companies, for the speed of the advance had placed a severe strain on the administrative services. The lines of communication now stretched some three hundred miles back to the Rear Maintenance Area in Normandy. With the Battalion advancing about fifty miles a day, Captain Stray, the Quartermaster, found it necessary to go back against the main stream of traffic as much as sixty miles to collect rations and petrol. This put a great strain on his staff and the M.T. drivers, but not once during the very rapid pursuit did the rifle companies go short of anything.

On September 6th the Battalion came under command of 151 Brigade once more and moved quickly to Brussels, with the task of protecting the south-east approaches to the city. All along the route the Belgians lined the road, throwing flowers and fruit at the trucks and shouting: "Allo Tommi." If anything they were more demonstrative than the French had been; the welcome which the Battalion had been given as it made its way through Northern France and Flanders was nothing compared to what it received as it motored into Brussels. The chief impediment to progress in the famous old capital was the inhabitants themselves, who swarmed over everything and everybody in hilarious and spontaneous welcome. The streets were blocked by waving and cheering crowds shouting: "Welcome our Liberators," "Welcome Tommy," "God bless the British." All, from the very young to the very old, were celebrating. It is hard to describe the joy on the faces of these people, but as the men listened to them, shook hands with them and, in some cases were hugged and kissed by Belgian girls, it made all the Battalion had come through during five long years of the war seem worth while.

That evening the welcome news was received that the Brigade would remain in Brussels for three days; in spite of the operational commitments everyone was to have as much rest and recreation as possible. Next day some small patrols were sent out as far east as the River Dyle and contact was made with the United States 2 Armoured Division in that area. However, there was still time for social engagements; all ranks soon made friends with the Belgians, and enjoyed their generous hospitality which often included the luxury of a proper bath.

CHAPTER THIRTY

THE BATTLE OF GHEEL

The bridgehead established—a counter-attack smashed—A Company in trouble—the Battalion positions penetrated—a night of confused fighting—the Germans withdraw—end of a hard struggle.

THIS relaxation was too good to last. In the early hours of September 8th, when numerous men were sleepily returning from parties given by the people of Brussels, the Battalion was warned to prepare for a 5 a.m. move. Actually, the column did not start off until 9.15 a.m., which was just as well as it enabled the companies to get all their men together. The route lay north-east through Louvain, and the column laagered up for lunch shortly after 12 o'clock. It seemed uncertain whether a further move would be made that day, but in the afternoon the Brigadier appeared with news about the fighting beyond Brussels.

Since the capture of Antwerp and Brussels, enemy opposition on the 30 Corps front had stiffened considerably. On the right, where the Guards Armoured Division had forced a crossing of the Albert Canal at Beeringen, the bridgehead had been heavily counter-attacked by German paratroops. At Antwerp all attempts to advance over the water obstacles north of the city had been unsuccessful. As the opposition increased it became necessary to get 30 Corps on to a narrower front, so troops of 12 Corps took over from 11 Armoured Division in Antwerp which enabled the Corps Commander to switch this division to the Beeringen Bridgehead. Soon after the completion of this move 50 Division was ordered to make a new bridgehead over the Albert Canal, and on the morning of September 8th 69 Brigade had crossed the canal between Steelen and Herenthals but was soon engaged in very stiff fighting. The Divisional Commander then decided to commit 151 Brigade and ordered the Brigadier to force another crossing of the canal with the object of capturing the town of Gheel.

The 8th Battalion was given the task of establishing a bridgehead for the Brigade in the vicinity of Steelen, and Lieut.-Colonel Oldman decided that A Company should do the initial crossing. When these preliminary orders had been given out, the Battalion moved on to Oosterloo, a village about two miles from Steelen, where it remained while A Company and Tactical Battalion H.Q. continued alongside the canal until they reached Steelen. As the banks of the canal were from fourteen to twenty feet high, A Company was able to move into the village without being seen.

It was not known what opposition would be encountered but the Higher Command did not anticipate that it would be very great. The

C.O.'s plan was for A Company to make a silent crossing to the left of a destroyed road bridge, with no supporting fire until opposition was met and the enemy positions located. 296 Battery, Royal Artillery was on call and Major Wakelin had established an observation post in the tower of Steelen church. As the infantry could not use the bridge, the crossing was to be made in assault boats which would be brought to the assembly area by Royal Engineers, but operated by the Battalion Assault Pioneer Platoon. Very little could be seen on the opposite side of the canal where there was no movement of either enemy or civilians.

The assault boats arrived by 4.30 p.m. and were soon made ready by the Pioneer Platoon. A Company now prepared to cross the canal. Meanwhile D Company had been called up and the company commander reported to Tactical Battalion H.Q., which was established in Steelen churchyard. He was ordered to follow A Company quickly and move out to the left flank when across the canal. The two companies were to advance to a position about four hundred yards beyond the canal, and then dig in; B and C Companies would then pass through them.

The A Company crossing was greeted by the fire of an enemy machine-gun, which fortunately was not very accurate. After about fifteen minutes the two leading platoons were across the canal, having suffered only three or four casualties, but as Company H.Q. was going over the fire became more intense, and Major Beattie was badly wounded as he climbed the bank on the enemy side. He was evacuated immediately, but the following day the Battalion was shocked to hear that he had died of his wounds. Beattie, one of the original Territorial officers, had been with the Battalion all through the war, except for a time in 1940 when he was in the Brigade Anti-tank Company. His death was a great loss to the 8th, as he had, in his own quiet friendly way, developed into a first-class company commander who could always be relied on to acquit himself well in any situation.

Major Beattie was unfortunately not the only casualty. After making some progress on the far bank A Company ran into heavy opposition. The Germans, who had been lying low perhaps expecting the usual British artillery barrage, now came to life. From their positions in the hedgerows and road embankment they opened deadly accurate fire with Spandaus and light mortars. Several A Company men became casualties, Lieut. Rood was killed, and Lieut. Robertson wounded for the second time in the campaign. In less than half an hour A Company had lost all its officers. The remainder of the company under the C.S.M. and Sgt. G. H. Self succeeded in occupying the objective against heavy opposition, and a number of prisoners was taken. The company was then bombarded by enemy mortars and swept by machine-gun fire. Taking two men with him Sgt. Self went out and silenced two Spandau nests. This quietened things down considerably and A Company was able to sit back and take stock of its position.

At 5.30 p.m., under cover of smoke put down by the artillery, D

Company began to cross the canal in the two remaining assault craft. The rest of the boats had either been sunk or rendered unusable in the first crossing; the disabled boats, with jagged holes in their canvas sides where the German defensive fire had caught them were abandoned by the Pioneers. In the crossing, D Company met less resistance than had A Company, and having formed up on the bank, moved forward quickly to come up on the left of the leading company. The forward sections were held up by some enemy in a farmhouse and Sgt. Wallbanks was killed by mortar fire. 17 Platoon immediately took cover and returned the enemy fire. Lieut. Wyatt ordered one section, supported by three Bren guns and the 2" Mortar, to give covering fire while the other two sections mounted a left-flanking attack against the farmhouse. This well-executed attack was too much for the enemy who ran off to the rear, leaving some dead and wounded in the vicinity of the farmhouse. Apart from Sgt. Wallbanks, 17 Platoon had no casualties.

During the crossing of the canal a gallant action by L/Cpl. J. Hunter won the Military Medal. His boat came under very heavy machine-gun fire from the bank and was sunk; two of his section were killed outright and three wounded. Hunter immediately dived into the canal wearing his full battle kit, grabbed hold of one of the wounded men and swam with him to the Steelen bank. By this time the Germans were sweeping the canal with heavy bursts of fire but Hunter ignored it to dive in again and rescue a second man. The enemy fire was ripping into the water all around him but he reached the bank safely. Then for a third time he plunged into the canal to bring the last man to safety.

It was now getting dark and the two forward companies started to consolidate their positions, not an easy task in the fading daylight. Meanwhile the rest of the Battalion had moved up. After an unopposed crossing B and C Companies advanced through A and D Companies to take up positions a little way forward. During this move C Company ran into heavy shell and machine-gun fire and Lieut. Niznick, the sole remaining Canadian officer, was killed and Captain Maier badly wounded. In the gathering darkness it was difficult to locate the enemy positions and the company dug in where it had been halted. The situation when the Battalion eventually settled down was that B Company(right) and C Company (left) were forward, with D and A Companies respectively a short distance behind them.

While the rifle companies were crossing the canal, the Carrier Platoon had moved along the bank on the home side to the village of Liessel. Moving across the canal on a ferry operated by 69 Brigade the carriers then dashed along the cinder path by the side of the canal to join the rifle companies in the 8th Battalion bridgehead.

The Anti-tank Platoon followed the example of the carriers and the guns were taken across by the Liessel ferry. The carriers were soon in action, moving up the main road to sieze two farmhouses in the A Company area. This served to reinforce the infantry company and to strengthen the right flank of the Battalion.

With the whole of the 8th across the canal, the Sappers began to construct a Class 9 bridge, consisting of two ramps supported on canvas rafts, with the ramps wide enough to take the wheels of a vehicle. The Engineers very soon came under fire from a German tank which had moved up on the right flank of the bridgehead. The tank was able to fire straight down the canal and was within range of the proposed bridging site with its 88-millimetre gun. The bridge should have been ready by 11 p.m., but owing to casualties among the sappers was not finally finished until 2 a.m. the next morning.

In the bridgehead the infantry companies sent out patrols to either flank, with the object of locating the enemy dispositions. The Germans, units of the German Air Force fighting as infantry, were not caught off their guard by any means. They reacted violently whenever their positions were approached. A small D Company patrol under Lieut. Wyatt moved down a lane leading away from the company positions, but was challenged by a German sentry. A sharp action followed during which Lieut. Wyatt was wounded. A few minutes previous to this, Lieut. P. Groom, second-in-command of the Anti-tank Platoon, had been hit near the same place by German Tommy-gunners when making a reconnaissance for the layout of his guns.

About 11 p.m. a sharp counter-attack developed against the positions held by A and C Companies and the Carrier Platoon. In particular the farms held by the Carrier Platoon came under heavy Spandau machine-gun fire. It was a clear night, bright with a brilliant moon. The brightness was increased by the glow of burning buildings, set on fire by a German 20-millimetre anti-aircraft gun which was continuously sweeping the area with incendiary shells. By the light of the moon and the flames, the carrier men could see the Germans advancing in open formation, They met them with the fire of at least twelve Brens. The Germans came to within twenty yards to throw their grenades, then suddenly broke up and retreated, taking their wounded with them. Their dead they left behind and next day the bodies of several enemy in air force blue could be seen on the ground.

The rest of the night was comparatively quiet. About 2 a.m. Lieut.-Colonel Oldman crossed into the bridgehead over the newly-constructed bridge which had just been completed by the Sappers, and made a tour of the positions. He found that in little more than nine hours, during which time the bridgehead had been established and consolidated, the Battalion had suffered fairly heavy casualties, totalling seven officers and twenty-two other ranks.

At first light on September 9th, 61 Divisional Reconnaissance Regiment, which had crossed the canal during the night, moved forward up the road to Gheel, but was held up in the area of Doornboom. The reconnaissance troops reported that the country to the north was strongly held by the enemy. About this time A Company of the 8th Battalion discovered that the group of houses known as Willaars was occupied by approximately fifty enemy. The fire of the whole 74th Field Regiment was directed on this target ; at least twenty-four guns went into action to bombard the houses and this heavy concentration must have caused many casualties. Meanwhile, the Class 9 bridge had been temporarily put out of action by the fire of the German tank down the canal.

During the morning the 6th D.L.I. crossed the canal to enlarge the bridgehead, and moving through the positions held by the 8th Battalion advanced without serious opposition. By 2.30 p.m. they were reported to be digging in on their objective, south of Gheel. The C.O. of the 8th now decided to reorganise the disposition of his companies.

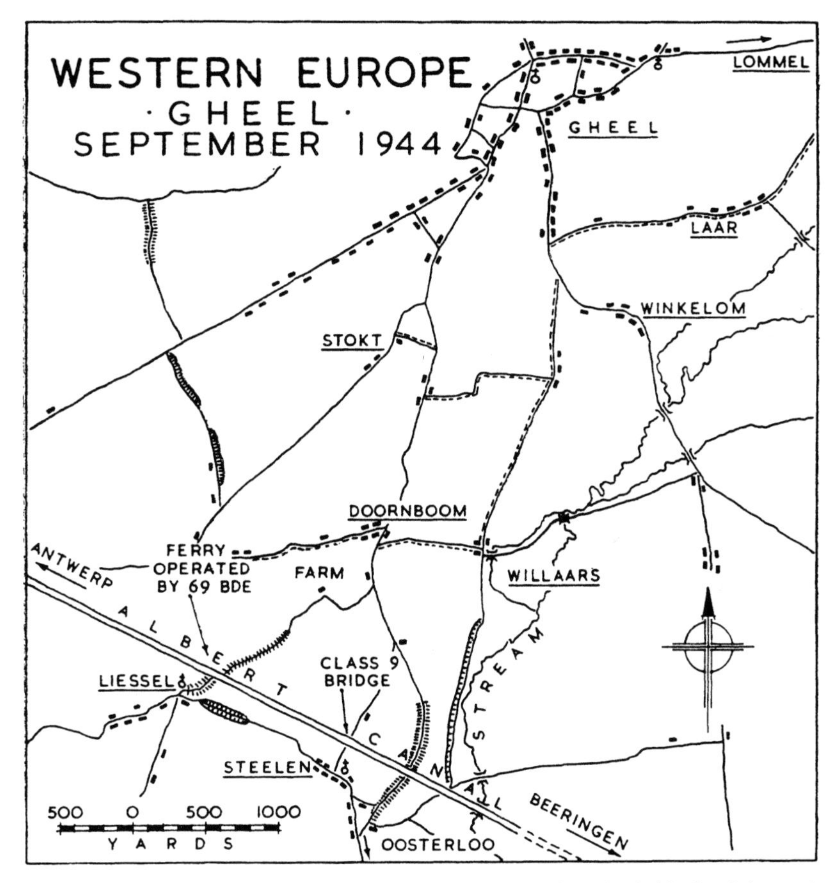

WESTERN EUROPE. The area south of Gheel showing the bridgehead beyond the Albert Canal which the 8th Battalion captured and held against fierce German resistance.

The Battalion front was broadened by moving D Company out to Willaars, now clear of the enemy, so that the right flank rested on a small stream which ran into the canal. On the left, the B Company platoons moved further forward. The centre was held by A Company and the Carrier Platoon, with C Company in the area of Doornboom. The Battalion soon settled down in its new positions. The rest of the day was disturbed only by occasional shelling and a quiet night followed.

Early the following morning sounds of battle could be heard to the north, and news came through that the 6th D.L.I. was being counter-attacked. All companies " stood-to," ready to go forward to assist the 6th D.L.I., but by 5 a.m. the latter reported that the enemy had been driven off by small arms and artillery fire. The Battalion "stood-down " and later in the morning a Reconnaissance Group from the 6th Green Howards reconnoitred the area prior to taking it over when the 8th Battalion moved forward. Meanwhile the enemy had again opened fire on the bridge and put it out of action.

The Brigade Commander, when he visited the Battalion in the afternoon, said that the tenacity and good fighting qualities of the German Air Force Division, fighting as infantry, had surprised the British Higher Command and it was now known that the enemy had been reinforced by a Parachute Regiment. On the other hand, elements of 8 Armoured Brigade, which had fought its way from the Beeringen Bridgehead, would soon be joining 151 Brigade.

The 9th D.L.I. now crossed the canal and set up Battalion H.Q. at Willaars while their rifle companies pushed on northwards. The leading troops met heavy opposition in the Winkelom area where they were held up. At the same time the 6th D.L.I., moving through Gheel, ran into strong resistance. The fierce German counter-attacks were broken up with very accurate artillery fire controlled by the 74th Field Regiment observers moving with the 6th D.L.I.

Lieut.-Colonel Oldman now ordered A and D Companies forward to an area one thousand yards north of Doornboom, to support the 9th D.L.I. in their advance. As the route lay over open country the two companies deployed, A Company moving off first. Some time elapsed before D Company followed, and as the leading sections crossed a track running from Winkelom to a group of houses known as Stokt they met some A Company men coming back along a hedgerow, considerably disorganised. This was followed almost immediately by the appearance of two German Panther tanks, not more than two hundred yards away. The D Company platoons made for the ditches and any other cover they could find, taking up fire positions to engage the tanks. Fortunately the Panthers moved away to the right and the commander of D Company, assisted by Corporal D. D. Michael of A Company, was able to collect together some of the stragglers from A Company, numbering about twenty men.

The leading company had apparently been caught in the open by the two German tanks, accompanied by about forty infantry. There was no cover of any sort and the first bursts of fire from the tank machine-guns killed Captain Ridealgh, the only officer left in the company, and killed or wounded several of the men. A Company had withdrawn in some disorder. As dusk was rapidly closing in, Major English, commanding D Company, ordered his men to dig in where they were and then reported the situation to Battalion H.Q., at the same time asking for anti-tank gun support.

Had it not been for Sgt. G. H. Self considerably more of A Company would have been missing. Self had immediately taken over command of the company when Captain Ridealgh was killed, and although the A Company platoons were overrun by tanks and enemy infantry he succeeded in getting the majority of his men through the German lines to safety. For his expert handling of an almost hopeless situation and for his gallantry in the initial capture of the bridgehead objective Sgt. Self was awarded the Distinguished Conduct Medal.

With D Company firmly in position, B and C Companies advanced across country at 9 p.m. to Stokt. This brought B Company up on the left of Major English's platoons while C Company, now reduced to two platoons under command of Major Chambers, came up on B Company's left. The move was completed without incident, but shortly after getting into position Lieut. Hannah of C Company was wounded in the legs by enemy machine-gun fire.

Just as it was getting dark a determined German counter-attack with about ten tanks and two hundred men was put in against the Battalion. Their objective was the Class 9 bridge over the canal. At this time the rifle companies of the 8th had just started to move forward to new positions and the Germans caught the 8th unawares. They came up the main road and, penetrating the Battalion positions between D and B Companies, reached the area of Battalion H.Q. The enemy, part of the force which had shot-up A Company that afternoon, was determined to create confusion, if nothing else.

Captain Hampson, hearing that there had been some casualties in A and D Companies, decided to take two carriers forward to bring back some of the wounded. He led the way up the main road towards Gheel, and behind him came Captain O'Conor with some Mortar Platoon carriers to reconnoitre a new position. Hampson went what he thought was the required distance, until he came to about sixty men sitting by the side of the road ; he could see them only dimly in the gathering darkness, and asked if they were D Company. His question was answered by three hand grenades being thrown into the carrier, which miraculously did no harm. A German came running at them, but Pte. C. Edwards shot him from ten yards, firing his rifle from the hip. The drivers then swung the carriers round and went back up the road at a fast pace. Captain Hampson stopped at main Brigade H.Q., which had not long been established in a field a little to the south of Doornboom, to report the incident, and asked the Brigade Major—Major The Viscount Long—if he could speak to Brigadier Gordon. The Brigade Major said the Brigadier was too busy, to which Hampson replied : " He will have to be damned busy if he does not want to hear what I have got to say." Having eventually passed on the information Hampson reported to Battalion H.Q. A few minutes later the Brigade H.Q. vehicles moved back at great speed to the safety of the south side of the Albert Canal.

Meanwhile, not being aware of what had happened to Hampson,

Captain O'Conor was proceeding along the road when the carrier in front of him blew up. He did not realise that it had been hit by a shell from a German tank about a hundred and fifty yards away. Deciding to investigate on foot, O'Conor told the carrier crew to wait for him a few hundred yards in rear. After going a short distance he heard a tank coming down the road from Gheel, and resolved to stop it for some information. He soon found himself addressing a Panther tank instead of a Sherman. On top of it were twelve German soldiers. It went on, apparently oblivious of O'Conor, who doubled into the cover of the hedge. He was at once surrounded by several Germans and taken prisoner.

The enemy tank which had passed O'Conor soon came up to the mortar carrier which had been detailed to wait. The crew, when they realised the position, started up, turned round, overtook the German tank and passed it quite unmolested. Another mortar carrier, however, was not so lucky and was hit, eventually blowing up. It was in this skirmish that Sgt. J. Martin was killed. He had been with the Mortar Platoon for years and was a very able section commander.

It was by this time appreciated that a full-scale counter-attack had been launched by the Germans and the D.L.I. Brigade was thrown on the defensive. Taking advantage of the thoroughly confused situation an enemy force of four tanks and about a hundred men had penetrated the Brigade positions to a depth of approximately eight hundred yards and had reached the area of 8th Battalion H.Q. Here the enemy found the way barred by a troop of tanks, the Carrier Platoon and the Battalion H.Q. personnel. It is probable that if they had been bold enough they could have reached the bridge under cover of darkness, but they halted half a mile short of it.

The situation remained confused during the night. No one knew where exactly was the enemy or in what strength. This prevented any attack being launched against them until next morning. Communications except by wireless between 8th Battalion H.Q. and the rifle companies were cut, and Lieut.-Colonel Oldman ordered everyone to stand firm until dawn, when the enemy who had infiltrated would be "seen off." The H.Q. personnel were formed into a battle patrol under Lieut. Cousins for the local protection of Battalion H.Q.

During the night the Germans sent up a number of parachute flares, and by the light of these the 88-millimetre gun on a Panther knocked out two Shermans which proceeded to blaze furiously. By the light of the fires, other German tanks which had moved up behind the 8th Battalion fired incendiary shells and solid shot at the houses round about. A section of men from the 6th Green Howards, obviously with no information as to the position, came up the road towards the enemy tanks. The Carrier men shouted to them but the advancing section did not hear because of the noise, and presently a high-explosive shell from the 88-millimetre gun exploded amongst them, obliterating almost all trace of the section.

The Carrier Platoon engaged the enemy tanks and infantry during the night without dislodging them. Towards morning a Sherman came slowly down the lane on the blind side of one of the Panthers until it was about a hundred and fifty yards away. The gunner took careful aim ; the first shot hit the turret and ricocheted off. He fired again quickly and missed. Meanwhile the big 88-millimetre gun on the Panther was traversing in the direction of the Sherman. The British gunner, who must have been sweating with anxiety behind his gun, fired again and just hit the back of the Panther, which burst into flames. The crew baled out and were shot or captured. About this time a party of Germans put in a silent attack which overran 17 Platoon of D Company, in position on the main road south-east of Stokt. There was confused fighting and when C.S.M. W. P. Brown went forward from Company H.Q. to find out what had happened, he was hit in the stomach by a burst of machine-gun fire and seriously wounded. No one ever found out what happened to 17 Platoon ; all the men were either killed or captured.

After a very cold night, dawn came with a heavy mist lying close to the ground. This prevented full counter measures being launched against the enemy as early as had been hoped. About 10 a.m. the Germans decided that their position was precarious and began to fall back. They tried to break out towards Gheel by way of C Company's area. Unfortunately it had not been possible to get anti-tank guns to C Company the previous night, and as luck would have it the first German tank passed across the rear of the company beyond the range of a Piat.

Enemy infantry now appeared and there was a brisk exchange of small arms fire. Shortly afterwards another tank passed in the same direction, some of the German infantry managing to scramble on to it. All the C Company weapons which could be brought to bear, fired at this excellent target, and the enemy was not slow to fire back. Presently what appeared to be another tank—it was later discovered to be a self-propelled gun literally covered with German infantry—came straight for C Company's Headquarters, but stopped about fifty yards from it. At once Sgt. J. K. Middleton, who was commanding a section of the Carrier Platoon, crawled about thirty yards with a Piat and with his first shot hit and knocked out the gun, killing ten Germans. Not content with this he then proceeded to machine-gun the remainder of the enemy infantry although he was outnumbered by at least thirty to one. The Germans were routed ; they turned and ran for it leaving their dead on the ground and also all their weapons. For this action and for his conduct during the remainder of the battle Sgt. Middleton was awarded the Military Medal. There were now a few odd parties of enemy running about the place, trying to get back to their own lines, and about twenty of these were taken prisoners by C Company. The company suffered three casualties, one of whom was Pte. W. Smith, Major Chambers' batman, who was hit in the shoulder. An old Territorial, Smith had been all through the war and was one of those rare individuals who never showed fear, no matter how bad the situation.

The German infiltration having been effectively dealt with the situation now quietened down, and companies were able to have the first hot meal for about thirty-six hours. The anti-tank gun lost when A company was dispersed by the German tanks the previous evening was recovered, though its carrier was burned out.

But if the German attempt to capture the bridge over the canal had failed, their efforts to drive the 6th D.L.I. out of Gheel had been more successful. The 6th D.L.I. had suffered heavy casualties from shelling and mortar fire and was now weak in numbers. Their forward positions were overrun, but they managed to retain a hold on the south-eastern part of the town. The Brigade Commander ordered that they be relieved by two companies of the 8th D.L.I.

At 5 p.m. B and D Companies moved up into Gheel to take over from the 6th D.L.I. Just before reaching the town 16 Platoon of D Company was surprised to see a section of Germans wander somewhat unconcernedly across the road about a hundred yards ahead. Pte. Holliday immediately dropped to the ground, fired two bursts from his Bren gun, and killed or wounded every man in the enemy section. By 10 p.m. B and D Companies had taken over from the 6th D.L.I., and the remainder of the 8th Battalion had moved up nearer to Gheel. One company of the 6th Green Howards was put under command and ordered to take up a position between D Company and the 9th D.L.I. on the right.

The enemy kept up incessant shelling of the area and also managed to infiltrate a number of snipers who worked themselves into positions where they were able to pick off several men of B and D Companies. The anti-tank gun detachment with these companies, commanded by Corporal A. Boyle, was sniped and also had grenades thrown at it. Boyle positioned his men in a house near the gun and very soon they had located a number of the German snipers, several of whom they killed or wounded. The determined and accurate shooting of Boyle's section forced the remainder of the enemy to withdraw. As a result of his energy and initiative Boyle had most effectively stopped an infiltration movement which might have resulted in serious consequences for the Battalion. During the heavy shelling Major English had been wounded when going round his company area ; Lieut. J. Swarbrick took over command of D Company. At about this time Cpl. Douglas of the Anti-Tank Platoon had a miraculous escape for he was hit by a mortar bomb which failed to explode. Apart from a large bruise on his shoulder, he was unhurt ; Douglas must be considered one of the luckiest men alive.

When Major English was wounded the C.O. ordered the Carrier Platoon forward to strengthen the B and D Company positions. He also sent Major Woodruffe, the Second-in-Command, to co-ordinate the defences. The heavy shelling continued and L/Cpl. Hall, the wireless operator in the C.O.'s jeep which Major Woodruffe was using, was badly wounded. When operating his set Hall was interested only in the message he was passing, seemingly oblivious of the enemy fire falling around him.

During the evening Captain O'Conor reappeared at Battalion H.Q., having been reported missing. He had an amazing story to tell about events after his capture. After being hurriedly questioned by a German officer he was placed in the charge of two young soldiers of the Air Force Division. They did not seem to have a very clear idea where they wanted to go, and after tramping across country for about an hour were hopelessly lost. They talked a lot about Gheel and asked O'Conor in bad French who was in the town. He, knowing the 6th D.L.I. were, replied that the Germans held it. They then ordered him to take them there. O'Conor had some idea of the way but the two Germans began to get suspicious. However, by pretending that south on the compass was north, they knowing no better, he managed to reassure them. Half-an-hour later they walked into a Sherman tank in Gheel. The tank opened fire and the two young Germans immediately bolted. O'Conor shouted to the tank and persuaded the crew he was British. He later saw one of his captors, a prisoner of the 6th D.L.I. O'Conor's escapade was not yet finished as he was told to report to Captain Wood's H.Q. This company of the 6th D.L.I. was surrounded in Gheel, and O'Conor was ordered to hold a corner of the town square with some 6th D.L.I. troops. It was not before he and his men had resisted five counter-attacks that the company was relieved and O'Conor able to rejoin the 8th D.L.I.

The rest of the night passed quietly but at about 8.30 a.m. on September 12th there were definite signs of an enemy counter-attack. The shell and mortar fire was intensified and small parties of infantry could be seen forming up. The groups of enemy were scattered by heavy and accurate artillery fire directed by Captain Pitt of the 74th Field Regiment, it being thickened up by the fire of the 3″ Mortars. Captain Hampson spotted an enemy observation post in the top of the church spire. He ran across to a Sherman tank to get the commander to shoot at it. The tank gunner hit the spire about half way up with an incendiary shell, and in a few seconds it was blazing merrily. The German shelling noticeably decreased after this, and although small parties of enemy managed to infiltrate into the town, they were quickly driven out again by B and D Companies.

During the morning news was received that the Battalion was to be relieved by the 6th Royal Scots Fusiliers of 15 Division, 12 Corps, and shortly afterwards their representatives reported to reconnoitre the area. The C Company positions were taken over in daylight, but the two forward companies in Gheel had to be relieved after dark. The men moved back over the Bailey Bridge, which had now been built, and were taken in troop-carrying lorries to the village of Pael. Next morning 15 Division attacked through Gheel but found the Germans had withdrawn, and they were able to close up to the Escaut Canal very quickly.

So ended the battle of Gheel. It had been a long drawn-out affair, in which the 8th Battalion had met some of the best German troops in the shape of the Parachute Regiment ; forty-seven prisoners had been taken and many enemy dead left on the field. The situation had often been confused, with small sub-units cut off and fighting on their own.

It was a battle which required great resource and initiative on the part of junior leaders. Casualties had not been light, particularly among officers ; but, as Brigadier Gordon explained a few days later, the Brigade had played a vital part in the Army plan and made possible the launching of subsequent operations.

CHAPTER THIRTY-ONE

NORTHWARDS TO ARNHEM

THREE pleasant but busy days were spent in the Pael area. There was much cleaning up and reorganisation to do. Reinforcements of five officers and twenty other ranks were posted to the Battalion; Major A. G. R. Noble was given command of C Company, and Lieuts. E. C. R. Frith, J. D. K. Ross and R. A. Morrison, who had arrived with him, were also sent to C Company as platoon commanders.

On September 17th the details of the Second Army plan for the next large-scale operation in the Western Europe campaign were given out to all ranks. Field-Marshal Montgomery's object was to "bounce" a crossing over the Rhine, isolate that vast industrial region of the Ruhr, then to penetrate deeply into the heart of the Reich. Between the present bridgehead over the Escaut Canal at Beeringen, which had been captured by the Guards Armoured Division, and the eastern bank of the Rhine were five major water obstacles—two canals, the River Maas at Grave, the Waal at Nijmegen and the Lower Rhine at Arnhem. The essential feature of the plan was the laying of a carpet of airborne troops across these waterways on the general axis of the main road running through Eindhoven, Veghel, Grave, Nijmegen and Arnhem. The airborne troops were to be provided by the Allied Airborne Corps consisting of 1 British, 82 and 101 American Airborne Divisions, together with the Polish Parachute Brigade.

Along the corridor established by the airborne divisions, 30 Corps was to advance to the Arnhem bridgehead. The right flank was to be protected and widened to the east by 8 Corps, while 12 Corps had a similar task on the left flank of the corridor. The Guards Armoured Division was to be the spearhead of the 30 Corps advance with 43 Division following up and 50 Division in Corps Reserve. The role of the infantry divisions in this operation was to take over the ground gained by the armour and to hold the flanks of the corridor secure against enemy attack.

The 50 Division advance was led by 231 Brigade while the D.L.I. Brigade was in reserve. In accordance with this plan the Durham battalions moved to Lommel, where on September 18th they took over positions in the Beeringen bridgehead from 231 Brigade, with the task of protecting the De Groote Barrier bridge over the Escaut Canal. During the first night in the new area the German Air Force made a determined attempt to smash the vital bridge. Twenty-five planes came over but most of their bombs fell on D Company, when L/Cpl. M. Duggan of the Anti-tank Platoon was killed. The bridge was undamaged.

The Battalion stayed in this area for five days. Most of the time things were fairly quiet except when a reconnaissance patrol from D Company ran into a German machine-gun post and the patrol leader, Lieut. Swarbrick, was killed. Although the leading formations of 30 Corps had advanced beyond Beeringen, isolated pockets of enemy resistance still held out in the area of the bridgehead which the D.L.I. battalions had taken over. Towards the end of the Battalion's stay in the Escaut positions further reinforcements of one officer and fifty-seven other ranks arrived, so A Company was now re-formed under the command of Major T. Paterson.

The advance northward continued on September 23rd and as the D.L.I. Brigade, together with the other infantry formations of 30 Corps, pressed forward along the corridor news came through that the airborne troops had been and were still engaged in heavy fighting. The main operation had only been partially successful ; the bridges at Veghel and Grave had been captured, also at Nijmegen, but only after a desperate battle which followed a gallant assault by troops of the Guards Armoured Division and 82 United States Airborne Division. Between Arnhem and Oosterbeek, where the position was rapidly becoming extremely grave, the British 1 Airborne Division was surrounded, fighting against heavy odds.

During the 23rd the 8th Battalion passed through Valkenswaard and beyond to Eindhoven, a very pleasant, clean town which greatly impressed everyone. Eindhoven was a tribute to the accuracy of the R.A.F. bombers ; the town itself was undamaged, but on the outskirts, the Philips radio factory—with its groups of gutted buildings—had been partially destroyed by the Lancasters and Halifaxes. On the 24th the Battalion moved north-eastwards a distance of 4 miles and deployed round the village of Nunen. Carriers from the 8th Battalion contacted elements of 61 Divisional Reconnaissance Regiment at Stiphout, and later in the day C Company occupied positions in the town. Next day foot patrols probed eastwards two miles to Helmond where a platoon of C Company took up positions.

Whilst the 8th Battalion was having a comparatively quiet time during September 24th the enemy succeeded in cutting the main 30 Corps axis for the second time since the start of operations by the Second Army and airborne forces to reach the Rhine. The corridor was now long and extremely narrow, being in parts little wider than the main road along which the Guards Armoured Division had passed. It was therefore a comparatively simple matter for the Germans to come in with small mobile forces to cut the road, and it was proportionately difficult, owing to the traffic congestion, for the British to move up additional troops to protect the flanks of the slender corridor. Consequently 50 Division in reserve was not involved in the heavy fighting which was taking place further to the north. The cutting of the lines of communication delayed the passage of supplies to the beleagured 1 Airborne Division at Arnhem.

The advance along the corridor was not continued until September 27th and on that day the Battalion moved just over twelve miles northwards to Volkel, a village near Veghel, a few miles east of the main road which was the corps axis. The whole area was littered with gliders of the American 82 Airborne Division who were in position on the Uden road. In the afternoon General Dempsey, the commander of the Second Army, was passing through the village when he stopped to speak to men of the Carrier Platoon. Captain Hampson expressed his concern at the exposed position of the British Airborne troops at Arnhem ; the General agreed and said he had been obliged to order their withdrawal. This took place on the night of the 25th/26th when two thousand four hundred men were safely brought back across the Rhine.

At Volkel Lieut. W. H. W. Jalland, the sole survivor of the rifle platoon commanders who had landed with the Battalion on D Day, was taken away to be preserved in the comparative safety of Brigade H.Q. That night a memorable party was held in the Officers' Mess. Those who were there will remember it chiefly for that remarkable song " Darling Daphne, don't say No," which was introduced and sung by Captain H. Crossley of the 74th Field Regiment.

The period of comparative peace and quiet was soon to come to an end. Before the Battalion left Volkel reinforcements of seven officers and thirty-four other ranks arrived ; for although the 8th D.L.I., together with the rest of 50 Division, had played only a minor part in the advance of 30 Corps to Arnhem, the Battalion was earmarked for a more active role in the consolidation and defence of the salient at Nijmegen which had recently been established at such heavy cost.

CHAPTER THIRTY-TWO

THE NIJMEGEN SALIENT

On to the "Island"—the capture of Haalderen—Sgt. Michael and the H.L.I.—life in the salient—patrolling—miserable living conditions —wild rumours confirmed—back to England.

THE Battalion received orders to move from Volkel on October 2nd to relieve the 6th D.C.L.I. of 43 Division in the bridgehead which had been established at Nijmegen. On arrival at Nijmegen the rifle companies debussed and waited to cross the now famous bridge. It was a magnificent structure, like a larger edition of the Tyne Bridge at Newcastle. No one stopped to examine it very carefully because one always had the feeling of being in the target area. The Germans had a heavy gun in the Reichwald Forest which shelled the bridge from time to time. It was about 17 miles away and since the British had no gun capable of firing so far, and the R.A.F. Typhoons could not locate it in the forest, the gun had not been put out of action. When the Canadian Military Police arrived they summed up most people's feelings about the bridge by putting up notices which said : " If you are going fast— go faster."

In the afternoon the Battalion moved over the bridge to the land lying between the river Waal and the Neder Rijn (Lower Rhine) which came to be known as the Nijmegen " Island," and there took over from the 6th D.C.L.I. who were occupying reserve positions. That night and the next day was quiet until the evening of October 3rd when the Battalion area was heavily shelled by medium artillery ; the Second-in-Command, Major Woodruffe, was one of those wounded.

Early next morning 50 Division was ordered to assault and capture the eastern edge of the village of Haalderen. The object of the attack was to enlarge the Nijmegen bridgehead to the east and at the same time to gain observation over the flat, open ground beyond Haalderen. 231 Brigade was to go into action first, on the left, followed at 2 p.m. by 151 Brigade, with the 8th D.L.I. on the right and the 9th on the left. The attack was to be supported by a barrage moving one hundred yards in five minutes. Lieut.-Colonel Oldman's plan was to have two companies forward, A Company right and C Company left, with B and D Companies in reserve. The Carrier and Anti-Tank Platoons were to be called up when the rifle companies had reached their objectives.

Shortly before the D.L.I. battalions commenced the advance, news came through that the attack by 231 Brigade was going well. Promptly at 2 p.m. the 8th Battalion moved forward in extended order over ground which had been cultivated in small plots, and through numerous orchards. There was the deafening roar of low-flying aircraft as R.A.F. Typhoons swooped down to attack the German defensive positions with rocket fire. This close support by the planes was devastating; the screech of the rockets terrified the Germans.

Things were going well on the right flank of the Battalion advance where A Company, keeping within a hundred yards of the barrage, dealt quickly with all opposition. Sgt. W. Higginson, with long battle experience, distinguished himself in this action and captured several prisoners, at the same time setting a fine example to the newly joined young reinforcements in the company. On the left flank, however, C Company was not doing so well. The company had very few experienced men left and the advancing platoons faltered under the enemy fire. C Company suffered several casualties and D Company was ordered to move up to take over the C Company responsibility. This was an unenviable task for D Company as by this time the barrage was well ahead but the platoons advanced quickly. By 5.30 p.m. all the Battalion objectives had been taken and the men started to dig in.

In spite of the hold-up on the C Company front the attack had been a most successful one; in fact those officers and men who had been with the 8th all through the war described it as the easiest ever carried out by the Battalion. Twenty Germans had been killed by the rifle companies, another sixty taken prisoner. The Battalion had not suffered heavily in relation to its gains; thirty-nine other ranks and one officer—Lieut. Frith—had been wounded. Unfortunately, in the evening, Major Riley—B Company Commander—was killed by a shell when standing outside his H.Q. in Haalderen village. Riley had joined the Battalion after the battle of Le Plessis Grimault and in a short time had proved himself a very able company commander.

The next two days were very quiet except for intermittent shelling. Patrols were sent out by the Battalion, including a successful reconnaissance patrol under Sgt. D. D. Michael of A Company which obtained some valuable information. Michael, one of the old hands, was not content just to sit back and wait for the enemy to do something. Several times he went out on his own initiative and soon had an intimate knowledge of the area. This was invaluable when the 6th H.L.I. of 52 Division attempted to establish a position forward of Haalderen. One of the companies ran into difficulties and did not reach its objective. The company returned somewhat shamefaced to the village where Sgt. Michael, having already been to the H.L.I. objective, offered to guide the company commander and his men to the area. The H.L.I. officer accepted and Michael led the company out of Haalderen and on to the objective.

The 8th Battalion was relieved during daylight on October 7th by a battalion of 53 Division. The relief took place without interference, except that A Company—under observation from the enemy—was shelled during the change-over and Sgt. Wood's anti-tank gun could not be brought out until after dark. The companies marched back independently to the Colonial Barracks at Nijmegen where one night was spent. Next day the Battalion moved into a school which proved to be a very comfortable billet. Further reinforcements arrived and one of them, Major J. W. D. Armstrong, took command of B Company.

The next four days in Nijmegen were a welcome change from the "Island." The troops were able to soak off the accumulated dirt of weeks in steaming hot baths. Cinema and E.N.S.A. shows were arranged, and in the welcome, quiet atmosphere of the school billets—when there was not work to do or kit inspections to attend—the men were able to write home and do the dozens of odd jobs which always seem to get postponed "until tomorrow" in the front line. About this time the Battalion received its share of a large enemy dump of wines and spirits which had been captured by troops of 30 Corps and distributed to units by order of General Horrocks.

For the formations of the Second Army engaged in the defence of the Nijmegen salient October was the beginning of a long, static period, when units spent ten days or so in the line followed by three days rest either in Nijmegen or in Divisional Reserve at Elst. The period which the 8th Battalion spent out of the line was all too short ; on October 12th the Battalion moved back on to the "Island" to relieve the 1st Hampshires in the village of Aam, east of Elst.

The flat, marshy country in which the Battalion found itself was typical of the sectors on the island held by 50 Division and other formations of the Second Army. The majority of the few large villages and scattered farmsteads had already been reduced to ruins by the fighting, which meant that the troops had to "rough it" in the open. The Battalions who garrisoned that desolate salient during the winter of 1944 will long remember the weather and uncomfortable living conditions. The whole area was intersected by dykes which, having received no attention since the fighting started, were blocked in places by dead cattle. The country being flat, the rain lay where it fell and soon the dykes had filled to overflowing. In the autumn the orchards on the Island had provided some cover from enemy observation but when the first winds of winter stripped the trees of their leaves the German guns increased their activity. Men caught out in the open had to decide quickly whether an approaching shell would land close enough to make it imperative to jump into several feet of water in the nearest ditch, or whether they could take a chance and merely press themselves flat in a foot of squelching mud. However, the flat nature of the country did have its compensations, for the Mortar Platoon could see their enemy. This was a welcome change after the shooting off the map they had been obliged to resort to in Normandy.

During the static period on the Island there were several enemy attempts to drive in the Nijmegen salient, so that the units in the front line had to be continually on the alert. When the 8th Battalion was holding the forward positions vigorous patrolling was carried out. The majority were reconnaissance patrols ; the few fighting patrols did not meet with much success. Conditions for patrolling were far from ideal as the men had to carry ladders or planks with which to span the ditches, making as little noise as possible. These ladders made movement very difficult, and whilst patrolling had always been a nerve-racking, unpleasant job, it now became doubly so.

One patrol was sent out on the Battalion front with the task of finding out if a certain farmhouse, used as an observation post by the enemy during the day, was occupied at night. If the patrol found the farmhouse empty it was to lay mines and booby traps which would be set off by the unsuspecting enemy next day. When the 8th Battalion men reached the farmhouse it was to find that the enemy held it in strength. There was a sharp and noisy engagement during which two Germans were killed before the Battalion patrol had to withdraw.

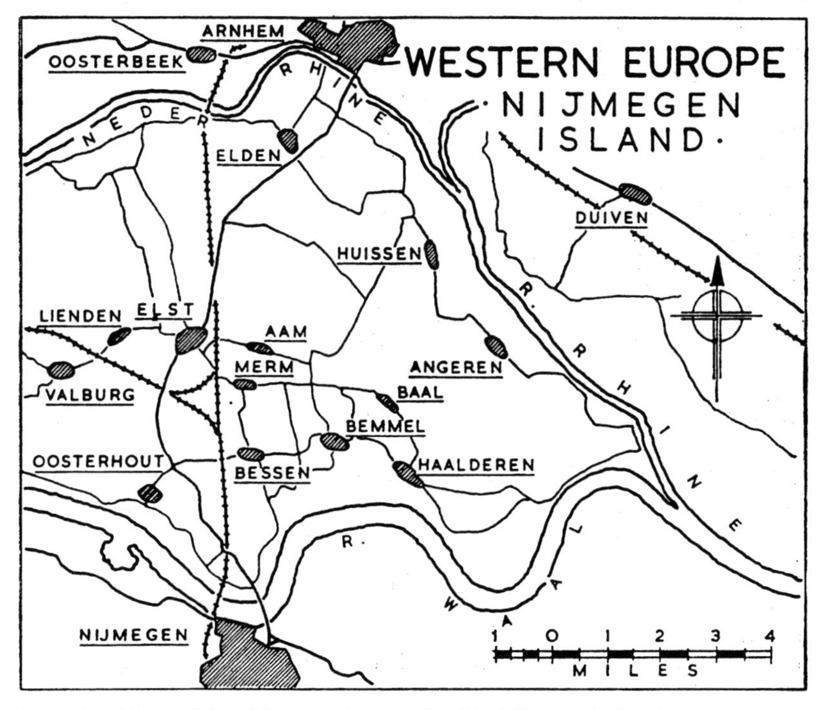

WESTERN EUROPE. The last days of the Battalion with the Second Army in Western Europe were spent on the Nijmegen " Island." During this period, which was static, the Battalion occupied several different front line positions north of Nijmegen and the River Waal.

Another reconnaissance patrol was sent out on a similar errand to find out if the enemy had a listening post in an orchard which lay in No Man's Land. The Battalion patrol approached the orchard warily ; at the same time a German patrol, probably briefed to find out whether British troops had a listening post in the orchard at night, crept towards the orchard from the enemy side. Inevitably the two patrols met and the D.L.I. troops, recovering from their surprise more quickly than the Germans, opened fire and forced the enemy to withdraw.

As the month of October drew to a close the weather became more cold and wet with every day, and living conditions for the troops were thoroughly miserable. The Germans could not have fared much better and at least both sides had a common enemy—the weather. Nevertheless, the war had to go on and the Higher Command decided that they wanted an identification Accordingly C Company of the 8th Battalion was ordered to carry out a raid on the night of October 26th/27th against enemy positions in the northern part of the "Island," in the area of the blown bridges over the Rhine, south of Arnhem. At this point the enemy occupied the very high railway embankment. It was planned that the British artillery would put down a concentration of fire on the embankment for ten minutes, then lift and engage known enemy positions elsewhere. This was to be the signal for C Company to rush over the embankment and pick up any live enemy encountered, or take every means of identification such as pay books from any dead bodies found. The company was then to return as quickly as possible. The whole operation was put under the command of Major H. N. Hopkins who had only recently arrived as Second-in-Command to replace Major Woodruffe. The raid started from the position held by 61 (Divisional) Reconnaissance Regiment, and when the artillery lifted from the railway line C Company scrambled over the top of the embankment and combed the area beyond. They did not find a single German, either alive or dead, so the company returned empty handed.

The 8th Battalion was relieved in the forward area on several occasions and moved back to Nijmegen or Elst for three days' rest. Actually, Nijmegen was not very popular because one had to run the gauntlet of enemy fire on the bridge in order to get there ; the heavy gun in the Reichswald had still not been put out of action. For the officers these rest periods, wherever they were, meant a lot of extra work. Stores, weapons and kit had to be checked ; baths, cinema and E.N.S.A. shows arranged.

The Divisional Commander and his Administrative Officer, Lieut.-Colonel T. Black, took a great deal of trouble to see that 50 Division had a very good share of whatever amenities were available, and the fact that the troops were so well looked after out of the line did much to raise morale. For the first time during the Western Europe campaign football and hockey matches were played, and during one visit to Nijmegen the Brigade had the services of the Durham Light Infantry Band, which had been sent out from the Regimental Depot at Brancepeth to tour the B.L.A. A Brigade church service was held in the Winter Gardens where the troops sang hymns to the accompaniment of the band. Afterwards the three Durham battalions marched past the Divisional Commander, who took the salute.

On the "Island" the living conditions became so unpleasant that it was necessary to arrange something in addition to three days out of the line every ten days. A regular system was instituted of sending several men from each company back to B Echelon for thirty-six hours, where they were able to get hot baths and a complete change of clothing ; also, a room was taken in a house so that the men could have a thorough rest. Leave parties, composed of men from the "Island", went into Brussels or Antwerp where 30 Corps had established Rest Camps and N.A.A.F.I. had taken over hotels to accommodate troops on leave. These hotels were extremely well run and the men who visited them had a very good time amidst pleasant surroundings, in spite of the flying bombs which arrived every few hours.

As the weeks passed, the routine of a period in the line with all its unpleasantness and discomfort followed by a short but welcome rest continued. During October and November many different defensive localities on the "Island" were occupied by the Battalion. The main burden during these weeks fell to the rifle companies. For them movement by day was restricted owing to lack of cover ; any undue activity inevitably brought down mortar and shellfire which often caused casualties, but the British guns and mortars were very active and sent back much more than was received. Meanwhile the patrolling continued and every night valuable information was obtained.

During November it became known that the enemy could flood the whole "Island" to a depth of several feet by blowing up the banks of the Lower Rhine. Therefore it was thought advisable to be prepared, so plans were made for Operation Noah should the enemy take this step. Civilians were evacuated from certain areas and houses were earmarked to which troops could be moved. Although these plans were never put into operation they were made use of in a modified form. Rain fell heavily during November, and the dykes, slit trenches and dugouts were soon waterlogged. Living conditions became most uncomfortable, so as many men as possible were put into houses and barns.

Towards the end of November, when the 8th had spent almost eight weeks in the Nijmegen area, rumours started to circulate in 50 Division—some of them to the effect that the whole Division was going back to England. To the handful of officers and men who had come safely through so much fighting with the 8th D.L.I. and who were beginning to wonder just how much longer their luck would last, these rumours seemed almost too good to be true. Nevertheless, they were confirmed when company commanders were ordered to prepare nominal roles according to four categories ; men who could be posted to other units immediately as riflemen, men requiring further training in infantry work, those for return to the United Kingdom with the Battalion, and finally, men suitable for garrison duties.

The news that the Division was to become a Home Service Division came as a great surprise to the majority but there were those who felt that perhaps 50 Division as a formation had at last reached a stage which, at some time or other, had been experienced by every fighting soldier in the Division. A man can stand so much but there comes a time when his own intuition tells him that unless something happens to halt or at least slow down the tempo of fighting against a ruthless and determined enemy, he will surely break under the strain.

The official explanation of the withdrawal of 50 Division from the front line was that owing to the urgent need for well trained infantry reinforcements, it had been decided to send the Division back to England to train personnel of other arms as infantrymen. To 50 Division as a formation it was a sad blow and a bitter disappointment ; it meant that this great division, which had been in the forefront of the fighting for two and a half years, would not be able to take part in the last battle to end the war in Europe. It also meant that, by splitting the men of the Division into four categories, only a very limited number could return with their units to England. This was probably the saddest aspect of what was, for all practical purposes, the disbandment of 50 Division. In the 8th D.L.I. a large number of men who had served the Battalion well for many months had to be sent to other units or to garrison duties in various parts of the B.L.A. The same thing applied in other units of the Division.

On November 30th the 2nd Gloucesters of 49 Division took over from the Battalion on the Island and the 8th moved back across the bridge into Nijmegen for the last time. The following day the Battalion was taken in M.T. to Oostvleteren in Belgium with the exception of S Company which went to Woesten, where the 8th had fought a sharp and difficult rearguard action during the B.E.F. campaign of 1940.

On December 8th Field-Marshal Montgomery visited the Battalion to decorate a number of N.C.Os. for conspicuous bravery in action. Afterwards, the man who in Sicily had said, " Wherever I go, I will send for my 50th Division," spoke to the Battalion and explained why, much to his regret, he had been obliged to order the Division back to England where it had a vitally important job of work to do.

In the days that followed the Army Group Commander's visit there were many farewells as gradually the strength of the Battalion was reduced, and the great comradeship and *esprit de corps* which had characterised the 8th was dispersed. The old spirit was to be carried on in England by those who returned with the Battalion but many felt the loss of good friends who were not among the lucky few.

On December 14th the 8th Battalion, now little more than a cadre started the journey back to England. Troop-carriers took the Battalion through Poperinghe to Ostende where the 8th embarked on H.M.S. *Queen Emma*. The following day the men with the Durham flash on their battledress sleeves marched down the gangway on to Southampton docks. It was the end of a journey which had started with the mighty invasion fleet from the same place on June 3rd and taken the 8th D.L.I. through six months of campaigning, during which time many successful battles had been fought for the liberation of Europe.

CHAPTER-THIRTY THREE

THE END OF THE ROAD

The first wartime Christmas at home—the old soldiers settle down—hard work training others—grand hospitality in Keighley—Uniacke Camp, Harrogate—another excellent Christmas—the 8th Battalion is disbanded.

THE day after disembarking at Southampton the 8th Battalion cadre arrived at Keighley in Yorkshire, the journey having taken just over twelve hours. The dozen or so officers and a hundred other ranks came with the dawn—at 5-45 a.m. At this stage of the war no one ever expected to arrive anywhere with the Army at a reasonable hour, even in England. On December 18th a week's leave commenced and for the first time since the outbreak of war the whole of the 8th Battalion, though a considerably depleted unit, spent Christmas at home. The seven days leave passed all too quickly and the officers and men returned to their new task of training drafts from other arms of the service as infantry. The Battalion was still commanded by Lieut.-Colonel H. Oldman.

The majority of the 8th Battalion cadre which returned to England were either pre-war Territorials or men who had joined the Battalion with the K.O.S.B. draft in December 1939. They had served continuously with the 8th throughout the war, and whereas others had left the Battalion for various reasons these "regulars" had hardly missed an action. This in itself is a record of which they can all feel justly proud. Their names are well known to all connected with the Battalion : Major Chambers and Captain Stray ; R.Q.M.S. Lightfoot and C.S.M. Cairns ; Sgts. Birbeck, Carter, Churcher, Burnhope, Swallow and Thompson ; Cpls. Carter, Miller and Wood ; Ptes. Bilton, Leeming, Nicholson, Newton, Nattrass, Openshaw and Richardson. If any names have been omitted from this list, it has not been intentional.

Whilst the 8th had been on leave a number of officer and N.C.O. instructors had arrived in Keighley ; the N.C.Os. came from various Infantry Training Centres and most of them had spent long periods overseas or were of low medical category. With this welcome addition the 8th settled down and prepared to receive a draft of six hundred R.A.S.C. men. There were training areas to visit, schemes to organise, field-firing and indoor ranges to construct. It was hard work and the old members of the 8th D.L.I. found it difficult to reconcile themselves to soldiering in England after being abroad for so long. It was not possible to get things done as quickly at home as it had been abroad, and the Battalion soon found itself tied and restricted by the usual red tape.

The 8th was organised into five companies—A,B,C,D and E. The sixth company consisted chiefly of N.C.Os. and potential N.C.Os. from the whole of 151 Brigade. When the R.A.S.C. men arrived most of them disliked the idea of becoming infantry but after a while they settled down and took a keen interest in their new training. However, a number of them were completely useless, from a medical point of view and in fact from any other point of view. Some of the R.A.S.C. units had grasped this opportunity of getting rid of their " bad hats ", and at least one draft had obviously been " hand picked." The Battalion had more trouble in the town of Keighley with a number of these men than at any time during the campaigns overseas. Fortunately the people of Keighley did not condemn the whole Battalion because of the behaviour of a few and looked after the 8th D.L.I. extremely well. They did everything possible, as the people in Oxfordshire and at Haverhill had done before them, to extend a welcome.

In January the programme consisted chiefly of weapon training and drill. As the work became more advanced the men fired all the platoon weapons, and an obstacle course was constructed as well as snap-shooting, Sten and rifle ranges. There were lectures and discussions and a certain amount of night work. The Battalion was visited by the Divisional Commander and, more frequently, by the Brigade Commander, and on one occasion the Commander-in-Chief Home Forces saw all the companies at various stages of training. As the work continued, a marked improvement in the men's morale was noticed. In February the R.A.S.C. men were taught fieldcraft—a most important subject to infantrymen—and then all companies were put through a battle-innoculation course which was made as realistic as possible. Machine-gun fire directed a few inches above the men's heads, and electrically-detonated charges gave them some idea of the sterner things to come.

The trainees then went to Hull where they took part in an intensive twenty-four hour street fighting course. They also went out on to Ilkley and Harden Moors where some of the things learned during the past few weeks could be put into practice. Rain and wind on the inhospitable Yorkshire moors could very easily have upset the training programmes, but the energy with which the instructors went about their job and the realistic nature of the exercises had the effect of keeping the men interested and the training standard at a high level. Unfortunately there was a fatal accident during February when Major J. W. D. Armstrong, a company commander who had joined the Battalion in Western Europe, was fatally wounded during training on Ilkley Moor.

By the middle of March the training was well advanced and all the trainees had been sent on embarkation leave. It had been hard work for instructors as well as trainees and the other side of the picture was one of well earned relaxation and the remarkable hospitality of the people of Keighley. The old hands in the Battalion, and none knew better than they, said that the town was the best of the many

Battalion billeting areas. The Yorkshire people had an amazing capacity for entertaining, and trying to keep pace with the Keighley hospitality was almost in the nature of a campaign. In fact a Keighley Star was suggested for those who were able to cope with the late hours, hearty meals and hectic parties in which the townspeople excelled. Needless to say there would have been a considerable number of applicants for the Star.

When the men returned from leave they took part in several company exercises. These were followed by a 48 hour exercise, and then on April 19th three hundred trainees were drafted to No. 1 Mobilisation Centre. The Battalion had completed its first job of work as a training battalion, and the instructors were satisfied that they had turned out reasonably good infantrymen. The next draft was made up of young soldiers who had just finished their primary training. They were good material, behaved themselves well, and the Battalion had a comparatively easy task turning them into infantry reinforcements. Before the end of April more than three hundred trainees had started a course, similar to that for the R.A.S.C. men, which continued throughout May and June. During July several drafts were despatched overseas and the Battalion found itself spending less time on the training of drafts and more on preparing and equipping them for overseas. There were now so few trainees that the programmes were reduced considerably and a great deal of cricket was played—with very creditable results. The 8th D.L.I. was gradually becoming more of a drafting battalion than a training unit.

Perhaps the most memorable date in August was the 15th—V.J. Day. It was now eight months since the 8th had left the Nijmegen salient. A great deal had happened in that time, and whilst the Battalion had been working hard at Keighley to turn out infantrymen the Allied armies in Western Europe and in the Far East had administered the *coup de grace*.

At the end of the month Lieut.-Colonel Oldman relinquished command of the Battalion which was then taken over by Lieut.-Colonel C. R. Battiscombe, an old friend of the 8th D.L.I. He had commanded the 6th D.L.I. in the desert until his capture when leading the attack of the D.L.I. composite battalion at Alamein. The days of the 8th were now drawing to a close and it seemed fitting in many ways that the Battalion should be commanded for the last few months by an officer so closely associated with the unit. The Battalion was also pleased to welcome back several officers who had been wounded or taken prisoner of war including Captain R. I. Pitt, captured with Lieut.-Colonel Battiscombe at Alamein, Major I. R. English, at Gheel, and Captain P. J. Lewis, wounded and taken prisoner at Primosole bridge. Since his capture in August 1942, Pitt had made several unsuccessful attempts to escape and was a constant source of worry to his captors. When he was moved to Germany after the Italian armistice Pitt escaped from a camp at Strasbourg and after six days freedom reached the French frontier, where he had the misfortune to ask directions from a civilian who turned out to be the local Gestapo chief. Captain Lewis, after three months in an Italian prison hospital, had escaped from a train on the way to Germany. He hid for several months in Italy, then crossed the mountains into Switzerland where he was interned together with several thousand other members of the Allied air forces and armies.

Training on a reduced scale was continued during September, and at the end of the month the Battalion heard that it was to leave Keighley. This was bad news and the men of the 8th started to plan farewell parties which would express their gratitude for the way in which the townspeople had looked after the Battalion. On October 1st an all-ranks dance was held in the Mechanics Institute ; it was a most successful dance, as were those organised by the Officers' and Sergeants' Messes. The people of Keighley could have been left in no doubt about the Battalion's feelings for that grand Yorkshire town.

In the middle of October the Battalion moved to Uniacke Camp, outside Harrogate, which was to be shared with the Royal Corps of Signals. This excellent hutted camp was built for the 1939 Militia and from the accommodation point of view could not have been better but the cheerless camp atmosphere was an unwelcome change from Keighley. Uniacke Camp was some distance from Harrogate, an admirable town in many ways but lacking the honest-to-goodness welcome of Keighley. Perhaps it was because the Battalion was not actually living in the town, but whatever Harrogate had to offer apart from its famous baths, was not made available to the Battalion on the same scale as had been the amenities of Keighley. However, on the opposite side of the road was Hildebrand Camp, occupied by the A.T.S., and this was some consolation for being stationed at Uniacke.

The main event of the month was on the 26th when a Guard of Honour was provided by two officers and twenty-five other ranks from each of the 6th and 8th Battalions for Field-Marshal Montgomery when he received the Freedom of Huddersfield. Major English, who had recently received well-deserved promotion to Battalion Second-in-Command, commanded the Guard which was largely made up of men who had been with the two battalions for several years and taken part in most of the battles in which the D.L.I. Brigade had been engaged. It was a wet, stormy day and there was a minor hitch when the Field-Marshal arrived ten minutes early without the Mayor of Huddersfield, having missed him on the outskirts of the town. Fortunately the Guard of Honour had already formed up, and the Field-Marshal carried out his inspection without the Mayor. After walking slowly along the ranks he spoke to the men who had fought under his command in North Africa, Sicily and Western Europe. They knew he was sincere when he said it was a grand sight for him to see there men who had been everywhere with him. Some of them were with the 8th in 1940 when Montgomery, then the commander of 5 Corps, had inspected the Battalion on coastal defence. They had travelled far since then and for most of the time under his brilliant leadership. It was a proud day for them in Huddersfield.

When Major-General D. M. Wimberley, D.S.O., M.C., Director of Infantry, visited the Battalion early in November to discuss training and trainees he told the remaining officers that the 8th D.L.I. would probably be going into suspended animation early in 1946. Throughout November and December training was continued, but it was not an easy task because each week the strength of the Battalion was reduced as members of the permanent staff, including many of the veteran members of the Battalion, were released. Most of the time was spent in preparing and equipping drafts for posting overseas. Nevertheless there was still work to be done and in mid-December Captain Lewis, with all the available officers and men in the Battalion, spent three cheerless days on Ovenden and Warley Moors searching for unexploded mortar bombs and grenades which had been used in exercises when the Battalion was at Keighley. Covering every inch of ground on two windswept moors was not exactly amusing, but there was a typical Yorkshire stone-built inn which apparently had no closing hours and consequently made the daily trip to the moors less of a penance.

On December 18th the C.O. went on leave and Major English took over temporary command of the Battalion. The final touches were put to the preparations for Christmas, and on December 24th the festivities commenced. There was an all-in Rugger game in the morning with H.Q. Company playing a combined team from B and F Companies ; it was a real free-for-all with no definite score. This was followed by a Battalion dance in the evening, organised by Lieut. E. Y. Cousins, which was excellent in every way and probably one of the best ever run by the Battalion. Refreshments were free, and Lieut. Bark consumed several pints of beer in quick succession, being under the impression that beer was free as well, until the news was gently broken to him that refreshments only included tea and cakes. The Padre, Captain G. Markham, visited the cinema during the evening and likened the dance to Dante's Inferno with "little groups of sinners sitting in corners, drinking and telling the old, old story to the A.T.S. from over the way." This most successful evening was a fitting closing celebration for the 8th Battalion and when the end came just after midnight everyone was sorry.

On Christmas Day the officers acted as waiters for the troops left behind in Uniacke and served a Christmas Dinner of turkey, roast pork, baked potatoes, Christmas pudding, mince pies, apples and oranges, chocolate—and free beer. Lieut.-Colonel Battiscombe had promised the troops who could not go home on leave, " the best time we can give you," and he certainly kept his word. The Christmas festivities were excellent in every way. The A.T.S., the Royal Corps of Signals personnel, and the Battalion entered right into the spirit of the holiday and competed with each other to provide the best entertainment.

Early in the New Year postings for many of the troops were coming in fast and by January 7th all the trainees had left the Battalion. Only the permanent staff remained under Lieut.-Colonel Battiscombe and a few officers. It fell to them to complete arrangements for closing down the Battalion by the 16th.

By this time there were very few veteran members of the 8th D.L.I. who had not been posted away or released from service during the past few weeks. Those who remained were proud to be with the Battalion at the end of the long, hard road which had covered thousands of miles and taken five years to travel. Most of them left the week-end before the 16th, and during their last few days at Uniacke Camp—with the majority of the barrack rooms deserted and the Officers' and Sergeants' Messes only partly occupied—there were more than a few who felt sadness at the breaking up of the 8th Battalion.

Today, in all parts of the British Isles and also abroad there are men who can look back over the years and reminisce about the greatness which was the 8th Battalion's during the Second World War, for of the three battalions in 151 Brigade none can feel prouder of its achievements. From the Battle of France in 1940 until the Nijmegen Salient in 1944 the Battalion had always been in the forefront of the fighting with 50 Division, and had built up a fine fighting record. Blessed always with the best of Commanding Officers and strong in the loyalty and steadfastness of its officers and men, the Battalion was the military equivalent of a " Happy Ship ". A man who can say in the years to come : " I fought with the 8th D.L.I." can do so with pride, for he is one of those who can look back on a fine job of work, well and truly done.

APPENDIX A

Roll of Honour

Every possible care has been taken to ensure that the details given below are accurate, but owing to lack of information in some cases, it is possible that there have been errors and omissions.

Abbott, R.	4459080	Pte.	Killed in action	Sicily	11.8.43
Ades, J.	6412537	Pte.	Killed in action	Western Europe	26.7.44
Alder, J.	4539583	Pte.	Killed in action	Western Europe	12.6.44
Allardice, D. W.	162336	Lieut.	Killed in action	Middle East	2.11.44
Allen, J. B.	14429619	Pte.	Killed in action	Western Europe	9.9.44
Allen, S. G. E.	14677484	Pte.	Killed in action	Western Europe	11.7.44
Ambrosino, A.	5675938	L/Cpl.	Killed in action	Western Europe	9.9.44
Apps, A. P.	4386185	Pte.	Killed in action	Italy	23.9.43
Archer, J. A.	4452014	L/Cpl.	Killed in action	Middle East	12.6.42
Armstrong, J. W. D.		Major	Killed on active service	United Kingdom	22.2.45
Arthurs, E.	14600537	Pte.	Killed in action	Western Europe	9.10.44
Ashbridge, T. S.	3607522	Pte.	Killed in action	Western Europe	11.9.44
Atherton, J.	4458994	Pte.	Died as a P.O.W.	Italy	8.10.44
Athey, C.	4457373	Pte.	Killed in action	Western Europe	9.9.44
Austin, R. R.	4452687	Pte.	Killed in action	Western Europe	23.11.44
Axam, F. C.	4031884	Pte.	Killed in action	Middle East	2.11.42
Bailey, A.	14286736	Pte.	Killed in action	Italy	17.1.44
Bailey, E. G. T.	3913877	Pte.	Died of Wounds	Middle East	17.7.43
Bailey, V. T.	259389	Lieut.	Killed in action	Middle East	21.3.43
Ball, J.	4461236	Pte.	Killed in action	Western Europe	19.6.44
Balmforth, E.	4464898	Pte.	Killed in action	Middle East	2.11.42
Bampton, S. L.	14432844	Pte.	Killed in action	Western Europe	9.9.44
Banks, J.	14429036	Pte.	Killed in action	Western Europe	21.7.44
Barbour, A.	3133790	Pte.	Killed in action	Middle East	2.11.42
Barefield, H. J.	5255209	Cpl.	Killed in action	Western Europe	1.8.44
Barnfather, F.	4443439	L/Cpl.	Died as a P.O.W.	Italy	2.12.43
Barraclough, J. T.	4461239	Pte.	Died of Wounds	Middle East	22.3.43
Barron, S. W.	4455454	C/Sgt.	Killed in action	Western Europe	20.6.44
Bateman, A. J.	14356397	Pte.	Killed in action	Western Europe	16.10.44
Bates, F.	4452336	Pte.	Died of Wounds	B.E.F. Campaign	21.5.40
Beal, H.	14398596	Pte.	Killed in action	Western Europe	11.6.44
Beattie, C. L., M.C.	75176	Major	Died of Wounds	Western Europe	9.9.44
Bell, W.	4458226	Pte.	Died of Wounds	Sicily	20.7.43
Beresford, F.	4467446	Pte.	Died of Wounds	Sicily	19.7.43
Berry, A.	3606222	Pte.	Died of Wounds	Western Europe	14.9.44
Betts, G.	4461243	Pte.	Killed in action	Middle East	2.11.42
Bishop, I.C.	5435838	L/Cpl.	Killed in action	Western Europe	4.10.44
Blackman, E. E.	5493059	L/Cpl.	Killed in action	Western Europe	4.10.44
Bolton, T. W.	4454732	L/Cpl.	Killed in action	Middle East	6.11.42
Bookless, G.	4627495	Pte.	Killed in action	Western Europe	17.11.44
Booth, R.	4458223	Pte.	Killed in action	B.E.F. Campaign	30.5.40
Bower, P. H.	76949	Capt.	Killed in action	Middle East	15.6.42
Bowman, T.	4452609	Pte.	Killed in action	B.E.F. Campaign	25.5.40
Bradford, W. T.	5389701	Pte.	Killed in action	Western Europe	9.8.44
Brannigan, M. J., M.M.	4449955	C.S.M.	Killed in action	Sicily	17.7.43

Briggs, H. B.	4461250	Pte.	Died of Wounds	Middle East	20.3.43
Broddel, T.	11424059	Pte.	Killed in action	Western Europe	19.6.44
Brown, R. H.	4455472	Cpl.	Killed in action	Middle East	12.6.42
Brown, T.	4456108	Pte.	Killed in action	B.E.F. Campaign	21.5.40
Buckfield, H. L.	6150802	Pte.	Killed in action	North Africa	5.8.43
Bulman, F. G.	164873	Lieut.	Died on active Service	United Kingdom	26.5.44
Burn, N.	4457384	Pte.	Died as a P.O.W.	Middle East	14.11.42
Burnett, D. H.	3191129	Pte.	Killed in action	Sicily	17.7.43
Burnside, J. T.	4538363	Pte.	Died of Wounds	B.E.F. Campaign	24.5.40
Burrows, G. K.	5443745	Cpl.	Killed in action	Western Europe	26.7.44
Burrup, S.	4470030	Pte.	Killed in action	Middle East	22.3.43
Burton, A. D.	982327	L/Cpl.	Killed in action	Western Europe	20.7.44
Burton, E.	4459083	Pte.	Died as a P.O.W.	Italy	14.11.42
Butler, M.	4270559	Sgt.	Killed in action	Western Europe	4.10.44
Butt, G. R.	4202204	Pte.	Killed in action	Sicily	18.7.43
Butterfield, A.	4449664	Pte.	Killed in action	Western Europe	30.7.44
Byrom, A. B.	4462393	Pte.	Killed in action	Western Europe	10.6.44
Cairns, G. T.	4459299	Pte.	Died of Wounds	Sicily	14.8.43
Calvert, W. M.	4470279	Pte.	Killed in action	Western Europe	4.10.44
Cantlay, J. A.	138526	Lieut.	Killed in action	Middle East	2.11.42
Carr, J. G.	3191134	Pte.	Died as a P.O.W.	Germany	7.4.45
Carr, J.	4458586	Sgt.	Killed in action	Sicily	17.7.43
Carr, R. R.	14379189	Pte.	Killed in action	Western Europe	11.8.44
Carse, H.	4451851	Pte.	Killed in action	B.E.F. Campaign	22.5.40
Carter, S.	5443102	Cpl.	Killed in action	Western Europe	24.7.44
Cartner, J. R.	3191135	Pte.	Killed in action	B.E.F. Campaign	31.5.40
Cautlon, G. A.	14681491	Pte.	Killed in action	Western Europe	11.6.44
Cavanagh, W.	4455679	Pte.	Died as a P.O.W.	Middle East	14.11.42
Challinor, L. G. S.	4134165	Pte.	Killed in action	Western Europe	11.6.44
Chappelow, W. J.	4462237	Pte.	Died on active Service	North Africa	12.10.43
Chelwick, F. T.	4032726	L/Cpl.	Killed in action	Sicily	3.8.43
Clapton, T. L. A.	509721	Major	Died of Wounds	Western Europe	12.6.44
Clark, N. W.	4462290	Pte.	Killed in action	Middle East	28.6.42
Clarke, F.		Lieut.	Killed in action	Sicily	17.7.43
Clarke, T.	4462291	Pte.	Killed in action	Sicily	17.7.43
Claye, D. H.	117991	Capt.	Died as a P.O.W.	Germany	23.9.44
Clayton, S. H.	4462065	Pte.	Died as a P.O.W.	Middle East	29.11.42
Clazey, F. O.	126486	Capt.	Killed in action	Western Europe	4.11.44
Clements, G. D.	3970430	Pte.	Died of Wounds	Middle East	2.4.43
Cloughton, S.	4457392	Pte.	Killed in action	Middle East	22.3.43
Clutton, H.	4193346	Cpl.	Killed in action	Sicily	17.7.43
Colledge, J.	4616675	Pte.	Died of Wounds	Western Europe	12.6.44
Connor, E. L.	3767326	Pte.	Killed in action	Western Europe	19.6.44
Conyers, R. A.	4626936	L/Cpl.	Killed in action	Sicily	18.7.47
Cornelius, F.	14610208	Pte.	Died of Wounds	Western Europe	11.6.44
Coulthard, B.	4451823	Pte.	Killed in action	Sicily	17.7.43
Cowan, T. H.	14645758	Pte.	Killed in action	Western Europe	11.6.44
Cowe, J. B.	3191139	Pte.	Died of Wounds	B.E.F. Campaign	31.5.40
Cowe, R.	4457658	Pte.	Killed in action	B.E.F. Campaign	21.5.40

Name		Number	Rank	Cause	Place	Date
Cowell, J. R.	.....	4451455	Pte.	Died as a P.O.W.	Germany	12.4.45
Craggs, M. O.	.....	4454201	C.S.M.	Died on active service	Middle East	12.1.44
Critchley, D.	.....	3654181	Pte.	Killed in action	Middle East	2.11.42
Cropper, D.	.....	4031588	Pte.	Killed in action	Western Europe	9.6.44
Crouch, S. J.	.....	14645695	Pte.	Killed in action	Western Europe	8.9.44
Cullen, L. T.	.....	14646231	Pte.	Killed in action	Western Europe	11.6.44
Curnow, J.	.....	5440862	L/Sgt.	Killed in action	Western Europe	11.6.44
Dale, W.	.....	4459358	Pte.	Killed in action	Middle East	2.11.42
Darwood, J.	.....	4447362	Sgt.	Killed in action	Middle East	22.3.43
Davidson, J.	.....	3191143	Pte.	Died of Wounds	B.E.F. Campaign	6.6.40
Davidson, P.	.....	4468160	Cpl.	Killed in action	Western Europe	9.9.44
Davies, O. A.	.....	289298	Lieut.	Killed in action	Western Europe	12.7.44
Davies, R.	.....	3782647	Pte.	Killed in action	Western Europe	9.9.44
Davies, W. H. W.		7958103	Pte.	Killed in action	Western Europe	11.6.44
Davis, J.	.....	4461277	Pte.	Killed in action	Middle East	22.3.43
Dees, E. L.	.....	88693	Lieut.	Died as a P.O.W.	Germany	25.1.41
Dent, R. H.	.....	4470045	L/Cpl.	Killed in action	Western Europe	4.10.44
Denton, F.	.....	3716743	Pte.	Killed in action	Western Europe	11.7.44
Dix, T. J.	.....	4462086	Cpl.	Killed in action	Middle East	22.3.43
Dixon, J. F.	.....	14675139	Pte.	Died of Wounds	Western Europe	10.9.44
Dixon, T......	.....	4462117	Cpl.	Killed in action	Western Europe	12.7.44
Dodds, W.	.....	4461285	Pte.	Killed in action	Sicily	11.8.43
Donohoe, P.	.....	4464192	Pte.	Died on active service	North Africa	1.8.43
Donoghue, J.	.....	3661008	Pte.	Killed in action	Western Europe	9.9.44
Dorrington, G. E.		14355081	Pte.	Killed in action	Sicily	5.8.43
Douglas, A.	.....	4461286	Pte.	Died on active service	United Kingdom	3.8.45
Downey, W. H.	.....	4457402	Pte.	Died as a P.O.W.	Middle East	14.11.42
Doyle, H.	.....	4468163	L/Sgt.	Died as a P.O.W.	Middle East	30.12.42
Doyle, J.	.....	3661541	Pte.	Killed in action	Western Europe	9.8.44
Draper, F.	.....	4447608	Cpl.	Killed in action	B.E.F. Campaign	1.6.40
Dudman, R. A.	.....	204386	2/Lieut	Killed in action	Middle East	2.11.42
Duggan, M. B.	.....	14629980	L/Cpl.	Killed in action	Western Europe	18.9.44
Dunkerley, W.	.....	4462119	Pte.	Killed in action	Middle East	28.10.42
Dunn, E. A.	.....	5345096	Pte.	Killed in action	Middle East	22.3.43
Dunning, L.	.....	4470153	Pte.	Killed in action	Western Europe	11.6.44
Dutton, J.	.....	4462087	Cpl.	Killed in action	Middle East	27.7.42
Dyer, A.	.....	4458991	Pte.	Killed in action	Middle East	29.6.42
Easten, R. C.	.....	4454420	Pte.	Killed in action	Middle East	2.11.42
Edwards, J.	.....	4458863	Pte.	Died as a P.O.W.	Middle East	14.11.42
Elliot, J. R.	.....	14229153	Pte.	Killed in action	Middle East	17.7.43
Ellison, L.	.....	4463441	Pte.	Died as a P.O.W.	Middle East	24.11.42
English, G. R.	.....	4455688	Sgt.	Killed in action	Middle East	22.3.43
Etherington, G. T.		4452553	Pte.	Killed in action	Western Europe	9.9.44
Evans, E.	.....	4462205	Pte.	Killed in action	Middle East	2.11.42
Evans, W. F.	.....	4467394	Pte.	Killed in action	Middle East	22.3.43
Evans, W. R.	.....	3718343	Cpl.	Killed in action	Western Europe	10.6.44
Evason, J. W.	.....	3913686	Pte.	Died of Wounds	Western Europe	11.6.44
Evenden, J. W.	.....	6411343	Pte.	Died of Wounds	Western Europe	13.7.44

Everson, J.	4468062	Pte.	Died as a P.O.W.	Middle East	14.11.42
Everton, G.	4458862	Pte.	Killed in action	Middle East	10.5.42
Fairbairn, D.	4461290	L/Cpl.	Died as a P.O.W.	Middle East	14.6.42
Fairbairn, R.	4461291	L/Cpl.	Died as a P.O.W.	Middle East	15.2.42
Farrar, S.	4543400	L/Cpl.	Killed in action	Western Europe	11.9.44
Field, F. R.	5677317	Pte.	Died of Wounds	Sicily	5.8.43
Finch, C. E.	5674354	Cpl.	Killed in action	Western Europe	2.7.44
Firth, H.	4470410	Pte.	Killed in action	Western Europe	19.6.44
Fishborn, J.	4456227	Pte.	Died of Wounds	Middle East	29.6.42
Fishburn, R.	4466437	Pte.	Killed in action	Middle East	22.3.43
Fitzpatrick, F.	4457415	Sgt.	Killed in action	Western Europe	11.6.44
Flaherty, L.	3661632	Pte.	Killed in action	Middle East	2.11.42
Flannigan, W.	3191152	Pte.	Killed in action	B.E.F. Campaign	26.5.40
Fletcher, A.	4462178	Pte.	Killed in action	Middle East	4.10.42
Fletcher, C. C.	4465265	Pte.	Died as a P.O.W.	Middle East	24.7.42
Fletcher, G.	4456133	Pte.	Killed in action	Middle East	26.3.42
Flynn, N.	4455810	Pte.	Died as a P.O.W.	Middle East	31.10.42
Ford, H. N.	14379205	Pte.	Killed in action	Western Europe	9.8.44
Foster, J.	4618582	Pte.	Killed in action	Western Europe	20.7.44
Fowler, D. H.	4467735	Pte.	Killed in action	Middle East	2.11.44
Fox, J. J.	14655690	Pte.	Killed in action	Western Europe	11.6.44
Fraser, A. M.	5444266	Pte.	Killed in action	Western Europe	19.6.44
Freeman, W.	4466445	Pte.	Killed in action	Middle East	12.6.42
Frost, A.	3390278	Pte.	Killed in action	Sicily	18.7.43
Frost, J.	4457412	Pte.	Died as a P.O.W.	Middle East	14.11.42
Galpin, W. C.	14661541	Pte.	Killed in action	Western Europe	11.6.44
Gandy, E.	3530858	Pte.	Died of Wounds	Western Europe	2.11.44
Gardner, R.	4461636	Pte.	Killed in action	Middle East	12.6.42
Gaze, A. S.	214646	2/Lt.	Killed in action	Middle East	12.6.42
Gedge, J. F.	88714	Lieut.	Killed in action	Middle East	22.3.43
Gee, J.	5442928	Pte.	Killed in action	Middle East	2.11.42
Gilbert, J.	4457684	Pte.	Killed in action	B.E.F. Campaign	30.5.40
Gill, E.	4455285	Pte.	Died of Wounds	B.E.F. Campaign	23.5.40
Gillan, R.	4461307	L/Cpl.	Killed in action	Middle East	22.3.43
Gillard, R. H.	289274	Lieut.	Killed in action	Western Europe	7.10.44
Gilmoore, F.	4462242	Pte.	Killed in action	Middle East	2.11.42
Godwin, J.		Lieut.	Killed in action	Sicily	11.8.43
Gordon, R.	4456129	Pte.	Killed in action	Middle East	2.11.42
Goring, R.	4035452	Cpl.	Killed in action	Sicily	17.7.43
Gradon, R.	4454365	Pte.	Killed in action	B.E.F. Campaign	27.5.40
Green, J.	4467271	Pte.	Killed in action	Middle East	2.11.42
Green, W. H	4466457	Pte.	Died as a P.O.W.	Middle East	1.12.42
Grierson, C. W.	3191159	Pte.	Killed in action	B.E.F. Campaign	21.5.40
Griffin, J.	4039957	Pte.	Died as a P.O.W.	Italy	31.7.43
Griffiths, R. R.	4457418	L/Cpl.	Killed in action	Middle East	2.11.42
Grimshaw, J.	4459025	Pte.	Killed in action	Middle East	29.6.42
Grix, S.	4450387	Cpl.	Killed in action	Middle East	2.11.42
Groves, J.	4465405	Pte.	Killed in action	Middle East	21.4.42
Guest, E. F.	4037582	Pte.	Killed in action	Middle East	2.11.42
Gunstone, C. F. J.	5675756	L/Sgt.	Killed in action	Middle East	22.3.43
Hadaway, J. F.	4454639	L/Cpl.	Killed in action	B.E.F. Campaign	21.5.40

Hadaway, L. F.	14214854	Pte.	Died of Wounds	Western Europe	30.11.44
Hall, J. N.	4455659	Cpl.	Killed in action	Middle East	14.11.42
Halliday, A. D.	3191248	Pte.	Killed in action	Middle East	27.7.42
Halliday, T. W.	14632851	Pte.	Killed in action	Western Europe	9.8.44
Hallsworth, J. W.	3660865	Pte.	Killed in action	Sicily	17.7.43
Hankinson, A.	14205728	Pte.	Killed in action	Middle East	8.6.43
Hardman, H.	3656782	Pte.	Killed in action	Middle East	2.11.42
Harland, J. W. B.	4456175	Pte.	Died of Wounds	B.E.F. Campaign	22.5.40
Harris, R. G.	14640632	Pte.	Killed in action	Western Europe	5.10.44
Haughton, W. H.	4036970	L/Cpl.	Killed in action	Middle East	22.3.43
Hay, W. M.	3191166	Cpl.	Killed in action	Western Europe	10.6.44
Hayes, E. J.	4039596	Pte.	Killed in action	Middle East	22.3.43
Hayward, L. W. J.	14632159	Pte.	Killed in action	Western Europe	19.6.44
Hazel, L. W.	4799746	Sgt.	Killed in action	Western Europe	9.9.44
Henry, E.	4461654	Pte.	Killed in action	Western Europe	9.8.44
Herauville, J. H.	5732285	Cpl.	Killed in action	Sicily	5.8.43
Herbert, W. E.	4031578	L/Cpl.	Killed in action	Middle East	2.11.42
Hickman, J.	4452899	Pte.	Killed in action	Middle East	2.11.42
Hicks, J.	4448010	Sgt.	Killed in action	B.E.F. Campaign	21.5.40
Highman, T.	4461657	Pte.	Died as a P.O.W.	Middle East	4.12.42
Hilton, T.	14641773	Pte.	Killed in action	Western Europe	2.8.44
Hitchman, D. C.	14630696	Pte.	Killed in action	Western Europe	10.9.44
Hood, R.	4465410	Pte.	Killed in action	Middle East	3.3.42
Hopkins, F.	4448944	Pte.	Died of Wounds	B.E.F. Campaign	26.5.40
Hopkinson, J. J.	4467339	Pte.	Died of Wounds	Middle East	1.4.42
Hub, J. H.	6480089	Pte.	Died on active service	Middle East	31.7.43
Hubble, A. F.	5052330	L/Cpl.	Killed in action	Middle East	22.3.43
Hunter, A.		Lieut.	Killed in action	Middle East	2.11.42
Hunter, J.	4463887	Pte.	Died as a P.O.W.	Middle East	29.6.42
Hurrell, V. A.	14659640	Pte.	Killed in action	Western Europe	13.7.44
Hurst, R.	252103	Lieut.	Killed in action	Middle East	14.10.42
Huscroft, N.	4456143	Pte.	Killed in action	B.E.F. Campaign	21.5.40
Hutchings, L. R.	5682303	Pte.	Killed in action	Western Europe	9.8.44
Hutchinson, J.	4456141	L/Cpl.	Died of Wounds	Sicily	17.7.43
Hutchinson, J. E. M.	4457424	Pte.	Killed in action	B.E.F. Campaign	21.5.40
Ingram, J.	4456233	Pte.	Killed in action	Middle East	24.5.40
Jackson, M. L. P. D.S.O.		Lt.Col.	Killed in action	Middle East	20.3.43
Jaines, L. J.	4035921	Pte.	Killed in action	Middle East	22.3.43
James, E.	3658244	Pte.	Killed in action	Middle East	22.3.43
Jardine, R.	4461190	Pte.	Died as a P.O.W.	Middle East	28.3.43
Jay, W. A.	5444928	Cpl.	Killed in action	Western Europe	19.6.44
Jenkins, F.	4450601	Pte.	Killed in action	Western Europe	19.6.44
John, P.	3910745	Pte.	Killed in action	Sicily	17.7.43
Johnson, H. N.	4461211	Pte.	Died of Wounds	Middle East	4.8.43
Johnson, J.	165875	Lieut.	Killed on active service	Middle East	6.43
Johnson, S.	4470081	Pte.	Died as a P.O.W.	Middle East	25.3.43
Jones, A. J.	3657155	Cpl.	Killed in action	Middle East	22.2.43

Jones, G. E.	4129333	Pte.	Died as a P.O.W.	Middle East	10.11.42
Jones, G. T.	4198235	Cpl.	Died of Wounds	North Africa	22.9.43
Jones, N.	4202761	Pte.	Died as a P.O.W.	Italy	18.7.43
Jones, T. J.	14676404	Pte.	Killed in action	Western Europe	11.6.44
Kailofer, J.	153376	Major	Died of Wounds	Western Europe	9.8.44
Kay, H.	3660957	Pte.	Killed in action	Western Europe	11.6.44
Keeble, F. A.	4461628	L/Cpl.	Died of Wounds	Middle East	8.6.42
Keenan, A.	4463655	Pte.	Killed in action	Middle East	1.7.42
Kershaw, K. H.	138521	Capt.	Killed in action	Sicily	17.7.43
Kidson, A. W.	78279	Lieut.	Killed in action	Middle East	2.11.42
Killen, C. F.	3773181	Pte.	Killed in action	Middle East	22.3.43
Kirton, S.	5248277	Sgt.	Died of Wounds	Western Europe	4.10.42
Langlands, J.	4463673	Pte.	Died as a P.O.W.	Italy	24.10.44
Lappage, V.	4451760	Pte.	Killed in action	B.E.F. Campaign	25.5.40
Lawn, P.G.	205608	Lieut.	Died of Wounds	Western Europe	16.6.44
Laws, A. W.	839627	Pte.	Killed in action	Middle East	2.11.42
Laws, H.	4461351	Pte.	Died of Wounds	Middle East	5.6.42
Lawson, W.	4441530	L/Cpl.	Killed in action	B.E.F. Campaign	1.6.40
Leadbitter, J. J.	4627195	Pte.	Killed in action	Western Europe	10.6.44
Lee, W. W.	14680249	Pte.	Killed in action	Western Europe	19.10.44
Lees, J.	4459096	Pte.	Killed in action	Middle East	29.6.42
Lewis, G. E.	3366511	L/Sgt.	Killed in action	Sicily	17.7.43
Liddle, J. H.	4456135	Pte.	Killed in action	Middle East	5.6.42
Linskill, J.	4466811	Pte.	Killed in action	Sicily	18.7.43
Lister, J. W.	4462481	Pte.	Killed in action	Middle East	27.7.42
Liversage, W. A.	4199417	Pte.	Killed in action	Western Europe	10.9.44
Lobley, J. F.	4458960	Pte.	Died on active service	Middle East	12.9.41
Lohan, G. H.	94156	Capt.	Killed in action	Sicily	17.7.43
Luckhurst, G. H.	5258628	Pte.	Killed in action	Western Europe	20.6.44
Luffman, P. H. Canadian Army	149840	Lieut.	Killed in action	Western Europe	1.8.44
Marsden, C.	4463685	Pte.	Killed in action	Middle East	21.4.42
Marsden, T. T.	4456097	C/Sgt.	Killed in action	Sicily	18.7.43
Marsh, J. H.	4698256	Pte.	Killed in action	Western Europe	11.6.44
Marshall, A. K.	4458291	Pte.	Died of Wounds	B.E.F. Campaign	25.6.40
Marshall, B.	5256073	Pte.	Killed in action	Western Europe	9.9.44
Martin, J.	4461357	Sgt.	Killed in action	Western Europe	10.9.44
Martin, R.	3191177	Pte.	Killed in action	B.E.F. Campaign	20.5.40
Maughan, T.	14681538	Pte.	Killed in action	Western Europe	9.8.44
Mawer, G. A.	4466829	Pte.	Died of Wounds	Western Europe	26.7.44
Mawson, J.	4452683	L/Cpl.	Killed as a P.O.W	Italy	8.12.43
May, G. F.	5510605	Pte.	Killed in action	Sicily	17.7.43
McAdam, T.	3191189	Pte.	Died as a P.O.W.	Middle East	14.11.42
McArdle, J.	4456515	Pte.	Died of Wounds	United Kingdom	1.6.40
McCoskrie, W.	3191192	L/Cpl.	Died of Wounds	Middle East	2.1.43
McDonald, J. T.	4040573	Pte.	Killed in action	Middle East	22.3.43
McEvoy, J.	3661975	Pte.	Killed in action	Middle East	2.11.42
McGahan, R.	4463715	Pte.	Killed in action	Sicily	8.8.43
McGivern, J. L.	4458328	Pte.	Died of Wounds	Middle East	11.4.42
McPherson, S.	4455710	Pte.	Killed in action	Middle East	2.11.42

McQuaid, G. G. E.	4446419	C.S.M.	Died on active service	Middle East	21.8.42
Mee, E.	4039234	Pte.	Killed in action	Sicily	17.7.43
Millar, M.	3191179	Pte.	Died of Wounds		15.2.44
Miller, E. S.	4464806	L/Cpl.	Killed as a POW.	Middle East	14.11.42
Milner, G.	14202636	Pte.	Killed in action	Middle East	22.3.43
Minto, D.	4458209	Pte.	Killed in action	B.E.F. Campaign	25.5.40
Mitchell, J. D.	4457745	Pte.	Killed in action	B.E.F. Campaign	21.5.40
Moane, T.	6026808	Pte.	Killed as a POW.	Middle East	5.7.42
Moody, W.	4458150	Pte.	Killed as a POW.	Middle East	17.8.43
Morgan, A.	3716963	Pte.	Died of Wounds	Western Europe	14.6.44
Morgan, P.	4466532	Pte.	Killed as a POW.	Middle East	17.8.42
Morrell, H.	4470099	Pte.	Killed in action	Middle East	22.3.43
Morton, G.	4447609	C.S.M.	Died as a POW. (escaped)	Middle East	27.7.44
Morton, J. W.	4447632	Cpl.	Killed in action	Middle East	2.11.42
Morton, L	4459547	Pte.	Killed in action	Sicily	17,7.43
Morton, W.	4452940	Pte.	Killed in action	B.E.F. Campaign	26.5.40
Moscow, B.	5622757	C.S.M.	Killed in action	Western Europe	18.6.44
Mould, J. D.	299741	Lieut.	Killed in action	Western Europe	11.6.44
Moxon, E.	4627333	Pte.	Killed in action	Middle East	17.7.43
Moyle, T. J. N.	14600494	Pte.	Killed in action	Western Europe	11.9.44
Moyle, W. H.	4451374	L/Cpl.	Killed in action	B.E.F. Campaign	21.5.40
Mullen, L.	69313	Pte.	Killed in action	Sicily	17.7.43
Nesbitt, G. R.A.CH.D., att.D.L.I.	163330	Capt.	Killed in action	Western Europe	6.7.44
Nesbitt, J. G. W.	4455259	L/Cpl.	Died of Wounds	Middle East	22.3.43
Newton, E. J.	4455524	Pte.	Died as a P.O.W.	Middle East	9.7.42
Niznick, H. Canadian Army		Lieut.	Killed in action	Western Europe	8.9.44
Noble, A. S.	4455543	Pte.	Killed in action	B.E.F. Campaign	21.5.40
Noland, H. A.	5260563	Pte.	Killed in action	Western Europe	4.10.44
Noone, A.	4463730	Pte.	Killed in Action	Middle East	22.3.43
Norris, S. E.	14659760	Pte.	Killed in action	Western Europe	11.6.44
O'Brien, W. S.	6215869	Pte.	Died as a P.O.W.	Italy	18.11.43
O'Donnell, W. J.	4036493	Pte.	Killed in action	Western Europe	9.9.44
O'Driscoll, P.	3456295	Pte.	Killed in action	Middle East	2.11.42
Ogden, F.	4455749	Pte.	Killed in action	Western Europe	4.10.44
Ogden, K.	4618214	L/Sgt.	Killed in action	Western Europe	10.6.44
O'Rourke, J.	3656444	Pte.	Killed in action	Middle East	2.11.42
Osborne, A.	4041652	Pte.	Died as a P.O.W.	North Africa	6.4.43
Palmer, J.	4452916	L/Cpl.	Killed in action	B.E.F. Campaign	21.5.40
Parker, G. E.	4461381	Pte.	Killed in action	Middle East	22.3.43
Parker, J. H.	138147	Capt.	Killed in action	Middle East	31.10.42
Pascoe, E.	5438085	Pte.	Killed in action	Western Europe	11.9.44
Parsons, A. A.	14642739	Pte.	Killed in action	Western Europe	4.10.44
Pattinson, G. E.	4449789	Pte.	Killed in action	Middle East	3.11.42
Pearce, J. W.	4465959	Pte.	Killed in action	Middle East	29.6.42
Pearson, H. M. M.	4457457	Cpl.	Killed in action	Middle East	23.3.43
Pearson, J. H.	4464361	L/Cpl.	Killed on active service	Middle East	8.6.43

Pearson, R. B.	4455527	Pte.	Died of Wounds	B.E.F. Campaign	21.5.40
Peel, R. W.	4461386	Pte.	Died as a P.O.W.	Middle East	17.8.42
Pentney, D. M.	176813	Lieut.	Killed in action	Middle East	22.3.43
Peters, J.	4459040	Pte.	Died as a P.O.W.	Middle East	4.7.42
Peterson, J. W.	4461388	Pte.	Killed in action	Middle East	4.6.42
Petitt, V. E.	14646157	Pte.	Killed in action	Western Europe	2.8.44
Phipps, R. T.	4039257	Pte.	Died of Wounds	Middle East	23.3.43
Pilkington, R. H.	14681549	Pte.	Killed in action	Western Europe	10.6.44
Pitts, L. R.	14641052	Pte.	Killed in action	Western Europe	11.9.44
Pratt, W. J.	4455499	Pte.	Killed in action	B.E.F. Campaign	22.5.40
Prescott, J.	3653331	Pte.	Killed in action	Sicily	17.7.43
Proctor, N.	4451490	Pte.	Killed in action	Sicily	17.7.43
Pryor, D.	14399635	Pte.	Killed in action	Western Europe	2.8.44
Raine, A.	4455444	Pte.	Killed in action	B.E.F. Campaign	23.5.40
Ralph, J.	3603138	L/Sgt.	Killed in action	Sicily	17.7.43
Ranson, J., M.M.	4452022	C.S.M.	Killed in action	Middle East	22.3.43
Rawlings, H. A.	4468079	Cpl.	Killed in action	Sicily	8.8.43
Rawlings, R. H.	5836852	Pte.	Killed in action	Sicily	17.7.43
Raybould, A. H.	11420052	Pte.	Killed in action	Western Europe	10.6.44
Redshaw, R.	4454458	Pte.	Died of Wounds	B.E.F. Campaign	28.5.40
Reed, G. R.	4466565	Pte.	Died of Wounds	Middle East	2.11.42
Reed, J. R.	4451814	L/Cpl.	Killed in action	North Africa	8.4.43
Rice, W. B.	3911496	Pte.	Killed in action	Western Europe	9.8.44
Richardson, T. A.	189227	Lieut.	Killed in action	Middle East	20.3.43
Richmond, J.	2987711	Pte.	Died as a P.O.W.	Middle East	14.11.42
Riddall, R. M.	2987614	Pte.	Died as a P.O.W.	Middle East	14.11.42
Ridealgh, W.	285508	Capt.	Killed in action	Western Europe	11.9.44
Ridgeway, F. G.	5672907	L/Sgt.	Killed in action	Middle East	22.3.43
Riley, C. A.	53496	Major	Killed in action	Western Europe	4.10.44
Roberts, D.	4463787	Pte.	Killed in action	Middle East	18.7.43
Roberts, J.	14403257	Pte.	Killed in action	Western Europe	4.10.44
Robinson, B.	4449615	Pte.	Died of Wounds	B.E.F. Campaign	3.6.40
Robinson, J.	4463781	Pte.	Killed in action	Middle East	22.3.43
Robinson, J. W.	5391278	Pte.	Died of Wounds	Western Europe	7.10.44
Robinson, R.	4450537	Pte.	Killed in action	Sicily	17.7.43
Robinson, R. H. R.	130757	Lieut.	Killed in action	Middle East	8.6.42
Rood, S. C.	281609	Lieut.	Killed in action	Western Europe	9.9.44
Roseberry, F.	4461405	Pte.	Killed in action	Sicily	5.8.43
Rourke, W.	14609111	Pte.	Killed in action	Western Europe	11.6.44
Rudol, N.	4470391	Pte.	Killed in action	Sicily	11.8.43
Rylatt, F.	4626958	Pte.	Killed in action	Sicily	17.7.43
Saile, J. W.	6402911	Pte.	Died of Wounds	Western Europe	15.6.44
Samms, T.	4456088	Pte.	Died of Wounds	Western Europe	4.7.44
Scott, J. T.	4461094	L/Cpl.	Died of Wounds	Middle East	11.11.42
Scott, W.	4454279	Pte.	Died as a P.O.W.	Germany	16.2.41
Selley, R.	5435233	Sgt.	Died of Wounds	Western Europe	19.6.44
Shaw, A.	4461409	Pte.	Died as a P.O.W.	Middle East	27.7.42
Shields, J.	4461412	Pte.	Died as a P.O.W.	Middle East	13.6.42
Sill, A.	4456086	Pte.	Killed in action	B.E.F. Campaign	21.5.40
Simcox, G. A.	4037065	Pte.	Killed in action	Middle East	22.3.43
Simpson, J. W.	3190669	L/Cpl.	Killed in action	B.E.F. Campaign	22.5.40

Simpson, C	4544449	Pte.	Killed in action	Sicily	8.8.43
Simpson, F. J.	4455300	L/Cpl.	Died of Wounds	Middle East	2.11.42
Slaney, E.	4346785	Pte.	Killed in action	Middle East	22.3.43
Smith, E.	3607542	Pte.	Killed in action	Middle East	22.3.43
Smith, J. H.	3657834	Pte.	Died of Wounds	Sicily	4.8.43
Snowball, T.	4456252	Pte.	Killed in action	B.E.F. Campaign	21.5.40
Snowdon, R.	5957027	Pte.	Killed in action	Sicily	17.7.43
Sorbie, A.	14623330	Pte.	Killed in action	Western Europe	10.6.44
Soulsby, F.	6850602	Pte.	Killed in action	Sicily	18.7.43
Southworth, H.	4460224	Pte.	Killed in action	Western Europe	10.6.44
Spears, E. R.	6103344	Cpl.	Killed in action	Western Europe	15.10.44
Splevins, R.	4455842	Pte.	Killed on active service	United Kingdom	3.10.40
Spry, J. N.	4463025	Pte.	Killed in action	Middle East	22.3.43
St. George, A. J.	63626	Capt.	Killed in action	Western Europe	19.6.44
Stanger, K.	4546300	Pte.	Killed in action	Western Europe	20.7.44
Steele, F.	3660815	Pte.	Killed in action	Sicily	17.7.43
Stephenson, M.	4461420	Pte.	Died as a P.O.W.	Middle East	14.11.42
Stevenson, G.	4450312	Pte.	Killed in action	Middle East	27.6.42
Streeter, W.	4450994	L/Cpl.	Killed in action	Middle East	22.3.43
Stringer, M.	4459113	Pte.	Killed in action	Middle East	29.6.42
Sturman, W. L.	4469927	Pte.	Killed in action	Sicily	17.7.43
Sutherland, J. T.	4449009	Pte.	Died of Wounds	B.E.F. Campaign	31.5.40
Swarbrick, J. J.	303298	Lieut.	Killed in action	Western Europe	18.9.44
Talbot, A. B.	4461424	L/Cpl.	Died as a P.O.W.	Middle East	13.6.42
Tasker, D.	4622474	Pte.	Died on active service	Middle East	14.8.43
Taylor, E.	4619119	Pte.	Killed in action	Sicily	5.8.43
Taylor, E. C. E......	14626573	Pte.	Killed in action	Western Europe	19.6.44
Taylor, J. T.	4463832	Pte.	Killed in action	Western Europe	9.8.44
Taylor, R.	4453045	Cpl.	Killed in action	Middle East	27.7.42
Thirtle, R.	4457045	Pte.	Killed in action	Middle East	29.6.42
Thomas, G.	5674821	Pte.	Killed in action	Western Europe	13.7.44
Thompson, D. J.	5620938	Pte.	Killed in action	Western Europe	11.9.44
Thompson, F. J. W.	3719012	L/Cpl.	Killed in action	Western Europe	5.7.44
Thornton, R.	4452627	Pte.	Killed in action	B.E.F. Campaign	25.5.40
Todd, S.	4456103	Pte.	Died of Wounds	Middle East	15.11.42
Turnbull, I. S.	72976	Capt.	Killed in action	Middle East	2.11.42
Turnbull, T.	4466618	Pte.	Killed in action	Middle East	22.3.43
Turner, H. F.	5955902	Pte.	Killed in action	Sicily	17.7.43
Vasey, J. C.	4466620	Pte.	Killed in action	Sicily	18.7.43
Virgo, F. C.	4459224	Pte.	Killed in action	Middle East	8.6.42
Waggott, H.	86523	Lieut.	Killed in action	Western Europe	11.6.44
Wallbanks, S., M.M.	3718643	Sgt.	Killed in action	Western Europe	8.9.44
Walker, J. G.	164854	Capt.	Killed in action	Western Europe	18.6.44
Walton, G. M.	4464870	Pte.	Died as a P.O.W.	Middle East	7.7.42
Wardle, J.	14409515	Pte.	Killed in action	Western Europe	11.9.44
Wardle, S., M.M......	4451703	C.S.M.	Died of Wounds	Sicily	13.8.43
Waring, G.	4037086	Pte.	Killed in action	Middle East	22.3.43
Waterhouse, J.	2080445	Pte.	Died of Wounds	Middle East	27.9.43
Watson, C.	4438568	Sgt.	Killed in action	B.E.F. Campaign	31.5.40

Watson, S. R.	4462897	Pte.	Killed in action	Sicily	17.7.43
Watson, T.	4457501	Pte.	Killed in action	Sicily	8.8.43
Watson, T.	5629154	Pte.	Killed in action	Sicily	17.7.43
Wattam, R. H.	4455456	Pte.	Killed in action	B.E.F. Campaign	29.5.40
Weedon, H.	14379260	Pte.	Killed in action	Western Europe	9.8.44
Wegener, W. E.	3972303	Pte.	Killed in action	Sicily	4.8.43
Welch, H.	217759	Lieut.	Killed in action	Western Europe	19.6.44
Welsh, J.	4447012	Cpl.	Killed in action	Middle East	2.11.42
Wharton, P.	4455463	Pte.	Died as a P.O.W.	Germany	10.5.45
Wheatley, J. N.	130394	Capt.	Killed in action	Western Europe	11.6.44
White, W. G.	6026850	Pte.	Killed in action	Sicily	8.8.43
White, W. H.	3656977	Pte.	Killed in action	Middle East	22.3.43
Whitehill, T.	3913213	Pte.	Killed in action	Middle East	22.3.43
Whitfield, G.	4463869	Pte.	Killed in action	Middle East	29.6.42
Whitfield, G. E. C.	4448802	Cpl.	Died as a P.O.W.	Middle East	1.6.43
Wibberley, N.	14681574	Pte.	Killed in action	Western Europe	20.6.44
Wicks, F. J.	4457688	Pte.	Died of Wounds	Middle East	11.6.42
Wilkinson, W.	4463871	Pte.	Died on active service	Middle East	3.10.41
Williams, G.	4450425	Pte.	Died of Wounds	Western Europe	22.8.43
Williams, H. F.	4196530	Pte.	Died of Wounds	Sicily	22.8.43
Williams, S. H.	5674618	Cpl.	Killed in action	Western Europe	9.9.44
Williamson, A.	6026123	L/Cpl.	Killed in action	Sicily	5.8.43
Wilson, H.	4534957	Sgt.	Died on active service	United Kingdom	24.2.44
Wilson, R.	5260166	Pte.	Killed in action	Western Europe	11.9.44
Wilson, W.	3718815	Pte.	Killed in action	Western Europe	11.6.44
Winch, R. B.	5672263	Pte.	Died of Wounds	Western Europe	10.9.44
Wood, A. A.	160885	2/Lieut	Died on active service	Middle East	8.10.41
Wood, E. W.	4456259	Pte.	Died as a P.O.W.	Germany	24.4.41
Wood, R......	4461449	Pte.	Killed in action	Middle East	2.11.42
Woodcock, T.	4626970	Pte.	Killed in action	Middle East	22.3.43
Woods, J. H.	4457500	L/Cpl.	Killed as a POW.	Germany	27.2.45
Woodworth, G. E.	3661445	Pte.	Killed in action	Middle East	2.11.42
Wright, G. H.	4465899	Pte.	Killed in action	Middle East	14.6.42
Wylie, T.	4463357	L/Cpl.	Killed in action	Middle East	22.3.43
Wylie, A. R. H.	4457710	Pte.	Killed in action	B.E.F. Campaign	22.5.40
Yearsley, K.	3718651	L/Cpl.	Killed in action	Sicily	5.8.43
York, A. L.	5048052	Sgt.	Killed in action	Middle East	2.11.42
Young, C. T.	4464724	Cpl.	Killed in action	Middle East	29.6.42
Younger, R.	4461456	Pte.	Died as a P.O.W.	Middle East	14.11.42

APPENDIX B

Honours and Awards

B.E.F CAMPAIGN 1939/40

DISTINGUISHED SERVICE ORDER.

Lieut.-Colonel R. S. McLaren.

MILITARY CROSS.

Captain The Rev. T. F. Duggan (R.A. CH. D. att. 8th D.L.I.)

DISTINGUISHED CONDUCT MEDAL.

Sgt. J. Carruthers.

Sgt. A. Skorochod, (French Military Mission att. 8th D.L.I.)

MENTION IN DESPATCHES.

Lieut.-Colonel C. W. Beart, M.C.
Major R. S. McLaren.
2/Lieut. D. H. Claye.
2/Lieut. I. R. English.
R.Q.M.S. T. Lightfoot.
C.S.M. J. Curry.
Sgt. A. T. Semple.
Cpl. H. Fletcher.

MIDDLE EAST

DISTINGUISHED SERVICE ORDER.

Lieut.-Colonel M. L. P. Jackson.

BAR TO THE MILITARY CROSS.

Captain I. R. English, M.C.

MILITARY CROSS.

Major H. S. Sell.
Captain I. R. English.
Captain H. Glasper.
Captain P. J. A. Lucas.
Lieut. P. J. Lewis.
Lieut. R. Place.

DISTINGUISHED CONDUCT MEDAL.

R.S.M. A. Jennings.
Sgt. A. Cairns, M.M.

BAR TO THE MILITARY MEDAL.

Sgt. W. Crawford, M.M.

MILITARY MEDAL.

C.S.M. G. E. Wood.
C.S.M. M. J. Brannigan.
C.S.M. J. Ranson.
Sgt. W. Crawford.
Sgt. I. McDermott.
L/Sgt. G. Hill.
Cpl. S. Hart.
Cpl. M. Pearson.
Pte. T. M. Swallow.
L/Cpl. A. W. Bark.
Pte. C. Beattie.
L/Cpl. W. Charlton.
Pte. J. Brown.
Pte. G. R. Fearon.
Pte. W. Higginson.
Pte. B. Holmes.
Pte. D. D. Michael.
Pte. J. W. Wood.

MENTION IN DESPATCHES.

Lieut.-Colonel C. W. Beart, M.C.
Major H. S. Sell.
Lieut. D. A. Neale.
R.Q.M.S. T. Lightfoot.
C.S.M. J. Ranson.
Sgt. T. G. Ayrton.
Sgt. R. Dickinson.
Sgt. J. Malone.
Sgt. T. E. Tennant.
Sgt. J. Thompson.
Cpl. T. Fenwick.
Cpl. J. Peveller.
Pte. R. Goodwin.
Pte. P. H. Lake.

SICILY

Distinguished Service Order.

Lieut.-Colonel R. P. Lidwill.

Military Cross.

Captain C. L. Beattie.
Captain D. A. Neale.
Lieut. P. G. Hampson.
Captain J. A. Leybourne.
Captain A. Noble (R.A.M.C. att. 8th D.L.I.)

Military Medal.

C.S.M. J. R. Hannah.
Sgt. C. J. W. Mackmin.
Cpl. W. D. Scriven.
Pte. C. B. Simpson.
C.S.M. S. Wardle.
L/Sgt. D. J. Richards.
L/Sgt. F. Mitchinson.
L/Cpl. G. F. Shepherd.
L/Cpl. F. H. Spink.
Pte. R. G. Goodwin.

WESTERN EUROPE

Second Bar to the Military Cross.

Major I. R. English, M.C.

Military Cross.

Lieut. P. M. Laws.

Distinguished Conduct Medal.

Sgt. G. H. Self.

Bar to the Military Medal.

Cpl. W. Higginson, M.M.
Cpl. D. D. Michael, M.M.

Military Medal.

C.S.M. J. E. Ineson.
Sgt. J. K. Middleton.
L/Sgt. S. P. Wallbanks.
L/Cpl. J. Hunter.
Pte. J. Cawley.
Sgt. S. F. Martin.
L/Sgt. R. Richmond.
Cpl. S. L. Brydges.
Cpl. B. Thomas.
Pte. F. Protano.

Mention in Despatches.

Lieut. S. C. Rood.
Sgt. F. W. D. Lauderdale.
Pte. D. Cropper
Sgt. C. Churcher.
Cpl. A. Boyle.
Pte. W. J. Flaxman.

FOR ESCAPING WHEN A PRISONER OF WAR

Member of the Order of The British Empire.

Major R. S. McLaren, D.S.O.

Distinguished Conduct Medal.

Cpl. R. Bainbridge.
Cpl. W. Roberts.
Cpl. J. A. Martin.

Mention in Despatches.

Captain P. J. Lewis, M.C.
Captain T. Preacher.

HALF-YEARLY HONOURS

Member of the Order of The British Empire.

Captain (Q.M.) W. G. Stray.

British Empire Medal.

Sgt. T. G. W. P. Coffin.

The following were granted Immediate Commissions in the Field :—

Sgt. A. W. Bark, M.M.
C.S.M. H. Glasper.
Sgt. J. Carruthers, D.C.M.
C.S.M. J. R. Hannah, M.M.

Note :—Ranks are those held at the time of the award.

ROUTES FOLLOWED BY THE 8TH

ON IN WESTERN EUROPE 1944